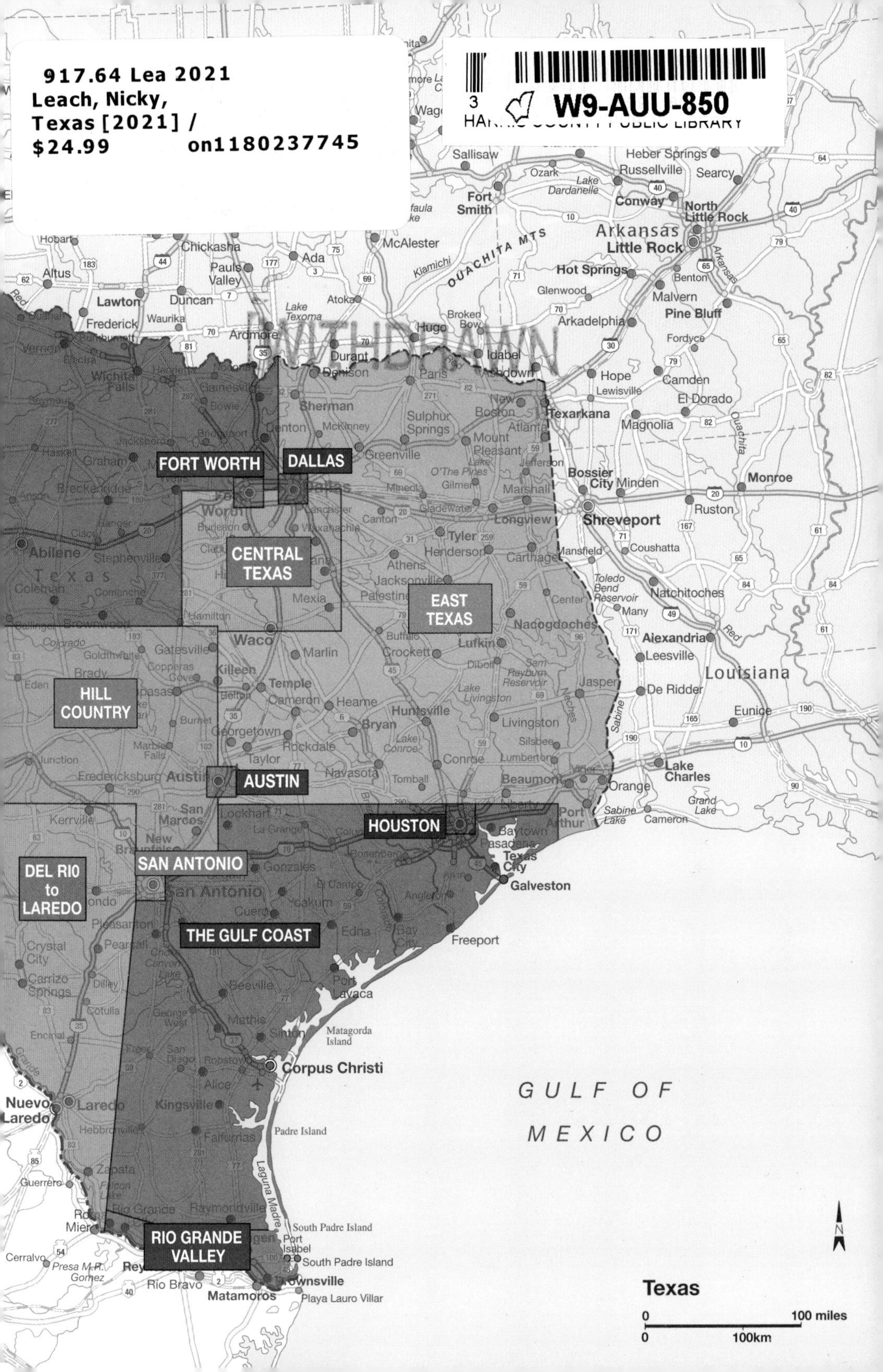
Texas
0 100 miles
0 100km
FORT WORTH
DALLAS
CENTRAL TEXAS
EAST TEXAS
HILL COUNTRY
AUSTIN
HOUSTON
SAN ANTONIO
DEL RIO to LAREDO
THE GULF COAST
RIO GRANDE VALLEY
GULF OF MEXICO
Arkansas
Louisiana
OUACHITA MTS
Little Rock
North Little Rock
Hot Springs
Pine Bluff
Fort Smith
Conway
Texarkana
Shreveport
Bossier City
Monroe
Alexandria
Lake Charles
Beaumont
Port Arthur
Galveston
Texas City
Baytown
Pasadena
Freeport
Waco
Tyler
Longview
Lufkin
Nacogdoches
Abilene
Wichita Falls
Sherman
Denison
Lawton
Corpus Christi
Laredo
Nuevo Laredo
Brownsville
Matamoros
South Padre Island
Port Isabel
Padre Island
Matagorda Island
Laguna Madre
Kingsville

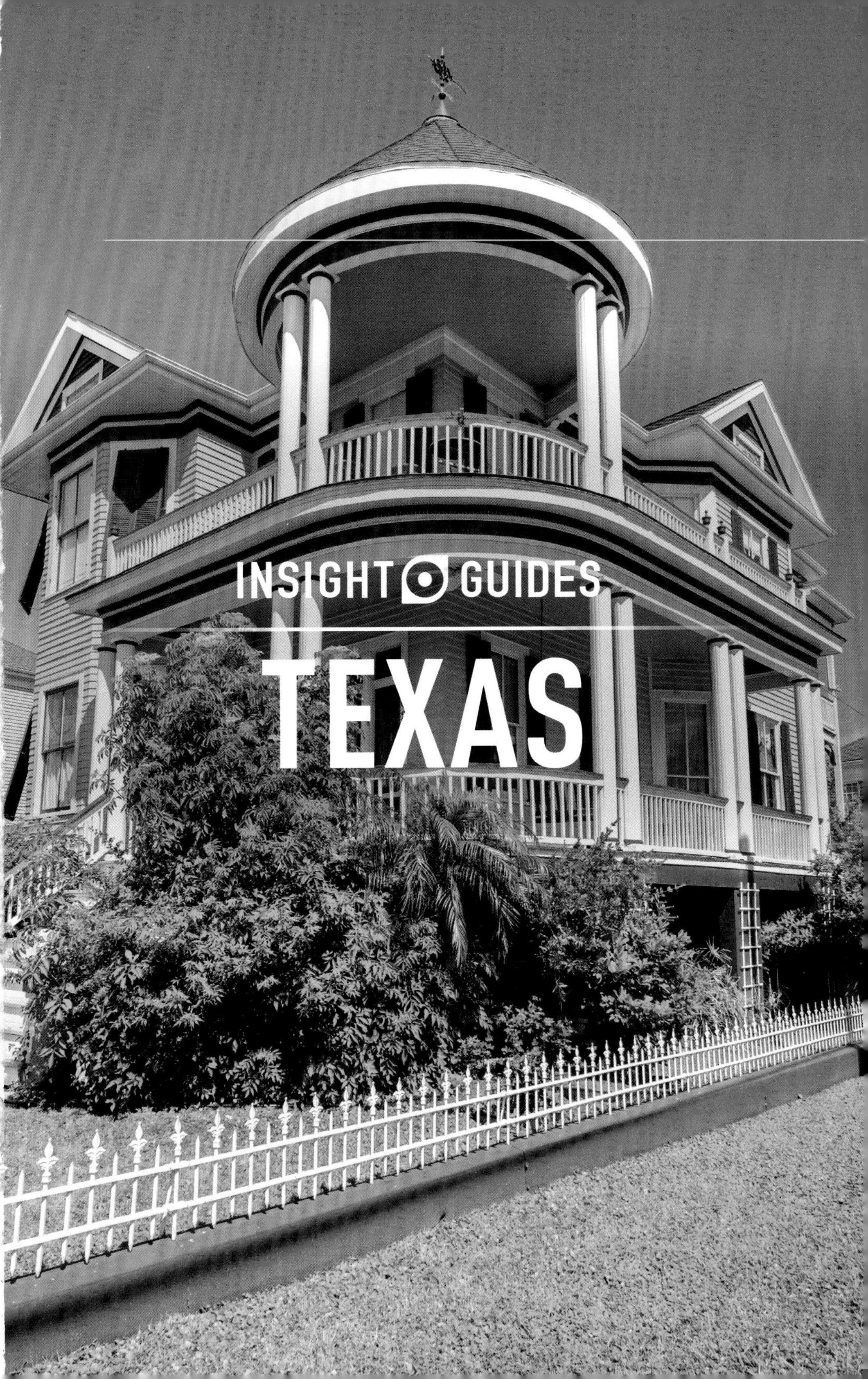

INSIGHT GUIDES

TEXAS

CONTENTS

Introduction

History & Features

Places

Travel Tips

Maps

LEGEND
Insight on
Photo story

THE BEST OF TEXAS: TOP ATTRACTIONS

△ **The Alamo, San Antonio**. The birthplace of the revolution that led to the nine-year Texas Republic in 1836, this somber Spanish mission chapel is the heart of Texas pride in exuberant San Antonio. See page 164.

▽ **The River Walk, San Antonio**. Stroll or take a boat tour along an enchanting European-style riverside promenade in downtown San Antonio that captures the lights, color, and history of the largest Hispanic city in Texas. See page 164.

△ **Nacogdoches, East Texas**. Its Caddo Indian name betrays the ancient origins of this attractive historic town, home to a state university, nature trails, museums, antique stores, and nearby Caddo Mounds State Historic Site. See page 202.

△ **The Menil Collection and Rothko Chapel, Houston**. Passionate art collectors the Menils' personal collection of art is displayed in an intimate setting in a stunning building by Renzo Piano. The interfaith chapel contains a collection of paintings by Mark Rothko. See page 186.

△ **Padre Island National Seashore, the Gulf Coast**. Texas's favorite beach destination beckons vacationers with its warm Gulf Coast waters, soft white sand, sea shells, and vivid sunsets. There are also whooping crane and sea turtle populations. See page 223.

◁ **State Capitol, Austin**. Brasher, taller, and more conservative than its Washington replica, Texas's State Capitol offers tours, political spectacle and granite beauty, plus excellent history and art museums on the adjoining UT campus. See page 144.

△ **Palo Duro Canyon State Park, West Texas**. West Texas's Grand Canyon rivals Arizona's top attraction for sheer beauty and its rugged desert canyon features, colorful rocks, historic cabins, and links to famed painter Georgia O'Keeffe. See page 286.

△ **NASA's Johnson Space Center, Houston**. Mission Control for the program that trained astronauts for moon landings and space shuttle travel, the still glamorous space center explores the space race, its achievements, and today's emphasis on medical research. See page 194.

▽ **Dallas Arts District, North Texas**. The largest arts district in the US takes up nine blocks of downtown Dallas, a sensory experience that includes world-class museums, galleries, and performing arts, restaurants, and unique pocket parks. See page 106.

▽ **Big Bend National Park, West Texas**. This huge, remote park in far West Texas's Big Bend Country protects teeming wildlife, shadowed canyons, and Wild West historic sites along the Rio Grande bordering the US and Mexico. See page 265.

THE BEST OF TEXAS: EDITOR'S CHOICE

Cadillac Ranch, Amarillo.

BEST MUSEUMS AND GALLERIES

Cadillac Ranch (Amarillo). Visit this humorous art installation featuring four partially-buried Cadillacs beside the interstate and add some graffiti of your own. See page 287.

The Orange Show Center for Visionary Art (Houston). This folk art museum is dedicated to the orange and is a community arts center supported by the likes of ZZ Top. See page 186.

Amon Carter Museum (Fort Worth). Artworks by Frederic Remington and Charles M. Russell, who specialized in depicting life on the range, are the highlights here. See page 120.

Nasher Sculpture Center (Dallas). This lovely outdoor setting in the Dallas Arts District displays artworks by Giacometti, Matisse, Miro, and other world-class sculptors. See page 107.

The Menil Collection and the Rothko Chapel (Houston). A world-class art collection combining Medieval and Byzantine art and contemporary works by Rothko, whose paintings have their own building. See page 186.

Museum of the Gulf Coast (Port Arthur). This museum interprets the Gulf Coast and its famed native sons and daughters, including Janis Joplin and Clarence Frogman Henry. See page 201.

Bullock Texas State History Museum (Austin). Texas's colorful history – from American Indians to six different flags – comes alive in this three-story museum next to the State Capitol. See page 145.

BEST WILDLIFE WATCHING

Galveston, Mustang, Padre Islands. Three of Texas's 350-mile (560km) -long barrier islands offer history, a chance to see rare whooping cranes, beachcombing, and camping. See page 214.

The Austin Bats. Ann W. Richards Congress Avenue Bridge in the Texas capital is home to a huge colony of Mexican freetail bats, which swirls forth at dusk in a crowd-pleasing spectacle. See page 147.

Big Thicket National Preserve. Rivers, pine woods, and desert come together in this large national preserve along the Texas–Louisiana border that is home to pileated woodpeckers and common night-hawks. See page 295.

High Island, Bolivar Peninsula. Texas Audubon operates four bird sanctuaries on High Island, an oak-dense upland used by neotropical migrant birds during their spring migrations. See page 214.

Bats over Ann W. Richards Congress Avenue Bridge, Austin.

BEST FESTIVALS AND EVENTS

Texas wildflowers.

Austin City Limits Music Festival. Around 150 bands perform over three days each September/October on the shores of Town Lake in downtown Austin, the self-proclaimed "Live Music Capital of the World." See page 144.

Kerrville Folk Festival. Springtime homage to folk and acoustic music, in the heart of Texas Hill Country. See page 154.

Cinco de Mayo and Diez y Seis. Mexican independence holidays celebrated on May 5 and September 16 each year. See page 52.

Spring wildflowers. Driving in the Hill Country to see bluebonnets, primroses, and other Texas flora is a time-honored Lone Star tradition. See page 158.

Juneteenth. Commemorating June 19, 1865, when Texas slaves learned they were free, this is a popular Galveston Festival. See page 214.

Willie Nelson's 4th of July Picnic. Fireworks, hot sun, cold beer, hours of music, and Willie Nelson make for an only-in-Texas blowout. Various locations. See page 81.

BEST TASTES OF TEXAS

Here is but a small selection of the many restaurants serving the best of Texas cooking around the state.

Barbecue. The Salt Lick (Austin).

Chicken-Fried Steak. Mary's Café (Strawn).

Tex-Mex. Molina's (Houston).

Gulf Coast Seafood. Gaido's Seafood Restaurant (Galveston).

Southern Comfort Food and Soul Food. Threadgills's (Austin).

High End Texas/Southwestern. Fearing's (Dallas).

Barbecue pit at the Salt Lick, Austin.

Reddish egret, Aransas National Wildlife Refuge.

BEST STATE AND NATIONAL PARKS

Big Bend National Park. This remote desert park in far West Texas showcases towering mountains, deep canyons, wild rivers, and the Chihuahuan Desert. See page 265.

Lost Maples State Natural Area. A Hill Country treasure, this park has rare out-croppings of bigtooth maples and Texas madrones, which provide some of the state's most beautiful fall colors. See page 298.

Palo Duro Canyon State Park. A dramatic slash in the Panhandle, Palo Duro Canyon has a long natural and cultural history that inspired the painter Georgia O'Keeffe. See page 301.

Franklin Mountains State Park. Skyline drives reveal dramatic views of El Paso and neighboring Juárez, Mexico from the nation's largest city park. See page 249.

Aransas National Wildlife Refuge. A birdwatchers' paradise along the middle of the Texas Coast, and home to the largest migrating colony of endangered whooping cranes. See page 300.

San Antonio Missions National Historical Park. This Unesco World Heritage Site had its origins in this ruggedly beautiful chain of churches along the San Antonio River (of which the Alamo is but one) in the San Antonio metropolitan area. See page 176.

Caddo Lake State Park. One of only a few natural lakes in Texas, this lake is a watery wilderness of cypress-shadowed sloughs and channels for canoers, kayakers, and anglers to explore to their hearts' content. See page 295.

The natural Hamilton Pool is a popular tourist destination in rural Travis County.

Chef at The Big Texan Steak Ranch.

Big Bend National Park.

Pearl Brewery, San Antonio.

WHERE BIG IS BEAUTIFUL

The myths are magnificent, but so is the reality. What appeals most about Texas – and Texans – is the huge diversity.

For many people, Texas is America – the one place where the American dream is still alive, where the values and traditions that helped build the nation are still a viable part of the culture. Think of all the American icons that come from Texas: the cowboy, the sheriff, the six-shooter, the 10-gallon hat, the maverick, the oil baron, the longhorn, and the open range, just to name a few. And how many times have you seen the big-hearted, drawling Texan used to represent Americans as a whole, slapping the world on the back and inviting it over for a barbecue? Distortions they may be, but they evoke an image of an America recognized around the world.

But to really get to know Texas, forget entirely about the "Big Texas" of legend and concentrate on something smaller. Texas has seven distinct regions (surprisingly few of which feature empty desert) and a plethora of cultural influences (as you'd expect from a state that boasts of having been governed by "Six Flags"). Sure, you'll encounter lonesome cowboys, wealthy oilmen, Hispanics, and American Indians – but expect the unexpected: a Vietnamese fishing community along the Gulf Coast, a Czech farming town out on the plains, Cajun enclaves in the piney woods bordering Louisiana, a ghost town that comes alive for country music in the Hill Country, and a community of contemporary New York artists in a dusty border town. Texas is even growing its own hipster culture in burgeoning Austin these days, as moneyed Silicon Valley types, students, natural foods purveyors, and musicians rub shoulders with politicians in what was once a small, out-of-the-way state capital.

Neon Lone Star flag.

Texas – it's a little bit country, a little bit rock and roll, and all heart. So gas up the iron horse – you'll certainly need to do a lot of driving – and hit the open road for adventures that will stoke your imagination for years to come.

A NOTE TO READERS

At Insight Guides, we always strive to bring you the most up-to-date information. This book was produced during a period of continuing uncertainty caused by the Covid-19 pandemic, so please note that content is more subject to change than usual. We recommend checking the latest restrictions and official guidance.

The Texas State Capitol, Austin.

THE LONE STAR STATE

Cultural traditions, economic realities, and the sheer distances involved mean that Texas could actually be five different states under its Lone Star.

Texas is truly a country within a country, befitting a state that was once its own republic. For starters, there's its size. At 268,000 sq miles (696,000 sq km), Texas is larger than many nations, including every country in Western Europe. It takes days just to drive from one side of the state to the other, passing through landscapes that shift from southern swamps and dripping forests to high plains and hilly ranch country to vast western desert, where the West really seems to start.

The variety of landscapes and the sheer size and space make for a chili gumbo of experiences, from small town to megacity, canyon country to gulf beaches, borderlands to heartlands, 21st-century skyscrapers and malls to historic missions and forts and villages that hark back to 19th-century Europe. There is a sense of room to stretch out and grow, even though in reality, most Texans live urban lives, and that has had a definite effect on how Texas sees itself, and others, in turn, see it.

Texans are inordinately proud of their state, and see themselves as Texans first, Americans second. There's a Texas way of doing things, but that takes on a different flavor depending on where you live in Texas, and that, for most visitors, is exactly why a visit here is so enjoyable.

Kicking back at the end of the day, Alpine, Texas.

DISTANCE AND DIFFERENCE

Traveling the entire state really does take a good deal of time. There are over 79,000 roadway miles (127,138km) 3,239 highway miles (5,212km), for example, between Texline on the northern border of the Texas Panhandle, and Brownsville at the mouth of the Rio Grande across from Mexico. From Texarkana in the northeast corner, beside the Arkansas border, to El Paso at the state's extreme western tip is 810 miles (1,300km).

As you cross this vast surface, everything changes: the configuration of the earth, the economy, time zones, and even the seasons. It is feasible to be snowbound in Amarillo one day and the next day to be sunbathing on the beaches of South Padre Island. Out west, in the mountainous areas of Big Bend and Fort Davis, or the Guadalupe Mountains adjoining New Mexico, the state's tallest peaks, the torrid summer endured in most of the state is pleasantly tempered by altitude. It takes only a little traveling around to understand why Texans never think of their province as one place, one thing, or one society.

CATTLE AND OIL

Cattle, then oil, originally fueled the state's economy and made it what it is, and both can be found, or have thrived, in almost every part of the state. In the early days, land and cattle were pretty much the only assets of the fledgling republic, which wasted no time in converting them into money, selling land to the federal government and longhorn steers by the millions to buyers in the American North and West.

Oil and gas, of course, are almost everywhere in the state, with only a handful of Texas's 254 counties not having found oil or natural gas within their boundaries. Texas is the largest petroleum-producing state in the US, and it has been estimated by economists that, if Texas were an independent nation, it would rank as one of the world's five largest petroleum-producing countries. Oil production took a hit during the recession, but thanks to oil- and gas-rich Eagle Shale deposits in South Texas and the potential for drilling in the newly discovered Barnett Shale in North Texas, it's back and it's booming again, driving a thriving economy that attracts new residents lured by jobs, lack of state tax, an inexpensive cost of living, and generous benefits for new business.

Though a sense of the past comes from human works – the buildings, roads, and other monuments resulting from centuries of creative efforts – what is under the land has often been more important in Texas than what is on top. Beginning 250 million years ago, during the Permian era, faults, folds, intrusions, and other geological movements formed the hidden reservoirs and basins that contain the great supplies of petroleum, natural gas, coal, salt, sulfur, and other minerals. Drilling has uncovered oil and gas in even older formations such as the Mississippian in North Texas and much younger Cretaceous era deposits in South Texas. It's clear that for Texas, its geology has been its destiny.

Big Bend National Park.

Not only has Texas increased in wealth and importance as a result of its subsurface minerals but also, in its most important agricultural region, the High Plains, water pumped to the surface from aquifers has transformed a desert into one of the world's great cotton- and food-producing areas.

FIVE STATES

When the old Republic of Texas became part of the United States in 1845, it retained the right to divide itself into as many as five states, should it so decide. Although Texas has so far not taken up this option, it still lurks at the back of some minds. Certainly breaking up the state would make this huge behemoth more manageable. As it is, in practice, the so-called "Five States of Texas" are mostly recognizable by the manner in which the inhabitants earn their living, the crops they farm, and their attitude toward their own and other people's customs, religions, and traditions.

BOUNDARIES

The exact boundaries of North, South, West, East, and Central Texas may vary, but the inhabitants of each region seem to accept the fairly general definitions. For example, when a Texan mentions West Texas, it is not just the geographical portion of the state that is being described; it is also a collection of traditions associated with that part of Texas and attached to its residents. And each major region contains its subregions, which are also recognizable to most Texans, including the Gulf Coast, the Rio Grande Valley, the Hill Country, the Texas Panhandle, and the High Plains, although these subregions have not acquired their own unique cultural patterns in the ways the larger geographic regions of Texas have.

WEST TEXAS GAMBLES

West Texans are considered highly individualistic, quick to react, but free with their purse and time. In West Texas one is seldom told, "I don't have time to see you now." Because so many of the region's leaders have associated themselves with ranching and the oil business, West Texans are seen as people willing to gamble – forced to gamble, in fact, by the nature of their enterprises. Ranching, whether cattle or sheep and goats, is a cyclical undertaking, dependent on the fluctuations of both the weather and the market.

Oil is famous for not always being where the prospector drills, but it can also reward its finder, and the landowner, with instant wealth. Most West Texas ranches today depend on oil and gas from their vast acres for economic survival. But all over Texas, the sight of the "horsehead" pump is common, some towering as high as a three-story building, pulling oil from those ancient Permian reefs and seabeds many meters below the surface. You'll see more pump jacks than cowboys, even in West Texas, which was once informally known as "Big Ranch Country."

These days, you're also likely to see a great many wind turbines in the state: if Texas were a country, it would rank fifth in the world for wind power capacity. Right now, it produces one-quarter of all US wind-power electricity. Wilderado Wind Ranch, off I-40 near Amarillo, is the largest in the state, with 161 turbines capable of producing enough electricity to power 50,000 households.

View from South Padre Island.

The stark flatness of the area, the open spaces that seem to go on forever, and the huge sky are often startling to newcomers, who will immediately understand the meaning of the term "high lonesome". Texans make a distinction between the part of West Texas that stretches from the western edge of Hill Country, southwest of Austin, to El Paso, in the state's southwestern corner, bordering Mexico and New Mexico, and the northwestern Panhandle, which includes the cities of Lubbock and Amarillo, along old Route 66 (now I-40), and into New Mexico.

Workers on the 6666 ranch, Guthrie.

SOUTHERN FOLK

East Texas natives, especially old timers, are held by the rest of Texas to be shrewder, more southern-rural, and often gifted with a special kind of earthy humor and wisdom.

This is the part of Texas most like the Old South back in the time of its agricultural dominance, with former cotton plantations and slow, unhurried ways. Here, you'll find a more humid climate, dense forests, swamps, and wide, slow-moving rivers, while, at its western edges, some 500 miles (800km) away, lie arid deserts, barren mountains, and streams that, although they turn into "gullywashers" when full, are often dry.

Even today, East Texas is a region of mostly smaller towns and many rural communities of the crossroads variety, consisting of a general store, a service station, a couple of churches (usually Protestant), and maybe a schoolhouse, left empty when the country schools were consolidated years ago. East Texas, incidentally, has produced some of Texas's better-known writers and other artists, many of them working from the strong sense of tradition that seems to come with the land. The late William Goyen's writings were filled with East Texas imagery. Alvin Ailey, the renowned choreographer, was born in East Texas. And sculptor James Surls is based in East Texas and uses woods found in the area as his main medium.

DOWN TO THE BORDER

South Texas starts (in the Texas mind) at San Antonio and continues southward to the Rio Grande, which forms the natural and official US–Mexico border, or as it is known, *La Frontera*. Along its edges, it supports two separate cultures: the long, well-populated curve of the Gulf Coast and that other world of mostly Hispanic Texans along *La Frontera*. South Texas was the birthplace of the Texas cowboy, who began as a Mexican *vaquero* (the Western term "buckaroo" is a corruption of the Spanish word), and of the 19th-century cattle drives made famous in story, film, and song. It remains a spread-out, sparse land, containing several of the state's major ranches, including the famous historic 825,000-acre (334,000-hectare) King Ranch on the far southwestern border.

Several huge Hispanic land grants in South Texas, granted by the king of Spain to the ancestors of current holders for services rendered centuries ago, remain today. That kind of centuries-old tradition strongly influences the attitudes of South Texans, who have the reputation of being easy-going yet fiercely loyal when it comes to "*familia y fe*" (family and faith) and political leaders. The lower Rio Grande Valley, called simply "The Valley" by Texans, furnishes a significant percentage of the citrus fruit and vegetables for sale in the US.

One of two major new oil deposits in Texas has recently been discovered in South Texas in the younger Cretaceous-era Eagle Ford Shale underlying most of this region. While the shale reaches the surface in North Texas, the oil-bearing portions are deeper down and occur entirely in South Texas, where most drilling is taking place. It is now one of the leading oil drilling regions in the country.

SELLING THE GOODS

North Texans share fewer traditional traits, probably because of the region's long-time role as merchant to the rest of Texas and the Southwest. North Texas is famous for its mega shopping, including the flagship Neiman Marcus department store in Dallas, and sells everything from clothing to electronics. Because the metroplex of Dallas–Fort Worth is so huge and wealthy, North Texans see themselves as more sophisticated than other parts of Texas, although the statement meets fierce and determined resentment if repeated too often: citizens of Austin in Central Texas and Houston in East Texas are not known for their high opinion of Dallas, though almost everyone praises Fort Worth for its old-fashioned charm and ranching traditions.

The local economy may be transformed by the recent discovery of the Mississippian-era Barnett

Wall mural near Mission Concepción.

Numerous playwrights have lived and worked in North Texas. Preston Jones wrote A Texas Trilogy and Don Coburn wrote The Gin Game, a Pulitzer Prize-winner. Larry L. King's musical Best Little Whorehouse in Texas was a hit in the 1970s and 80s.

Shale, much older than the Permian era deposits found in West Texas. The Barnett formation is rich in natural gas, as well as having oil in significant quantities. Extraction has been controversial, however, as most of the formation lies under Dallas–Fort Worth within extremely hard shale.

IN THE MIDDLE

In the past, Central Texas has not been as well defined geographically as other parts of the state. That's certainly not the case now. Its lovely, rolling, wildflower hills, freshwater lakes, viticulture scene, traditional German- and Czech-influenced small towns, and scenic backroads have become a major Texas destination for cultural travelers – and those who just enjoy a more relaxed and human-scale way of life.

Hill Country, as it's known, is within a stone's throw of the state capital of Austin, famed for its own (taller) version of the US capitol, a growing high-tech sector, and the University of Texas, whose students have helped foster an exciting live music scene, natural and gourmet foods (this is home base for Whole Foods), and a fun and funky attitude to everything, from outdoor pursuits to culture. Its alternative vibe, neatly summed up by the "Keep Austin Weird" slogan adopted by the city's many small businesses, is in marked contrast to the conservative nature of the rest of the state.

Dallas skyscrapers.

Friday night football is popular across Texas. Buzz Bissinger's book Friday Night Lights tells the true story of a high school football team that boosted morale in the depressed town of Odessa. The book spawned a cult film and TV series.

Central Texas has contributed a large proportion of political figures to the lore of the Lone Star State. Foremost among them, of course, is Lyndon Baines Johnson (LBJ), US Vice President under John F. Kennedy, who ascended to the presidency under tragic circumstances in 1963, won election on his own terms, and presided until 1969, passing a remarkable amount of important legislation, including Civil Rights. LBJ was born in Hill Country and taught school there. He never attempted to pull up those roots during his journey to the White House, and visiting his ranch (as well as the Lady Bird Johnson Wildflower Center in Austin founded by the first lady in Austin) is one of the most enjoyable destinations as you tour the region.

Country road, West Texas.

A Civil War era map of Texas and the Gulf of Mexico.

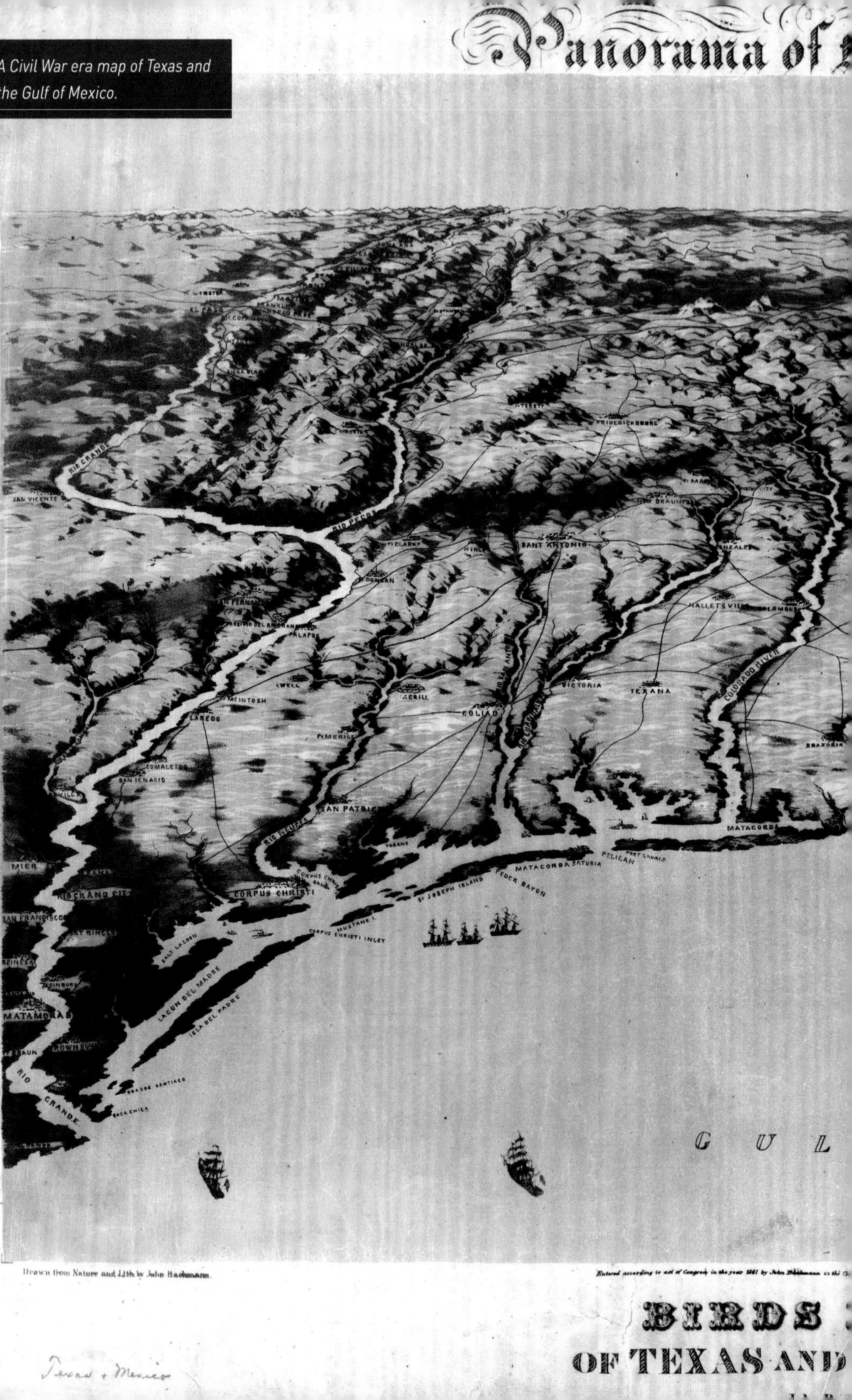

e Seat of War.

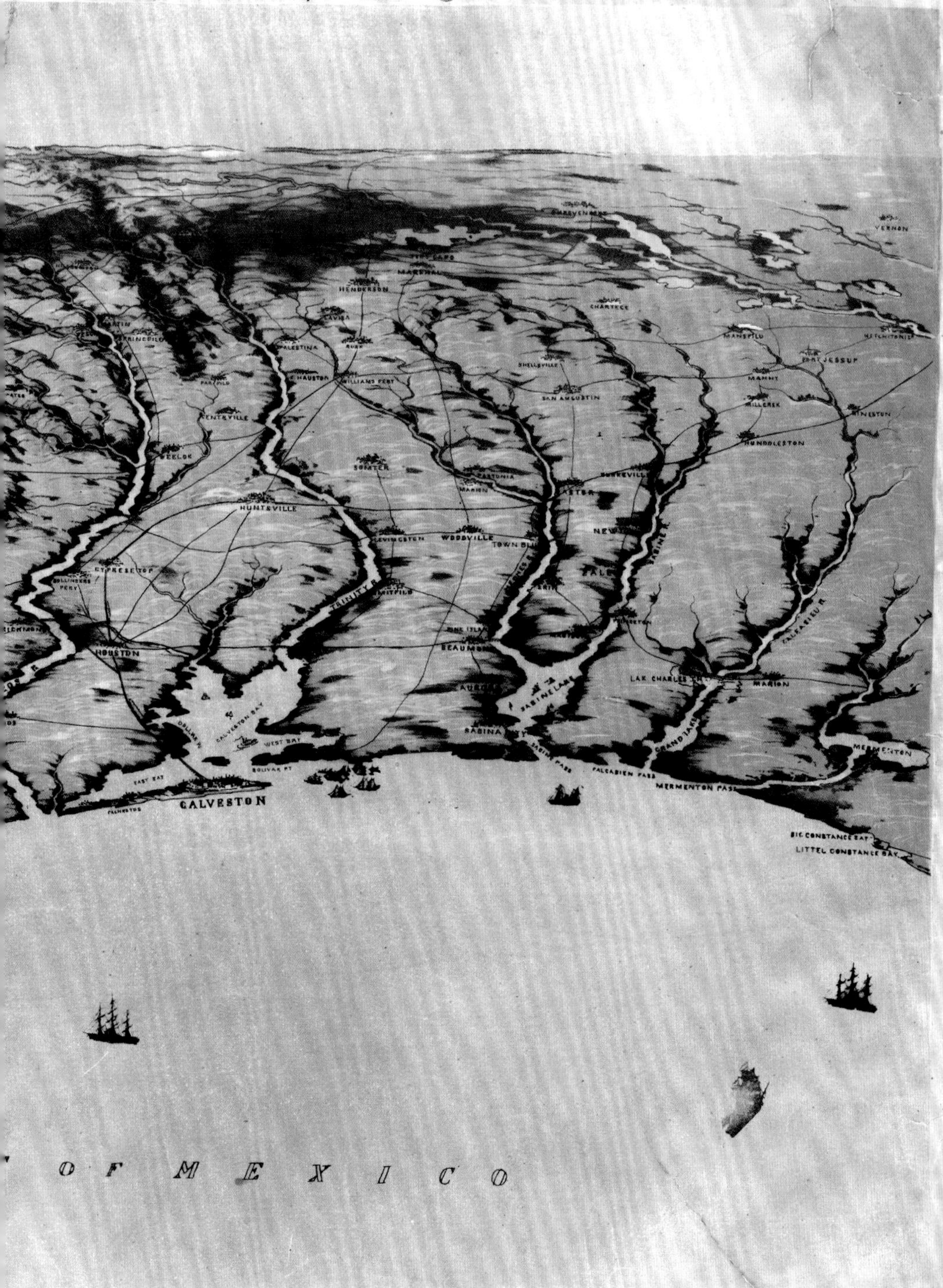

f the District Court of the U.S. for the Southern District of New York.

YE VIEW

ART OF MEXICO

DECISIVE DATES

1519
Spain lays claim to the region comprising the present state of Texas.

1685
La Salle lands in Matagorda Bay and sets up a short-lived French colony.

1718
Governor Martín de Alarcón leads a small group which establishes the mission San Antonio de Valero (the Alamo) and the Presidio San Antonio de Bexar along the San Antonio River.

1758
Construction begins on the present Alamo chapel.

1793
San Antonio de Valero mission is closed and its lands are divided up among Indian families.

1803
A Spanish cavalry unit from San Carlos del Alamo de Parras occupies the mission as a garrison.

The storming of the Alamo.

1823
Stephen F. Austin brings the first 300 families to help Mexico settle Texas.

1824
Mexican constitution promises Texas statehood.

1830
Law of April 6 toughens restrictions on immigration from the US into Texas, heightening tensions between Anglo settlers and Mexico.

1834
Santa Anna is elected president and starts to centralize the Mexican government.

REVOLUTION

1835
Texas revolt begins; San Antonio is occupied. The Texas Rangers are officially instituted.

1836
Santa Anna invades. Texas declares independence. Siege and battle of the Alamo. All defenders of the mission are killed. Santa Anna is later defeated at San Jacinto. Texas becomes an independent republic.

1839
Austin, formerly the village of Waterloo, is established as the new nation's capital.

1841
Republic of Texas' President Mirabeau Lamar sends a small armed force to New Mexico in a vain attempt to seize territory from Mexico.

1842
Santa Anna retaliates by twice seizing San Antonio, leading to an expedition by mutinous Texas volunteers that ends in disaster at Mier.

1844
US Senate rejects annexation treaty with the Republic of Texas, dashing hopes until the election of US President James K. Polk, who revives the annexation effort; it passes the following year.

1846
Ending almost a decade of independence, Texas joins the US. War breaks out between Mexico and the US.

1848
War ends. The Rio Grande becomes a permanent international boundary in the Treaty of Guadalupe Hidalgo.

1850
US Army repairs the Alamo.

1853
The Buffalo Bayou Brazos and Colorado – the first railroad

chartered by Texas – begins operating.

1854
The state establishes two Indian reservations.

1858
The army imports camels for use in the arid western part of the state.

1861
Texas secedes from the Union in favor of the Confederacy. The Alamo is used by the Confederate Army during the war between the states.

Battle of Resaca de la Palma, 1848 (Mexican-American War).

1865
Final battle of the Civil War fought near Brownsville, Texas, after the war's official end. Announcement at Galveston that slavery has been abolished.

1866
Large-scale cattle drives to the north begin.

1870
Texas is readmitted to the Union.

1873
Record annual rainfall (109ins/279cm) at Clarksville.

1875
Comanche Chief Quanah Parker loses his last fight and is forced onto a reservation, effectively ending Indian wars in Texas.

1876
Charles Goodnight founds the J.A. Ranch at Palo Duro Canyon, the first cattle ranch in northwest Texas.

1884
Fence cutting wars; new laws ban the practice.

1888
The Alamo chapel, having been used as a warehouse, is sold by the Catholic Church to the state.

1894
Oil is discovered at Corsicana.

EARLY 20TH CENTURY

1900
Hurricane destroys half of Galveston and kills 6,000 people.

1901
Mining engineer Captain A.F. Lucas discovers the Spindletop gusher near Beaumont.

1905
State of Texas grants custodianship of the Alamo to the Daughters of the Republic of Texas.

1907
Neiman Marcus department store opens in downtown Dallas.

1910
First military flight in a Wright Brothers plane at Fort Sam Houston.

1916
Pancho Villa and his men cross the border to raid Texas communities.

1917
Race riots occur in Houston. Texas legislature votes to impeach Governor Jim Ferguson for mismanagement of state funds.

1920
Texas–Mexico border skirmishes come to an end.

1925
Miriam "Ma" Ferguson, wife of impeached Governor Jim Ferguson, becomes the first female Governor of Texas. She is re-elected for a second term in 1933.

1930
Oil strike by C.M. "Dad" Joiner 100 miles (160km) east of Dallas becomes the East Texas Oil Field, the largest petroleum deposit on earth at that time.

1932
Texan Babe Didrikson Zaharias wins three Olympic gold medals.

1933
Texan Wiley Post makes first solo flight around the world.

1934
Career of Depression-era bank robbers Bonnie Parker and Clyde Barrow ends in a hail of bullets, after a 102-day manhunt led by Texas Ranger Frank Hamer.

POST-DEPRESSION TEXAS

1947
Fiery chain explosions demolish much of the coastal refinery town of Texas City, killing almost 600 and injuring almost 4,000.

1953
Dwight D. Eisenhower becomes the first Texas-born President of the US.

1956
George Stevens' movie of Edna Ferber's novel *Giant* is released to wide popularity, forever fixing the myth of tough Texas oilmen in American folklore.

1958
Texas Instruments' Jack Kilby ushers in the electronics age with his revolutionary development of the silicon chip.

1959
Lubbock-born rock 'n' roll singer Buddy Holly dies in an airplane crash.

1962
NASA opens Manned Spacecraft Center at Houston.

1963
President John F. Kennedy is assassinated while touring Dallas in a motorcade with Texas Governor John Connally. Kennedy's Texan-born Vice-President, Lyndon B. Johnson, is elevated to presidency.

1964
Lyndon B. Johnson wins election for the presidency in the largest landslide in US history.

1969
Apollo 11 commander Neil Armstrong calls Houston from the moon.

1976
Houston Democrat Barbara Jordan becomes the first African-American woman to deliver a keynote address at a party conference.

1978
Dallas TV drama series begins and is soon screened all over the world.

1985
Larry McMurtry's novel *Lonesome Dove*, about a Texas cattle drive, is published to immense popular and critical acclaim; TV adaptation follows.

1988
Sometime Houstonian George H.W. Bush is elected US President.

1993
Federal agents storm the compound of the Branch Davidians sect near Waco, resulting in more than 80 deaths. El Paso author Cormac McCarthy wins the National Book Award for *All the Pretty Horses*.

1998
Murderess Karla Faye Tucker becomes the first woman to be executed in Texas since 1863.

2001
Texas Governor George W. Bush, Jr, son of George H.W. Bush, is sworn in as the 43rd President of the US. Tropical Storm Allison claims 23 lives. Thousands lose their jobs as Houston-based energy company, Enron, collapses.

2005
When Hurricane Katrina devastates the city of New Orleans in neighboring state Louisiana, East Texas takes some 200,000 refugees, most settling in Houston. The majority are still living there.

Spindletop oil field, 1915.

2006
The Dallas Cowboys start construction on a new stadium, moving the team from the suburb of Irving to the suburb of Arlington.

2007
Former First Lady Texan and conservationist, Lady Bird Johnson, dies at age 94.

2008
Hurricane Ike hits the Gulf Coast island of Galveston, causing destruction and power outages in Galveston and parts of nearby Houston for 21 days. The adjoining Bolivar Peninsular, a popular birding and vacation spot, is hard hit.

2009
The Texas Board of Education approves a science curriculum that opened the door for teachers and textbooks to raise doubts about evolution.

2010
Charlie Wilson (b.1933), former Texas congressman (1973–96), dies. His deal-making funneled millions of dollars in weapons to Afghanistan to back rebels fighting the Soviet Army. Tom Hanks starred as Charlie Wilson in the 2007 film *Charlie Wilson's War*, based on the 2003 book by George Crile.

2011
The underdog Dallas Mavericks defeat the Miami Heat four games to two, to capture their first ever NBA championship.

2012
Texas governor Rick Perry ends his presidential campaign and endorses Newt Gingrich's candidacy for the 2012 Republican presidential nomination.

Former president George W. Bush.

2013
A fiery explosion rips through the West Fertilizer Co. in West (pop. 2,700), north of Waco, injuring more than 200 people and causing $100 million in damage. The Czech government later donates $200,000 in aid to assist West, in solidarity with the many people there with Czech roots.

2014
TransCanada begins delivering oil from Cushing, Oklahoma, to customers in Nederland, Texas, through the southern portion of the controversial proposed Keystone XL pipeline.

2015
Senator Ted Cruz announces his candidacy for the Republican nomination for President of the United States, but withdraws after losing to rival candidate Donald Trump in the Indiana Primary.

2016
First case of Zika virus in the US reported in Texas.

2017
Hurricane Harvey causes over 70 deaths and catastrophic damage in the Houston metropolitan area. A gunman kills 26 people after opening fire at a church in Sutherland Springs in South Texas.

2018
Five package bombings kill two people in Austin. Outspoken Texas congressman Beto O'Rourke tours all 254 Texas counties in his campaign for Senate against Ted Cruz, which he ultimately loses by a narrow margin.

2019
Texas makes headlines for the inhumane treatment of migrant children separated from their parents at the border and placed in detention center "cages". The El Paso Wal-Mart mass shooting leaves 22 people dead and the Midland-Odessa drive-by shooter kills seven. White police officer Amber Guyger is jailed for shooting and killing her unarmed black neighbor, when she mistook his apartment for her own.

2021
Joe Biden is inaugurated as the 46th President of the United States. Winter brings brutal weather conditions, with at least 26 people passing away. Millions are cut of power and experience water disruptions. Many are forced to spend nights in vehicles. Republican senator, Ted Cruz, causes outcry as he leaves the state for a holiday in Mexico while the exceptional weather takes over the state. The Covid-19 pandemic hits Texas hard. In April, it is reported that the state has the second-highest rate of cases, behind California.

The famous six flags of Texas.

SIX FLAGS OVER TEXAS

Control of Texas has been handed from one external power to another, but independence and self-determination remain the watchwords of its people.

Pass through a few Texas towns large enough to have an independent school system, and the names on the schools will begin to take on a familiar sound: Austin, Crockett, Fannin, Bonham, Lamar, Travis, Houston. Every town will have buildings or streets carrying one or more of those names, too.

Schoolchildren, taught Texas history by legislative decree, grow up on stories about its legendary heroes. Today, with thousands of Hispanic and black students, schools are beginning to be called by the names of ethnic heroes such as Benito Juárez, Emiliano Zapáta, or Martin Luther King. Historical mythology is strong in all ethnic groups.

Unlike New England or the Atlantic seaboard states, Texas had no single source of settlement. White men came quite early to some parts of the state and arrived 350 years later to the others. The famous "Six Flags Over Texas" theme is rooted in historical fact. Each flag – those of Spain, Mexico, France, the Republic of Texas, the Confederacy, and the United States – represented a separate, if brief, period of the state's history.

The Texan coast may have been sighted by Amerigo Vespucci as early as 1497, but there is evidence of much earlier inhabitants – some possibly as far back as 37,000 years. Archeological studies have revealed no grand past civilizations in Texas such as were found in Mexico and Central and South America, but there were cliff dwellers in the Texas Panhandle, and cave dwellers left traces of their fascinating paintings for us to ponder throughout West Texas. The Caddoconfederations encountered in East Texas by the first Europeans were an agricultural people.

Stephen Fuller Austin rallies colonists against the Karankawas c.1824.

COLONIZATION

Along the Gulf Coast, from Galveston Bay southwestward to Corpus Christi Bay, lived the nomadic Karankawas. Said to be practitioners of ceremonial cannibalism, and always incredibly fierce, they had been wiped out by the white man's diseases and bullets by the 1850s. The American Indians that the Texas settlers battled against were Plains tribes who rode in from the north on horses descended from those brought to the New World by early Spanish explorers.

One of these Spanish explorers, Alvar Núñez Cabeza de Vaca, was cast ashore on what is believed to have been Galveston Island, working his way across Texas for eight years before finally reaching Spanish Mexico in 1536.

He and three other shipwrecked survivors of the Narvaez expedition, including a Moroccan slave named Esteban, later known as Estevanico, were enslaved by the Karankawas. But after escaping, they gained such reputations as medicine men that, when they approached a strange tribe, everyone turned out to welcome them.

When Cabeza de Vaca and Esteban returned to civilization with tales of cities of gold and pearl in El Norte, the myth of the Seven Cities of Cibola became the motive for several Spanish expeditions to Arizona, New Mexico, and Texas. These golden cities, and the equally mythical Gran Quivira, were never found, of course, but the search for them led to Spanish colonization of the Southwest.

Sam Houston, Governor of Tennessee and Texas.

THE ALAMO

The Alamo's defenders were recent arrivals from England, Ireland, Scotland, and Denmark, as well as the United States, and their 26-year-old commander, William B. Travis from South Carolina, wrote three days before he died that "the citizens of this municipality are our enemies." His associates included opportunists such as Jim Bowie, remembered for his namesake knife, and the legendary Davy Crockett, a three-term congressman from Kentucky who sought his fortune in the West after his presidential ambitions evaporated. The independent Texas for which they fought and died survived just nine years before being subsumed by the United States.

It was France laying claim to the area around Matagorda Bay that caused the Spanish to begin settling Texas. In 1685, French explorer René Robert Cavelier, Sieur de La Salle, had landed on the Texas coast and built a fort. By the time Spanish authorities in Mexico heard of the French intrusion, La Salle had been killed by his own men and the colony wiped out by American Indians. Nevertheless, the nervous Spanish began to build missions on the border between French Louisiana and Spanish Texas.

In East Texas they met Caddo Indians, who greeted them with the cry "Tejas!" Thinking this was the name of a large tribe, the Spanish explorers called the area *Tejas*, or Texas. Later, settlers realized the word was a widely used greeting meaning "friend".

SPANISH HERITAGE

Despite owning Texas for nearly three centuries, the Spanish settled it only for protection, in narrow strips along the coast and the rivers. Even San Antonio, the major Spanish settlement, was more important militarily and as a mission than as a commercial center.

Spain's mark, however, is still strong in Texas, with many of the outstanding geographical features and major rivers bearing Spanish names. Numerous Spanish missions still stand, at least partly restored, and various Spanish legal terms and property laws survive as Texas statutes.

Perhaps the most important Spanish inheritance was passed to cattle ranching. Almost every practice and piece of equipment used by ranchers has a Spanish name and origin. These range from *chicote* (a rawhide whip) to *tumbador* (someone who throws calves ready for branding).

The older regions of greatest Spanish colonization, from San Antonio and Laredo south, especially those along the Rio Grande, still show evidence of this influence in their architecture, language, religion, and everyday customs.

Between 1811 and 1821, Spain found itself continually putting down rebellions in Texas.

In 1811, the young Santa Anna, later to be the scourge of the Alamo but then still a junior officer, was in one of these disciplinary forces. At the same time, the Spanish authorities recognized that the sparsely occupied parts of Texas were always under threat unless developed, so they encouraged immigration. Moses Austin was among the men who applied for an *empresario* grant but, when he died just after receiving it, his son, Stephen Fuller Austin (today known as the "Father of Texas"), renegotiated it in his own name and brought in 300 settlers.

Those first colonists are to Anglo-Texas what the passengers of the *Mayflower* are to Massachusetts: the proudest bloodlines go back to "The Old 300." In 1821, Mexico gained its independence from Spain and, within the next decade, 41 *empresario* contracts were signed, permitting the arrival of nearly 14,000 Anglo-Americans to supplement the original Spanish population. Eventually, hundreds more settlers joined the Austin colonists.

THE TEXAS NATION

"Texians" (as they were then called) never learned to get along well with the Latin laws, religion, and political practices of Mexico. Aggravated by the unpopular Law of April 6 1830, which aimed to restrict Anglo immigration, the Anglo-American majority in Texas led a rebellion against what were considered despotic governmental practices in 1835. In reality, the despotism was mainly created by Mexican dictator Santa Anna.

The Texas Revolution lasted only eight months, but it gave Texas the myth and image that Texans are exhorted to live up to. It was this short but successful period of rebellion that created the Texas Valhalla, with such heroes as Ben Milam, James Fannin, Jim Bowie, William B. Travis, James Bonham, Davy Crockett with his fellow Tennesseeans, and General Sam Houston.

From the Texas Revolution came the stories of the Alamo (still largely a matter of conjecture), those 13 fateful days in 1836 when 189 patriots held out against the fierce onslaught of 4,000 Mexicans, who eventually overran the fort, killing all its defenders, save for a few women, children, and slaves.

Minimizing his losses, Santa Anna said: "It was but a small affair," and ordered that the bodies of the heroes be burned. His aide, noting that he took many casualties, losing many of his best men, muttered: "Another such victory and we are ruined."

The Caddo Indian cry "tejas" ("friend"), from which the state derived its name, has been translated over the years into the Texas state motto: "friendship."

Texas battle flag in Austin's State Capitol.

Forty-six days later, the Texans got their revenge. Along with a group of American volunteers, and led by General Sam Houston, they avenged their fallen at San Jacinto.

Taking Santa Anna and his 1,500 men by surprise, Houston's force, though greatly outnumbered, routed the Mexicans within minutes. "Remember the Alamo," they shouted to each other as they charged, and it has never been forgotten. Santa Anna was captured, 600 of his troops were killed, and Texas was free. A new republic was born.

The period that followed sowed the seeds of the feelings of loyalty for which Texans are so famous. And no matter how diverse their lives, or how far from Texas they may wander, all Texans hold the Alamo in common ownership.

For less than a decade, from 1836 to 1845, the Republic of Texas was an independent nation with its own flag, its own ambassadors, its own president and congress, and, after some moving around, its own specifically designed national capital at Austin. It is true that millions of Texans today may recall the republic only occasionally, but they have never entirely forgotten it.

Their self-reliance and fierce loyalty (which

The dome of the Texas Capitol building, Austin.

has not always endeared Texans to their fellow American citizens) come from that decade of independence. The state seal and the Lone Star flag, which is still displayed as frequently as the national banner, remain from that independent government.

FIRST PRESIDENT

Commander of the army Sam Houston was elected as first president of the new Republic of Texas, his 5,119 votes far outnumbering the total votes of his rivals (Henry Smith, 743; Stephen F. Austin, 587).

The Mexicans were still to cause major trouble in the next decade, when, in 1842, they invaded Texas and briefly captured San Antonio before withdrawing. And there was also the American Indian problem.

Sam Houston had lived among the Cherokee, and understood their mentality more than most. He wanted to stabilize the situation, and proposed a guarantee of tribal rights through legal title to their lands. But he found that he was unable to keep the promises he made to the Cherokee. When Houston's term expired, the new president, Mirabeau Lamar, proposed that all American Indians be expelled from East Texas: "Nothing short of this will bring us peace and safety," Lamar thundered, "the white man and the red man cannot live in harmony together... Nature forbids it..."

The republic expanded rapidly, tripling its population, but the influx of slaves – brought by southerners settling on the Gulf Coast to develop the cotton crop – led to disputes when Texans voted to join the Union in 1845.

As part of the annexation arrangement, the US Congress assumed the Texas Republic's $10 million in debts and allowed Texas to retain possession of all undistributed land (although, in the 1840s and 1850s, much of it was still in the possession of the Comanche). There were no federal taxes in effect, but Texas had no wealth, only land. It sold to the US its rights to New Mexico and Colorado, and Sam Houston and other conservatives supported the Boundary Act on the grounds that the state had more desert land than it could use.

Pressing for funds for frontier defense, Texas persuaded Congress to give it an extra $7.75 million in 1855. With the money, the state launched a major building program of state structures, courthouses, schools, transportation systems – all of which was achieved without imposing taxes. This then conditioned Texas to look for sources other than taxes to finance its activities, a situation that continues today.

By 1860, when Sam Houston was elected governor for a second term, Texas was again in debt. The following year, when the Civil War broke out, Houston was forced to resign after he refused to swear allegiance to the Confederacy. Houston died in 1863. Three months after his burial, the Confederate legislature of Texas passed a resolution: "His public services through a long and eventful life, his unblemished patriotism, his great private and moral worth, and his untiring, devoted and zealous regard for the interests of the state of Texas command our highest admiration, and should be held in perpetual remembrance by the people of this state."

NEWCOMERS

During the period of revolution, resettlement, and republic, thousands of people came to Texas to get away from whatever their life had been "back home." They weren't always fleeing from the law. More often, the new Texans came west to escape failure or some sort of unhappiness that could be left behind. This is very much a continuing tradition as, even today, Texas becomes home for thousands who leave other parts of the nation every month to seek new opportunities in the Lone Star State. A high percentage of the dead at the Alamo, and a majority of the unfortunates who were slaughtered earlier at Goliad, were recent arrivals in Texas; even Davy Crockett, the superhero of the Alamo, had only been in Texas for a few weeks. The tradition of the newcomer hero has a long history.

At the time of the Civil War, most Texas settlers were from the agricultural South. A plantation economy, with its accompanying slavery,

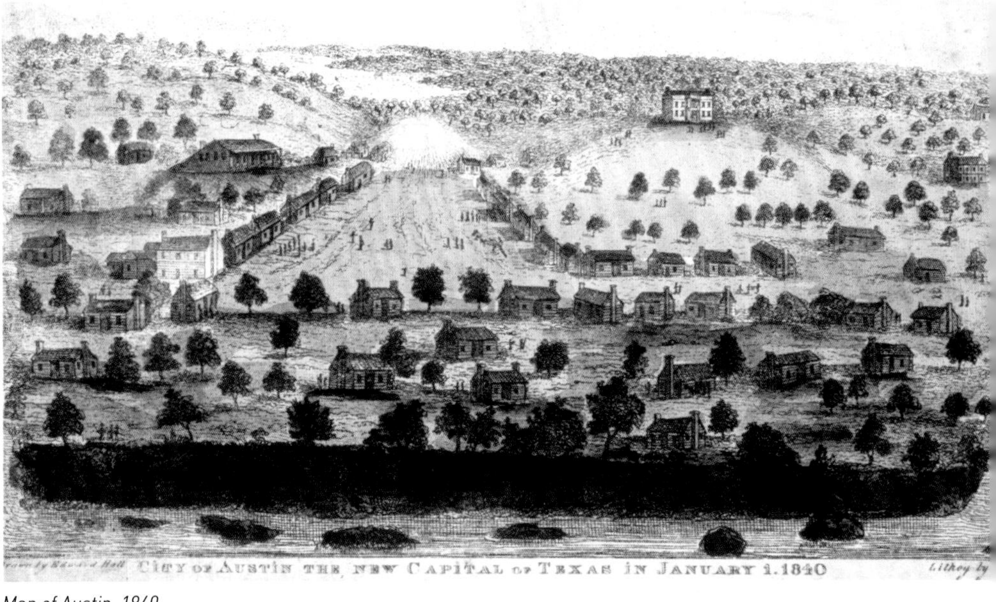

Map of Austin, 1840.

SAM HOUSTON

Sam Houston's victory at the Battle of Jacinto over Mexican General Santa Anna, in April 1836, secured Texas's independence from Mexico and, using the rallying cry "Remember the Alamo," avenged the deaths of the ragtag band of martyred revolutionaries at the Alamo two months earlier. Houston was the only American to be elected governor of two different states – Tennessee (1827–9) and Texas (1859–61) – and the only Southern governor to oppose secession and refuse to swear an oath of allegiance to the Confederacy when Texas seceded from the Union in 1861, following the outbreak of the Civil War.

Houston was a complex character. He was born in Virginia and moved to Tennessee, where he lived among the Cherokee, married into the tribe, and was later adopted as a citizen. He resigned the governorship of Tennessee and moved to Arkansas, only to become embroiled in politics again, which led to his migration to Texas. Following his removal from office as Texas governor, he moved to Huntsville, where he died in 1863. Houston was honored after his death with a memorial museum, four US warships named USS *Houston* a US Army base, a national forest, a historical park, a university, and a prominent roadside statue outside Huntsville. Best known, of course, is the city to which he gave his name – Houston in East Texas – the fourth largest city in the US.

controlled East Texas and the Coastal Plains, where cotton was a profitable crop. Thus, Texas was overwhelmingly drawn into the Civil War on the side of the Confederacy. It was never torn by any major battles, and, after the war, sectional wounds healed quicker in Texas than in any other southern state. Within a decade, newcomers from northern states were not only arriving in great numbers but were assuming positions of business and economic leadership.

Unusually, Texas owns nearly all of its public lands. Technically, if the federal government wishes to create a park it has to ask the state's permission.

Bird's eye view of Houston, 1873.

BARBED WIRE

By the 1880s, would-be ranchers from all over the world were flocking to Texas, but overstocking, followed by a severe drought, led to the inevitable bust. People believed that stock had to be conserved and contained. Fencing was primarily constructed from the osage tree at the time, but this changed in 1874, when an Illinois man, Joseph F. Glidden, was granted a patent for new fencing material that consisted of barbs wrapped around a single strand of wire. There were hundreds of competing designs, but Glidden's eventually won out. You can learn more about barbed wire at the Devil's Rope Barbed Wire Museum in McLean, Texas.

OPPORTUNITY FRONTIER

When the Union blockaded the Gulf Coast during the Civil War, Texas managed to smuggle some cotton across the Rio Grande for shipment to world markets, but the blockade was serving another purpose then unknown. Unable to export its cattle even to the Confederate Army, Texas's herds built up to more than 3 million during the Civil War. Once the war was over, there was tremendous demand for this beef in northern and western states.

Texas went through relatively little of the sorrow and desperation of the Reconstruction period. And because it was the only ex-Confederate state that offered its southern sister states hope of a new beginning, southerners flocked there. The 15 years that followed Appomattox saw Texas emerge as the opportunity frontier of the whole nation, north and south alike. It has retained that position, and has continued to uphold that reputation.

Families from every social level picked up and moved to Texas, pushing forward the old frontier boundaries until, like a flooding river, newcomers swept out onto the prairies and battled American Indians for the wealth of grass and soil that was once thought to be the "Great American Desert." This movement to the frontier created two new Texas myths: one was the frontiersman and his sturdy pioneer wife, and the other was the cowboy.

THE END OF THE OPEN RANGE

Texas was readmitted to the Union in 1870 and, with the 1875 surrender of Comanche chief Quanah Parker at Fort Sill, Oklahoma, the far western portion of the state was finally ready for ranching on a large scale. Barely a decade later, though, the wide-open spaces were being fenced and confined as settlers and sheep farmers fought to contain the open range.

In 1894, oil was discovered at Corsicana by workers drilling for water. With the discovery of the major gusher at Spindletop in 1901, Texas entered the new century with an economic boom.

THE GREAT CATTLE DRIVES

With hardy livestock and even hardier cowboys, life on the great cattle trails of the 19th century was no picnic but remains one of the iconic images most associated with Texas.

The first cattle known to have entered Texas were 500 cows that had been brought in by Spanish conquistador Coronado in 1541. Subsequent explorers also brought cattle, which gradually wandered into the wilderness. By 1757, Reynosa (pop. 269) had 18,000 head of cattle. A fat cow was worth four pesos in 1779, with hides and tallow more valuable than beef. Mission Espiritu Santo, on the banks of the winding Guadalupe River, between present-day Victoria and Mission Valley, was the first great cattle ranch in Texas. Around 1770, it claimed 40,000 head of cattle.

The definitive Texas cow was the longhorn – a hybrid breed from Spanish *retinto* (criollo) stock and English Hereford and Bakewell cattle that were brought in from Ohio, Kentucky, and other southern and midwestern states in the 1820s and '30s. Their long horns had a spread of 5–6ft (1.5–2 meters), with some spanning a full 8ft (2.5 meters) from tip to tip. They were apparently "tough to eat and tougher to handle" but, with their long legs and hard hooves, were ideal trail cattle that gained weight even on the way to market.

By the mid-19th century, great hordes of Texas longhorns that had been roaming freely, and shaped by nature and environmental conditions, were being gathered into herds for the trail drive north. Cattleman Edward Piper made what may have been the first northern drive in 1846, moving a herd from Texas to Ohio. He was followed almost immediately by many other contractors, especially after the end of the Civil War.

The drive cost the herd's owner about $500 per month, worked out on the basis of about 75¢ per head of cattle for three months. Eight to 20 hands were needed to trail a herd of 2,000–3,000 cattle, about one man per 250–350 animals, with crews including a trail boss and cook plus a horse wrangler (usually a young boy), to handle the six or eight mounts needed for each man. The all-important trail boss had "as many duties as the captain of a steamboat." He arose early to wake and assign the men, ensured there were always enough provisions, settled all disputes, kept counting the cattle to see none had been lost, and rode ahead to check on water supplies. Exploring ahead, the boss would ride part way back and, from some hilltop, wave his hat to indicate which direction the herd should take.

Cattle herd fording a river, c.1860.

The herd itself was usually a mix of beeves – mature steers – and cows (which walked with a less steady stride). It had a head (point) and feet (drag), with swingmen watching the "shoulders" and flank men watching the "hips." Riders bringing up the drag, sometimes physically pushing the laggards ahead, were enveloped in dust, especially on the alkali flats, and kept a "wipe" (bandanna) across their faces. The best place to learn cuss words, recalled one veteran, was always on the drag.

Cattle drives began in early spring when new grass was emerging but before the rivers were swollen with heavy run-offs. In the north, drives had to be completed before the autumn snowfalls. Once under way, the trail drive would cover up to 16 miles (26km) per day, although a herd making only 10–12 miles (16–19km) could take a leisurely lunch by grazing and thus put on some weight en route. The easiest part of each day was the afternoon, when the thirsty cattle were eager to reach water – the basic secret of successful trailing being the grazing and watering: well-fed cattle were less likely to stampede.

A nodding donkey pumps crude up from the ground.

MODERN TIMES

After the legacy of the longhorn came the bounty of black gold, and with it an increasingly urban sophistication for the rural state of Texas.

The greatest change in the way Texas lived and viewed itself began in 1901, when the Spindletop oil field near Beaumont, in the far southeastern corner of the state, blew in with billions of barrels of oil each year. Spindletop was where the world's modern petroleum industry was born. No field like it had been dreamed of before and, with the later development of the East Texas oilfield in Rusk County, it ensured that Texas, and the world, would never be the same again.

With the Spindletop discovery, the state had jumped from an agricultural economy to a financial-industrial economy. At first, Texans were slow to recognize change, and many still haven't fully accepted it. To this day, the struggle between rural and urban values continues to divide the state. In the 1960s, the trend toward suburbanization increased, as more and more farmers preferred to live in town and visit their fields by car. Indeed, nearly 80 percent of Texans now live in urban areas, a fact not always apparent from the many movies and novels about the state that turn on the romance of the past.

Since Spindletop, Texas has rarely failed to lead the US in petroleum production. In the early days, it was the global leader. This has added to the state's tendency to measure itself not against sister states but against the world.

OIL AND POLITICS

The 1960s produced a series of events bigger even than the state itself. The traumatic assassination of President John F. Kennedy in Dallas in 1963 swiftly led to the swearing in of Kennedy's Vice President, Lyndon B. Johnson – a Texan – as the 36th US President. The year before had seen the opening of NASA's Manned Spacecraft Center at Houston, and, before the decade was

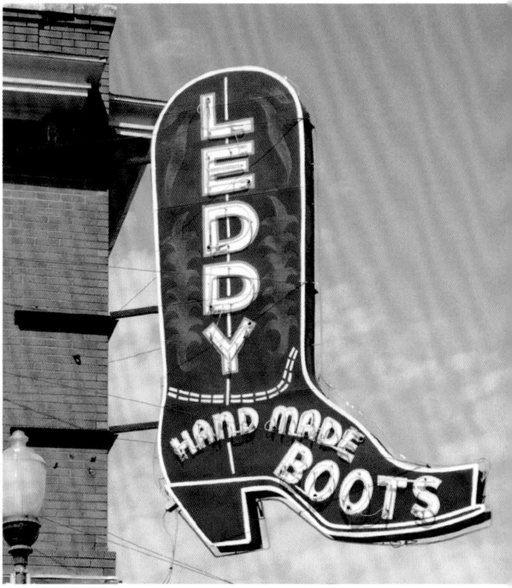

Cowboy boot store, Fort Worth.

over, Apollo 11 astronaut Neil Armstrong was transmitting the first words from the surface of the moon: "Houston, Tranquility Base here. The Eagle has landed." Somehow, it seemed appropriately Texan in style.

In the 1970s, while price freezes, gas shortages, and civil rights became as familiar concepts to Texans as to the rest of the country, the state continued to grow. In 1973, it became the fourth most populous state in the Union. The Arab oil embargo increased domestic production in Texas oilfields. Towns such as Lubbock, Abilene, and Odessa doubled in size.

After a slump in prices and a major global recession, things have been looking up in oil and gas. In 2008, the first extractions began from the

Eagle Ford Shale, which extends from the US border with Mexico into East Texas. Some 3 billion barrels of oil are projected to be found in the Eagle Ford formation, and the average well is thought to contain some 2.36 billion cubic feet of gas. By the end of 2015, production had skyrocketed to almost 1.2 million BOE (barrel of oil equivalent) per day and now extends into 24 counties in Texas, making it the most productive oil and gas field in the US.

In addition, substantial oil and gas deposits have been located in the ancient Mississippian Barnett Shale formation beneath the Dallas–Fort

Senator Kay Bailey Hutchison.

Worth area of North Texas, although drilling here may prove trickier as the shale is very hard and it lies beneath the metroplex.

Texas is well known for its brash politics and larger-than-life politicians – not so surprising given the outsize personality of the state. Texas has been either the birthplace or adopted home of four US presidents – Dwight D. Eisenhower, Lyndon B. Johnson, George H.W. Bush, and George W. Bush, not to mention presidential candidates, including most recently Governor Rick Perry and Senator Ted Cruz, who both ran in 2016.

Texas has had two female governors – Miriam Amanda Wallace "Ma" Ferguson in the 1920s and Ann Richards 1991–94; in 1993, Texas elected its first female US senator, Kay Bailey Hutchison – and in 2017 she was appointed the US Ambassador to NATO. In fact, strong, practical women are a feature of the Lone Star state; they form the backbone of many a venture, as was evident in the TV series *Dallas*. The late political commentator and humorist Molly Ivins is a case in point: like Ann Richards, she could go toe-to-toe with any Texas good ol' boy and put them in their place. Texas even had one of the country's first women's museums, a Smithsonian Institution affiliate located in Fair Park, Dallas, until 2011.

SUPERLATIVE TEXAS

Texas facts and figures are seldom expressed in other than superlative terms: *The* biggest; *The* best. And Texas planners tend to think along the same lines. That's one of the reasons why such a high percentage of recent US building and real estate development has taken place in cities like Dallas, Houston, and Austin. There has been uncontrolled growth in some areas, but this has not discouraged Texas developers.

Today, in the wake of the Iraq War and volatile prices, oil is of critical importance. Aside from that, though, it is an element of Texas's identity. Even in nonproducing counties, the commodity plays a vital part in local business because of the jobs and buying power it creates. Dallas is a perfect example: it is a city legendary the world over for its involvement in the oil business, but it is located in a section of Texas that has never produced any, although that may change now that the Barnett Shale formation is considered by some experts to be largest onshore natural gas field in the US.

Texas's rich oil and gas resources have traditionally been a double-edged sword. On the one hand, oil has brought immeasurable wealth to the state, especially now that domestic sources of energy are so highly valued, but until the economy began to diversify in recent years, the reliance on oil had made the state vulnerable. The crash in world oil prices caused hardship in Texas in the early 1980s and was followed by the shock of the Savings and Loan crisis of the late 1980s, when over a million Texans lost their homes.

As a result, state leaders have recognized the importance of economic diversification and have gone out of their way to attract high-tech firms. Computer chip fabrication, software development, and tech companies have found a receptive home in Austin, and Dallas has become a significant financial market. San Antonio and Austin are also becoming major tourist destinations in the US. Consequently, Texas has weathered the Great Recession much better than most places in the US, making it one of the top places creating new jobs (albeit largely in the minimum wage sector), building new infrastructure, and growing in population and demand.

THE NEW ECONOMY

Everything – from the fashion industry to movie and television production to a burgeoning art market – is currently taking root in Texas, and all of these new players are challenging the oil industry's long tenure at the head of the state's economic pyramid. The new economy is based on a sounder combination of technology, manufacturing, and finance.

Texas has taken over national leadership in many phases of the chemical industry (not just petrochemicals). It has remained an important aerospace center, and is attracting more technological manufacturing firms. Still a major farm and ranch center, it contains the most farmland

Governor Rick Perry.

BILLIONAIRE POLITICS

While it may seem that big money buys political favors in places like Texas (and beyond), not all billionaires in Texas politics can be considered the "guys in black hats." Ross Perot, an Independent candidate for the US Presidency in 1992 and 1996, brought deep pockets and his own strong agenda on fiscal policy, overseas job losses, and opposition to gun control to the table and won the support of numerous undecided and disaffected voters looking for a different choice.

During the 1992 election, he garnered 18.9 percent of the vote, and 8 percent in his subsequent candidacy, a healthy percentage for a third-party candidate. Perot came out against the North American Free Trade Agreement (NAFTA) in his campaign, citing the loss of US jobs to Mexico, and also focused on education. The state's controversial "No Child Left Behind" campaign requiring extensive mandatory testing in schools was adopted by George W. Bush as governor and then at the national level during his presidency – a policy that has had mixed success.

Perot philanthropy has endowed several institutions in Texas, including the Perot Museum of Nature and Science in the Dallas Arts District, but the man himself has now disappeared from politics. He supported Republican Mitt Romney in the 2012 election.

of any American state and ranks third among the states in total agricultural income. It is first in the production of cotton, cattle, sheep, goats and, in most years, rice. In addition, alternative energy production from wind power is now big business in Texas, which has enthusiastically adopted huge wind generating farms through its Central and West sections. Wind power facilities account for almost 22 percent of the state's total generating capacity.

The state's location in the Sunbelt is also enticing. All kinds of corporations are shifting their headquarters to the Lone Star State, not just for its more favorable climate but also for its access to world markets, its central location, and its eagerness to acquire fiscal and industrial families. Major international corporations, too, have opened branches in Dallas and Houston.

Wind turbines on the Lone Star Wind Farm, Abilene.

FIRST IN JOBS, BOTTOM IN SOCIAL SERVICES

It doesn't hurt that business taxes are low in Texas, and there is no state income tax – although a high sales tax ensures that those on low incomes, generally making one of the country's lowest minimum wages, end up paying a disproportionately higher amount of their income in taxes than corporations and the wealthy.

This, indeed, is one of the ironies of the Texas Miracle that has gripped the country during the Recession years: companies and job seekers are flooding there, swelling the demand for goods and services, but the apparent success is tempered by other forms of taxation that make living in the state more expensive than at first appears.

Texas is also bottom of the league in social services, particularly health care, since this is one of the states that refused to expand Medicaid for its lowest income residents under the Affordable Care Act, otherwise known as Obamacare. For that matter, it ranks 34th in education and 33rd in crime among other states. Those at the bottom of the social scale struggle more in Texas than in many other states, even though the state's ability to attract business and grow jobs has helped its economy greatly overall.

TEA PARTY POLITICS

The widening gulf between rich and poor in Texas – and the country as a whole – is not news for anyone who has been following the split along Republican and Democratic lines in US politics in recent years. Much of it can be put down to the rise of a small number of older, conservative voters in the Republican Party's minority Tea Party faction. Texas politicians Governor Rick Perry, US

Senators John Cornyn and Ted Cruz, and former House Majority Leader and Congressman Tom Delay have been driving forces in this new factional politics. All have brought their hard-line, religious-based agendas to the national stage as they have risen through the ranks and been elected, driving a wedge into the old school Republican party, which in turn has fractured the US political discourse.

That's not to say that all of Texas is Republican and ultraconservative, just a very vocal and powerful minority. Texans are largely urban nowadays, and its cities – the largest and most rapidly growing in the US – are overwhelmingly liberal and vote Democrat. Rural areas with large numbers of Hispanics, such as South Texas, along the US border with Mexico, also are Democrat, but tend not to vote – an issue now on the radar of both Republicans and Democrats – and Texas demographics influence the outcome.

The fast-growing Hispanic and urban liberal populations are, in fact, changing Texas's political demographics, as has already happened in other western states that have traditionally voted Republican, such as Colorado. In San Antonio, this has already come to pass – the city's former Democratic mayor Julián Castro gained national attention in 2012 when he was the first Hispanic to deliver the keynote address at a Democratic National Convention. Castro ran for president briefly in 2020, but despite his progressive views, he couldn't make significant connections with Democrat voters and ultimately dropped out.

SPORTING ARTISTS

These days, art districts are part of every major city in Texas, offering a huge variety of traditional and modern art. That's true even in far-flung places such as West Texas, where Marfa,

A man exercises his right to bear arms.

A TEXAS PRESIDENT

Lyndon Baines Johnson (1908–73) was born into a Texas Hill Country farming family. Ruthlessly ambitious, he became a senator in 1948 and John F. Kennedy's Vice-President in 1960. Three years later, aboard Air Force One, he was sworn in as US President, just 99 minutes after Kennedy's assassination in Dallas. Johnson had a landslide victory in the 1964 election, but his years at the White House, dedicated to creating "the Great Society", were darkened by the shadow of the Vietnam War. Vociferous domestic opposition to the conflict led "LBJ" to step down in 1968, and he retired, with his wife, Lady Bird, to their Texas ranch.

a little ranch town in Big Bend Country, has been taken over by contemporary artists, and in Amarillo, home to the famous Cadillac Ranch art installation in a field west of town.

Oil and developer money supports many artistic endeavors in Texas, and some of the best art collections and well-endowed museums in the country, if not the world, can be found in Dallas and Houston and other cities funded by the likes of Trammell Crow and the Menils.

Texans work hard and play hard. Most are mad about sports, particularly baseball and football. Soccer is increasingly popular with younger Texans, more of whom are playing the game. The state received its third Major League Soccer team in 2021, when Austin FC was added to its existing teams, Houston and FC Dallas.

Dallas Cowboys game.

Texas athletes of both sexes have established themselves as stars and record-holders in track and field, swimming, gymnastics, golf, baseball, basketball, tennis, motor and horse racing, bicycling, sailing and polo. There is scarcely a Texas town that cannot volunteer the name of some native son or daughter who has gone on to receive national or international sporting acclaim. And visitors who participate in such activities as golf or tennis will find doors opened to them.

INCREASINGLY URBAN

Although in the eyes of the United States, as well as the rest of the world, the prevailing image of Texas remains rural, its 28.7 million residents are overwhelmingly urban. Life today in the larger Texas cities has scant connection with the Texas of history and romance. Nevertheless, urbanites were fascinated, along with everybody else, by the TV drama *Dallas,* which – despite the cast working in high-rise offices – pictured the ranch as the center of Texas family life, even if the Ewings were not exactly an average family. The series was revived in 2012 but unfortunately its principal star, Larry Hagman, passed away during filming.

Dallas ranks as one of the largest fashion marketing centers in the country. Home to the flagship Neiman Marcus store, famed for its selection and customer service, Dallas has some of the best shopping in the US, and has long attracted celebrities to its upscale malls and glittering boutiques. Small towns in the metro area are also benefiting, including places like Denton, north of Dallas, a university town with a popular live music and arts scene and funky stores, much like Austin.

A MINI-US

As Texas has grown, it has acquired the vices and problems it long scorned as "big city" or "foreign". It now has three of the largest US cities, so slums, pollution, and traffic are a part of the urban scene.

Texas is said to be modern America in microcosm, bowing to changes while proclaiming a rugged individualism, celebrating past glories but with one foot firmly in the future and pragmatic about what it takes to thrive in the 21st century. Perhaps this is the best way for personal independence in the US to survive – honoring traditions while, at the same time, regarding them with a flexible state of mind.

In recent years Texas has shown that it handles various issues differently to elsewhere in the United States. The Covid-19 pandemic, for example, brought millions of cases to the state with hospitals being overwhelmed with patients. The Republican leader of the state also rejected lockdowns. In March 2021, social distancing requirements were removed, along with the state's mask mandate. The following month, it was declared that the state had the highest number of Covid-19 cases in the country, behind California. Vaccination in Texas is also behind the country's average.

Cy Twombly Gallery, Houston.

Cowboys at daybreak.

Metal-art vendor at the San Antonio Stock Show and Rodeo.

TEXANS

People from all over the world have made Texas – the land of opportunity – their home, bringing with them their own individual cultures and traditions.

Anglo immigrants established the overall trends of the state's cultural development, when they wrested the area from Mexico in the 19th century. But there have been other cultural influences: Texas is crosshatched with a complicated pattern of regional and ethnic divisions. The state welcomes people from many countries, and as a result it has one of the top rates of foreign immigration in the US.

"Anglos" – American citizens – who settled in Texas before annexation, were mainly from the South, although, even within this group, there were major cultural differences. Immigrants from the Deep South, where slavery was deeply rooted, tended to settle east of San Antonio, in the wetter agrarian sections of East Texas. Those from the mid-Atlantic states, where slavery was less pervasive, tended to settle north and west of the Colorado River in North and West Texas.

Like southerners today, these settlers held a wide range of political, religious, and moral views, some of them in direct opposition to each other, and to those of foreign Anglo emigrants from the British Isles and central and eastern Europe.

AMERICAN COWBOY IMAGE

For a long time, the homesteading, agrarian Anglos east of San Antonio set the tone for the whole state. East Texas was not just southern – it was an extension of the Deep South. In the early 20th century, thanks to the ubiquitous presence of the cowboy in the societal media of the day, this southern influence in the popular imagination waned, replaced by that of the West, with its powerful icons. Denim overalls and cotton growing gave way to cowboy boots and cattle raising as essential elements in the international image of Texas – at least until the wildcatter and the oil baron joined the cowboy in the Lone Star pantheon. Non-Southern dishes like chicken-fried steak, tortillas, and chili have by and large replaced the traditional offerings of grits, greens, and cornbread on the Anglo table in Texas.

A cowgirl poses by a supersize truck at Rodeo Austin.

Recent immigrants seem to prefer the state's cowboy image to its connection with the Confederacy. Although for the most part cowboys are a thing of the past, the cowboy image seems more in keeping with the state's vitality than the cultivation of southern memories. And, because being a cowboy was never an exclusively Anglo experience, but actually arose from Mexican and Tejano communities, it tends to run right across Texas's many ethnic boundaries.

Anglo-Southerners are not just being

westernized; they are disappearing. Whites of Old South descent make up less than half the population, especially after heavy immigration from California, the Midwest, and the Northeast during the mid-1990s boom years.

The composition usually called "Anglo" is likely to consist of several European and possibly some non-European elements. Texas was the location of the earliest Polish community in the United States and some of the first Irish ones. The largest group of immigrants to come directly from Europe was German.

Visitors at the Zapata Fair.

HISPANIC ASCENDANCE

In his book of essays, *In a Narrow Grave*, Larry McMurtry put forward the view that Texas cities are always improved when the Hispanic culture influences the Anglo. If this is true, Texas cities must be improving: their Hispanic populations are increasing steadily. San Antonio, Houston and El Paso are among the top US metropolitan areas in total Hispanic population, and Texas follows only California in the number of Hispanics: people with Spanish surnames make up 38 percent of its population. And that is just legal residents: Texas has the country's second highest number of illegal immigrants, most from south of the border (around 1.5 million, according to the Department of Homeland Security). Border immigration issues remain some of the most emotional and contentious politically in the US, made all the more so by the explosion in numbers of unaccompanied young children crossing the border, only to be rounded up and placed in detainment centers. President Trump's proposal to build a wall along the entire US–Mexico border increased tensions on both sides of the border. However, with Joe Biden now in power, the US Department of Defense said it was going to cancel the construction of parts of the border wall that Trump had been building.

In big cities like Dallas and Houston, where black people used to be the largest minority, Hispanics are surpassing them. In the state as a whole, Hispanics overtook black people as the dominant minority group in the late 1940s.Texas gained nine Hispanic residents per one white resident in 2018 alone. It is possible that by 2022, Hispanics will become the largest population group in the state.

It's clear that Spanish-speaking people are gradually re-Hispanicizing the state, following much the same immigration patterns as Anglos. Hispanics are no longer confined behind the imaginary boundary that once kept them west and south of the San Antonio River. Today there are *barrios* in Dallas and Fort Worth, Corpus Christi, El Paso, and even in the Texas Panhandle, bringing Mexican and Central and South American customs and traditions across the length and breadth of the state. Hispanics are integrated into every element of public and private life in the state. Cinco de Mayo and Diez y Seis, two holidays celebrating Mexican independence, and Día de los Muertos are widely celebrated outside of Hispanic communities as well.

Hispanic influence is strongly felt throughout the state in every aspect of daily life, and increasingly in politics; Republican senator Ted Cruz is the first Latino in that office in Texas, and the first Cuban-American. Hispanics traditionally lean Democrat, and their increasing numbers and clout have shifted American politics in western states like California and Colorado. Until now, though, voter turnout among eligible Texan Hispanics has been low, but appears to be increasing with 40.5 percent turning out for the 2016 presidential election, and 830,000 more Latinos voting in the Senate elections in 2018 than in 2014. Both major parties accept the realities of changing demographics and lobby for the Hispanic vote.

What is clear is that the influx of liberal urban residents from California to booming cities like Houston, Austin, and San Antonio, along with growing numbers of more politically active Hispanics, is likely to shift state politics yet again.

More than any other minority group, Spanish-speaking Texans have made their cuisine part of the mainstream of Texas life and, increasingly, that of the rest of the nation. Tacos, enchiladas, fajitas, and all the rest of the Tex-Mex menu (a culinary style derived from the cross-cultural influences of the border regions of both countries) are found as often on the Texas table as chuck roast and sweet tea.

AFRICAN-AMERICAN HERITAGE

The state's other major minority group, African-Americans, have lived in Texas since it was ruled by Spain. When Cabeza de Vaca was shipwrecked on the Gulf Coast in 1528, an African slave named Esteban was with him. Black people, enslaved or free, were found in subsequent Spanish settlements, and intermarriage resulted in a significant *mulatto* population in Spanish Texas.

The first large infusion of black people came after the Republic of Texas was established. The Mexican stand against slavery had made owners reluctant to import their human chattels, and the absence of slavery had created a haven for free black people. But, after independence, slavery became legal, and former Deep Southerners began to bring in slaves. Slavery tended to be concentrated east of the Texarkana–San Antonio line, where the Anglo masters were settled, and where the agrarian economy was more conducive to farms and plantations.

Following Emancipation (which Texas slaves learned about on June 19, 1865 – two and a half years after its issue, giving rise to the state holiday of Juneteenth), and into the 20th century, black people often lived a rural life on scattered farms or in small black "freedman" communities. Today, as they move to cities within Texas and elsewhere, the rural communities that preserved black culture are dying out or, as in the case of Austin's historic Clarksville neighborhood, becoming gentrified by an influx of affluent white homeowners.

The popularly accepted idea that black people were not an important part of western frontier life ignores some significant black history. Many runaway slaves and free black people joined American Indians and lived among them, not just on the frontier but beyond it.

The black soldiers of the ninth and 10th Cavalry and the 24th and 25th Infantries who fought American Indians were called "Buffalo Soldiers" by the tribes (owing to the coarse, kinky quality of the troopers' hair). After they mustered out of the service, many of these soldiers stayed out West to ranch, raise crops on dryland farms, or work as cowboys. Despite this role played by black soldiers in the Indian Wars and the settling of West Texas, most Texans continue to associate black

Two sisters dressed up for a charrería, San Antonio.

people only with the southern strands of Texas's history. The Spanish-ruled Mexicans were the first non-Native American Texans, or *Tejanos*, and descendants of these original settlers form a small, stable, and often wealthy core of the Spanish-speaking population of Texas. Sometimes intermarrying with wealthy Anglos, these *Tejanos* have succeeded in preserving a culture distinct even from the rest of the Spanish-speakers.

Black communities are more often urban in modern times, so their political and cultural influence is most strongly felt in the cities. Southern Dallas, eastern Fort Worth, and southern Houston have African-American majorities, and Texas's most famous African-American politician, the late US Senator Barbara Jordan, came from the heart of Houston's inner city black wards. Following the devastation of Hurricane Katrina in 2005, nearly 200,000 refugees from New Orleans were taken in by the city of Houston, most of them African-American. The vast majority settled in the city permanently, and the city is now 22 percent black. Today, Texas has the largest black population among all states.

AMERICAN INDIAN POPULATION

American Indians lived in what would become Texas for centuries before Europeans arrived. A paleohunter burial in the Permian Basin, dated to the Folsom culture, 12,000 years ago, was discovered in 1953 and the remains labeled "Midland Minnie"; Lubbock Lake Landmark is on another Folsom site.

Texans tend to think their American Indian population simply dispersed to other states, when, in fact, many Texas tribes were destroyed. Among them were the Hasinai Caddo of East Texas, the southwestern most branch of the powerful Mississippian Mound Builder culture, part of the powerful Mississippi Valley trading empire 1,200 years ago. The Caddo word for friendship (*tejas*) gave the state its name. Caddo Mounds State Historic Site near Nacogdoches interprets the Caddo culture today and preserves several mounds.

Unusual place names in Texas are a clue to its rich American Indian history – with places like Nacogdoches, Waxahachie, Wichita Falls, Anahuac, and Comanche Lake. Some 50 tribes once lived in present-day Texas, including the Alabama, Apache, Atakapan, Bidai, Caddo, Cherokee, Chickasaw, Choctaw, Comanche, Coushatta, Hueco, the Karankawa of Galveston, Kiowa, Lipan Apache, Muscogee, Natchez, Quapaw, Seminole, Tonkawa and Wichita.

It is a heartbreaking fact of European settlement that the country's diverse First Peoples, who had lived for centuries on their lands, were either wiped out by disease or war or subdued and removed to reservations. Today, however, American Indian populations are rebounding somewhat in Texas, compared with a century ago, and can be found in pockets throughout the state and on three federally recognized reservations.

The Alabama and Coushatta, two southern tribes, migrated to East Texas and now live as one tribe. In West Texas, Ysleta del Sur Pueblo in El Paso is home to a group of Pueblo Indians, the Tigua, who fled over the border from New Mexico along with Spanish missionaries during the 1680 Pueblo Revolt and did not return. In the Rio Grande Valley, the Kickapoo

Members of the Pacuache-Tilijaya Coahuilteca tribe perform a traditional dance.

migrate annually from Mexico across the Rio Grande to Eagle Pass.

Dallas and Houston also attract numbers of American Indians, especially from the Cherokee and Navajo nations of neighboring Oklahoma and New Mexico.

SPANISH AND IRISH ARRIVALS

The Irish were among the first Europeans in Texas. In fact, Hugo O'Conór was a governor of Spanish Texas in the late 18th century. Where O'Conór came from and how he ended up in the employ of the Spanish are questions to which the answers are lost. More Irish people arrived in Texas in the 1820s and '30s, when the Spaniards granted what are now the counties of Refugio and San Patricio (St Patrick) to Irish settlers. The Mexican government evidently wanted an Irish Catholic buffer between the areas of Protestant-born Anglo settlements and the Spanish-speaking Catholics.

After the Republic of Texas was declared in 1836, Europeans viewed the area as more stable politically than when it was part of Mexico. Leaders of the Republic encouraged immigration more actively than the Mexican government had. Whether Texas would be annexed by the United States was then unknown, but these factors combined to open Texas up to a flood of Europeans whose imagination had been captured by the Texas Revolution. From the beginning, the Texas government saw to it that new settlers received land, and immigrant aid groups, like the Adelsverein, who settled New Braunfels and Fredericksburg, organized migration to Texas. However, the group was not well administered and ran short of badly needed relief funds.

GERMAN FARMERS

The largest European group in Texas, the Germans' first permanent settlement was Industry, in Austin County, west of Houston, so-called for its cigar factory. Many Germans settled in the port cities of Galveston and Indianola. Typically, they wrote home an "America letter" that described – often with exaggerated, if not downright false, hopefulness – the human happiness, fertility, and wonderful climate of Texas. Their letters were shared among a village or other group of acquaintances from which braver Germans, despite the danger, would set out. German immigrants tried to bring along an entire support group, motivated in varying degrees by wanderlust, political idealism, and the desire for social and economic improvement. Some stayed in the relatively urban ports, while others settled for a while in the interior where there were friends and relatives. After they had found their bearings, they proceeded to establish daughter communities. Constrained by the settlement patterns of previous groups

A cowboy heats rosin on his gloves in preparation for a rodeo.

and the threat of Comanche raids farther west, most Germans made their homes in a 10-county strip north of San Antonio, designated as the "German Belt," which became the center of German influence in the state.

German immigrants came from all walks of life. Some were peasant farmers, while others were well educated. Some brought with them libraries that were extensive for the time and place, and they belonged to learned organizations such as the Goethe Society. Some formed orderly farming communities, while others organized into utopian-style communes, such as Bettina, now disappeared, and Tusculum, now known as Boerne.

In *Journey Through Texas*, famed landscape architect Frederick Law Olmsted, who traveled throughout the South from 1856–7, wrote with surprise and admiration about the intellectual attainments of the German colonists in Texas. He described their primitive but neat log cabins, plastered and stuccoed, and their books, musical instruments and paintings. Olmsted hoped their liberal influence would move Texas out of the Old South sisterhood of slave states.

Olmsted recorded: "One of the party said to me: 'I think if one or two of the German tyrants I could mention could look in upon us now, they would display some chagrin at our enjoyment...' I have been assured, I doubt not, with sincerity, by several of them, that never in Europe had they had so much satisfaction – so much intellectual enjoyment of life, as here."

A Texas polka band.

Most of the Germans disliked slavery. In fact, at least 19 German-born Union sympathizers were killed by Confederate troops near the town of Comfort in 1862. Nor did they wish to annihilate American Indians, who considered Germans a distinct tribe, superior to the loathsome Spaniards, Mexicans, and Anglo-Americans. German influence can still be felt today in the music (polkas and conjuntos), the bock and lager-style native-Texas beers, and the architecture (the churches, courthouses, and "Sunday Houses") of Central Texas and the Hill Country.

LATIN-SPEAKING COMMUNITIES

In the German agricultural villages of Sisterdale, Bettina, and Comfort, Latin was spoken in everyday life; the communities are remembered as "Latin colonies", and, understandably, they mystified their Anglo neighbors at the time. It is just as well that the neighbors understood little of what the Germans had to say, for their beliefs were on the whole very different from those of Anglo-Southerners. Not only were many of them opposed to slavery, as Olmsted noted, but several communities – Sisterdale and its daughter village of Comfort, in particular – were the centers of free thought and agnosticism. Many of the German settlers were Lutheran, and a few Catholic, but their free-thinking may have been unique on the frontier.

Broad German influence continues to this day in certain parts of Texas. Until the 1950s, the Tex-Deutsch dialect, an amalgam of English and German, was spoken in many settlements of San Antonio, such as the King William District. Today it has almost disappeared, and the Germans of the Texas Hill Country are becoming more like the Anglo majority and less like a true minority group.

Deliberate attempts to preserve German festivals have resulted in the regular celebration of the Fredericksburg Easter Fires and the *Wurstfest* in New Braunfels. The Easter Fires are lighted on the hills surrounding Fredericksburg on the Saturday before Easter. While local legend holds these fires were originally set by Comanche Indians, scholars have demonstrated that they were probably a custom brought from southern Germany which can be traced to pagan roots. The *Wurstfest* in New Braunfels usually comes in fall, at more or less the same time as the German *Oktoberfest*. Sausage and beer consumption, and a *gemütlich* sociability, link this New World celebration to the boisterous beer halls and *kellers* of Munich.

SLAVS IN CENTRAL

The Texas State Historical Marker at Serbin, Texas, makes interesting reading: "Trilingual (Wendish-German-English) community founded in 1854 by 588 Wends under the leadership of the Rev. John Kilian. The Rev. Kilian (Evangelical Lutheran) named the place Serbin because the Wends were descendants of Lusatian Serbs (or "Sorbs"). A thriving town 1865–1890; it had grocery, dry goods, jewelry, drug and music stores, shops of wagon maker, blacksmith, saddler, post office, three doctors, two dentists. On Smithville–Houston Oxcart Road – sending out cotton, other produce, and hauling in staples. Decline began about 1890 as railroads bypassed settlement by several miles."

eastern counties still have the largest rural populations of Czechs in the US. Czech settlements are generally agricultural, and most Texas Czechs have made their names and fortunes as farmers. Not as numerous as the Germans, the Czechs have nevertheless preserved many of their culinary traditions, including baking kolaches, a delicious pastry, for which many people make a pilgrimage to Hill Country.

Several Czech communities hold celebrations to honor their heritage. Annual festivals in West,

Young cowgirls at the Rodeo Austin Livestock Show.

Taylor, and Ennis draw city-dwellers to eat sausage and sauerkraut and dance the polka.

While German communities have adapted more and more to the dominant Anglo culture, other small groups, have been similarly absorbed. A group of Polish Catholics followed their priest southeast of San Antonio in 1854 to set up the first Polish colony in the US, Panna Maria. Later, several more Polish towns were established in Texas.

Two other major Slavic groups in the state are Wends and Czechs. Czechoslovakia was dissolved in 1993, but the groups here retain a strong affiliation with the Czech Republic, as was clear when that country stepped in and donated funds to assist with rebuilding after 2013's explosion at the refinery in West, home to many Czechs. Together, several central and

Wends are a German-speaking group who left their homes in Prussia in the 1840s. Those in Texas settled in two counties east of Austin: Lee and Fayette. The church and farm were the centers of Wendish life. Today, most Wends have left the smaller towns for the city, but their colony in Texas was the only such community in North America.

CAJUN IMMIGRATION

French colonization of Texas was sporadic. While La Salle and other French explorers were among the early visitors to Texas, and Jean Lafitte and his pirate band established an early enclave in

Galveston, the French influence seen today has mainly come from a group of French-American settlers who traveled to Texas from Louisiana. The Cajuns are descendants of Acadians, French settlers who were removed from their Canadian homeland by the British in the 1760s to '80s. After resettling in French-owned Louisiana, they developed their own culture, combining French, Spanish, American Indian, and Creole elements.

At the turn of the 20th century, the discovery of oil in East Texas lured Cajuns to the area. Texas Cajuns retained – (and still retain) – their regional French patois, their string band music, and bayou-bred culinary traditions, and a certain *laissez les bon temps rouler* (let the good times roll) outlook toward life. They lend a distinctive flavor to the East Texas and Gulf Coast areas where they have settled. Jambalaya, gumbo, and crawfish étouffée are eaten throughout the bayou country of East Texas. Cajun music is also enjoying renewed popularity. Usually played on accordions and guitars, and sung in the Cajun French patois, this music enlivens many East Texas dancehalls.

Contestants at the annual World's Largest Rattlesnake Roundup.

TEXAS BARBECUE

Barbecue is a big deal in Texas – each region has its own favored style of preparing beef and those associated with East and Central Texas have fanatical followings. In East Texas, beef is marinated in a sweet, tomato-based sauce and slow-cooked over hickory wood until it falls off the bone, southern style; the South Texas variant features molasses-style sauces to keep the meat moist. Central Texas, meanwhile, is all about dry barbecue, western-style, where meat is rubbed with spices and cooked over pecan or oak wood; in West Texas, they cook their barbecue over mesquite instead, giving it a distinctive smoky taste. Lastly, *barbacoa*, Mexican-style barbecue, features a variety of meats from hogs to goats, which are barbecued in a pit in the ground covered with maguey leaves.

German settlers in Central Texas were instrumental in boosting the popularity of sausage and barbecue. They often gathered on market days and holidays to sell their produce or celebrate, and whether revisiting a large market city such as San Antonio or just celebrating at one of their villages, they roasted a calf, sheep, or goat. Some people believe that another unique Texas preparation, chicken-fried steak, is of German derivation, citing its obvious similarities with schnitzels, breaded and pan-fried cuts of meat.

ASIAN INGENUITY

Asians are the most recent group to be added to the Texas mix. They first came to the state on their eastward trek after the California gold rush. Chinese laborers worked on the railroad, but were abandoned by the rail companies when the tracks were finished. Isolated in a strange world, the Chinese were then usually hired as cheap labor to undercut emancipated black people.

> *Kickapoo Indians enjoy special dispensation from both US and Mexican governments, allowing them to roam freely across the border between the two countries.*

The first wave of Chinese immigrants did not have much lasting impact on Texas, since US immigration laws banned most Chinese women from the country. Some agricultural laborers in Robertson County intermarried with local women, producing the "Black Chinese" of Calvert. More or less permanent Chinatowns were formed in El Paso, and later in San Antonio, but restrictive immigration policies kept the Asian population to a low level in Texas until fairly recent times.

In the early 20th century, Japanese settlers started experimental rice-farming communities along the coast, while Chinese and Japanese merchants set up small businesses in San Antonio and other cities. Until recently, Asian-run groceries served the black community, but a new influx of Southeast Asians has made Asian products more profitable.

The Asian migration of the 1970s, the result of the Vietnam War, included Vietnamese, Cambodians, and others. Many settled on the Texas Gulf Coast, where they fish in areas traditionally harvested by other groups, particularly Anglos.

Misunderstandings and prejudice at first resulted in several killings and other ugly incidents that involved the influence of the Ku Klux Klan. However, the coast is now fairly calm, and Texas seems ready to add another piece to its mosaic of cultures. The most famous assimilation story may be that of Dat Nguyen, the son of Vietnamese "boat people" who grew up to be a star defensive player on "America's Team", the Dallas Cowboys.

While a distinctive Vietnamese culture might seem most likely to thrive in fishing settlements along the coast, not all Vietnamese live in these areas, nor do they all earn a living by fishing. Many of the latest immigrants are technicians and other highly trained people who have settled in Texas's urban areas (the Asian populations of Austin and Houston more than doubled in the 1980s and '90s). Others are found in rural communities as professional workers, farmers, and ranchers.

Mardi Gras in Bandera.

OTHER ANGLO RESIDENTS

Other smaller groups have blended into Anglo culture. A substantial Scandinavian population immigrated to Texas; Greeks settled along the coast, particularly around Galveston; and a small Italian contingent lived in the larger cities but also had agricultural settlements in the Brazos Valley. Jewish migration took place in the 19th century, when German and eastern European Jews came to Texas. Today, Jews are an urban group in the state. However, the small town synagogues in Brenham and Corsicana are reminders of their long Texas history. Jewish merchants founded several thriving Texas mercantile chains.

Sgt. Danny Young, a Texas Ranger from Jasper.

THE TEXAS RANGERS

Efficient, tough, and uncompromising: the Texas Rangers are a remarkable band of law enforcers – a legion of heroes with a reputation second to none.

For most of the first century of Texas history, the Texas Rangers were almost synonymous with that history. No police force in the country had the prestige of the Rangers. The *WPA Guide* noted in 1940: "The man in the tan trousers and shirt, wide-brimmed Western hat, black tie, leather holster and sidearms not only commands respect but admiration."

Today, although Rangers uniform is largely just Western dress, the Rangers badge, carved from 1940s-era silver Mexican five-peso coins, is one of the most famous law enforcement emblems in the world. Texas Rangers were "one of the most colorful, efficient and deadly bands of irregular partisans on the side of law and order the world has ever seen," one historian noted "...called into being by a society that could not afford a regular army." Many of these adventurers were famous before reaching their thirties, men who showed "an utter absence of fear," superb psychologists at understanding not only the enemy but also the men around them.

There is an apocryphal story still told of a 1930s oilfield boomtown in East Texas caught up in the grip of a riot. Frantic with fear, the local sheriff wired the governor in Austin for help in the form of the Texas Rangers. A day later, the train pulled into the boomtown station, from which alighted a single Ranger. "They only sent one?" asked the incredulous sheriff. The Ranger did not bat an eye. "You've only got one riot, don't you?" he replied.

In the 1880s, Texas Ranger Captain Bill McDonald, who was known for his readiness "to charge hell with a bucket of water", confronted three gunmen who had tried to ambush him. He dropped one, and, after taking bullets through his left side and right wrist, was busy cocking his pistol with his teeth when the other two outlaws fled. "No man in the wrong can stand up against a man in the right who keeps on a-coming," was the romantic assessment of this episode by a fellow Texas Ranger.

Rangers badge.

ORIGINS OF THE FORCE

"In 1823", wrote journalist Pamela Colloff in the April 2007 issue of *Texas Monthly* magazine, "Stephen F. Austin hired ten men 'to act as rangers for the common defense.' Nearly two centuries later that group – known as the Texas Rangers – is alive and well, having adapted from being frontier lawmen to an elite investigative force, trading their horses and bedrolls for cell phones and laptops." In 1835, the Texas legislature instituted the Texas Rangers as an official body: 56 men in three companies, each with a captain and two lieutenants.

The Head Ranger, a major, was subject to the army's commander-in-chief. Earning the same pay as the army ($1.25 a day), Rangers supplied their own mounts and rations and had to be equipped with "a good horse (and) one hundred rounds of powder and ball" at their own expense. They protected the frontier against raiding Mexicans, and fought against outlaws and Indians.

When Sam Houston was reelected in 1841, he realized that the Rangers were the most effective and economical way of protecting the frontier, when Captain John Coffee "Jack" Hayes and 150 Rangers helped repel an 1842 invasion from Mexico.

A few years later, the 1846 US War with Mexico brought the Rangers worldwide fame. "Armed to the teeth," they successfully guided the US Army to Monterrey and were at home in the remote deserts of northeastern Mexico, where, battling guerrillas, they earned a fearsome reputation as *los diablos Tejanos* (the Texan devils). Between 1845 and 1875, Rangers fought in the big and little wars against Indians and Mexicans, as well as tracking down robbers and horse thieves.

19th-century Texas Ranger, Benjamin McCulloch.

RANGERS IN THE REPUBLIC

Throughout the years of the Republic of Texas (1836–45), the Rangers worked as scouts and couriers during the first presidency of Sam Houston, who fostered friendship with the Indians. But, from December 1838, under the presidency of Mirabeau B. Lamar, 13 new Ranger companies were commissioned, which "over the next three years... waged all-out war against the Indians", according to *The Handbook of Texas*.

The army and the Rangers were often at odds, due to conflicting sets of rules and orders; the former sought to police the frontier and keep peace, while the Rangers rode to push back and punish the Indians.

REVOLVER REVOLUTION

In 1851, when 21-year-old former sailor Samuel Colt began manufacturing the first .34-caliber six-shooter weapon, nobody seemed particularly interested. Then one of the revolvers found its way into the hands of a veteran Ranger, Captain Samuel Walker, who saw its potential for a man fighting on horseback. At his suggestion, Colt designed a heavier .44-caliber gun (later .47), which became the standard weapon for US cavalrymen.

The first to use Colt's new six-shooter on the Plains Indians was the aforementioned Captain Jack Hayes, a 23-year-old former Tennesseean who had arrived in Texas as a surveyor, before he was appointed by President Lamar to be Chief of Rangers at San Antonio. All the ideal requirements for a Texas Ranger seemed to come together in this handsome, quiet "gentleman of purest character," and, when he ended his service, at 34, he was the model to which all Rangers aspired. One Comanche war chief swore never to confront Hayes, "who has a shot for every finger on his hand." Largely thanks to Hayes and his men, the Rangers learned to embrace the most advanced technology of each era, which has enabled them to stay relevant to their times.

The law enforcement team that tracked down notorious outlaws Bonnie and Clyde.

TAKING OUT BAD MEN

After the end of the US War with Mexico (February 2 1848), the Rangers went into a decline and were little used. One Ranger captain, arriving to help a community fight off the Indians, said that all he was doing afterward was hearing complaints from farmers about Rangers killing their hogs. At the onset of the Civil War (1861), many joined the Confederate forces.

State Democrats, back in power in 1874, declared Texas was "overrun with bad men," and, to counter these, plus Indian attacks on the western frontier and border raids by Mexicans, the Rangers were regenerated. Their Special Force unit gained a fearsome reputation, on one occasion stacking a dozen dead rustlers "like cordwood" in a Brownsville square "as a lethal response to the death of one Ranger." Among the 3,000 desperados they "thinned out" was the multiple killer John Wesley Hardin.

Although present-day Rangers wear the familiar "star in a wheel" badge, it was adopted officially only in 1962, when enough Mexican five-peso coins were donated to the DPS to provide badges for all 62 Rangers working at that time.

The Rangers endured another lean period at the beginning of the 20th century, when the force was trimmed down to just four 20-man companies.

But the 1910 revolution against Mexico's president Porfirio Diaz created unrest at the border. Then the onset of World War I, with its need to counter German intrigues and protect internal Texas security, was followed by Pancho Villa's raid on Columbus, New Mexico, in 1916, which fueled antagonisms between the two nations.

EXECUTED WITHOUT TRIAL

In responding to these challenges, sometimes, critics charged, the Texas Rangers' actions were high-handed, and they were not being held accountable. If an ethnic Mexican, be he a Tejano US citizen or Mexican national, was found armed, he was often accused of banditry and killed outright. In 1915, a group of Rangers, having captured a carload of Mexicans suspected of robbing a train near Brownsville, took them into the bushes and shot them. The indiscriminate killing of approximately 5,000 Hispanics between 1914 and 1919 (according to *The Handbook of Texas*) became a source of "scandal and embarassment" and, in 1919, prompted a legislative investigation that discredited Ranger tactics. The force was overhauled by recruiting "men of high moral character." Higher salaries – as well as more restraints – were introduced.

Texas Ranger Hall of Fame and Museum, Crawford.

BONNIE AND CLYDE

Bonnie Elizabeth Parker and Clyde Chestnut Barrow were Dallas outlaws who led a gang to rob stores and gas stations, and eventually a dozen or so banks, in the Depression era. Pursued relentlessly by the Texas Rangers, they killed at least nine officers and several civilians before being gunned down in a shootout in Louisiana in 1934. The romantic relationship of Parker and Barrow, and photogenic glamor exuded by the 20-somethings – played up in the 1967 movie Bonnie and Clyde starring Warren Beatty and Faye Dunaway – were at odds with the grittier reality of their lives on the run but fueled the legend that endures to this day.

THE PROHIBITION YEARS

Prohibition found Rangers patrolling the border against tequila smugglers, protecting Federal tick inspectors, monitoring labor and Ku Klux Klan demonstrations, and taming the lawless oil boomtowns. The Rangers were often at odds with local lawmen, who preferred to leave gambling casinos and illegal drinking joints alone.

In 1932, the Rangers ill-advisedly backed Governor Ross Sterling in the Democrat primary, and, when his opponent, Miriam "Ma" Ferguson, took office, all 44 Rangers were fired or resigned in protest. Ferguson politicized the force, handing out Ranger badges as political favors to contributors and cronies. Salaries were slashed, and Texas became a haven for the likes of George "Machine Gun" Kelly and Bonnie (Parker) and Clyde (Barrow). Parker and Barrow were eventually hunted down by renowned Ranger Frank Hamer.

NEW QUALIFICATIONS

In 1935, under Governor James Allred, the Rangers became part of the Texas Department of Public Safety, which included the Texas Highway Patrol. New qualifications were laid down for Rangers, who had to be between 30 and 45 years of age (later extended to 50), 5ft 8 inches (1.74 meters) tall, and "perfectly sound" in mind and body. Each Ranger was required to be "a crack shot" and underwent extensive training in ballistics and investigation techniques.

Rangers were spread throughout the state, becoming plain-clothes officers and sometimes a sort of rural constabulary. When World War II arrived, they were kept busy rounding up enemy aliens and helping protect vulnerable sites. Their attitude toward America's Mexican neighbors changed as a modern era between the two countries began.

The job of the Rangers widened enormously in the 1960s, when the 8,000 cases they had been dealing with annually almost doubled, due to increasing urbanization. Rangers became involved on both sides of labor and civil rights issues. Rangers sometimes acted as strikebreakers against farmworkers in South Texas, even while they helped guarantee voting rights and civil rights in other areas. Some of the old complaints began to resurface, as the Rangers again began to hear accusations about their attitude toward brown-skinned citizens.

One early writer once said of the Texas Rangers that they "could ride like Mexicans, shoot like Tennesseans and fight like the very devil."

A Texas Ranger patrolling the US–Mexico border.

Today, the Rangers remain an elite force, with over 100 applications for every vacancy, most of which are never advertised. In 2020, the Rangers included166 men and womenwho make up six companies within the Texas Department of Public Safety. They are supplied with powerful cars, sophisticated weapons, and forensic and communications equipment. Noted *Texas Monthly*: "A typical day [for the Rangers] looks more like CSI than *The Lone Ranger*."

Cowboy chase.

DON'T FENCE ME IN

The real Texas cowboys bore little resemblance to the Indian-fighting, songs-around-the-campfire heroes created by Hollywood.

To much of the world, the cowboy is the embodiment of the American character; stoic, self-reliant, loyal, taciturn, hardy, and – sometimes – reckless or violent. His iconic status has outlasted two world wars, the Space Age, rock 'n' roll, the arrival of the internet, and the whole of the 20th century and 150 years after his brief heyday his heroic aura remains undiminished.

He has been celebrated in books such as Owen Wister's *The Virginian*, Teddy Blue Abbott's *We Pointed Them North*, and Larry McMurtry's *Lonesome Dove*; in the paintings and sculptures of Charles Russell and Frederic Remington; in the photographs of Erwin E. Smith and Richard Avedon; in song, from cowboy ballads collected by Texas folklorist John Lomax to the chart-topping hits of Waylon Jennings and George Strait; and on film in John Ford's *The Searchers*, Howard Hawks's *Red River* – both starring John Wayne – and Fred Zinnemann's *High Noon*.

The zenith of the American cowboy was brief, roughly the last 25 years of the 19th century. And, contrary to the tall-in-the-saddle imagery perpetuated by the movies and television, the typical cowboy was a wiry man – be he Anglo, African-American, or Hispanic – of slight stature whose six-shooter was most typically drawn to defend against a rattlesnake or coyote, not a bandit or Indian.

He was a blue-collar working man, a laborer who toiled for seldom more than a dollar a day. But what set him apart from the rest of mankind, in his eyes, was that he was first and foremost a horseman, heir to a centuries-old tradition.

"The cowboy's contempt of the farmer was not unmixed with pity," wrote *Lonesome Dove* author Larry McMurtry. "Cowboys could perform terrible labors and endure bone-grinding hardships and yet consider themselves the chosen of the earth; and the grace that redeemed it all in their own estimation was the fact that they had gone a-horseback."

Cowboy buckles with ornate engravings.

Though his lineage belongs to history, he has an enduring hold on our imagination, and his descendants still practice his craft today.

THE WORKING COWBOY

Underneath the storybook and movie glitter, there was always a real working cowboy, and there still is today. Not until the Comanche and Kiowa were largely "subdued" in the mid-1870s by the army and the Texas Rangers could much of the vast Texas prairie be safely opened to rancher, and so the working cowboy did not fight nearly as many Indians as we see him fighting in the movies.

When he was on the trail, the cowboy lived out under the stars and he had a closeness to nature. He supplied his own strong code of frontier ethics in a land with no established law, and he enforced it with a gun – though the gunfighter was a rare and endangered species in the West, compared to the ubiquitous cowboy.

The history of the working cowboy begins with the introduction of cattle into the New World by Spanish explorers as early as the 16th century.

Texas cowboys in traditional costume, c.1890.

> *The boot was one of the cowboy's tools: he had no need of the exotic leathers and elaborately stitched tops seen on today's fashionably macho and expensive footwear.*

Most of the details of cattle ranching had been worked out by the Spaniards in northern Mexico and southern Texas by the time the first Anglos came into the area in the 1820s.

The Spanish cattle-ranching vocabulary was assimilated by the early Texas cattlemen, along with the rest of Spanish/Mexican cattle culture. Words like *la reata* (lariat or lasso), *remuda* (string of riding horses), *corral* (holding pen for cattle) and *dally* (from "dar la vuelta," or "take a turn") are still in use today. Words for land forms, such as *mesa* (literally, "table" – a high desert plateau or tableland) and *arroyo* (gully or dry wash), were also adopted.

COWBOY COSTUME

Much of the Texas cowboy's costume came from the *vaquero*, as the Mexican cowboy was called. The angled high-heeled boots helped to keep a cowboy's feet in the stirrups when he was riding his horse. The narrow toes of the boots and the slick, treadless leather sole were designed to slide easily into the stirrup, while the boot tops were 12–16 inches (30–40cm) high and perfectly plain in design. The leather was good quality and durable.

Being generally concerned with the well-being of his animals, the Texan cowboy replaced the sharp, revolving roweled spurs favored by the *vaquero* with larger, blunt wheels, in order to protect his horse's flanks. The jingle of spurs was "saddle music" to the cowboy. While the *vaquero* usually wore spurs only for work, many a Texas cowboy felt naked without them, and only removed them upon entering his house.

For a long time, cowboys wore a very characteristic pair of striped breeches. These gave way in the 1870s to the blue denims manufactured by the Levi-Strauss Company of San Francisco. A cowboy covered his breeches with heavy leather leggings, called chaps, when he rode through brushy country. "Chaps" is a corruption of the Spanish word *chapparal*, meaning heavy brush.

The bandana, an oversized neckerchief, was the Swiss army knife of the West. It was invaluable to cowboy and *vaquero* alike: it kept the sun off the back of his neck and mopped the sweat from his face; it could be a sling for a broken arm or a mask to filter the acrid dust; wrapped around a couple of biscuits, a bandana could serve as a lunchpail.

The tall-crowned, wide-brimmed *sombrero* worn by the *vaquero* was never favored by the Texas cowboy; nor was the fabled 10-gallon hat ever worn by anyone but movie cowboys. There was a wide variety of headwear among real cowboys, from the cavalry-style fedora to the shapeless farmboy's hat, but, by the 1870s, the hats made by John B. Stetson of Philadelphia had become standard western wear.

Cowboys who worked for a dollar a day would pay $10–20 for a good hat and $20–30 for a good pair of boots.

Shirts were widely varied, some no more than homemade flour-sack affairs. As likely as not, they were covered with a vest. The sleeveless vest gave warmth and protection, but did not bind the cowboy's arms while he worked. For cold weather, a cowboy wore a blue denim jacket or a fleece-lined leather shortcoat. An oilcloth slicker kept off the rain. A cowboy rarely carried more than one change of clothes, which he packed into a bedroll.

TRAIL DRIVING DAYS

The cowboy's life was a hard one. As many a "greenhorn" quickly learned, a cowboy had to have common sense and a head for survival.

The heyday of Texas cowboying was the trail-drive years from the mid-1860s through the 1880s. Prior to this time, the cattle business in Texas was rather low key. It centered on Spanish-style ranches that were loosely run and generally unfenced – prime conditions for creating "mavericks" in the rich South Texas grasslands where the hardy longhorn cattle could easily survive on their own.

After the Civil War, a flood of immigrants from the South entered Texas, many of them young single men looking for a new life. They found it as cowboys.

The price of cattle in the industrial cities of the North was as much as $40 a head, whereas, in South Texas, longhorns could be bought for $4 apiece. Thus, there was plenty of work for cowboys, driving cattle from Texas to the railheads in Kansas, from where beef was shipped to city markets. The great cattle trails of the era – the Chisholm Trail, the Goodnight-Loving Trail, the Western Trail, and others – came into being to transport cattle across the unfenced plains to railheads or army posts in New Mexico, Kansas, Missouri, or even Wyoming and Montana.

A cowboy's work began in spring with the cattle roundups or "cow hunts." Nursing calves followed their mothers as the cattle were herded into holding pens. There the animals were separated by their brands and claimed by their owners. Young calves were marked with the same brand as their mothers. They came to be known on the trail as "dogies," from the short rope that tethered the newborn calf to its mother. As herds became larger and cattle thieves began to alter brands, some ranchers took to cutting notches in the ears of their cattle as a secondary form of identification.

TRAIL BALLADS

After all the rounding up and branding, the trail drive began. Many a cowboy ballad was composed on the open trail, as the cowboys sang to comfort their cattle and keep them from stampeding. Cowboy ballads were usually laments about loneliness, lost love, and the hard life on the trail. Many, such as *Streets of Laredo*, derived from English or Celtic ballads. "The chief contribution made by white men of America to the folk-songs of the world," observed Texas folklorist J. Frank Dobie, are "the cowboy songs of Texas and the West... rhymed to the walk, the trot, and the gallop of horses."

A rider at a Mexican-style rodeo, or charrería.

Hollywood Western stars like the late Gene Autry and Roy Rogers capitalized on this aspect of cattle trail life, making their careers as "singing cowboys." But historians point out that a hard day's drive more usually ended with conversation around the fire, or perhaps a game of poker. Few cowboys would have had room in their saddlebags for musical instruments any larger than a harmonica or a concertina.

BEGINNING THE DRIVE

To start a drive, small herds of cattle rounded up in South Texas by four or five cowboys would be driven toward a pre-arranged point, at which point a trail herd was formed. The trail drives then followed well-known routes that were determined by designated passes or river fords. Small operators with only 10 or 12 cowboys went up the same trails used by big outfits with 50 or more cowhands. The biggest drive recorded, in 1869, set out from Texas with 15,000 head of stock. Between 1865 and the mid-1880s, some 10 million animals went up the trails, the largest artificial migrations in history.

Prize longhorn steer, Zapata County Fair.

With the sale of the cattle in Abilene, Kansas (or Dodge City, Denver, Cheyenne, or Kansas City), the cowboys were paid for the first time on their long ride from Texas. For many of them, all the nights of sleeping on the ground and days of herding cattle over the open plains were erased in wild drinking and carousing in brothels. When the last dust of the trail drive had been washed away, the cowboys mounted up for the long ride home.

Not all cowboys wasted their money in the saloon and the bordello for, as often as not, the wages of the trail drive were used to buy cattle back in South Texas or in Mexico. A cowboy might also take his pay in cattle when he returned home, driving them north as part of a larger herd the following summer. In this way some working cowboys, such as the legendary Charles Goodnight, became great ranchers. They invested their profits in land and cattle, building up small spreads of their own.

THE FENCED RANGE

When J.F. Glidden was issued the first patent for barbed wire in 1874, it portended the end of the open range and the great cattle drives. At the same time, the railroad was expanding. In Texas, Fort Worth became the major railhead. Slaughterhouses and packing companies were built in Fort Worth and San Antonio, making it unnecessary to drive cattle to Kansas. Additionally, the introduction of refrigerated boxcars meant beef could be shipped longer distances. Amarillo and Abilene became active markets in West Texas.

Charles Goodnight composed this epitaph for his friend in 1929: "Bose Ikard served with me for four years on the Goodnight-Loving Trail, never shirked a duty or disobeyed an order, rode with me in many stampedes, participated in three engagements with the Comanches, splendid behavior."

It was not uncommon for a rancher to marry a woman much younger than himself, his own younger years being given to building up a ranch that would support a family. Charles Goodnight, at age 91, married Corinne Goodnight, a woman 65 years his junior. This practice left many women widowed and in charge of ranches. Some women took an active part in the management of Texas ranches and still do so today, making up 37 percent of all Texas farmers and ranchers.

Hard work was and is still a major part of life for the ranch cowboy. In addition to the spring roundup and branding, the ranch cowboy had to look after his cattle year-round. Cowboys still practice their riding and roping, but now they work in the corral or inside the fences of the ranch, rather than on the open range. In the fall and winter, cowboys ride the fence lines in order to mend them. Winter is also a time for repairing saddles, bridles, and other pieces of important ranch equipment.

GIGANTIC SPREADS

It was in the era of the open range that the great ranches of Texas began to form. The King Ranch in South Texas is the largest in the state, and bigger in size than Rhode Island. Texans measure the ranch's current size as 1.23 RIs (Rhode Islands), or 825,000 acres (333,390 hectares). It was founded in 1853 by a former Rio Grande steamboat captain, Richard King. Even though the original boundaries of the ranch are no longer the same, the King Ranch is substantially intact and still

The enormous King Ranch in South Texas was modeled so closely on the Spanish rancho that patrón King even led an entire village out of Mexico to work on it.

Cowhands take a break from branding longhorns at the Lonesome Pine Ranch.

BRANDING

Brands are used to identify cattle from individual ranches. Branding requires skill and experience because, if the branding irons are pressed too hard, the mark will go too deep and leave sores. There are other preliminaries, too: the male calves have to be castrated (the roasted testicles, also known as Rocky Mountain oysters, are a prized snack), and horns have to be trimmed to prevent the animals injuring each other.

Each Texas ranch had its own distinctive brand, which was registered with the Cattleman's Association, and established brands were recognized by their distinctive pattern everywhere on the range. Before the Civil War, it was not uncommon for a South Texas rancher to start a herd by rounding up unbranded cattle and giving them his brand. "Mavericks," or unbranded cattle, are said to have gotten their name from Samuel Maverick, the Matagorda County entrepreneur of the 1840s.

In historic times, brands were not widely used by Spanish and Mexican ranchers because their ranchos operated on the patrón system. The patrón, in the manner of a feudal lord, owned all the cattle and land within the "fiefdom" of his rancho, so there was very little need to establish his ownership by branding. If the cattle were on his land, they were his.

BLACK COWBOYS

It is a lesser-known fact that some of the best cowboys to come into Texas were black Americans leaving the war-ravaged states of the South.

A cowboy at the National Black Rodeo Finals.

African-Americans in the West often met the same prejudice they faced elsewhere. Few acquired property or social distinction. But, to a range boss, character and willingness to work trumped skin color. It was estimated that about one-quarter of the cowboys on the northbound trail drives between 1866 and 1895 were black.

Many of the early black cowboys had been born as slaves or sons of slaves and eventually found more freedom on the open ranges than in urban areas. Others were army veterans from the corps of black cavalrymen called "Buffalo Soldiers." After the Civil War, some 5 million head of loose stock roamed the Texas plains and cowboys of all skin colors were in high demand. Some ranches east of the Trinity River had all-black crews, and many became horsebreakers, but very few achieved the elevated status of foremen or managers. A handful became federal peace officers or took up careers as rodeo performers. One Texas-born African-American cowboy, Bill Pickett, achieved enormous fame by inventing the rodeo sport of bulldogging (or steer wrestling). A life-size bronze statue of Pickett subduing a steer stands today in the historic Stockyards District in Fort Worth.

Bose Ikard, a slave born in Mississippi in 1843, was brought to Texas by his master in 1852 and learned the cowboy trade on a ranch near Weatherford. Freed as a result of the Civil War, he went to work for the famed western rancher Charles Goodnight, eventually becoming the cattle baron's right-hand man. Goodnight said he trusted Ikard "farther than any living man." Ikard's story was among those told in fictional fashion in the novel and TV mini-series by Texas author Larry McMurtry, *Lonesome Dove*.

Another former slave, Isom Dart – who was born Ned Huddleston in Arkansas in 1849 – had an early career stealing horses in Mexico and swimming them across the Rio Grande to sell in Texas. Later, his gambling and fighting in northwest Colorado entangled him with the law. After that, he changed his name to Isom Dart, bought a ranch, and tried to go straight but was tracked down and killed, at the age of 51 by bounty hunter Tom Horn.

The 1993 made-for-television movie *Return to Lonesome Dove* featured a fictional character named Isom Pickett, who was a composite of the real life Dart and Bill Pickett.

A cowboy and bronc buster named Nat (or Nate) Love was one of many who claimed to have been the original model for Deadwood Dick, saying he had acquired the nickname by winning a roping contest in Deadwood, South Dakota in 1876.

Today's black cowboys can showcase their skills through a series of African-American rodeos, sponsored by the Cowboys of Color, the Bill Pickett Invitational Rodeo, and other organizations.

In recent years, black cowboys have begun to assume their rightful roles in the cinematic history of the West via such actors as Woody Strode (*Sergeant Rutledge, The Man Who Shot Liberty Valance*), Morgan Freeman (*Unforgiven*), Danny Glover (*Lonesome Dove, Silverado, Buffalo Soldiers*), Louis Gossett, Jr. (*Return To Lonesome Dove*), and Jamie Foxx (*Django Unchained*). Mel Brooks famously used his 1974 parody Western, *Blazing Saddles*, to send up modern racial attitudes.

family owned. There are organized tours, and any highway that goes to Kingsville will cut through some part of it.

The celebrated XIT Ranch in the Texas Panhandle was started by midwestern and British land and cattle syndicates and was the largest range in the world under fence. In the 1870s and '80s, the state sold the land to the syndicates to finance the present State Capitol in Austin. Originally a monstrous 4.54 RIs (more than 3 million acres/1.25 million hectares), the XIT was split up in later years as the out-of-state investors went their separate ways. At its peak, the ranch was bounded by more than 1,500 miles (2,413km) of fencing.

Texas ranches have become more mechanized and modernized. The only contemporary ranch of any size doing business in the 19th-century way is the Kokernot 06, between Fort Davis and Balmorhea in Davis County.

However, large modern-day Texas ranches such as the Matador, the 6666, the Waggoner, the Y.O, and, of course, the mighty King Ranch still endure and thrive, though some have had to incorporate oil exploration and tourism into their traditional livestock vocations.

COWBOY SPECTACULARS

Rodeo is the sport of cowboys, developing naturally out of their skills and tasks as they worked with livestock. Early rodeos were just informal gatherings of locals who all pitched in to provide the livestock, riders, and entertainment. Pecos, in the Big Bend Country of West Texas, claims to have held the first rodeo in 1883 (strongly disputed by Prescott, Arizona, which claims to have hosted a rodeo since 1888). Rodeo is now controlled by the Professional Rodeo Cowboys Association (PRCA), which sanctions more than 650 rodeos each year all over the United States – even in places such as New York City. There are national finals held annually in mid-December in Las Vegas, Nevada, and the top rodeo cowboys make six-digit salaries competing in as many as 125 competitions a year.

Over the fence at a Texas rodeo.

SAVING THE LONGHORN

With the introduction of barbed wire fencing and the end of unlimited free range grass in the 19th century, it became more economical to raise cattle that developed faster than longhorns, which, by the 1920s, had been almost bred out of existence. Shorthorns and Herefords predominated.

Longhorns were saved from probable extinction by Will C. Barnes and other Forest Service men, who collected a small herd of breeding stock for Oklahoma's Wichita Mountains Wildlife Refuge. A few years later, oilman Sid Richardson financed the acquisition of small herds for Texas state parks. Eventually, cattlemen rediscovered the longhorn's longevity, its resistance to disease, fertility, ease of calving, ability to thrive on marginal pastures, and also the fact that its leaner beef was in tune with the times.

One result of the cattle drives was that ranches were established not only in the uninhabited parts of Texas but also on the hitherto remote plains of the Middle West and in the Indian Territory that is now the state of Oklahoma. As the tribes were pushed farther and farther back, even the mountains and desert plains in the far western parts of the state, beyond the Pecos River, became valuable property. These are the major cattleman's strongholds today, and they contain some of the largest ranches in the state.

The traditional rodeo events are bull riding, bareback bronc riding, calf roping, steer wrestling, saddle bronc riding and, for women, barrel racing. In the 1930s and 40s, there was an extensive women's rodeo circuit. Women competed in the same events as men and added gymnastic trick riding, too. Today, the Women's Professional Rodeo Association is the longest running women's professional association and each October the WPRA World Finals take place in Waco, Texas. There is still today a thriving circuit of African-American rodeos officiated by several organizations.

African-Americans made their way to the frontier after the Civil War, and many signed on as admired, hard-working cowboys for famous outfits in Texas.

Rancher and renowned chuck wagon cook, Cliff Teinert.

Rodeo contests can be held indoors or out, but the basic requirement is a large, dirt-floored corral or arena, with chutes along one side and escape gates for the livestock opposite them. The arena is surrounded by stands, and behind the stands are barns and holding pens. Bull and bronc riders mount up in small pens that open directly into the arena.

When the gate swings open, a rider tries to stay on the animal for eight seconds. Half of the points scored in a ride come from the total time the rider stays mounted; the other half are awarded for the competitor's style and daring.

Rodeo can be dangerous: the animals are wild, and often try to trample or gore dismounted riders. The rodeo cowboy's best friend is the clown, who runs into the arena to distract the mount while the rider is on the ground. Elaborately inscribed belt buckles, displaying the cowboy's name and the event, are presented as trophies.

COWBOY HERITAGE

The world of the cowboy and the Wild West has been preserved in several modern museums dedicated to its memory. One of the finest

SAMUEL MAVERICK

Samuel Maverick moved to Texas in 1835, where he became a land speculator, buying land at 15¢ per acre, and by 1842, was said to be the biggest landholder in the state. Later that year, Maverick was caught during the invasion of San Antonio and imprisoned in Mexico for seven months. On his return, he reluctantly accepted 400 cattle from a neighbor in lieu of a debt, thus becoming a rancher.

Without much interest, Maverick placed the cattle on his Gulf ranch under the care of his black slaves, who reported that their boss was unenthusiastic about applying a burning iron to flesh. The slaves branded about one-third of the growing herd and the others often strayed to the mainland, where they were seized by less scrupulous ranchers, "mavericker," who stamped them with their own brand.

Some ranchers hired "maverickers" to brand as many as 18 "mavericks" per day, at 50 cents to a dollar apiece. Eventually, in 1854, Samuel Maverick sent a party of vaqueros to round up his herd, which numbered several hundred, and moved it to Rancho Conquista, a spread he'd acquired on the San Antonio River, 50 miles (80km) from the city.

Disenchanted with the cattle business, Maverick sold his herd, but the use of his name to describe stray cattle lives on today to signify people who make their own way in life, independent of the crowd.

collections can be found in the Panhandle-Plains Historical Museum in Canyon, Texas. The T-Anchor Ranch Headquarters, built in 1877, is on the museum grounds. Another fine collection is in the Longhorn Museum in Pleasanton, which claims to be "the birthplace of the American cowboy." Exhibits in this museum document the cowboy and his American Indian and Hispanic antecedents. San Antonio has The Trail Drivers Association and the Institute of Texan Cultures, both displaying collections of cowboy – and cowgirl – memorabilia. Austin's modern

In 1884, the cattle-driving Pryor brothers were contracted to deliver 45,000 head in 15 separate lots, earning themselves a handy net profit of around $20,000.

Bullock Texas State History Museum details the Lone Star State's frontier past. The XIT Museum in Dalhart chronicles the history of that famous old ranch, while the National Cowgirl Museum and Hall of Fame in Fort Worth has a collection celebrating women in the West. Also in Fort Worth, the Amon Carter Museum (in that city's Cultural District) and the smaller downtown Sid Richardson Museum feature large quantities of Western art and photographs, including masterpieces by Charles Russell and Frederic Remington.

The National Ranching Heritage Center on the campus of Texas Tech University in Lubbock is the home of 20 buildings representing ranch housing from the Spanish days to the large family ranch houses of 1890s cattle barons. Almost any county historical museum in any town in cattle country preserves some artifacts from the trail driving and cowboy era.

LOST SKILLS

The visitor looking for working cowboys today is at something of a loss. Modern equipment has made many of the cowboy's traditional jobs obsolete. Consequently, contemporary cowboys and ranchers have learned to combine traditional roping and riding skills with modern tools, from DNA breeding research to computers and "green" technology. A modern cowboy might ride the range on an all-terrain vehicle, with a cellphone in the pocket of his Levis. The best ranch to visit is the Y.O. Ranch near Kerrville. The King Ranch offers tours, as do some of the surviving West Texas spreads. Dude ranches in the Bandera area also offer a taste of ranch life. But, a rodeo is the most accessible form of cowboy life available today.

BEWARE OF IMPOSTERS

Not all the folks you see strolling around in boots and jeans are cowboys. People who look

Herding longhorn cattle.

like cowboys may never have been astride a horse. Cowboy hats, Western-cut shirts with pearl snaps, big buckles on tooled leather belts and leather boots are standard fashion for many modern Texans. By contrast, some of today's younger working cowboys wear "gimme" caps and T-shirts emblazoned with the names of rock 'n' roll bands. Find a fellow who takes things too far by adding a swagger and some big talk to this costume and you have what's popularly referred to as a "drugstore cowboy." He's the cowboy who spends more time at the drugstore lunch counter than he ever does astride a horse. A real cowboy is apt to say of such a fellow, "He's all hat and no cattle."

Luckenbach musician David Harris.

MUSICAL TRADITIONS

From country, blues, and folk to conjunto, western swing, and good ol' rock 'n' roll – musically, Texas has it all.

The enduring glory of the music from the Lone Star State is rooted in its free-form eclecticism, its gumbo of cultural influences, and a cheerful disregard for the artificial boundaries erected between musical genres in other parts of the country. Texas has always been a crossroads, and over the past 300 years Texas music has been informed and enriched by Anglo-Celtic ballads, Mexican norteño, Appalachian mountain folksongs, African/Caribbean blues, Cajun and zydeco music from the wilds of Louisiana, Bohemian oompah polka bands, and British Invasion pop, not to mention the various practitioners of punk, rap, reggae, jazz, techno, funk, pop, and rock who have managed to find a home within the joyfully elastic boundaries of the state's musical community. The constant cross-fertilization of distinct ethnic sources accounts for both the diversity and the similarity of traditional Texas music.

Country music legend Willie Nelson.

HOME OF COUNTRY

The tendency to think of Texas as the home of country and western and cowboy music is understandable (no matter what those folks in Nashville say). Texans have made some of the most important contributions to the development of country music. Texan Vernon Dalhart's 1924 recording of "*The Wreck of the Old 97*" was the first million-selling country album; Bob Wills and his Texas Playboys took western swing to the world; Ray Price and Ernest Tubb formulated the hard-edged honky-tonk sound, which dominated country music in the post-war era; the Dixie Chicks, from Dallas, became the best-selling female group of all time.

When they came to the South, the early Anglo-Irish settlers brought with them a vigorous heritage of folk songs, ballads, and fiddle music. In Texas and the surrounding region, unique southwestern forms soon developed, such as the cowboy songs that were documented extensively in the early 20th century by the Texan John A. Lomax, one of America's earliest and most prodigious folk-song collectors.

Texans also developed distinctive instrumental styles, such as the swinging, fluid Texas fiddle style that can be heard at the many annual fiddle and bluegrass contests across the nation. One of the Texas fiddle style's earliest practitioners, the legendary A.C. Eck Robertson, was also one of, if not the, first country musicians to record commercially. In the early 1920s, he waxed such classics as "*Sally Gooden*" and "*Brilliancy.*"

The continued vitality of country music in Texas is seen in the ongoing popularity of small dance halls that are dotted throughout the state, such as Austin's Broken Spoke and Gruene Hall in the Hill Country near New Braunfels, the oldest dance hall in the state. And of course, there's also a revolving cast of larger nightclubs in the major cities, including Billy Bob's Texas in Fort Worth, which bills itself as the "world's largest honky-tonk."

One nightclub, the late-lamented Armadillo in Austin, became the launch pad for famous musicians like Janis Joplin and Willie Nelson and the beginning of Austin's fame as the live music capital of the US. Its heyday in the 1970s (it closed in 1980) saw the emergence of Texas's "outlaw country" music scene, led by native Texan "outlaws" Willie Nelson and Waylon Jennings and others, including Michael Murphey, Guy Clark, Townes Van Zandt, and Jerry Jeff Walker. Outlaw country flew in the face of Nashville conformity by blending rock, country and blues, and appealing to younger rock audiences. The fact that its name alluded to the slightly dangerous lifestyles of its leading exponents also added to the allure.

Today, a new "Texas Music" country rock movement mixes regional pride and an edgy vibe with a high-octane rock. Performers such as Ashley McBryde, The Scooter Brown Band, and The Steel Woods have all toured brought their Southern sounds with them on US tours.

Musicians in Terlingua.

AUSTIN CITY LIMITS

Austin rivals Nashville as the country music capital of the United States. When it comes to popularity, nothing beats the annual live recordings of the popular PBS television show *Austin City Limits*, which celebrated its 40th season in 2014 and is now the longest running music series in US television history. Taped over 13 weeks each season, the award-winning show has featured nearly 1,000 musicians on its outdoor concert stage on the campus of UT in downtown Austin, with the state capitol picturesquely lit up behind the performers.

In recent years, ACL, as it is known, has reached out to embrace alternative rock, rhythm and blues, and singer-songwriters. The show and old UT theater where it was originally taped were inducted into the Rock and Roll Hall of Fame in 2010. In 2011, ACL moved to the purpose-built Moody Theater and Studio downtown, a venue with a larger seating capacity. ACL itself retains a taping audience of 800 (the original capacity), however; the rest of the seating is used for the ALC Live concert series.

Willie Nelson, who was the very first musician to take the stage at ACL, when he was a relative unknown, achieved the status of American institution many years ago. Nowadays, his weathered visage has become iconic, and his laconic vocal style and fluid guitar playing still refreshing and instantly recognizable. Nelson is honorary godfather to a generation of storytelling Texas singer-songwriters, including Billy Joe Shaver, Rodney Crowell, Steve Earle, Lyle Lovett, and Robert Earl Keen.

UNCONVENTIONAL

While Texas continually generates conventional country stars who succeed in logging big chart hits – including George Jones, Ernest Tubb, and Ray Price over three decades ago, and more recently the Dixie Chicks, George Strait, Miranda Lambert, and Kacey Musgraves – it is the iconoclasts who make the most compelling music. Grandfathered by Buddy Holly, they make Texas music that belongs to no one genre. Joe Ely, Jimmie Dale Gilmore, and Butch Hancock, from Lubbock, mix folk, country, and rock in their performances and collectively as The Flatlanders. They and other West Texas musicians like Waylon Jennings and Roy Orbison (and, before them, Bob Wills) take perverse pride in bending musical rules and leapfrogging stylistic boundaries. The same can be said for genre-hopping Brave Combo, based in Denton, a small university town north of Dallas known for live music offerings that rival those of Austin.

Pioneer of western swing, Bob Wills was one of Texas's most durable musicians. His career stretched from the 1920s all the way into the 1970s.

WESTERN SWING

Texas's most original contribution to country music may be western swing. It grew out of jazz and was developed in the early 1930s by two Fort Worth bands, Milton Brown and his Musical Brownies and the Light Crust Doughboys. The latter was co-founded by Bob Wills, who perfected the genre in his band Bob Wills and His Texas Playboys. Wills turned traditional string band dance music on its head by introducing elements of hot jazz, blues, pop, and Tex-Mex ranchera strains. Soloing and improvisation were encouraged, and Wills' twin-fiddle attack, augmented by a keening steel guitar and the soulful vocals of Tommy Duncan made for one of the swinginest sounds in any genre. Wills sometimes even included brass in his line-up. The western swing torch is carried today by performers such as the Hot Club of Cowtown and Asleep At the Wheel.

THE BLUES, R&B, AND HIP-HOP

"Blues came to Texas, lopin' like a mule," sang the famous Texas bluesman Blind Lemon Jefferson. Texans were certainly indispensable to the style's development. After the Civil War, freed slaves and free migrant black people followed the harvests and worked in the sugar plantations and lumber camps of East Texas. Their field hollers and acoustic "country blues" informed the music of Texas bluesmen like Mance Lipscomb, Huddie "Leadbelly" Ledbetter, and Sam "Lightnin'" Hopkins.

Houston-born global superstar Beyoncé.

In the 1930s, Dallas' Aaron "T-Bone" Walker was one of the first electric blues guitarists to coin an original style: the single-string solo. A master showman (he did splits while playing the guitar behind his head), Walker was a pivotal influence on B.B. King, Eric Clapton, and others. Walker's contemporary, the late Clarence "Gatemouth" Brown, bristled at being called "just" a bluesman, when he played country, jazz, and Cajun music as the spirit moved him.

After World War II, Houston and Dallas/Fort Worth became the state's hotbeds of electric, urban blues, and rhythm and blues. The Duke and Peacock record labels in Houston waxed hits by Bobby "Blue" Bland, Junior Parker and "Big Mama" Thornton, while the "Texas Tenors" – a group of hard-charging saxophonists led by King Curtis, Illinois Jacquet, and David "Fathead" Newman – set the standard for sax players in R&B, soul, and jazz bands. Other great jazzmen who hail from Texas include the avant-garde master Ornette Coleman, ragtime king Scott Joplin, and keyboardist Teddy Wilson. Many of these greats played in Dallas' Deep Ellum neighborhood, which has kept up the tradition over the last century, and still remains a musical mecca for bands and artists to play on their tours through Texas. Today, Houston's R&B heritage is carried on by superstar Beyoncé and her sister Solange Knowles, while Dallas is proud to call R&B artist Erykah Badu one of their own.

Falco Jiménez, pioneer of conjunto.

Houston, along with New Orleans and Atlanta, has become headquarters for rap and hip-hop in the South. After the success of the Geto Boys in the 1990s, Houston hip-hop (characterized by its slowed-down, hypnotic, "screwed" grooves) is dominated by the influence of the late D.J. Screw, and current performers Travis Scott, Mike Jones, Paul Wall, Chamillionaire, Slim Thug, Baby Bash, Chingo Bling, and Bun B.

Though not under the hip-hop or R&B umbrella, Texas has produced some notable pop artists like Selena Gomez, Jessica and Ashley Simpson, Demi Lovato, and Todrick Hall.

FROM BLUES TO ROCK

Texas has also had younger white artists who draw their inspiration from the blues, a trend that stretches from Port Arthur's Janis Joplin – who was part of Austin's folk revival scene in the 1960s before moving to California, where her rapid rise to stardom ended in a tragic death – through vocalists like Fort Worth's Delbert McClinton and late guitarist Stevie Ray Vaughan. The Vaughan brothers, Jimmie and Stevie Ray, amassed an international reputation as electric blues guitarists of the first order – Jimmie with the Fabulous Thunderbirds and Stevie Ray with his band Double Trouble.

ZZ Top, from Houston, also emerged from the blues rock scene of the 1970s and notched huge hits by combining John Lee Hooker–style boogie with Texas braggadocio. Texas rock is a wellspring of raucous, often bizarre music, stretching from the 1960s-era psychedelic anthems of the 13th Floor Elevators to the avant-punk noise of the Butthole Surfers in the 1980s and 1990s, grunge rock of the Toadies in the 1990s, the pop rock bands, Bowling for Soup and Fastball of the late 90s and 2000s, and today's heavy metal band Pantera. Leon Bridges of Fort Worth and Gary Clark Jr. of Austin pay tribute to Texas' blues, soul, and rock history with their soulful sounds.

CONJUNTO AND TEJANO

Like their Anglo-American counterparts, Mexican immigrants and Tejanos (Texans of Hispanic heritage) brought a vast store of folk songs and ballads, many in the styles of norteño, mariachi, or corridos. Tejanos were innovators and helped develop a distinctive Tex-Mex dance music called conjunto. While the distinguishing instrument of conjunto, the accordion, was introduced to Mexicans by the Germans in the 1840s, by the late 19th century they had developed their own accordion style, while retaining the polka and waltz melodies of their European antecedents. Conjunto was not insulated from other ethnic traditions. The early performer Narcisco Martinez, who is sometimes called "the Father of

Conjunto Music," even recorded a version of the Bob Wills standard "San Antonio Rose." Corridos, the storytelling songs of the border country, have kept pace; recently a new strain has arisen, the narcocorrido, chronicling the exploits of drug smugglers and outlaws. Conjunto has had an interesting influence on Texas rock 'n' roll, which could be heard in the early 1960s in the Tex-Mex rock 'n' roll hits ("She's About a Mover", "Mendocino") of the Sir Douglas Quintet. Doug Sahm, and Augie Meyers, two of the SDQ founders, went on to form another Tex-Mex group in the 1990s, the Texas Tornados, which featured conjunto master accordionist Flaco Jiménez and vocalist Freddie Fender. San Angelo's Los Lonely Boys are perhaps the most well-known American Chicano rock band of today, playing what they call "Texican rock n' roll."

Tejano, an amped-up, electrified rock 'n' roll cousin of conjunto, received national attention when its brightest young star, Selena Quintanilla Perez, was killed in 1996. While a clear successor to Selena has yet to emerge, Tejano's popularity has continued to simmer in the dance halls and music festivals of the Rio Grande Valley, Corpus Christi, and South Texas, like Fiesta de la Flor, a two-day music festival in honor of the late Selena.

CAJUN AND ZYDECO

Before and after World War II, immigrants from Louisiana flowed west in search of work in the oil refineries of Houston and the East Texas cities of Beaumont, Orange, and Port Arthur bordering Louisiana. The two musical forms they brought with them, Cajun and zydeco, are roughly analogous to country music and the blues. White Cajun musicians tended to adhere to the traditional sounds of the button accordion, the triangle, the fiddle, and the guitar. The peppery, volatile dance music called zydeco is powered by the keyboard accordion and a heavy rhythm section. It was introduced to Texas by black Creoles from the Lafayette, Louisiana area (principally Clifton Chenier, the late "King of Zydeco").

CLUBS AND FESTIVALS

The club scene is capricious, with venues opening and closing, or changing ownership or location. Most of the larger cities have free alternative weekly newspapers, such as the *Austin Chronicle* and the *Dallas Observer*, which are good sources for club and concert listings. Texas's annual music festivals are well advertised. The Texas Folklife Festival every June offers a sampling of authentic traditional Texas music, as well as revival forms. For folk music, the Kerrville Folk Festival in May is mandatory, and every kind of global and regional pop music can be found at Austin's gigantic South By Southwest festival every March. Since 2012, the Austin City Limits Music Festival has earned a permanent spot on the music fan's calendar every September. Willie Nelson's 4th of July Picnic is a holiday event as revered as parades and fireworks.

South By Southwest festival.

TEXAS MUSIC STORES

Good online sources of information on Texas and Americana artists include www.nodepression.com, the community website for the now defunct magazine of the same name, and www.lonestarmusic.com, which also publishes a bi-monthly magazine. Free newspapers such as the *Austin Chronicle* and *Dallas Observer* contain listings. One of the best independent record stores in the country, with an exhaustive selection of Texas music, is Waterloo Records in Austin. The Arhoolie record label is particularly rich in archival recordings of old-time Cajun, folk, blues, country, zydeco, and conjunto artists.

The Fort Worth Museum of Science and History.

TEXAN ARCHITECTURE

From adobe huts and primitive log cabins to glistening glass towers, the state's architecture is a fascinating mix of the functional and the inspired.

In Texas today, the words "Remember the Alamo" also have a special relevance to Texas architecture. For most of the 20th century, and especially in recent years, a battle has been waged between people who want new Texas architecture to reflect native values and styles and those who want to move beyond regionalism to the very cutting edge of international design.

It's an issue that is not likely to be resolved soon, because, at a deeper level, it is a struggle over the image of Texas itself. The conflict between regional design and international design isn't just about architecture; it's part of an ongoing struggle between rural and urban Texas, between native architects and outsiders, and between the mythical Lone Star State and the real, contradictory, contemporary Texas.

BEGINNING WITH ADOBE

To remember the Alamo in San Antonio is, of course, to remember the Spaniards, Texas's first European settlers. The Spaniards gave architectural life to the creamy white limestone of Central Texas, and introduced skill and efficiency to the simple adobe technique of American Indians of the Southwest. Although the late 19th-century Spanish architect, Antonio Gaudí, would have approved of the native method of globbing one handful of mud on top of another to make a wall, the 18th-century Spanish friars taught them how to mold heavy, regular adobe bricks in wooden frames.

Adobe, together with wood and stone, was used by native people, and later Spaniards, all along the lower Rio Grande. It was easier to make adobe bricks than to quarry stone, and an adobe wall protected the interior of a house or church from the heat just as well as stone. Adobe is sturdy and, with its insulation properties – warm in winter and cool in summer – well suited to the hot, dry southwestern climate, as long it is maintained and water is not allowed to seep in and undermine the walls.

Mission San José.

Adobe is an aesthetically pleasing and tactile material, which by its very nature offers many stylistic uses inside and out. For instance, because traditional adobe walls are laid thick – usually around 2ft (0.6 meters) – windows are deeply recessed and may serve as window seats or built-in shelves; plastered adobe can also be used to make built-in seating (*bancos*), display nooks (*nichos*), half-dividing walls, bed platforms, and steps, giving interiors a smooth, sculpted, all-of-a-piece quality that is organic, artistic and endlessly versatile.

THE MISSIONS

The Spanish missionaries in Texas, used to the Renaissance churches of their homeland, took pains to create an architecture that went beyond function. They wanted their buildings to express beauty in the wilderness. The Alamo mission is remembered as the bloody place where early Texans sacrificed their lives for freedom, but the building itself, in the heart of downtown San Antonio, is the image of quiet repose. The stone arches and carved niches suggest that the Alamo deserved a different kind of fame. The bell tower and "rose window" of San Antonio's San José Mission are proof that the Spaniards intended not just to survive, but to glorify, too.

A breezeway at Quinta Mazatlan, a historic adobe mansion in McAllen.

FARMHOUSE STYLE

Such a claim can hardly be made for the early Anglo-American settlers of the 1820s and 1830s. When farmers from Tennessee, Kentucky, Mississippi, and Alabama rolled into Texas, they brought with them the only architecture they knew – the plain log house and its cousin, the functional frame house of roughly hewn boards. There was nothing extra in these houses, nothing to make life on the Texas frontier a little sweeter or softer.

And yet, as is often the case with architecture, function led people to design structures that were, if not beautiful, still comfortable in the landscape. The deep porch offered protection against the sun, the dog or possum "trot" (an open breezeway between two essential rooms or cabins) was used for such things as curing meat and for sleeping outdoors, and the steeply pitched gable roof protected the house from the pounding rain. These features not only eased the hardships of frontier life, they created a simple, graceful, appealing style.

Even the Germans who emigrated to Texas from the 1840s onward modified their age-old method of building stone and wood *(Fachwerk)* houses in order to incorporate elements of the Anglo farmhouse. Their hewn frameworks were joined with mortise-and-tenon joints secured by wooden pegs. In the 1850s, famed American architect Frederick Law Olmsted, traveling to San Antonio, slept in New Braunfels in a "small cottage of a single story, having the roof extended so as to form a verandah, with a sign hanging before it, *Guadalupe Hotel, J. Schmitz.*"

FORMALITY AND GRACE

Before the Civil War, most people in Texas did not live in houses as snug and pleasant as those of the Germans in Central Texas. They were only too glad to leave behind their relatively crude houses when life grew easier, and when the classic Greek Revival and later Victorian styles were brought into the eastern, central, and southern parts of the state.

The Greek Revival put classical columns on the porches of even the simplest log houses, and gave a touch of southern formality and grace to larger buildings. Greek Revival is found in Austin (for instance, in the Governor's Mansion), but it flowered in East Texas. Crockett, Jefferson, Marshall, Tyler, and Houston all have charming and varied examples of the Greek Revival style, which remained popular into the 1870s when Victoriana became all the rage. The Victorian buildings of Nicholas Clayton of Galveston, and the Richardson Romanesque courthouses of James Riley Gordon in many of the county seats (look for his buildings in such places as San Antonio, Waxahachie, La Grange, Stephenville, Sulphur Springs, Giddings, and New Braunfels) are evidence of the growing influence of gentility. When Texans began to concern themselves with porticoes and turrets, high culture had clearly arrived.

The Greek Revival Bayou Bend, Houston.

MODERN TEXAS

Beaux-arts eclecticism held sway in Texas briefly, just long enough to influence some public and university buildings. The trickledown popularity of the Arts and Crafts Movement in Britain found expression in thousands of Texas bungalows.

During the Great Depression, courthouses and other public buildings were built by government labor. Their blocky, repetitive shapes and flat reliefs in the Art Moderne style make it easy to date such monumental buildings as the Fort Worth City Hall and the distinctive courthouses of Travis, Brazoria, and Eastland Counties to this period.

Not many skyscrapers were built in Texas before and during the 1920s and '30s. A few did go up, such as Houston's Esperson Building in the popular Eclectic style and Dallas's Adolphus Hotel (1912) and the Magnolia Building (1922), in the Beaux-Arts style.

One of the most elegant Victorian buildings in Texas, Austin's Driskill Hotel, designed by Frederick E. Ruffini, is still open for business.

Within a period of about 50 years, roughly between 1870 and 1920, domestic architecture in the state began to mature. Indeed, wealthy Texans systematically demonstrated that what was fashionable in Paris or London was fashionable in Houston, or even on the ranch. The set for the 1956 film

Giant (about a Texas rancher and oilman) captured this spirit of brashness, while the movie's Second Empire mansion, silhouetted against endless West Texas ranchland, carried it to absurd limits.

IN SEARCH OF A STYLE

Central Houston's famed River Oaks residential section, established by the Hogg brothers in the 1920s around River Oaks Country Club, and next to the Galleria, is one of the wealthiest and most exclusive communities in the country. With its carefully manicured lawns and gardens, oak-shaded streets, and elegant homes, it has long been a model for planned communities throughout the US.

It could be said that some of the grand homes here, variants on the English Tudor and American Colonial style specified by the planners, reflect a self-consciousness often associated with the nouveau riche tasked with building a home for the first time. Even when the stylistic adaptations are imaginatively and tastefully handled, and local stone such as pink granite has been used, at times it's possible to detect a feeling of uncertainty in some of the design choices. It may be that some newly rich Texans feel the need to rise above their architectural roots – sullied as they were by poverty, struggle, and, not infrequently, illiteracy – and do so by co-opting a pastiche of styles as they gradually work out their own.

In this, however, Texans are by no means unusual – just more obvious, perhaps, given the numbers of super wealthy residents in the state. River Oaks is one of the top 10 planned communities in the nation, with homes worth an average $1.5 million and a top draw for famous residents since it opened.

Gresham Castle, Galveston.

DON'T FORGET THE KIMBELL

Fort Worth's much-admired Kimbell Art Museum, opened in 1972, draws from the past in subtle ways. Its barrel vaults, which allow light to stream down along interior walls, may recall the silos that architect Louis Kahn admired in the Texas landscape, but this is, at best, conjecture. What makes the Kimbell appropriate to Texas is its strength, tranquility, and aura of permanence. It looks back to the years before Texas dressed its buildings up in the styles of the East, beyond the Victorian and Greek Revival periods to the simple, functional early Texas buildings. It is regional in the finest sense of the word. Remember the Alamo, but don't forget the Kimbell.

EXTERIOR INFLUENCES

In the 1920s and '30s, small groups of architects – in California, New York, and Spring Green, Wisconsin (at Frank Lloyd Wright's Taliesin compound) – formulated new ideas about Modern architecture that would eventually make it acceptable for Texans to look upon their architectural heritage without shame. Their new ideas ranged from the "organic naturalism" of Wright's "Prairie Style" to the "machines for living" of the Frenchman Le Corbusier, but all of them respected what was functional in architecture – and opposed what was merely applied and decorative. In this light, the functional and formal aspects of missions and ranch houses were reevaluated. If early Texans had allowed "form to follow function" out of necessity, a later generation of Texans made a conscious choice to do so. The result was the flowering of Texas architecture in the mid-20th century.

It was at this time that Texas buildings began to show not contempt but deference to their older neighbors. San Antonio architect O'Neil Ford, who, along with others, became interested in the accurate restoration of Spanish Colonial architecture, taught Texans to respect the scale and character of indigenous buildings, and to appreciate the native materials used in them. Ford's own Trinity University campus in San Antonio (begun in 1949), a group of brick buildings that beg comparison with Italian hillside villages, is faithful to the nature of the hilly Texas landscape. His Johnson City Post Office (1970) is a modified ranch house of limestone blocks with a wide front porch and a sloping roof. His Cowboy Artists of America Museum in Kerrville (1983) is both a fortress built of creamy limestone and a gallery of near-forgotten building techniques. Throughout his life (he died in 1982), Ford had great influence on Texas architects. His teachings still form the basis of the regionalist school of thought.

Chinese-born architect I. M. Pei, responsible for some of the most distinctive Modern architecture in Texas, is also famous for the Louvre's glass pyramid in Paris.

A meticulously restored Sinclair gasoline station in Albany.

BOXY TOWERS

Ironically, the Modern emphasis on function, which prepared the way for a new appreciation of Texas's early buildings, was also responsible for giving birth to the attitude that the architecture of the past did not stack up well against the box. When the German Bauhaus architects sold Americans on their philosophy in the 1940s, cities like New York and San Francisco began to build boxy skyscrapers.

Texas cities were still young at that time, and possessed a few fine old buildings and almost no tradition of urban architecture. Thus, when cities like Houston and Dallas began to expand, much of their growth took the logical form of the Modern glass box. Their new urban buildings delivered a message as honest as that conveyed by the early settlers' houses: unadorned simplicity was still at home in Texas. Later, the boxes were criticized for their brutality.

Early Texas structures were admired for their utility and for their rural beauty, but they certainly didn't influence high-rise architecture in the heyday of the box. A golden sunset reflected by the limestone facades of Central Texas could evoke the memory of Coronado and his search for the Seven Golden Cities; or a lonely wind whistling through a broken windmill near an isolated ranch house could conjure up romantic images of the hard frontier life. But what, after all, did rough-cut limestone blocks or pitched roofs have to do with multistory, steel-framed buildings?

During the years dominated by the glass box, Houston architecture came into its own. The Tenneco skyscraper (1963), with its exposed steel frame, and One Shell Plaza (1965), with its clean white facades, were as sophisticated and current as any new buildings anywhere.

Famed architect Philip Johnson set the stage for his Houston breakthroughs with his Amon Carter Museum in Fort Worth (1960), which has the stately order of a Greek temple. Later, by breaking up the rigidity of the Bauhaus box with the trapezoidal towers of his Pennzoil Place and his round-cornered Post Oak Central buildings (both 1976), Johnson drew international eyes to Texas architecture. The state that was famous for its rugged individualism at last had a Modern architecture that expressed it.

Even the more conservative Dallas received oddly shaped, shimmering, reflective glass buildings and a city hall (dedicated 1978) that broke out of the box completely. I.M. Pei's design, which took the form of an immense triangle balancing on one edge, sent cantilevered floors of offices precariously (it seemed) out over a plaza. O'Neil Ford was outspokenly annoyed by the Dallas City Hall, believing its effectiveness depended on playing tricks with the viewer's expectations. It was intentionally unnerving. Ford and his opinions are relevant to the shift in taste in skyscraper design in the early 1980s.

Once again, with his Houston skyscrapers, Philip Johnson led the way for developer Gerald Hines, but this time he did more than break out of the box. His designs now referred openly to the architectural styles of the past. His lighthouse-like Williams Tower, with Art Deco setbacks, and his Gothic Republic Bank tower were the world's first Postmodern skyscrapers.

And that wasn't all. By sheathing Republic Bank in red granite, Johnson made an oblique reference to Texas's many granite public buildings. His 1983 Crescent complex in Dallas (offices, hotel and shopping court) was said to draw inspiration from early Texas architecture. The regional architecture that pragmatists like O'Neil Ford had championed became popular with Postmodern architects, interested in its romantic connotations.

The Kimbell Art Museum, Fort Worth.

IN SEARCH OF REGIONALISM

Regionalist architecture is still practiced by Texas architects on a small scale in rural areas, but many large urban commissions still go to outsiders. In recent years, the green glass Wells Fargo Bank Plaza, by Skidmore, Owings and Merrill; the steel and glass Four Leaf Towers, by Cesar Pelli;

and the silvery granite needle of I.M. Pei's JPMorgan Chase Tower were added to Houston's skyline.

Dallas, meanwhile, has become more daring. I.M. Pei designed two 60-story rockets of glass docked in a water garden downtown. Philip Johnson's last project, the Cathedral of Hope's Interfaith Peace Chapel, was completed in 2011, six years after the architect died. With its soaring, smooth white sculptural forms, Johnson considered the building his memorial, the capstone of his career. The Perot Museum of Nature and Science, designed by award-winning Thom Mayne of Morphosis, in Victory Park, looks like a huge floating cube on a landscaped plinth. The sustainable building has received the highest green rating.

The Long Center for the Performing Arts.

AUSTIN'S CRANES

As Texas grows, its architecture changes. San Antonio has a new library and a repurposed historic buildings such as the 1929 Art Deco-style Alamo National Bank Building on the River Walk, restored and converted to a flagship historic hotel by Drury Hotels. Ruby City, a contemporary art museum, founded by the Pace salsa heiress, Linda Pace, was designed by Pace herself, but the building known for its angular and crimson red exterior from the walls to the concrete, was brought to life by architect Sir David Adjaye OBE.

Three hours away in Houston, the city is working to repurpose many of its old buildings into architectural marvels of the future. They've taken an old Post Office building and transformed it into POST Houston, a 555,000-square foot (51,000 square meter) commercial hub on 16 acres (6.5 hectares) of land, complete with a 6-acre (2.5 hectares) rooftop park. It opened in mid-2020.

The place to find exciting contemporary architecture, though, is the vibrant state capital of Austin, previously known for its many Victorian buildings – most famously, the Driskill Hotel, built as a showstopper by a cattle baron with deep pockets. Austin is experiencing a huge construction boom, and the local joke goes that the new state bird is the crane. Among the many significant contemporary residential and commercial buildings are the Long Center for the Performing Arts; the Kimber Modern Boutique Hotel; Mueller Central, a on-going redevelopment of the old Austin airport; and Soaring Wings, a home located in Westlake Hills outside Austin.

One of the new office buildings on Congress Avenue is made of pink granite from the same quarry as that building with a gable roof. Organic architecture is shown, including the rustic pedestrian bridge over the river and the Lost Pines Chapel in the woods.

Texas bluebonnets on a railroad track.

House in Galveston.

11th St Cowboy Bar, Bandera.

Corona
Extra
Find your beach
Budweiser

Tubing on the Guadalupe River.

INTRODUCTION

A detailed guide to the entire state, with principal sites clearly cross-referenced by number to the maps.

Texas has it all: sophisticated cities, beautiful beaches, colorful deserts, sleepy border towns, wide open plains, and dramatic mountains. In both geography and culture, it is a microcosm of the entire country. Texas contains as much diversity and internal contradictions as any other part of the United States. You'll find wild rodeos and honky-tonks, but also fine museums and elegant restaurants; towering glass skyscrapers and bustling sidewalks, but also quaint Victorian homes and old-time country fairs.

Texas is a place where all sorts of social, economic, and geographic boundaries intersect, and each part of the state has a distinct character. You'll notice the influence of the Old South in East Texas, and the vibrant mix of Mexican and American cultures along the Rio Grande in southern Texas. You'll find that Texans are still struggling with the conflict between rural and urban values, and that there are more "cowboys" walking the streets of Houston or Dallas than there are on the range.

Tours of Texas generally start in the north, in the Dallas–Fort Worth Metroplex, two cities that have grown into a single bustling metropolitan area. The Metroplex has been a major business center for years, but recently the cities have made strides in the cultural arena as well. Fort Worth's museum district houses some of the finest collections in the state and the Dallas Arts District is the largest contiguous urban arts district in the nation.

Four hours south of the Metroplex in Central Texas lies Austin, the state capital, famous for its live music and liberal attitudes. Houston in southeast Texas is the state's largest city, however – and with its rich ethnic mix, great wealth, exciting architecture, and thriving arts community, it is also one of the liveliest. People don't often think of Texas as a coastal state, but Texans have been enjoying the warm breezes, glorious sunshine, and brilliant blue waters of the Gulf of Mexico since the early 20th century. America's "Third Coast" has over 300 miles (500km) of white, powdery beaches, quaint Victorian villages, modern resorts, bustling fishing towns, and major ports.

As you head south and west to the Rio Grande, in South Texas, Texas's Hispanic roots are clear. San Antonio is the urban capital of Hispanic politics and culture in Texas but it is in the small towns along the Rio Grande that the Tex-Mex blend of *la frontera* is most distinct.

The scene alters as you go west of Dallas. In Central Texas, the land opens. In West Texas the plains give way to desert. El Paso has more in common with its New Mexican neighbors than with its eastern sister cities.

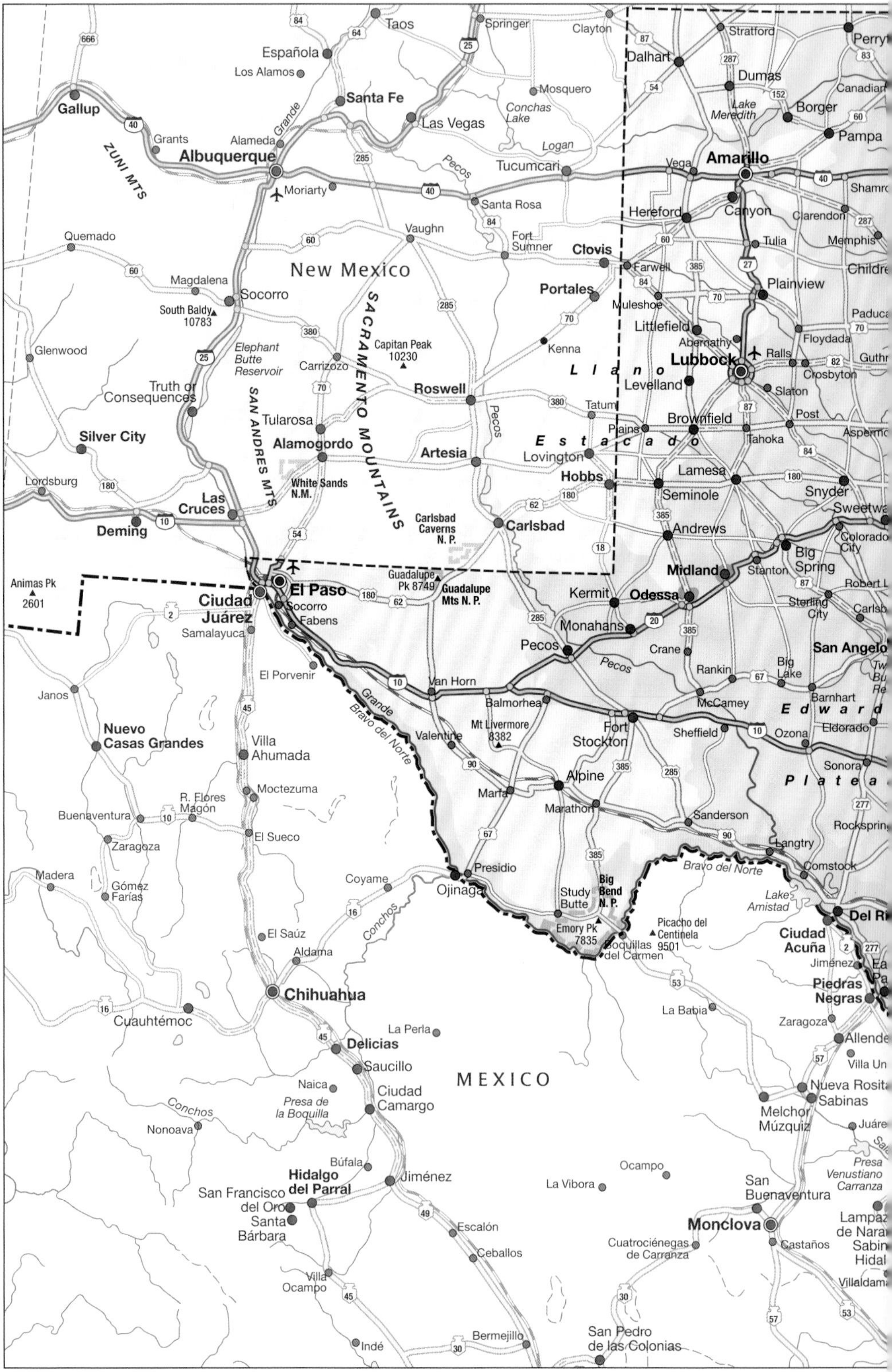
New Mexico
MEXICO
Taos
Española
Los Alamos
Santa Fe
Las Vegas
Springer
Clayton
Mosquero
Conchas Lake
Logan
Gallup
Grants
Alameda
Albuquerque
Grande
ZUNI MTS
Moriarty
Tucumcari
Santa Rosa
Pecos
Vaughn
Fort Sumner
Clovis
Portales
Quemado
Magdalena
Socorro
South Baldy 10783
SACRAMENTO MOUNTAINS
Capitan Peak 10230
Elephant Butte Reservoir
Carrizozo
Kenna
Glenwood
Truth or Consequences
SAN ANDRES MTS
Tularosa
Roswell
Silver City
Alamogordo
Artesia
White Sands N.M.
Lordsburg
Las Cruces
Deming
Carlsbad Caverns N. P.
Carlsbad
Animas Pk 2601
El Paso
Ciudad Juárez
Socorro
Fabens
Samalayuca
Guadalupe Pk 8749
Guadalupe Mts N. P.
El Porvenir
Janos
Nuevo Casas Grandes
Villa Ahumada
Moctezuma
R. Flores Magón
Buenaventura
El Sueco
Zaragoza
Madera
Gómez Farías
Coyame
Ojinaga
Presidio
Conchos
El Saúz
Aldama
Chihuahua
Cuauhtémoc
La Perla
Delicias
Saucillo
Naica
Presa de la Boquilla
Ciudad Camargo
Nonoava
Búfala
Hidalgo del Parral
Jiménez
San Francisco del Oro
Santa Bárbara
Escalón
Ceballos
Villa Ocampo
Indé
Bermejillo
Grande
Bravo del Norte
Van Horn
Balmorhea
Valentine
Mt Livermore 8382
Marfa
Alpine
Marathon
Fort Stockton
Study Butte
Big Bend N. P.
Emory Pk 7835
Boquillas del Carmen
Picacho del Centinela 9501
Pecos
Kermit
Odessa
Monahans
Midland
Stanton
Big Spring
Crane
Rankin
McCamey
Sheffield
Big Lake
Ozona
Sanderson
Langtry
Comstock
Lake Amistad
Ciudad Acuña
Jiménez
Piedras Negras
Zaragoza
Allende
Villa Un
Nueva Rosita
Sabinas
Melchor Múzquiz
La Babia
Ocampo
La Vibora
San Buenaventura
Monclova
Castaños
Cuatrociénegas de Carranza
San Pedro de las Colonias
Presa Venustiano Carranza
Lampaz
de Nara
Sabin
Hidal
Villaldam
Dalhart
Stratford
Dumas
Lake Meredith
Borger
Perry
Canadian
Pampa
Amarillo
Vega
Hereford
Canyon
Clarendon
Shamro
Tulia
Memphis
Childre
Farwell
Plainview
Muleshoe
Littlefield
Abernathy
Lubbock
Ralls
Floydada
Paduca
Crosbyton
Guthr
Levelland
Slaton
Llano Estacado
Tatum
Plains
Brownfield
Post
Tahoka
Aspermo
Lovington
Hobbs
Lamesa
Seminole
Snyder
Sweetwa
Andrews
Colorado City
Robert L
Sterling City
Carlsb
San Angelo
Barnhart
Edwards Plateau
Eldorado
Sonora
Rockspring
Del R
Bravo del Norte

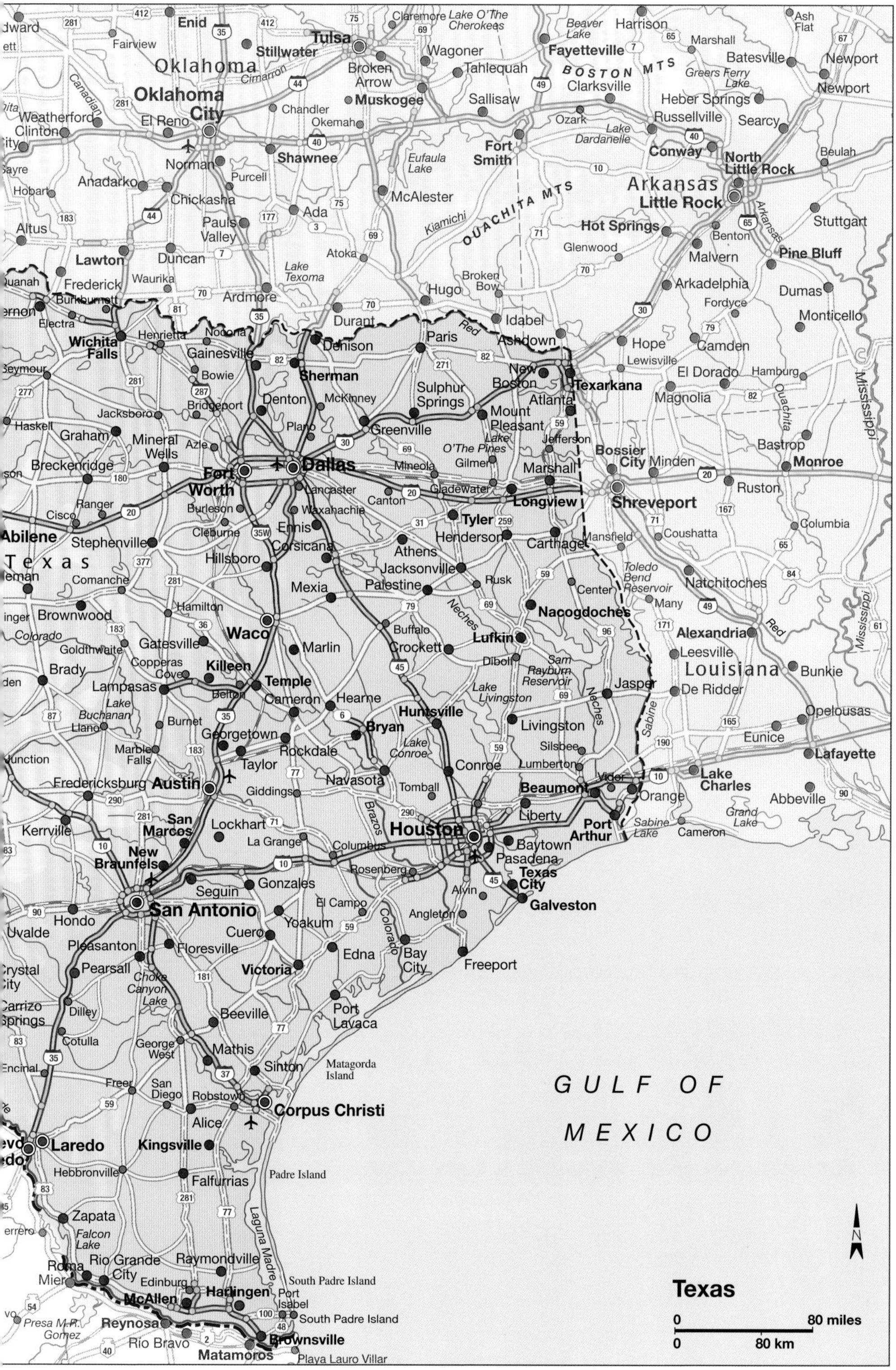
Oklahoma
Oklahoma City
Tulsa
Enid
Stillwater
Fairview
Cimarron
Canadian
Weatherford
Clinton
El Reno
Chandler
Okemah
Broken Arrow
Muskogee
Wagoner
Tahlequah
Claremore
Lake O'The Cherokees
Sallisaw
Shawnee
Norman
Purcell
Anadarko
Chickasha
Hobart
Altus
Lawton
Pauls Valley
Duncan
Ada
Atoka
McAlester
Eufaula Lake
Kiamichi
Fort Smith
Waurika
Frederick
Ardmore
Lake Texoma
Durant
Hugo
Broken Bow
Idabel
OUACHITA MTS
BOSTON MTS
Beaver Lake
Harrison
Fayetteville
Clarksville
Ozark
Lake Dardanelle
Russellville
Marshall
Batesville
Greers Ferry Lake
Heber Springs
Searcy
Newport
Ash Flat
Conway
North Little Rock
Beulah
Arkansas
Little Rock
Hot Springs
Benton
Glenwood
Malvern
Stuttgart
Pine Bluff
Arkadelphia
Fordyce
Dumas
Monticello
Hope
Camden
Lewisville
El Dorado
Hamburg
Magnolia
Ouachita
Mississippi
Texarkana
Ashdown
Paris
Red
Denison
Sherman
Gainesville
Nocona
Henrietta
Burkburnett
Electra
Wichita Falls
Quanah
Vernon
Seymour
Bowie
Bridgeport
Denton
McKinney
Plano
Sulphur Springs
New Boston
Atlanta
Mount Pleasant
Lake O'The Pines
Jefferson
Greenville
Jacksboro
Haskell
Graham
Mineral Wells
Azle
Breckenridge
Fort Worth
Dallas
Mineola
Gilmer
Marshall
Gladewater
Longview
Canton
Lancaster
Waxahachie
Burleson
Ranger
Cisco
Abilene
Stephenville
Cleburne
Ennis
Corsicana
Tyler
Henderson
Carthage
Athens
Hillsboro
Jacksonville
Rusk
Texas
Coleman
Comanche
Mexia
Palestine
Hamilton
Brownwood
Colorado
Goldthwaite
Gatesville
Waco
Marlin
Buffalo
Crockett
Neches
Lufkin
Nacogdoches
Center
Diboll
Sam Rayburn Reservoir
Lake Livingston
Brady
Copperas Cove
Killeen
Belton
Temple
Cameron
Hearne
Lampasas
Lake Buchanan
Llano
Burnet
Georgetown
Bryan
Huntsville
Lake Conroe
Livingston
Jasper
Marble Falls
Rockdale
Taylor
Navasota
Conroe
Silsbee
Lumberton
Junction
Fredericksburg
Austin
Giddings
Tomball
Beaumont
Vidor
Orange
Kerrville
San Marcos
Lockhart
La Grange
Brazos
Houston
Liberty
Port Arthur
Sabine Lake
Baytown
Pasadena
New Braunfels
Columbus
Rosenberg
Texas City
Galveston
Alvin
Seguin
Gonzales
San Antonio
El Campo
Yoakum
Hondo
Uvalde
Cuero
Angleton
Colorado
Pleasanton
Floresville
Edna
Bay City
Freeport
Crystal City
Pearsall
Choke Canyon Lake
Victoria
Carrizo Springs
Dilley
Beeville
Port Lavaca
Cotulla
George West
Mathis
Sinton
Matagorda Island
Encinal
Freer
San Diego
Robstown
Corpus Christi
Alice
Laredo
Nuevo Laredo
Kingsville
Hebbronville
Falfurrias
Padre Island
Zapata
Laguna Madre
Falcon Lake
Guerrero
Rio Grande City
Raymondville
Roma
Mier
Edinburg
Harlingen
McAllen
Port Isabel
South Padre Island
Reynosa
Presa M.R. Gomez
Rio Bravo
Brownsville
Matamoros
Playa Lauro Villar
Shreveport
Bossier City
Minden
Ruston
Monroe
Bastrop
Mansfield
Coushatta
Columbia
Toledo Bend Reservoir
Natchitoches
Many
Alexandria
Leesville
Louisiana
Bunkie
De Ridder
Opelousas
Eunice
Lafayette
Lake Charles
Abbeville
Grand Lake
Cameron
Sabine
Red
GULF OF MEXICO
Texas
0 80 miles
0 80 km
N

The Hunt Oil building.

DALLAS

Swanky Dallas is beginning to outlive its tragic history, and today is home to cutting-edge architecture, the country's largest arts district, and the world's best shopping.

Known for its glitz and glam and financial sector, the tragedy of President Kennedy's assassination here in 1963, and a certain popular TV program from the 1970s selling excess, the gleaming city of Dallas has risen above its infamy in recent years and is showing promising signs of becoming an exciting place to live and visit.

Dallas has always had boatloads of money, but now it is showing that it can corral its excesses and focus its energy and can-do attitude into a coherent whole. As a result, it is fast becoming a diverse city of planned neighborhoods linked by well-thought-out green spaces with world-class buildings, museums, and performing arts venues, and vibrant reclaimed arts and historic districts. In its more gentrified areas, it has the kind of edge more commonly seen in places like Austin.

DOWNTOWN

Downtown Dallas is quite compact – but only relatively speaking. The easiest way to explore it is to hop on the D-Link, a free bus system with routes through Downtown, Bishop Arts, and parts of Deep Ellum, or on the expanding light rail system. This rail system (DART) shares Union Station with Amtrak and here, beside the Stemmons Freeway (I-35) in the southwest corner of town, is a good place to begin. In the summer, you could opt to take the underground system of tunnels called the Dallas Pedestrian Network. The 3 miles (4.8km) of tunnels connect some of Dallas' most notable buildings and are open during the weekdays.

Four stepped, perpendicular glass boxes house the **Hyatt Regency Hotel**, connected to which is the 560ft (172-meter) **Reunion Tower** ❶ (300 Reunion Boulevard E; tel: 214-712-7040; www.reuniontower.com; Sun–Thu 10.30am–8.30pm, Fri–Sat until 9.30pm).

Main attractions

- Reunion Tower
- Sixth Floor Museum
- Perot Museum of Nature and Science
- Dallas Arts District
- Fair Park
- Southfork Ranch

Maps on pages 102, 110

The bronze longhorns in Pioneer Plaza.

The sixth floor of the Texas School Book Depository building, from where Lee Harvey Oswald shot President Kennedy.

Topped by a geodesic dome with 260 lights, the tower adds a dramatic nighttime star to the city's skyline. An observation deck and two revolving restaurants are accessible via fast elevators and the views, understandably, are the best in Dallas.

The city began in this area, in the **Cabin of John Neely Bryan** ❷ beside the nearby Trinity River, which Bryan mistakenly believed to be navigable for trade all the way to the Gulf of Mexico. An earlier colony, La Réunion, founded by French settlers, had failed, largely because the colonists had been artisans in Europe, not farmers. Bryan, however, survived and lived long enough to welcome, in 1872, the first passengers arriving on the Houston and Texas Central Railroad. This was the beginning of the city's major expansion.

Between 1880 and 1890 Dallas' population tripled to 38,000, the mule cars that transported passengers around town were replaced by electric trams, *The Dallas Morning News* began publication, and the forerunner of the annual State Fair of Texas took place. Bryan's reconstructed cabin now sits on a grassy sward across from the Old Red Courthouse, now the Old Red Museum, on Elm Street.

Just east of the Reunion Tower is the city's huge **Kay Bailey Hutchison Convention Center** ❸, flanking a grassy hillside that is home to *A Herd of Longhorns*. This exhibit, which shares **Pioneer Plaza** ❹ with an ancient cemetery,

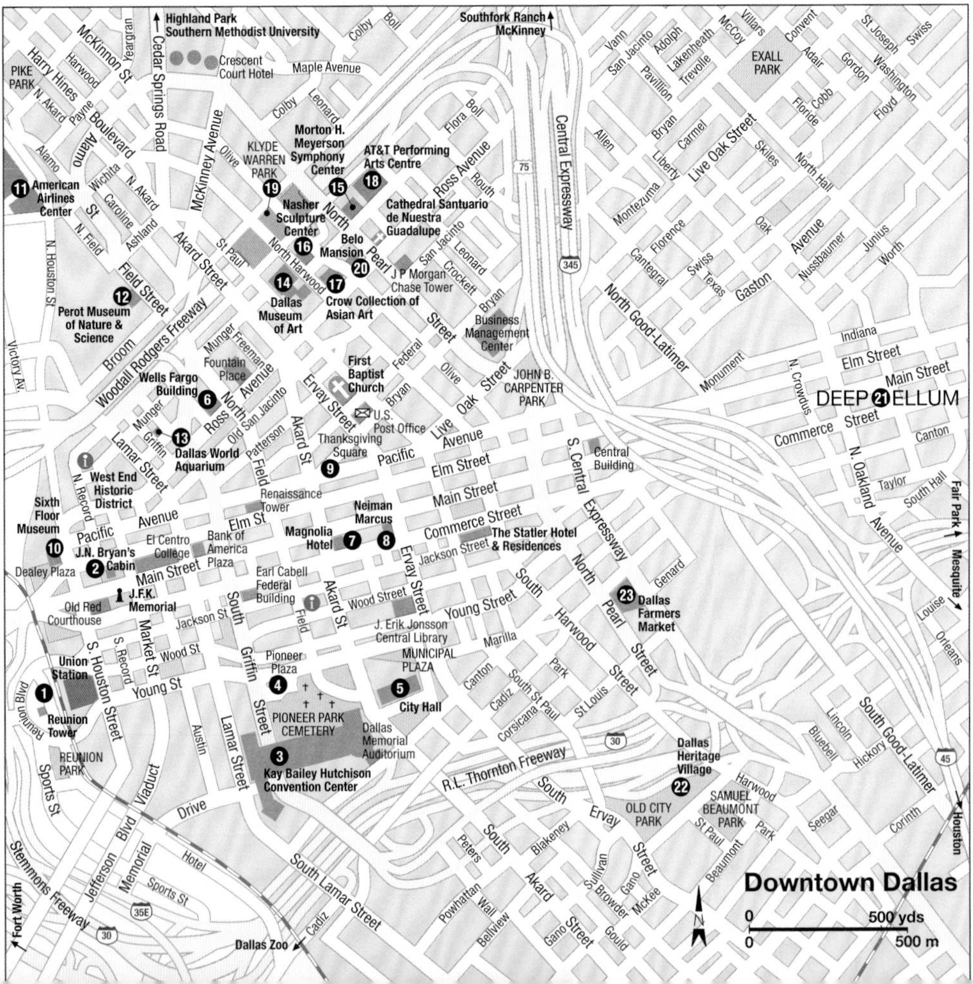

is collectively the world's biggest bronze monument, although that is up for debate. Created by Texan sculptor Robert Summers, it depicts dozens of longhorns and three cowboys and sprawls down a realistic cattle trail in a setting enhanced by native plants and a stream that cascades over a miniature limestone cliff. Beyond the Plaza, facing the public library, the futuristically stepped-back **City Hall** ❺ is the work of Chinese-American architect I.M. Pei.

From the Reunion Tower's observation deck, it is easy to be impressed by Dallas's architecture. This tangible display of big-money investment began way back in 1908, when Texas law demanded that every insurance company doing business in the state should keep a substantial part of its assets in Texas.

Insurance remains essential to the city's economy, along with banking, merchandising, and, most recently, high technology. For many years, Dallas was the world's largest inland cotton market and all the farmers of North Texas did their banking here. Following World War II, the city began its accelerated growth. Two large aircraft factories were built in the suburbs, and, for a time in the 1950s, oil companies swarmed to Dallas, where banks were eager to finance them. Eighteen Fortune 500 companies, including Exxon, J.C. Penney, and Kimberly-Clark, currently have their headquarters in the Dallas area.

Northeast, on Main Street, is the **Bank of America Plaza**, a 72-story giant outlined with 2 miles (3km) of green neon, while the sharp angles of I.M. Pei's 60-story **Wells Fargo Building** ❻ (Field Street and Ross Avenue) near Fountain Place catch the eye from everywhere in the city. Also distinctive are the octagonal Thanksgiving Tower (Elm and Ervay) and the J.P. Morgan Chase Tower (Pearl and San Jacinto), whose slit tower had to be modified to cut down its wind tunnel effect.

Almost hidden by the huge behemoths surrounding it, is Pegasus, the neon flying red horse trademark that sits atop the **Magnolia Hotel** ❼ (1401 Commerce Street). (Formerly the Magnolia Petroleum Building, this was the tallest building in the south when it went up in 1922.) Its original flying horse first presided here in 1934 and was replaced in 1999. In 2015, the original Pegasus sign was discovered in a shed at White Rock Lake. After extensive restorations, it now sits in front of the Omni Hotel Dallas. Behind the Magnolia Hotel, at Main and Ervay, is the flagship department store of **Neiman Marcus** ❽ and, two blocks north, close to the light-rail line, is **Thanksgiving Square** ❾ a tranquil oasis designed by architects Philip Johnson and John Burgee.

JFK MEMORIAL

Just north of Reunion Tower is the **West End**. With many of the city's oldest buildings restored as shops and cafés, the area is filled with museums like the **Dallas Holocaust and Human Rights Museum** and the **Museum of**

Fact

The Pioneer Plaza exhibit covers over 4 acres (1.6 hectares) and pays tribute to the Texas trail-driving days. It was unveiled in 1994.

The Texas School Book Depository building.

NEIMAN MARCUS

Purveyors to the wealthy, Neiman Marcus has endured for over a century as America's most trusted department store because it goes the extra mile for its customers.

The Dallas-based Neiman Marcus department store, world-renowned for its Christmas Book offering such "His and Her" gift suggestions as $1,600 mummy cases or pairs of matched camels ($16,000), prides itself on unstinting service. At the request of one customer, for example, the store discreetly investigated Queen Elizabeth's stocking size so that she could be sent a pair of nylons.

Customers were made and kept, Stanley Marcus once explained, "by [the] ability to remember small details, such as anniversary dates... a promise to get a certain evening bag for a specific social occasion... a promise that the dress bought for a girlfriend would be billed to the Mr and not the Mrs account." This was not trivia: "... it's what specialty store retailing is all about."

The world-famous Neiman Marcus department store.

Stanley, one of the sons of co-founder Carrie Marcus, has been probably the person most responsible for developing the store's modern image, but Neiman Marcus – now a chain with outlets in 43 US locations – was a success from its start in 1907. Soon after that, Nebraska-born Al Neiman teamed up with (and married) Kentucky-born Carrie Marcus who, aged 21, had already proved herself to be the most successful saleswoman at the Dallas department store A. Harris & Co.

Together with Carrie's brother, Herbert, the trio set up a sales promotion business in Atlanta that was so successful they found themselves looking for further investment opportunities. They considered investing in a new bottled drinks company, Coca-Cola, but decided to set up a retail business instead. It became a family joke down through the years that Neiman Marcus was founded on a bad business judgment.

They soon set up their Neiman Marcus store in central Dallas. Neiman, the flamboyant and egotistical buyer, traveled regularly between Dallas and New York City, acquiring clothes and constantly clashing with his partners over style and design. In the 1920s, Herbert bought him out for $250,000 and the Neiman marriage broke up at the same time.

At first, the store's wealthier clientele was, to a large extent, the state's cotton aristocracy but, just after the Great Depression began (as the store was completing a major expansion), oil was discovered in East Texas. This produced a new group of millionaires who soon became Neiman Marcus customers.

In *The Grand Emporiums: The Illustrated History of America's Great Department Stores*, published in 1979, author Robert Hendrickson wrote that Neiman Marcus operated on the premise that "if we can please the 5 percent of our customers who are the most discriminating we will never have any difficulty in satisfying the other 95 percent who are less critical."

Certainly millions of recipients of the store's Christmas Book seem satisfied. Eight customers, for example, splashed out on the $11,200 Chinese junks offered one year. One page of the catalog is devoted to "How to Spend a Million Dollars at Neiman-Marcus," although other pages offer gifts for $25 and under.

Illusions, restaurants, bars, and boutiques. If walking is too much trouble, visitors can take horse-drawn carriage rides around the area.

Head up Houston Street, past the unmistakable Old Red Courthouse (behind which, at Main and Market, is the simple **John F. Kennedy Memorial**, a cenotaph designed by Philip Johnson), and ahead on the left is the most visited site in Dallas: the former Texas School Book Depository building, from which Lee Harvey Oswald shot President Kennedy.

The **Sixth Floor Museum** ⑩ (411 Elm Street; tel: 214-747-6660; www.jfk.org; Tue–Sun 10am–6pm, Mon noon–6pm; timed entry, tickets may be purchased online up to two hours in advance) overlooks Dealey Plaza, through which President Kennedy was riding in a motorcade on November 22, 1963, when he was assassinated. Oswald – later arrested and murdered on live television while in police custody – fired the fatal shots from a corner window on the building's sixth floor, a site roped off in the museum.

The museum, which gets an average of 400,000 visitors each year, houses exhibits about JFK's campaign; his social and economic programs; the space race; and the "Red Threat". Reproductions of newspaper stories from around the world are on show, including the full-page advert in *The Dallas Morning News* on the day of his visit to the city, in which his right-wing enemies accused him of communist sympathies. Cameras used by spectators watching the motorcade can be seen, as can the famous Zapruder camera and some of the footage it recorded of the assassination. A videotape of the dramatic events of that day includes a tearful Walter Cronkite announcing the President's death. A cellphone tour of the museum and Dealey Plaza is available.

Don't underestimate the time needed to see the museum: it is immensely interesting (and moving) and, to the uninitiated, serves as a quick course about a significant era in US history. Among the messages in the visitors book is one from a child who wrote that the assassination was the first time he had seen his father cry.

VICTORY PARK

The West End continues north of the DART rail line, whose station at Pacific and Lamar (shared with a bus transfer station) is almost surrounded by parking lots. Here bars, saloons, restaurants, and cafés keep pedestrian traffic on the move.

Anchoring the popular 72-acre (29-hectare) Victory Park development in the West End is the striking **American Airlines Center** ⑪ (2500 Victory Avenue; tel: 214-665-4797; www.americanairlinescenter.com), a state-of-the-art sports stadium that superceded Reunion Arena as the home of the major sports franchises. It is surrounded by hip restaurants, shops, and hotels, including the gleaming 33-story W Hotel. Designed by architect David Schwarz in retro style,

Fact

President John F. Kennedy was on his way to make a speech at the Dallas World Trade Center when he was assassinated. The shots rang out at 12.30pm; the President was pronounced dead in hospital at 1pm.

A friendly manatee at the Dallas World Aquarium.

with Art Deco touches, it was built at a cost of $420 million on land that was once home to an old city dump, a meat packing plant, and an old power plant. New transportation links all around have revitalized the area.

Victory Park is the largest Environmental Protection Agency brownfield project in the United States. Its latest attraction is the **Perot Museum of Nature and Science** ⓬ (2201 N. Field Street; tel: 214-428-5555; www.perotmuseum.org; Mon–Sat 10am–5pm, Sun 11am–5pm), which was gifted to the city by the Perot family. Designed by award-winning architect Thom Mayne of Morphosis Architects, the building sits on a large plinth above a landscaped park of native Texas plants. Inside, six floors of hands-on exhibits are a draw for kids and imaginative adults alike. **Dallas World Aquarium** ⓭ (1801 N. Griffin Street; tel: 214-720-2224; www.dwazoo.com; daily 10am–5pm) is another popular attraction in the West End, housed in two former warehouses. Inside you'll find the world's largest freshwater aquarium, containing manatees, turtles, giant catfish, and more, as well as a saltwater aquarium with rays and sea turtles, among others. The other major draw here is a South American rainforest, featuring exotic plants and wildlife, from toucans and sloths to monkeys and crocodiles, along its jungle walkway.

THE DALLAS ARTS DISTRICT

The crown jewel of Dallas's downtown is its 68-acre (28-hectare) **Arts District** (www.dallasartsdistrict.org), the largest in the country. Spread over 19 landscaped city blocks, with a growing number of world-class museums housed in spectacular buildings, this is a wonderful place to stroll, enjoy music, theater and other entertainments, and get a bite to eat.

One block northeast of the distinctively shaped Fountain Place (Wells Fargo Building) is **Dallas Museum of Art (DMA)** ⓮ (1717 N. Harwood Street; tel: 214-922-1200; www.dma.org; Tue–Sun 11am–5pm, Thu until 9pm; free), designed by Edward Larrabee Barnes. Its collection is impressive:

Exhibits at the Nasher Sculpture Center.

it exhibits American artifacts dating from the pre-Columbian and Spanish eras; Greek and Roman antiquities; a model of a boat from the Egyptian Middle Kingdom, *c.*2000 BC; a magnificent Hindu shrine of silver and wood; plus 18th-century Gilbert Stuart and Copley portraits, 19th-century landscapes, and works by Toulouse-Lautrec, Léger, Picasso, Mary Cassatt, Georgia O'Keefe, Giacometti, Edward Hopper, Andrew Wyeth, and the Modernists. One room alone includes millions of dollars' worth of art by Courbet, Boudin, Pissarro, Degas, Cézanne, Monet, Rodin, Van Gogh, and Vuillard. Contemporary artists represented include Pollock, Rothko, Stella, and Warhol.

The **Morton H. Meyerson Symphony Center** ⓯ (2301 Flora Street; tel: 214-849-4376; www.mydso.com) is another Dallas institution that has been financed by Ross Perot and serves as home to the Dallas Symphony Orchestra. Nearby is the **Nasher Sculpture Center** ⓰ (2001 Flora Street; tel: 214-242-5100; www.nashersculpturecenter.org; Tue–Sun 11am–5pm). This $50-million building and outdoor sculpture garden houses the fabulous modern sculpture collection of the late Raymond and Patsy Nasher, including more than 300 works by Calder, de Kooning, di Suvero, Giacometti, Hepworth, Kelly, Matisse, Miró, Moore, Picasso, Rodin, Serra, and others. The museum was designed by world-renowned architect Renzo Piano, in collaboration with landscape architect Peter Walker.

Adjacent stands the **Crow Collection of Asian Art** ⓱ (2010 Flora Street; tel: 214-979-6430; www.crowcollection.org; Tue–Sun 11–5pm; free) surrounded by a score of valuable sculptures, including Rodin bronzes, and displaying an important collection of Asian art. Note the enormous Ellsworth Kelly painting in the building's east lobby and the 68-ton (62-metric ton) steel sculpture by Eduardo Chillada, which was requested by the building's architect, I.M. Pei. In front of the building, and flanked by the 1898 Cathedral Santuario de Nuestra Guadalupe, is Artists' Square, a venue for craft shows, with a stage for concerts and cultural events.

Also nearby is the **AT&T Performing Arts Center** ⓲ (2403 Flora Street; tel: 214-880-0202; www.attpac.org). Built at a cost of $354 million, this huge center offers performances of opera, musical theater, classic and experimental theater, ballet, and other forms of dance. Three major architectural firms designed portions of the attractive modern center, including British firm Foster and Partners. The architectural jewel of the center is the **Margot and Bill Winspear Opera House** (tel: 214-443-1000; www.dallasopera.org), home of the Dallas Opera.

UPTOWN

Linking the Arts District to Uptown, on the other side of the freeway, is **Klyde Warren Park** ⓳, a 5-acre (2-hectare) urban green space between Pearl and St. Paul streets. In an inspired piece of urban planning, it's built right over

Tip

Note that it is not the custom to hail taxis in Dallas. Cabs should be requested by telephone.

THANKSGIVING SQUARE

Pocket parks offer relief from the busy man-made environments of urban downtowns, and Dallas has several such spots, including Klyde Warren Park on the edge of the Arts District. None are more soul-soothing, though, than Thanksgiving Square, which occupies the triangle between Bryan Street, Pacific Avenue, and Ervay Street. Championed by four local businessmen in 1964, and funded through a nonprofit foundation, the park opened in 1976 as "a place where people can use gratitude as a basis for dialogue, mutual understanding, and healing." This lovely oasis is now a beloved local feature and a popular destination. It was designed by renowned architect Phillip Johnson and includes a meditation garden, waterfalls and grass, a Wall of Praise, a bell tower with three bronze bells designed in the form of the Liberty Bell that ring every hour, a museum of thanksgiving, and a small but striking interdenominational Chapel of Thanksgiving. The whitewashed spiral chapel is inspired by Middle Eastern architecture. Inside is the famous Glory Window, the largest stained-glass window in the world. It was designed by Gabriel Loire of Chartres, France – a city renowned for its cathedral and the stained glass within – and features brighter colors as the spiral reached its apex. The window famously appears in a shot in director Terrence Malick's 2011 film *The Tree of Life*.

Fact

The multi-million dollar Morton H. Meyerson Symphony Center is home to the Dallas Symphony Orchestra, rated one of the finest orchestras in the US.

the Woodall Rogers Freeway and is a vibrant gathering space where people do yoga, play chess, attend book signings, listen to concerts, and relax. Food trucks congregate here, so this is a good place to take a breather.

At Olive and Ross, **Belo Mansion** ⑳, a building now housing the Dallas Bar Association, was, in 1932, the funeral home where the body of Clyde Barrow once lay. The 25-year-old bank robber and his companion, 23-year-old Dallas-born Bonnie Parker, were both shot dead driving down a Louisiana country road. Their four-year crime spree had earned them headlines throughout the country. The gas station at 1620 Eagle Ford Road, built by Clyde's father, has been replaced with a new structure, but the Barrow house behind it still stands.

To head into Uptown, take one of the venerable 90-year-old streetcars (with velvet seats and stained-glass windows) that start from outside the DMA and run along bustling, brick-tiled **McKinney Avenue**, which is lined with restaurants, boutiques, and galleries, and is a happening nightlife spot during the week and weekends.

Klyde Warren Park.

NORTH DALLAS

Visitors come from all over the US to shop in Dallas and, of course, thousands of locals spend countless hours in the malls that continue to spring up, largely in the northern part of the city. The very first was **Highland Park Village**, a pseudo-Colonial complex with outdoor cafés, posh stores such as Hermes, and an old theater now converted into a movie theater. It was designed by William David Cook, who also designed Beverly Hills, and is America's second-oldest shopping center. It is on Mockingbird Lane near the Dallas north Tollway. A couple of miles north, on Northwest Highway abutting US 75, is **NorthPark Center**, filled with such prestigious stores as Neiman Marcus, and Nordstrom.

Nearby, on the other side of US 75, is the shopping area known as **Mockingbird Station**, home to some local craft shops, boutiques, and restaurants, as well as an **Angelika** movie theater, which shows many art films that aren't on general distribution. DART trains can take you to this area from downtown.

One of only three theaters built to a design by Frank Lloyd Wright, Dallas Theater Center's **Kalita Humphreys Theater** is on Turtle Creek Boulevard. Not far away is one of the most expensive institutions of higher learning in Texas, **Southern Methodist University (SMU)**.

One of SMU's benefactors was the late Algur H. Meadows, an oil magnate who in middle age began using his large fortune to build up a private art collection. He was aggrieved to discover that he was the owner of a number of Spanish School paintings wrongly attributed to masters, and that many of his supposed Braques, Picassos, and Modiglianis were in fact counterfeits by the Hungarian master forger Elmyr de Hory. Meadows righted his collection with the help of an art historian and kindly donated it to the university. The hundred or so Spanish paintings displayed at SMU's **Meadows Museum** (5900 Bishop Boulevard; tel: 214-768-2516; www.meadowsmuseumdallas.org; Tue–Sat 10am–5pm, Sun 1–5pm), by such masters as Murillo, Velázquez, Goya, and Miró, constitute one of the finest collections of Spanish art outside Spain.

Also on the SMU campus is the **George W. Bush Presidential Library and Museum** (2943 SMU Boulevard; tel: 214-346-1650; www.georgewbushlibrary.smu.edu; Mon–Sat 9am–5pm, Sun noon–5pm). This vast facility contains the full archive of the younger Bush's two terms as president (2000–08) and displays clothing and other personal articles. Its Decision Points Theater provides an interesting insight into how President Bush made decisions about important events such as the September 11, 2001 terrorist attack and the Iraq War. President Bush has no connection to SMU; the university simply outbid other locations to host the library.

OPULENT HOTELS AND STORES

Dallas has some world-famous hotels, among which are the **Rosewood Mansion on Turtle Creek** and the Hotel **Crescent Court** nearby. The latter, which is more "public," is so opulent that even the house cats live in their own designer "mini hotel" on the grounds. The surrounding Turtle Creek area has some of the classiest homes in the city, as does Mockingbird Lane, which heads west from Highland Park to Love Field airport. The iconic **Statler Dallas, Curio Collection by Hilton** reopened in 2018 following a major restoration project, while further west along Commerce Street another Dallas landmark, the Beaux Arts Adolphus Hotel, is supposedly haunted by the ghost of a jilted bride. Farther north is the upscale **Galleria Dallas** (13350 Dallas Parkway; tel: 972-702-7100; www.galleriadallas.com; Mon–Sat 10am–9pm, Sun noon–6pm), modeled after a prototype in Milan and housing a Westin hotel, dozens of restaurants, hundreds of shops, and an ice rink.

FAIR PARK

East of US 75, and running roughly parallel to it, is Greenville Avenue, whose lower end (called "Lower Greenville") is jammed with hip bars and pool halls. It's the area to find beer gardens and ethnic restaurants of all kinds, although **Deep Ellum** ㉑, farther south, offers a more concentrated experience (drive or take a taxi down Elm Street from midtown). The 12-block area, which housed a community of freed slaves after the Civil War, has always attracted the avant garde. Deep Ellum has been renowned for its blues and jazz clubs since the 1920s. It was here that famous Texan bluesmen like Blind Lemon Jefferson and Huddie "Leadbelly" Leadbetter began their careers. The neighborhood's current incarnation traces back

McKinney Avenue trolley.

Deep Ellum Outdoor Market.

Dallas Farmers' Market.

to the"outlaw parties" in renovated warehouses that a group of musicians organized in the 1980s. Clubs began to open up, followed by art galleries, funky shops, and eating spots. Deep Ellum's music tradition continues today with multiple live music venues, guaranteeing you can find a concert or band playing any day of the week. Many visit Deep Ellum to explore the murals that grace nearly every building, or to check out the neighborhood's art galleries, boutiques, tattoo parlors, nightclubs, bars, book store, hostel, and some of the city's best restaurants.

Across I-30 from Deep Ellum is **Fair Park**, site of the 1936 Texas Centennial Exposition, which celebrated the battle at which Texans won their independence from Mexico. For three weeks beginning in late September each year, the largest cowboy in the world, Big Tex, greets visitors to the State Fair of Texas.

Fair Park is an interesting place to visit, as it contains the largest collection of Art-Deco buildings in the country. Among the attractions are the **Texas Hall of State** Ⓐ (3939 Grand Avenue; tel: 214-421-4500; www.dallashistory.org; Tue–Sat 10am–5pm, Sun 1–5pm; free), complete with mammoth murals and statues of heroes; the 68,000-seat **Cotton Bowl Stadium** Ⓑ, home of the annual Red River Showdown or the University of Texas–University of Oklahoma rivalry football game; the **Children's Aquarium at Fair Park** Ⓒ (tel: 469-554-7430; www.childrensaquariumfairpark.com; daily 9am–4.30pm), with sharks, piranhas, and 5,000 other marine and freshwater creatures; an amusement park dominated by what is one of the country's biggest Ferris wheels; and several theaters. Next to the park's band shell, pleasant gardens and a conservatory make up the **Texas Discovery Gardens** Ⓓ (tel: 214-428-7476; www.txdg.org; daily 10am–5pm), which include a collection of plants indigenous to Texas.

The **African American Museum** Ⓕ (3536 Grand Avenue; tel: 214-565-9026; www.aamdallas.org; Tue–Fri 11am–5pm, Sat 10am–5pm; free) has 1,000 exhibits relating to African-American culture in Texas, and one of the nation's best folk art collections.

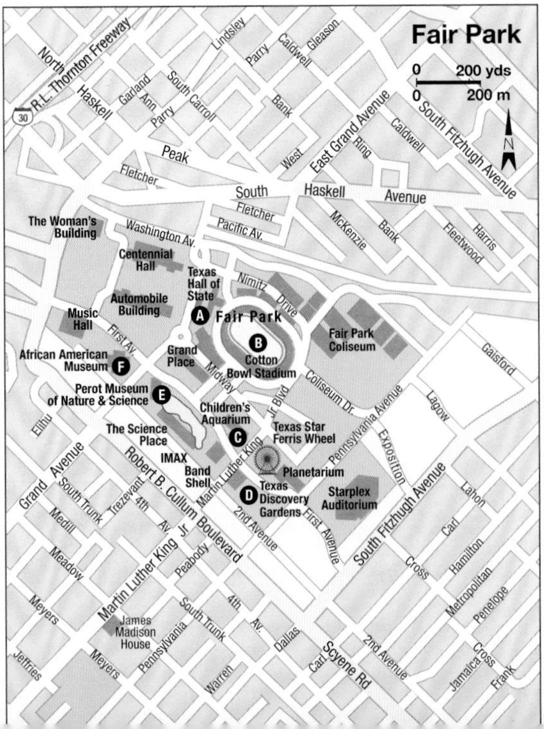

Not far away is **Dallas Heritage Village** ㉒ (1515 S. Harwood Street; tel: 214-421-5141; www.dallasheritagevillage.org; Tue–Sat 10am–4pm, Sun noon–4pm), which has a collection of century-old buildings and a Victorian bandstand on its village green. Nearby is the enormous **Dallas Farmers' Market** ㉓ (920 S. Harwood Street; tel: 214-664-9110; www.dallasfarmersmarket.org; open daily), one of the largest fresh produce markets in the US.

East of Fair Park is the little community of **Mesquite**, which stages a rodeo every Saturday evening between June and August. Here, you can eat Texas barbecue and watch champion cowboys compete at roping, steer wrestling, and bareback riding (tel: 972-285-8777; www.mesquiterodeo.com).

White Rock Lake, located northeast of Fair Park, attracts Dallas locals every day. The 1,015 acre-lake (410 hectare) has 9.6-miles (15.4km) of trails, a dog park, kayak and paddleboard rentals, and is a popular destination for sailing. During the summer, locals kayak to the lakefront Dallas Arboretum and Botanical Gardens to enjoy a summer concert series. The Dallas Arboretum is a great destination in itself with popular annual events like the largest floral festival in the southwest.

BISHOP ARTS DISTRICT

One of Dallas's most interesting up-and-coming areas is in the North Oak Cliff area, immediately south of downtown. Developed as warehouses and shops in the 1930s, this area was once a popular tram stop for shoppers but was on the decline in the 1990s, when local entrepreneur Jim Lake began buying up properties and letting them out rent-free in order to bring the area back to life. It seems to be succeeding. The two-block area that is now known as **Bishop Arts District** is becoming a popular place for boutiques, restaurants, and edgy businesses, and a dynamic place to live, work, and visit. Work has continued on the infrastructure to make this a walkable historic district, including the addition of murals, pedestrian areas, and landscaping. The increasingly popular Oak Cliff Film Festival has received national attention, and some of Dallas's most eclectic restaurants are here.

South of Bishop Arts is the Oak Cliff neighborhood which has had a historically large Hispanic population. To experience this local culture, make your way to **Jefferson Boulevard**. This main drag is lined with Latino-owned restaurants, taco shops, *quinceañera* stores, music shops, art galleries, and **Mercado369** (369 Jefferson Blvd; http://mercado369.com), a market selling one-of-a-kind art and homemade wares by Latino artists from South, Central, and North America. It's also where you'll find the **Texas Theatre** (231 W Jefferson Blvd; 214-984-1546; www.thetexastheatre.com), the historic theater where Lee Harvey Oswald was apprehended by police officers. Today, people visit Texas Theatre for its eclectic and artsy film screenings or small concerts, enjoying the on-site bar in the lobby before and after shows.

WEST DALLAS

In the southwestern part of town is the **Dallas Zoo** (650 SRL Thornton Freeway; tel: 469-554-7500; www.dallaszoo.com; daily 9am–5pm), which offers a 20-minute narrated monorail safari through half a dozen African habitats. The Simmons Hippo Outpost is designed like a watering hole and has an underwater viewing window through which visitors can watch its magnificent residents bathing.

West Dallas has slowly been coming into its own. The **Design District** is a neighborhood renowned for its furniture and design showrooms, as well as high-end art galleries on Dragon Street, which host a Third Thursday Art Walk each month. In addition to breweries and restaurants, you'll also

Bishop Arts District.

discover the **Latino Arts Project**, an arts museum with rotating exhibits highlighting Latino art.

Nearby is **Trinity Groves**, a 15-acre (6 hectares) dining and entertainment district set next to the Trinity River. A large warehouse-like building houses a treasure trove of restaurants that offer all types of cuisine from barbecue to steak, Asian, Mexican, seafood, and Italian. With indoor and outdoor seating, diners have views of the Downtown Dallas skyline and the Margaret Hunt Hill Bridge. Following their meal, they can explore a funky park on the Ronald Kirk Pedestrian Bridge which connects to Downtown Dallas, or check out the breweries and art galleries that have sprung up in the area. This area is set to grow tremendously under the Trinity River Corridor Project which is aiming to make the floodway a Dallas destination with additional development, including a massive urban park that will be 11 times larger than Central Park.

Not too far away is **Oak Lawn**, positively referred to by locals as "the Gayborhood." Oak Lawn is Dallas' LGBTQ-friendly neighborhood that offers a welcoming and inclusive atmosphere among the restaurants, bars, and night clubs along Cedar Springs Road, as well as at the nearby Cathedral of Hope (https://cathedralofhope.com), the world's largest LGBTQ-inclusive church. The **Rose Room** (3911 Cedar Springs Road; 214-526-7171; http://theroseroomdallas.com) is perhaps the most famous of spots on Cedar Springs for its world-renowned drag show on the weekends. Dallas previously held their Pride parade along Cedar Springs before moving it to Fair Park.

The gift shop at Southfork Ranch.

OUT OF TOWN

The television series *Dallas*, which ran from 1978 to 1991, and was revived in 2012, probably did more to spread the city's fame than anything else, even if the image of greedy oilmen and dysfunctional families was not what the city fathers might have chosen. It made **Southfork Ranch** (3700 Hogge Road, Parker; tel: 972-442-7800; www.southfork.com; open daily), actually in Parker, half an hour's drive north of downtown via US 75 (take the Parker Road exit), where the Ewing clan supposedly lived, familiar to viewers in around 100 countries. Today, Southfork remains the area's major tourist attraction. The family who lived there was forced to move out by the hordes of tourists, and the ranch has now become a must-see tourist attraction and venue for weddings and special events (there is a hotel nearby). Tram tours start at the visitor center and include JR's Den. When JR Ewing (Larry Hagman) passed away during filming of the series in 2014, his memorial was held at the ranch.

McKinney (pop. 181,330), a historic county seat 20 miles (32km) northeast of Dallas, is growing so fast that it has now become a suburb of Dallas. Nevertheless, it remains a fine example of a small town, with numerous Victorian houses, that has worked hard at retaining its old-time flavor. Victorian and Greek Revival houses around Chestnut Square, dating back to 1853, are furnished in period style and can be toured (tel: 972-562-8790; www.chestnutsquare.org; Thu and Sat 11am). In the sleepy center of town, many old buildings – with their tin ceilings preserved – have been refurbished as shops selling arts and crafts. On Kentucky Street, the Collin County Jail (1880), popular with moviemakers, once housed Frank James of the infamous James gang. The **Heard Natural Science Museum and Wildlife Sanctuary** (1 Nature Place, McKinney; tel: 972-562-5566; www.heardmuseum.org; Tue–Sat 9am–5pm, Sun 1–5pm) pays tribute to its founder, Bessie Heard (1884–1988), scion of a venerable local family, meticulously documenting her life. The museum sits in a 287-acre (116-hectare) wildlife sanctuary with trails, a garden, and a picnic area.

The Dallas Cowboys once called **Irving** home, before they moved from Texas Stadium to AT&T Stadium. Despite losing "America's Team" to Arlington, Irving has managed to become a destination in its own right, thanks to its nearby location to Dallas-Fort Worth International Airport. The **Mandalay Canal Walk** (215 Mandalay Dr.; tel: 972-556-0625) at Las Colinas attracts couples for romantic walks on the paved waterfront or rides in gondolas before eating at one of the restaurants on the canal front. Nearby is the **Toyota Music Factory** (300 West Las Colinas; tel: 214-978-4888; https://toyotamusicfactory.com), an entertainment complex with a concert venue, restaurants, and bars. Everyone from Bill and Hillary Clinton to Ringo Starr and His All Starr Band have graced the stage at The Pavilion at the Toyota Music Factory.

Every year, DFW descends on Plano for the annual Plano Balloon Festival (www.planoballoonfest.org) held in September. Forty hot air balloons take to the sky over the weekend, offering a spectacular view of Dallas-Fort Worth.

Mandalay Canal Walk in Las Colinas, Irving.

Stockyards National Historical District.

FORT WORTH

From cowtown to cultural and commercial center, Fort Worth has become a modern, sophisticated city but has never forgotten its dusty, cattle-trading roots.

Fort Worth, which began life as a bastion against rampaging Comanche Indians, spent its first half century as a rough and tumble frontier town, dusty and lawless. The bad guys were quick to take advantage of the situation, and the area became a haven for bandits, outlaws, and military deserters. One neighborhood famous for its notorious residents – including bank robbers Butch Cassidy (George Parker) and the Sundance Kid (Harry Longabaugh) – was known as Hell's Half Acre until its destruction in the early 1900s.

The thing that brought international fame and fortune to what had been just another dusty Western backwater, however, was the longhorn steer. By 1870, large numbers of cowboys had begun to take their rest and pleasure in Fort Worth as they drove great herds of longhorns along the Chisholm Trail from the South Texas ranches to railheads in Kansas. In Fort Worth, the trail's last major stop, they bathed, drank, gambled, and whored to forget their arduous, lonely, and monotonous trail driving. After resting and having provisioned themselves, the cowboys went on their way with thousands of cattle, through dust or mud.

With the arrival of the Texas and Pacific Railroad in 1876, hundreds of miles were cut off the cattle drives, and eight lines eventually connected Fort Worth with northern markets. The cattle were, of course, the worse for wear – and thinner – for every mile they traveled, thus cattle freighted from Fort Worth were in much better condition than they would have been had they struggled all the way to Kansas. Acres of pens were built to receive the herds, which were fattened up before transportation.

Attendant industries such as meatpacking – the Armour and Swift companies became major players – developed here and remained Fort Worth's most important source of income through the 1920s. However, just as improvements

Main attractions

Stockyards National Historic District
Kimbell Art Museum
Amon Carter Museum
National Cowgirl Hall of Fame
Six Flags Over Texas

Map on page 116

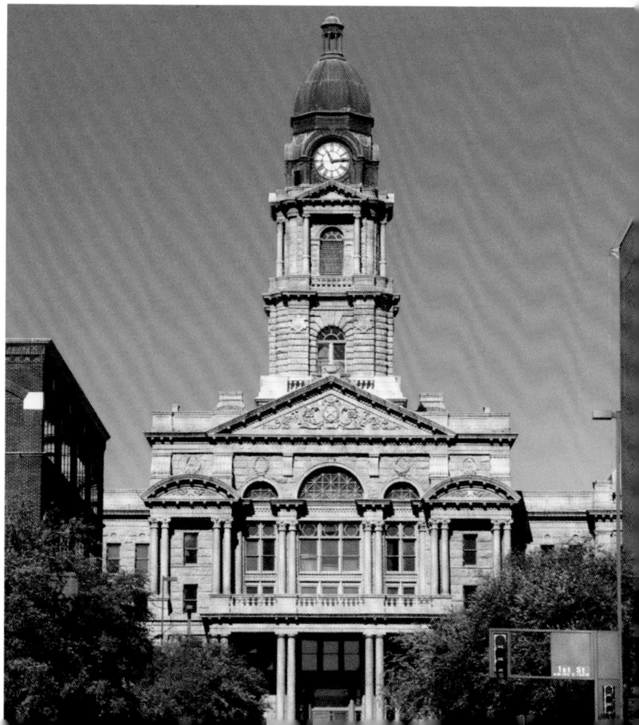

Tarrant County Courthouse.

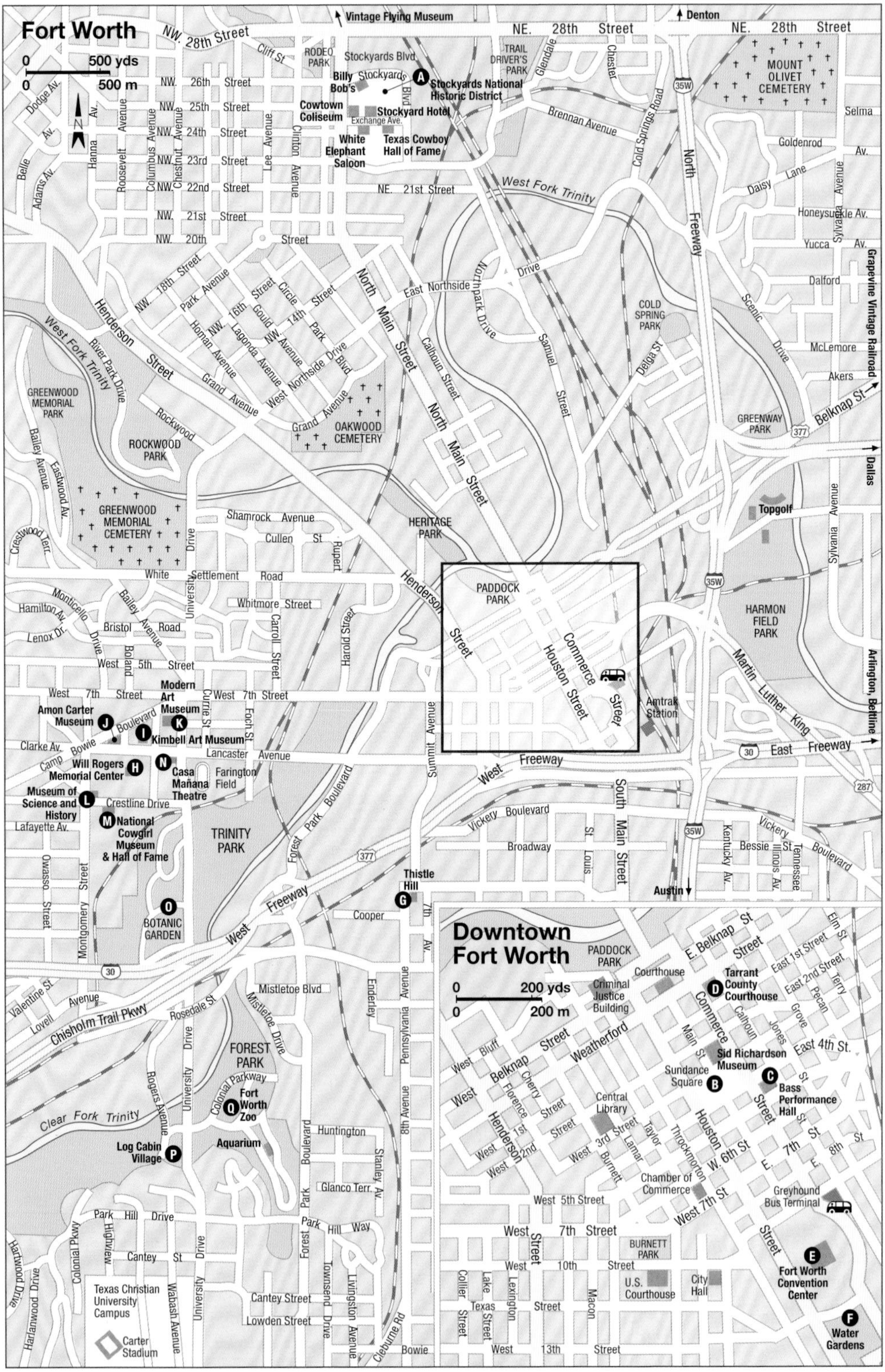
Fort Worth
0 500 yds
0 500 m
Vintage Flying Museum
Denton
NW. 28th Street
NE. 28th Street
NE. 28th Street
Cliff St
RODEO PARK
Stockyards Blvd
TRAIL DRIVER'S PARK
Glendale
Chester
MOUNT OLIVET CEMETERY
Billy Bob's
Stockyards Blvd
Stockyards National Historic District
Cowtown Coliseum
Stockyard Hotel
Exchange Ave.
White Elephant Saloon
Texas Cowboy Hall of Fame
Brennan Avenue
Cold Springs Road
North Freeway
Selma
Goldenrod Av.
Daisy Lane
Sylvania Avenue
Honeysuckle Av.
Yucca Av.
Dalford
Grapevine Vintage Railroad
McLemore
Akers
Belknap St
Dallas
Dodge Av.
Belle Av.
Adams Av.
Hanna Av.
Roosevelt Avenue
Columbus Avenue
Chestnut Avenue
NW. 26th Street
NW. 25th Street
NW. 24th Street
NW. 23rd Street
NW. 22nd Street
NW. 21st Street
NW. 20th Street
Lee Avenue
Clinton Avenue
NE. 21st Street
West Fork Trinity
NW. 18th Street
Park Avenue
NW. 16th Street
Circle Park Blvd
14th Street
Gould Avenue
Homan Avenue
Lagonda Avenue
West Northside Drive
Grand Avenue
North Main Street
East Northside Drive
Northpark Drive
Calhoun Street
Samuel Street
COLD SPRING PARK
Delga St
Scenic Drive
GREENWAY PARK
Henderson Street
River Park Drive
West Fork Trinity
GREENWOOD MEMORIAL PARK
Rockwood
ROCKWOOD PARK
OAKWOOD CEMETERY
Bailey Avenue
Eastwood Av.
Crestwood Terr.
GREENWOOD MEMORIAL CEMETERY
Shamrock Avenue
Cullen St
Rupert
HERITAGE PARK
Topgolf
Sylvania Avenue
University Drive
White Settlement Road
Henderson Street
PADDOCK PARK
HARMON FIELD PARK
Hamilton Av.
Monticello Drive
Lenox Dr.
Bristol Road
Whitmore Street
Carroll Street
Harold Street
Commerce Street
Houston Street
Amtrak Station
Martin Luther King Freeway
Arlington, Beltline
West 5th Street
Boland
West 7th Street
West 7th Street
Modern Art Museum
Amon Carter Museum
Boulevard
Currie St
Foch St
Summit Avenue
Kimbell Art Museum
Clarke Av.
Camp Bowie
Lancaster Avenue
East Freeway
Will Rogers Memorial Center
Casa Mañana Theatre
Farington Field
West Freeway
Forest Park Boulevard
South Main Street
Museum of Science and History
Crestline Drive
Lafayette Av.
National Cowgirl Museum & Hall of Fame
TRINITY PARK
Vickery Boulevard
Broadway
St. Louis
Kentucky Av.
Bessie St
Illinois Av.
Tennessee
Vickery Boulevard
Owasso Street
Montgomery Street
Thistle Hill
Austin
Cooper
7th Av.
BOTANIC GARDEN
West Freeway
Valentine St
Lovell Avenue
Chisholm Trail Pkwy
Rosedale St
Mistletoe Blvd
Mistletoe Drive
Enderly
Pennsylvania Avenue
FOREST PARK
Colonial Parkway
Fort Worth Zoo
Rogers Avenue
University Drive
Clear Fork Trinity
Log Cabin Village
Aquarium
Forest Park Boulevard
Huntington
Stanley Av.
8th Avenue
Glanco Terr.
Park Hill Drive
Park Hill Way
Colonial Pkwy
Highview
Cantey St
University Drive
Hartwood Drive
Harlanwood Drive
Texas Christian University Campus
Wabash Avenue
Carter Stadium
Cantey Street
Lowden Street
Forest Park
Townsend Drive
Livingston Avenue
Cleburne Rd
Bowie
Downtown Fort Worth
0 200 yds
0 200 m
PADDOCK PARK
Criminal Justice Building
Courthouse
E. Belknap St
Street
Tarrant County Courthouse
East 1st Street
East 2nd Street
Elm St
Terry
Pecan
Grove
Jones
Calhoun
Commerce
Main St
East 4th St.
Sid Richardson Museum
West Bluff
West Belknap Street
Weatherford
Sundance Square
Bass Performance Hall
Cherry Street
Florence
Henderson
West 1st Street
West 2nd
Central Library
West 3rd Street
Lamar
Taylor
Burnett
Throckmorton
Houston Street
W. 6th St
E. 7th St
8th St
Chamber of Commerce
West 7th St
West 5th Street
Greyhound Bus Terminal
West 7th Street
Street
BURNETT PARK
West 10th Street
Fort Worth Convention Center
U.S. Courthouse
City Hall
Collier Street
Lake Street
Lexington
Texas Street
Macon
West 13th Street
Water Gardens

in transportation had brought the cattle business to Fort Worth, further improvements took part of it away. Larger trucks and better highways made centralized marketing and fattening of cattle unnecessary. Cattlemen could fatten and auction herds locally, for truck delivery.

THE STOCKYARDS

Today, Fort Worth's **Stockyards National Historic District** Ⓐ, its streets cobbled and gaslit, looks much as it did a century ago. Longhorns are even driven down the main avenue twice a day. The cattle pens have been restored and Exchange Street is lined with the shops of artisans hand crafting saddles, chaps, and boots, while horse and mule barns have been renovated into the Mule Alley, an area with shops, boutiques, and restaurants. Even today, in this sleek, modern city, one might still see a Stetson-wearing businessman or a lawman on horseback.

The **Texas Cowboy Hall of Fame** (2515 Rodeo Plaza; tel: 817-626-7131; www.tchof.com; Mon–Thu 10am–5pm, Fri–Sat 10am–7pm, Sun 11am–5pm) honors the greats of rodeo and other cowboy pursuits in Texas – 140-plus inductees to date, each of whom has a display with personal memorabilia. Other exhibits include the Sterqueil Wagon Collection, the John Justin Trail of Fame, the Chisholm Trail Exhibit, and the Zingrang Horse Bit Collection. An Induction Ceremony is held every January prior to the Fort Worth Stock Show & Rodeo.

At the famous **White Elephant Saloon** (106 E. Exchange Avenue; tel: 817-624-8273; www.whiteelephantsaloon.com), noted for its bullet-splintered floorboards, there's nightly country and western music, and the notorious 1887 gunfight between owner Luke Short and former marshall Jim Courtright is reenacted on February 8 each year. The **Stockyards Hotel** (where Bonnie and Clyde once stayed) has been decorated in "cattle baron baroque," its saloon bar stools sporting saddles, while the Mission-style **Cowtown Coliseum** (121 E. Exchange Avenue, tel: 817-625-1025), which since 1908 has featured performers as varied as Enrico Caruso and Elvis Presley, offers weekly rodeos. The world's first indoor rodeo was held here in 1918. Even the 6,000-capacity **Billy Bob's Texas** (tel: 817-624-7117; http://billybobstexas.com), which describes itself as "the world's largest honky-tonk," has live bulls posturing in its indoor ring, inviting visitors to see how long they can stay aboard the pesky critters.

Next to the old hog and sheep pens (now housing art galleries, shops, and eateries), **Grapevine Vintage Railroad** operates steam train trips (707 S. Main Street, Grapevine; tel: 800-457-6338; www.grapevinetexasusa.com/grapevine-vintage-railroad; see website for schedule), pulled by its 1896 engine to the little town of Grapevine (see page 125), 21 miles (34km) northeast.

Livestock auctions are still held weekly in Fort Worth and, in keeping with modern technology, entire herds of cattle are bought and sold via the internet. The city has also profited from

Live entertainment at Billy Bob's Texas.

Sundance Square.

Tip

The dazzling golf and entertainment complex Topgolf (2201 E. 4th Street; tel: 817-349-4002; www.topgolf.com/us/fort-worth; Mon–Thu and Sun 9am–11pm, Fri–Sat 9am–1am) offers climate-controlled hitting bays for those wishing to perfect their golf swing while enjoying a drink or a meal with friends.

the West Texas oil boom and serves as a base for many oil companies.

Although the size of sprawling Fort Worth (pop. 874,000) makes it a bit of a problem to negotiate without a car, it has only two other major areas that draw most visitors – the historic downtown area, 2 miles (3km) to the southeast of the Stockyards, and the Cultural District, a mile or two west of that. The three areas make up what is termed a "Western Triangle" and, sensibly, the city runs a shuttle called Molly the Trolley between them.

DOWNTOWN

At the heart of downtown, **Sundance Square** **B** (201 Main Street; tel: 817-222-1111; www.sundancesquare.com), between 2nd and 5th streets, at Throckmorton, is especially lively at night, with crowded bars and clubs and musicians entertaining the patrons of packed sidewalk cafés. In the old days, when rowdy cattlemen came here to celebrate, they were sometimes entertained by a tightrope walker negotiating a wire between the Plaza Hotel and the Adelphi Theater across the street.

Close by the original 1908 hotel, long ago converted into offices, is the **Sid Richardson Museum** (309 Main Street; tel: 817-332-6554; www.sidrichardsonmuseum.org; Mon–Thu 9am–5pm, Fri–Sat 9am–8pm, Sun noon–5pm; free), a permanent collection of Western art acquired by the late oilman. At one time, Richardson, who died in 1959 aged 67, owned 125 producing oil wells. His nephew, Perry Bass, and his sons acquired 38 square blocks of downtown after inheriting the Richardson fortune, and the Bass family – unsurprisingly among the nation's wealthiest individuals – have been major local philanthropists.

Surrounded by the collection's 56 paintings, primarily by Frederic Remington and Charles M. Russell, is a magnificent, silver-studded saddle by Ed Bohlin. It was given to Richardson by his close friend publisher Amon G. Carter. Almost everybody who's watched a Western movie has seen some of the art of Ed Bohlin, the

Fort Worth Water Gardens.

Swedish-born farmer who migrated to the US with the dream of becoming a cowboy. He was commissioned by Buffalo Bill Cody to repair leather harnesses used in his traveling show, and then moved to Hollywood to create saddles, holsters, and other leather tack for the studios. Among his customers were Roy Rogers, Tex Ritter, Gary Cooper, the Cisco Kid (Duncan Renaldo), and John Wayne, who habitually donned a Bohlin-made gunbelt and silver hatband. The **Nancy Lee and Perry R Bass Performance Hall** **C** (525 Commerce Street; tel: 817-212-4280; www.basshall.com), home of the city's symphony orchestra and ballet and opera companies, is an awesome masterpiece designed by the Washington architect David M. Schwarz and completed in 1998. It is hoped that the 2,056-seat hall will last 300 years – as long as some of its European counterparts: "Great concert halls," Schwarz muses, "are symbols of an age. If they're done well they reflect a great moment in history." Surmounted by Hungarian sculptor Márton Váró's gigantic granite angels, blowing 6ft (2-meter) trumpets, this hall is also noted for such extravagant decorative features as the cloud-filled, 80ft (25-meter) -wide Great Dome, which soars high above the auditorium. This, and the hall's other artwork, was the creation of Scott and Stuart Gentling.

Sundance Square is backdropped by the block-long (and very luxurious) Worthington Renaissance Fort Worth Hotel, which is convenient to everything downtown. A huge mural flanks the parking lot on 3rd Street: a three-story trompe l'oeil by Richard Haas of cowboys and longhorns on the Chisholm Trail.

HELL'S HALF ACRE

At one end of what was once Hell's Half Acre, not far from the history exhibits in the refurbished Fire Station No. 1 (120 N Pecan; tel: 817-392-3000; open daily; free), is the **Tarrant County Courthouse** **D** (100 E. Weatherford Street), dating from the late 1900s. At the other end is the **Fort Worth Convention Center** **E**, between Houston and Commerce. Opposite are the delightful **Fort Worth Water Gardens** **F** at Commerce and 15th streets, created by architect Philip Johnson and his associate, John Burgee, and imitated all over the country. Slabs are tipped at delicate angles to carry, direct, or stop water that is swirling, falling, sprinkling, or lying still. Closed in 2004 after a tragic drowning incident, the gardens later reopened with new safety features and a plaque commemorating the victims. The effects of the pouring, pounding water are not intended to rival nature – rather, they bring to mind leaking dams or streams of industrial coolant in flow to prevent meltdown.

CULTURAL DISTRICT

The third region of the city's Western Triangle, the Cultural District, is 1.5 miles (2km) west of downtown. Roughly halfway between the two areas can be

The Sid Richardson Museum is home to a collection of Western art, reflecting both the romance and the reality of the American West.

Kimbell Art Museum.

Fact

One of the most remarkable features of the Kimbell Art Museum is the clever use of natural light, which allows exhibits to be seen to their best advantage.

found **Thistle Hill** G (1509 Pennsylvania Avenue; tel: 817-336-5875; www.historicfortworth.org; tours Wed–Fri 11am–2pm, Sun 1–3pm), an imposing example of a cattle baron's mansion dating from the turn of the 20th century. Cattleman W.T. Waggoner began building the house at 1509 Pennsylvania Avenue for his daughter in 1903, and another cattleman, Winfield Scott (one-time owner of the Plaza Hotel), completed it in 1910. The landscaped grounds are as interesting as the house restoration, which contains period furnishings and original pieces.

Dominant in the Cultural District is the **Will Rogers Memorial Center** H (3401 W. Lancaster Avenue; tel: 817-392-7469), but, apart from the staging of specific events (such as the annual Southwestern Exposition and Livestock Show in January), this is less interesting than the major museums here.

One of these, the **Kimbell Art Museum** I (3333 Camp Bowie Boulevard; tel: 817-332-8451; www.kimbellart.org; Tue–Thu and Sat 10am–5pm, Fri noon–8pm, Sun noon–5pm; free), designed by the late Louis Kahn, has long been regarded as one of the top three museums in America. Kahn, revered by many of his fellow architects, also designed La Jolla's Salk Institute, and his work, according to *Contemporary Architects* "had an absolutely monumental impact on the development and redirectioning of progressive design."

Combining concrete, marble, glass, and vegetation with subtle modulations of natural light in a simple, exquisitely detailed whole, the Kimbell is human-sized with a wide collection that is constantly being expanded. There are single objects here that would, on their own, justify a visit: a Duccio, a Giovanni Bellini, Vuillards, a Cézanne, a Rubens, a Rembrandt, and a spectacular Oriental collection. The museum, founded with the art collection of oil tycoon Kay Kimbell on his death in 1964, explains its rationale: "the individual work of outstanding merit and importance is more effective as an educational tool than a large number of representative examples."

Situated nearby is the **Amon Carter Museum** J (3501 Camp Bowie Boulevard; tel: 817-738-1933; www.cartermuseum.org; Tue–Sat 10am–5pm, Thu 10am–8pm, Sun noon–5pm; free), the work of Philip Johnson, one of the many American architects who were influenced by the work of Louis Kahn. Founded by the publisher of the *Fort Worth Star Telegram* whose name it bears, the museum is best known for collections of paintings and bronzes by Frederic Remington and Charles M. Russell, who specialized in depicting life on the range and along the cattle trails.

In addition to the museum's collection of significant paintings by such revered American artists as John Singer Sargent, Thomas Eakins, Winslow Homer, and Georgia O'Keeffe, there are numerous intriguing paintings by anonymous 19th-century artists and some wonderful sepia prints. These feature gold mining scenes and were taken in an era when advances in photography had reduced the time needed for exposures

Modern Art Museum of Fort Worth.

to a mere 30 seconds. The pioneering "animal movement" photographer Eadweard Muybridge is also represented with an 1887 shot of a horse that shows all of its feet off the ground.

The permanent art collection of the **Modern Art Museum of Fort Worth** Ⓚ (3200 Darnell Street; tel: 817-738-9215; www.themodern.org; Tue–Sun 10am–5pm; Thu 10am–8pm) – ironically the city's oldest – includes works by such post–World War II favorites as Frank Stella, Mark Rothko, Clyfford Still, Morris Louis, Joseph Cornell, and even Pablo Picasso, with contemporary sculpture dotting the adjoining garden. The striking building was designed by Japanese architect Tadao Ando.

Fort Worth Museum of Science and History Ⓛ (1600 Gendy Street; tel: 817-255-9300; www.fwmuseum.org; Tue–Sat 10am–5pm, Sun noon–5pm) employs every inch of space to entertain and educate its visitors, with even its restroom walls adorned with charts explaining aspects of the human body. Notes by the fountains reveal that water covers three-quarters of the earth's surface, with only 3 percent of it fresh. The museum is exceptionally friendly to kids who can sit in a helicopter or dig for dinosaur bones.

Additional attractions are an Omnimax theater, astronomy programs and daily shows at the Noble Planetarium. Inside the science museum is the **Cattle Raisers Museum** (1600 Gendy Street; tel: 817-332-8551; www.cattleraisersmuseum.org; Tue–Sat 10am–5pm, Sun noon–5pm), where among other things you'll find famous branding irons and a "talking longhorn." One exhibit here explains the importance of the brand inspector in the never-ending fight against rustlers.

For information about the women who worked the ranches on horseback, there's the **National Cowgirl Museum and Hall of Fame** Ⓜ (1720 Gendy Street; tel: 817-336-4475; www.cowgirl.net; Tue–Sat 10am–5pm, Sun noon–5pm), whose 200-plus inductees include Henrietta Chamberlain King, co-founder of the enormous King Ranch; sharpshooter Annie Oakley; world champion bull rider Lynn Jonckowski; and trick rider and calf roper Dixie Reger Moseley.

Fact

The National Cowgirl Museum and Hall of Fame is devoted not just to women who have worked the ranches but also to entertainers like Dale Evans and Patsy Cline.

A trompe l'oeil mural by Richard Haas outside the National Cowgirl Museum and Hall of Fame.

THE CHISHOLM TRAIL

The great trail drives of the 19th century passed through Texas towns and characterized an era with their herds of longhorns, cowboys, and long days in the saddle.

From 1867 to 1884, the major route north for cattle was the Chisholm Trail, named for Jesse Chisholm who had established regular trade with northern American Indian camps.

At first the trail went by such names as the Kansas or Abilene Trail, but "Chisholm" soon became the common term for its entire length, from the Rio Grande to Central Kansas. It became the most favored route after fears about Texas tick fever led six states to close off other trails. (Texan longhorns had built up an immunity to the fever, but it had caused huge losses of cattle in other regions.)

Running from San Antonio through Austin, following what is, roughly speaking, today's I-35, and splitting up at Waco, the Chisholm Trail headed up to Fort Worth and turned eastward at Decatur, to the crossing at Red River Station, which marked the beginning of Indian Territory.

Author Wayne Gard, a former president of the Texas Historical Association, who wrote the definitive book on the Chisholm Trail, observed that it was like a tree, with the roots being the feeder trails from South Texas, the trunk the main route from San Antonio across Indian Territory, and the branches extending to the various railheads in Kansas.

In many places, such as Salado, the trail headed right up a town's main street. Only here, and at river crossings, were the cattle squeezed down to a group 50–60ft (15–18 meters) across and confined to a specific trail: they were normally spread out across possibly half a mile (nearly 1km) of prairie, grazing as they continued on their guided drift north.

Individual cattle tended to keep roughly the same position each day, but there was always an ambitious steer or two to take the lead, and usually a trail boss could rely on a favorite steer to give the herd a lead and be the first into the water at a river crossing.

Wayne Gard once told of a stampeding herd of 1,200 on a northbound trek, in the then small town of Dallas. The two steers that had led the drive stayed in place, remaining perfectly still, and eventually the frightened cattle returned to gather peacefully around them.

The writer J. Frank Dobie stressed the importance of one's companions. Two sayings on the range, he wrote, best expressed the utmost in trustworthiness: "He will do to tie to" and "He will do to ride the river with."

When the railroads eventually penetrated the state and made the Chisholm Trail an anachronism, Texas had more cattle than there had been at the beginning and, although drives continued until the mid-1880s, they were on a reduced basis. In the quarter-century of its existence, the Chisholm Trail saw the passage of more than five million cattle, plus a million mustangs.

Jesse Chisholm himself died in 1838. "No one ever left his home cold or hungry," said the epitaph over his grave. Today's US 81 follows the route of the old Chisholm Trail from Fort Worth right through to Newton, Kansas.

A map of the Chisholm Trail.

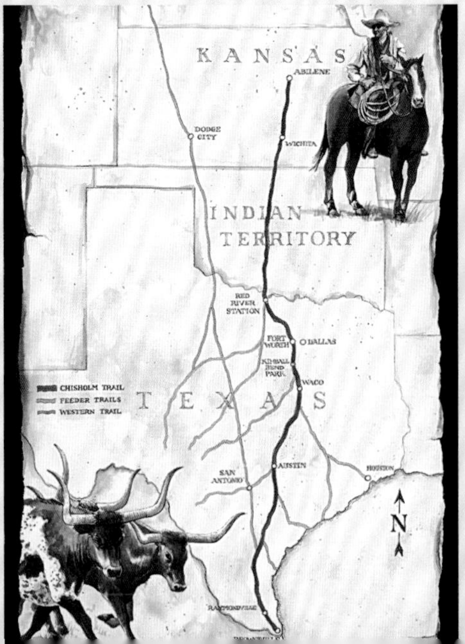

Casa Mañana Theatre N (3101 W. Lancaster; tel: 817-332-2272; www.casamanana.org) is a venue for Broadway-style musicals. Its roof is an early example of the geodesic dome invented by R. Buckminster Fuller, and it was one of the city's tributes to the 1936 Texas Centennial Celebration. Based on the triangle, and requiring no internal support, the geodesic dome grows stronger as it grows larger, can withstand hurricanes and, unlike domes in general, has good acoustics. A later example forms the top of the Reunion Tower in Dallas.

WALKS ON THE WILD SIDE

Several blocks to the south, near the intersection of I-30 and South University Drive, is the **Fort Worth Botanic Garden** O (tel: 817-392-5464; www.fwbg.org; open daily; free), a 109-acre (44-hectare) park watered by natural springs and containing more than 50 species of tree, all sorts of roses, and a Japanese Garden. Nearby is **Dickies Arena** (1911 Montgomery Street; tel: 817-402-9000; www.dickiesarena.com), Fort Worth's premier concert and event venue that opened in 2019. The legendary Fort Worth Stock Show & Rodeo will now be held here.

Farther south still on Colonial Parkway, west of University Drive, is **Log Cabin Village** P (2100 Log Cabin Village Lane; tel: 817-392-5881; www.logcabinvillage.org; Tue–Fri 9am–4pm, Sat–Sun 1–5pm), featuring seven homes from the 1850s, with costumed pioneers, a grist mill, and spinning wheels.

A short distance away is the **Fort Worth Zoo** Q (1989 Colonial Parkway; tel: 817-759-7555; www.fortworthzoo.org; Mon–Fri 10am–5pm, Sat–Sun until 6pm) in Forest Park. Set among natural habitats along winding paths are 540 species of animals, birds, and reptiles. The zoo's art gallery contains 28 enormous paintings by the German artist Wilhelm Kuhnert, who went to the East African bush for inspiration. Several American buffalo live here on a 3,400-acre (1,375-hectare) range of their own. There is a prairie dog "town," where small burrowing owls may be seen creeping in and out of abandoned prairie dog holes. Trails of many descriptions divide the refuge.

Aviation buffs will enjoy the **Vintage Flying Museum** at Meacham Airport (505 N.W. 38th Street; tel: 817-624-1935; www.vintageflyingmuseum.org; Fri 10am–5pm, Sat 9am–5pm, Sun noon–5pm). Some planes in this collection of historic aircraft and World War II memorabilia still fly, and each October the museum hosts a fly-in of rare and vintage aircraft.

ARLINGTON

Though a separate town, **Arlington** (pop. 396,400) has become something of an eastern adjunct to Fort Worth. Its many residents are fans of the Texas Rangers, and thus flock to watch the team play at **Globe Life Park**, a magnificent facility that was replaced by **Globe Life Field** on its completion in 2020. The stadium has a retractable roof and seating for 40,500 fans and standing-room-only areas for

Fact

One plot at Fort Worth Botanic Garden has been planted particularly for the strength and variety of its scent, in anticipation of blind visitors.

A store on Exchange Street, Stockyards National Historic District.

> **Fact**
>
> The Six Flags Over Texas amusement park specializes in white-knuckle rides, but there is plenty to entertain all ages, including mock shoot-outs, ice shows, and appearances by popular "Looney Tunes" characters.

another 2,000 people. Its estimated cost was $1.1 billion. Prior to Globe Life Field opening, the Texas Rangers created **Texas Live!**, (1650 E Randol Mill Rd; tel: 817-852-6688; https://texas-live.com) a next-door entertainment complex with accommodations, restaurants, bars, co-working spaces, offices, and a concert venue called Arlington Backyard. At the multi-level sports bar called Live! Arena, fans can watch the Rangers play on a 100-foot (30m) LED HD screen.

Globe Life Park will be retrofitted so it can used by XFL's Dallas Renegades and the North Texas Soccer Club. The nearby **AT&T Stadium** is home to the Dallas Cowboys football team and also hosts bowl games and major concerts. This immense structure has the world's largest column-free interior, as well as one of the 25 biggest high definition video screens in the world. Tours are available here.

FUN AND GAMES

Heading away from Globe Life Field, past Arlington's Convention Center, you reach **Six Flags Over Texas** (2201 Road to Six Flags St E; tel: 817-640-8900; www.sixflags.com/overtexas; open daily), at the junction of I-30 and Highway 360. This is the state's biggest tourist attraction and the original base of what is now a nationwide chain. The 212-acre (86-hectare) theme park devotes an area to each of the nations whose flag has flown over Texas – Spain, Mexico, France, Texas, the Confederacy, and the US – and there are other attractions, too. Next door, **Six Flags Hurricane Harbor** (1800 E. Lamar Boulevard; tel: 817-640-8900; www.sixflags.com/hurricaneharbortexas; open May–Sept) offers a cool respite from the searingly hot temperatures that summer visitors to Texas can always expect.

Louis Tussaud Waxworks and Ripley's Believe It or Not! (601 Palace Parkway; tel: 972-263-2391; www.ripleys.com/grandprairie; open daily) is to the east, in Grand Prairie, along I-30 at Beltline, and offers the usual garish waxwork and emporium fun. Farther afield is the **Colonel Middleton Tate Johnson Plantation Cemetery** (600 W. Arkansas Lane; tours can be arranged through the Arlington Historical Society, tel: 817-460-4001), a small family cemetery where a major figure in early Arlington history and his African-American slaves are buried. There is an historic log cabin on the site. At the entrance to the River Legacy Parks, near the lake at the west side of town, is the **River Legacy Living Science Center** (703 N.W. Green Oak Boulevard; tel: 817-860-6752; www.riverlegacy.org; Mon–Sat 9am–5pm). Housed in an attractive sustainable 12,000-sq-ft (1,115-sq-meter) building, it offers environmental exhibits for all ages.

On the far side of Highway 360, which runs north to south on the eastern edge of Arlington, are shopping opportunities at Grand Prairie Premium Outlets (2950 W Interstate 20), and the enormous Traders Village Flea Market (2602 Mayfield Road, Grand Prairie), which displays the wares of

The Texas Rangers take on the Houston Astros at Globe Life Park.

over 3,000 dealers at weekends. The return trip west to Fort Worth on I-20 passes the gargantuan Parks Mall (Cooper at I-20).

Arlington's downtown attractions are clustered within walking distance of each other around Main Street. These include the perennial Johnny High's Country Music Revue at the **Arlington Music Hall** (224 N. Center Street; tel: 817-226-4400; www.arlingtonmusichall.net) and the 200-seat **Theatre Arlington** (305 W. Main Street; tel: 817-275-7661; www.theatrearlington.org; Mon–Fri 10am–6pm). The **Arlington Museum of Art** (201 W. Main Street; tel: 817-275-4600; www.arlingtonmuseum.org; Tue–Sat 10am–5pm, Sun 1–5pm) concentrates on Texan artists.

GRAPEVINE

More than 50 19th-century buildings have been preserved and restored in the little town of **Grapevine**, which sits at the end of the Grapevine Vintage Railroad line that begins at the Fort Worth Stockyards. Named for the wild mustang grapes prevalent in the area, the town dates back to 1843 when General Sam Houston camped nearby before signing a peace treaty with American Indian tribal leaders. There are numerous wineries in the area, the nearest being the château-style **Delaney Vineyards** (2000 Champagne Boulevard; tel: 817-481-5668; www.delaneyvineyards.com; Tue–Sat noon–5pm).

Grapevine is dotted with historical markers, and much of its Main Street is listed in the *National Register of Historical Places*. The tourist office (636 S. Main Street; tel: 800-457-6338; www.grapevinetexasusa.com) is in the artfully reconstructed Wallis Hotel building, which was filled with traveling salesmen in the early 1900s. *The Sidewalk Judge*, a lifelike sculpture by J. Seward Johnson, sitting on a bench outside, is an irresistible photo opportunity.

Across Main Street, at No. 300, the old **Palace Theatre** (tel: 817-410-3459; www.grapevinetexasusa.com/palace-theatre) has been restored as a home for the Grapevine Opry, and in the next block is the former **Grapevine Home**

Fact

In celebration of the local wine industry, Grapevine stages an annual Grapefest every September.

Grapevine Vintage Railroad steam train.

Fact

The Fort Worth Stock Show and Rodeo (tel: 817-877-2400; www.fwssr.com) takes over Cowtown, as its known, for most of January and part of February.

Bank, which was robbed by some of the Bonnie and Clyde gang back in 1932. Many of the buildings on Main Street sell genuine arts and crafts. These include **Off the Vine** (324 S. Main Street; tel: 817-421-1091; www.offthevinetexas.com), a wine shop that also sells wine-related art, such as handblown goblets.

What's known as the **Torian Log Cabin**, built in 1845, inhabited until the 1940s and still primitively furnished, sits near the gazebo in Liberty Park at the northern end of the street. The more interesting old homes are behind Main Street at the other end: a group of Victorian houses on College Street. One block west back on Main Street are the Heritage Center and the **Grapevine Depot**, the latter serving as the town's railroad station before being converted into an historical museum.

The St Louis and Southwestern (Cotton Belt) Railroad depot once stood here and today, near the classic 1933 **Aeromotor Windmill**, which at one time pumped water for a nearby farm, is the terminal for the Grapevine Vintage Railroad, which runs daily between here and Fort Worth. At the blacksmith's shop, with its wild mustang grapevine, genial Jim White demonstrates forging brands while posing happily for visitors, and his neighbor, saddlemaker Aubrey Mauldin, presides over a leather shop filled with custom-made boots.

The cowboy boot is something special and the state produces more of them than any other place in the world. There were 600 Texas bootmakers at one time. Now only about one-tenth of that number still painstakingly cut and stitch every inch by hand, from pointed toe (to slip easily into the stirrup) to elevated arch and heel (to hold the foot firmly in place).

At the far end of the depot is **Grapevine Botanical Gardens at Heritage Park**, featuring such specimens as the swamp rose, the pink-flowered bouncing bet (once used as a soap substitute), and the crinum lily, all attracting butterflies and hummingbirds and making the garden a visitors' delight.

North of town, 19-mile (30km) long **Grapevine Lake** is a cool recreational oasis offering boating, swimming, fishing, and all kinds of water activities. Beyond the lake, off Highway 26 at 3000 Grapevine Mills Parkway, near the airport, is the huge, brightly lit Grapevine Mills shopping mall, which is not a bad place to while away a couple of hours between flights. A convenient shuttle bus runs to and from the airport.

Grapevine's two most notable hotels are **Gaylord Texan Resort & Convention Center** (1501 Gaylord Trail; tel: 817-778-1000) and the **Great Wolf Lodge** (100 Great Wolf Dr; tel: 800-693-9653). Families are attracted to Great Wolf Lodge for its indoor waterpark open year-round, while others visit Gaylord Texas Resort throughout the year for its dining options and events. However, the Gaylord is a notable Christmas destination in DFW as the interior is decorated with 2 million

Denton County Courthouse.

lights and stunning decorations, and the hotel offers winter fun activities like ice skating, snow tubing, and ICE!, a walk-through experience featuring extravagant ice sculptures of holiday characters in a wintery wonderland.

DENTON

Thirty-five miles (56km) northeast of Fort Worth, on US 35, is the attractive college town of **Denton** (pop. 136,000), home to two universities and one of the liveliest (and least known) live music scenes in the US. In fact, it rivals Austin for indie music, and is the hometown of well-known band Brave Combo whose musical style seems to draw from just about everywhere.

Its century-old limestone and granite courthouse dominates a square lined with renovated old buildings that now house eclectic cafés, music shops, funky boutiques, antiques stores, and specialty stores. The **Courthouse-on-the-Square Museum** (110 W. Hickory Street; tel: 940-349-2850; Mon–Fri 10am–4.30pm, Sat 11am–3pm; free) in the courthouse focuses on the history of the region. The town's pioneer founder, Captain John B. Denton, is buried beneath the lawn.

Numerous movies (including the 1998 film, *Armageddon*) have been shot in Denton, especially among the old homes of the Oak-Hickory Historic District. A free historic walking tour of downtown can be downloaded from Main Street Denton).

The A Train connects Denton to Dallas and the DART light rail and bus system. To the south of town, the **Texas Motor Speedway** (3545 Lone Star Circle; tel: 817-215-8500; www.texasmotorspeedway.com) will be of interest to auto-racing enthusiasts.

Also in this area is the **Texas Women's University** (TWU), the largest of its kind in the nation, containing the **Texas First Ladies Historic Costume Collection** (tel: 940-898-3644; Mon–Fri 8am–5pm), which displays gowns worn by the First Ladies of Texas. In the vicinity is the **University of North Texas** (tel: 940-565-2000), which has a fashion collection of its own, as well as a famous library.

Tip

Consider historic Denton as a base for a visit to Dallas or Fort Worth. Not only is it halfway between the two centers, but it also has numerous attractions of its own, including live music venues and a vibrant college scene. The A Train links Denton to Dallas's DART system.

Texas Motor Speedway.

An old gas station off Interstate 35.

CENTRAL TEXAS

Detour from the interstate south of Dallas, between Waxahachie and Austin, and discover quirky towns, artificial lakes, paleontological sites, distinctive architecture, absorbing museums, and Texas A&M.

Central Texas has long been known as the backyard of Texas – not such a bad thing in a state with so many glamorous frontyards. Too often travelers, unless headed for the lakes or elderly relatives, race from Dallas to Austin without even exiting the freeway. To really understand Texas, leave the interstate between Waxahachie and Austin and "come on around to the backyard."

WAXAHACHIE

Waxahachie ❶ (pop. 35,000), located 35 miles (56km) south of Dallas, is one of the latter's bedroom communities. Take the exit from I-35 East, the Dallas arm of the Fort Worth–Dallas "Y." The town's name derives from an American Indian word for "buffalo creek"; white settlers arrived here in the 1840s.

Much of the honey in Texas supermarkets comes from Waxahachie, a town that has become increasingly industrialized. Nevertheless, it still proudly preserves hundreds of Victorian and early 20th-century houses, many of which can be toured along a "Gingerbread Trail" marked on a free map. This is available from the **Waxahachie Convention and Visitors Bureau** (2000 Civic Center Lane; tel: 469-309-4040; www.waxahachiecvb.com).

Photographs and pioneer artifacts in the **Ellis County Museum** (201 S. College Street; tel: 972-937-0681; http://sites.rootsweb.com/~txecm; Mon–Sat 10am–5pm), a former Masonic meeting-house on **Courthouse Square**, are devoted to the history of Waxahachie. The red sandstone and granite 1895 **Ellis County Courthouse** (Mon–Fri 8am–5pm; free), a product of Texas courthouse architect James Reily Gordon, is one of the most-photographed buildings in the state. It cost $150,000 to construct – a substantial sum in the 1890s. According to legend, an Italian stonecutter who was working on the building is thought to have fallen in love with a Waxahachie

Main attractions

- Ellis County Courthouse, Waxahachie
- National Polka Festival, Ennis
- Armstrong Browning Library, Baylor University, Waco
- Texas Ranger Hall of Fame and Museum, Waco
- Central Texas Area Museum, Salado

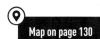

Map on page 130

Ellis County Courthouse.

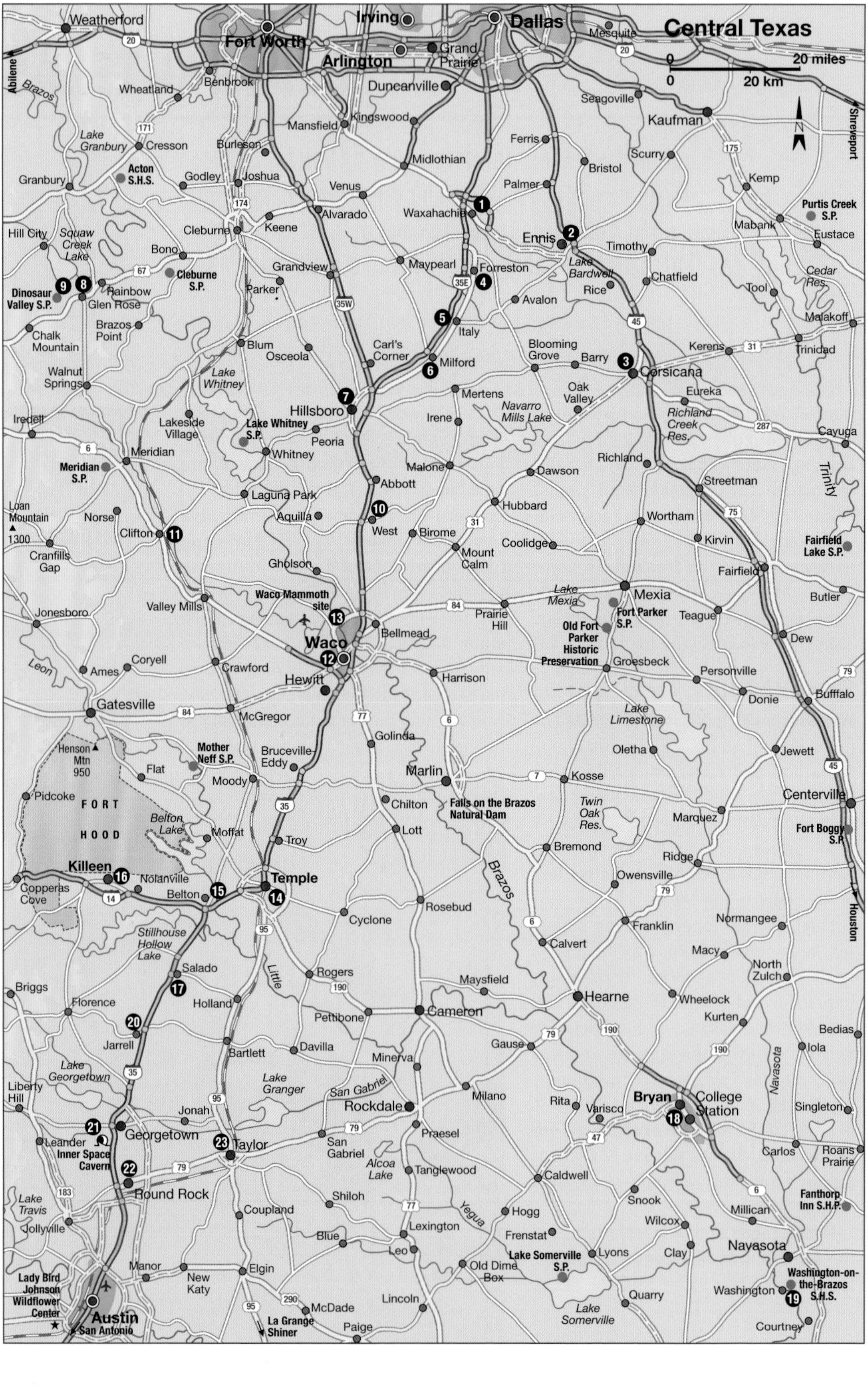
Central Texas
0 20 miles
0 20 km
N
Weatherford
Fort Worth
Irving
Dallas
Mesquite
Arlington
Grand Prairie
Abilene
Brazos
Wheatland
Benbrook
Duncanville
Seagoville
Kaufman
Shreveport
Mansfield
Kingswood
Lake Granbury
Cresson
Burleson
Midlothian
Ferris
Bristol
Scurry
Acton S.H.S.
Godley
Joshua
Granbury
Venus
Palmer
Kemp
Waxahachie
Purtis Creek S.P.
Alvarado
Keene
Cleburne
Hill City
Squaw Creek Lake
Ennis
Mabank
Eustace
Timothy
Bono
Grandview
Maypearl
Forreston
Lake Bardwell
Chatfield
Cedar Res.
Dinosaur Valley S.P.
Rainbow
Glen Rose
Cleburne S.P.
Parker
Rice
Tool
Avalon
Chalk Mountain
Brazos Point
Italy
Malakoff
Blum
Osceola
Carl's Corner
Milford
Blooming Grove
Barry
Kerens
Trinidad
Corsicana
Walnut Springs
Lake Whitney
Mertens
Oak Valley
Eureka
Hillsboro
Navarro Mills Lake
Richland Creek Res.
Iredell
Lakeside Village
Lake Whitney S.P.
Irene
Peoria
Cayuga
Meridian
Whitney
Meridian S.P.
Malone
Dawson
Richland
Trinity
Abbott
Streetman
Laguna Park
Hubbard
Loan Mountain 1300
Norse
Aquilla
Wortham
Clifton
West
Birome
Coolidge
Kirvin
Fairfield Lake S.P.
Cranfills Gap
Mount Calm
Fairfield
Gholson
Lake Mexia
Mexia
Butler
Waco Mammoth site
Valley Mills
Jonesboro
Prairie Hill
Fort Parker S.P.
Teague
Old Fort Parker Historic Preservation
Bellmead
Dew
Waco
Leon
Coryell
Groesbeck
Personville
Ames
Crawford
Hewitt
Harrison
Bufffalo
Gatesville
Donie
McGregor
Lake Limestone
Golinda
Henson Mtn 950
Mother Neff S.P.
Bruceville-Eddy
Oletha
Jewett
Flat
Moody
Marlin
Kosse
Pidcoke
FORT HOOD
Chilton
Falls on the Brazos Natural Dam
Twin Oak Res.
Centerville
Marquez
Belton Lake
Moffat
Lott
Fort Boggy S.P.
Troy
Bremond
Killeen
Nolanville
Temple
Ridge
Copperas Cove
Belton
Owensville
Rosebud
Cyclone
Normangee
Franklin
Stillhouse Hollow Lake
Calvert
Macy
Houston
Salado
North Zulch
Little
Rogers
Briggs
Maysfield
Florence
Holland
Hearne
Wheelock
Pettibone
Cameron
Kurten
Jarrell
Bedias
Gause
Iola
Bartlett
Davilla
Minerva
Navasota
Lake Georgetown
Lake Granger
San Gabriel
Liberty Hill
Milano
Rita
Bryan
College Station
Rockdale
Varisco
Singleton
Jonah
Georgetown
Leander
Inner Space Cavern
Taylor
San Gabriel
Praesel
Carlos
Roans Prairie
Alcoa Lake
Tanglewood
Caldwell
Round Rock
Lake Travis
Shiloh
Coupland
Snook
Fanthorp Inn S.H.P.
Yegua
Hogg
Millican
Jollyville
Lexington
Wilcox
Blue
Frenstat
Leo
Lake Somerville S.P.
Lyons
Clay
Manor
Elgin
Old Dime Box
New Katy
Lady Bird Johnson Wildflower Center
Washington-on-the-Brazos S.H.S.
Washington
Quarry
Lincoln
McDade
Lake Somerville
Austin
San Antonio
La Grange
Shiner
Paige
Courtney
20
171
174
67
35W
35E
45
31
175
287
6
75
84
79
77
7
35
14
95
190
183
290
47
1
2
3
4
5
6
7
8
9
10
11
12
13
14
15
16
17
18
19
20
21
22
23

telegraph operator, Mabel Frame, whose carved face is a recurring exterior motif.

The museum owns the red-brick Greek Revival **Jenkins Home** (604 W. Main Street; open during the Gingerbread Trail Historic Home Tour in early June), packed with antique fans, furniture, and Bohemian glass. It was built in 1904, at the height of Waxahachie's prosperity (based on cattle, grain, and cotton), a few years after the 1900 **Chautauqua Auditorium** (www.waxahachiechautauqua.org), part of the century-old nationwide Chautauqua educational movement begun in upstate New York and still offering cultural presentations here. Also from the same era is the ornate Roman Revival **Nicholas P. Sims Library** (515 W. Main Street; tel: 972-937-2671; www.simslib.org), with a richly decorated Carrara marble and gold interior.

Waxahachie's proximity to Dallas's already established film industry, its charming small-town feel, and its attractive period architecture have made it popular as a movie location. The 1985 *Peyton Place* remake was filmed here, as were the movies *Tender Mercies* and *Places in the Heart*.

POLKA FESTIVAL

Many of the state's Czech immigrants settled in Central Texas's fertile cotton-growing belt, and almost all did well as cotton farmers here. Their descendants make up approximately half the population of **Ennis** ❷, on I-45 between Dallas and Houston. Since 1966, Ennis has sponsored the **National Polka Festival** in May, attracting crowds of 50,000. A parade of 14 polka bands rolls down Main Street, which may be the widest in Texas – divided into East and West Main by railroad tracks, it is 340ft (104 meters) across. The town also has a **Railroad and Cultural Heritage Museum** (105 N.E. Main Street; tel: 972-875-1901; http://www.visitennis.org/attractions.htm; Tue–Sat 10am–4pm, Sun 1–4pm), which showcases the Czech influence as well as railroad history.

ON THE WATER

Since 1900, more than 200 lakes have been created in Texas. **Lake Bardwell**, or the Bardwell Reservoir, on Waxahachie Creek, 4 miles (7km) outside Ennis, was built by the US Army Corps of Engineers in the early 1960s. Like the other new lakes near Navarro Mills and Mexia, it is a popular recreation area, with pretty lakeside parks and camping. It also acts as the water supply for Ennis, Waxahachie, and Corsicana. Visitors from out of state – especially New Englanders, whose reservoirs are fenced and carefully patrolled – are often surprised to find Texans fishing, water-skiing, and sailing on theirs.

Corsicana ❸, the Navarro county seat, is 19 miles (30km) south of Ennis on I-45. It is named for Corsica, home of the parents of the Texas hero José Antonio Navarro of San Antonio, who signed the Texas Declaration of Independence and helped write the first constitution. The first Texas gusher was not drilled at Corsicana as is commonly believed. However, a 12-year oil boom began in 1894 when the city dug an artesian

The Ellis County Museum.

Delicious Czech pastries at Caldwell Kolache Festival.

well and struck oil instead of water. The strike made Corsicana the first oil boomtown in Texas, but today, it may be best known for the *Cheer* documentary on Netflix which highlights the championship cheerleading squad at Corsicana's junior college, Navarro College. A current attraction, **Pioneer Village** (912 W. Park Avenue; tel: 903-654-4846; www.cityofcorsicana.com/995/Pioneer-Village; Mon–Sat 8am–5pm, Sun 10–4pm) is made up of reconstructed 19th-century log buildings, including an American Indian trading post and slave quarters.

Corsicana is known for the "Deluxe" fruit cake made by the **Collin Street Bakery** (401 W. 7th Avenue; tel: 800-672-5216; www.collinstreet.com; open daily), featured on Food Network, which has been exported all over the world – 1.6 million fruitcakes per year, to be exact. An essential ingredient is the inimitable Texas pecan, more than a million pounds (just under half a million kilograms) of which are used by the bakery annually. Be warned: American-style fruitcakes are invariably very sweet and not to everyone's taste.

NAMELESS PLACE

Forreston ❹, 10 miles (16km) south of Waxahachie on the interstate, is the oldest town in the area. Another 5 miles (8km) south, near **Italy ❺**, the Confederates operated a hat factory.

Italy was originally called "Houston Creek," because Sam Houston was reported to have camped nearby. Reputedly, the post office would not issue a postmark unless the name of the town was changed and, after six different names had been rejected, settlers wrote back: "Let the post office be nameless, and be damned." The community was Nameless, Texas, from 1880 to 1890, and there is still a Nameless Schoolhouse and Nameless Road.

Houston Creek eventually became Italy – a tribute, it is said, to the sunny Central Texas climate. The population of Italy has never exceeded 1,950 souls, but it did receive the first fully endowed public library in Texas – the **Dunlap Library** (300 W. Main Street; tel: 972-483-6481) – from businessman S.M. Dunlap.

Texas bluebonnets, near Ennis.

HISTORICAL TOWNS

Back on I-35, or via State Route 22 from Corsicana, you arrive at **Milford 6**, a town settled in the 1850s that once adopted the good-humored city motto: "The home of 700 friendly people and three or four old grouches." It is nothing more than human nature to leave the freeway in the hope of catching a glimpse of one of the grouches. The town of **Hillsboro 7**, just below the point where I-35 West joins I-35 East from Dallas, has been a crossroads since the 1850s, when there was a dirt-floor, elm-pole courthouse here.

Today's limestone Hill County Courthouse was built in 1890, burned down in 1993, and was restored in 1999, with the help of a fund-raiser headlined by Willie Nelson, who grew up in nearby Abbott. At Hill Junior College, the Texas Heritage Museum and History Complex (112 Lamar Drive; tel: 254-659-7750; Mon–Fri 8am–4pm) displays paintings, photographs, and documents from the Civil War, around 200 guns and other weaponry from the Civil War to the present, and the uniform worn by Audie Murphy, the most decorated American soldier of World War II.

Northwest of Hillsboro on State Road 144 is **Glen Rose 8**, where it is rumored John Wilkes Booth once lived – under the name John St Helen – after he assassinated President Lincoln. Glen Rose is sometimes known as the "Petrified City," because petrified wood is a popular building material here. Local history is explained in the tiny hometown **Somervell County Museum** (101 Vernon Street; tel: 254-898-0640; Fri–Sat 11am–4pm; free).

JURASSIC PARK

Numerous dinosaur tracks can be found in Glen Rose and in the 1,500-acre (607-hectare) **Dinosaur Valley State Park 9** (1629 Park Road 59; tel: 254-897-4588; www.tpwd.state.tx.us/state-parks/dinosaur-valley; open daily 7am–10pm), 4 miles (6km) west of the town. The tracks are easy to spot, but there is a steep trail to the river. The Bosque River Valley was once coastal swampland and dinosaurs left their tracks – some of the best-preserved examples in the world

Fact

Texas-born Audie Murphy (1924–71) was able to build on his honorable service record by becoming an actor, starring in a series of war and Western films, most notably the Civil War movie *The Red Badge of Courage* (1951).

Hill County Courthouse.

Fact

Waco is best known for the 1993 FBI seige of the Branch Davidian compound to force out members of the breakaway Seventh Day Adventist Church sect who were suspect of weapons violations. The standoff lasted 51 days and ended in a fire that killed cult leader David Koresh and 76 people and triggered the Oklahoma City bombing two years later.

– in the limestone riverbed here. There are no "taildrag marks" in the dinosaurs trackway – the water here was deep enough for the dinosaurs' tails to float – but you can see where the mud oozed up between their toes. The park has facilities for camping, picnicking, hiking, biking, and horseback riding, and is one of the state parks in which part of the official state longhorn herd is kept.

WEST, TEXAS

The small town of **West** ⑩, halfway between Hillsboro and Waco, is sometimes confused with the region "West Texas," so it is often referred to as "West, Comma, Texas." Forty thousand people came here on September 15, 1896, to view the ridiculous, staged spectacular of two locomotives of the Missouri, Kansas and Texas Railroad crash into each other. Their throttles tied back to 50mph (80kmph), the trains exploded on impact, killing two spectators. The agent who dreamed up this reckless stunt was merely fired – and promptly rehired the next day.

On April 17, 2013, West was hit by tragedy when the West Fertilizer Company exploded, killing 15, injuring more than 160 people, and destroying or damaging more than 150 buildings. West has a large Czech population, like much of Central Texas, and shortly after the explosion, the Czech Republic donated $200,000 to assist with rebuilding the community. Officials later determined that the fire had been set on purpose.

If you stop in West, be sure to sample kolaches, the traditional individual fruit pies baked in multigeneration family bakeries in Texas's Czech communities. They are a treat that people drive miles to enjoy. You'll see savory versions in Austin's hipper areas, but there's nothing like stopping by the side of a backroad and enjoying a warm, fresh-baked fruit kolache with a cup of coffee.

THE BOSQUE

Twenty miles (32km) west of Hillsboro, across the Brazos River, is the region known as **Bosque County** (Spanish for "woods" and pronounced "boskay"). A number of Norwegians settled here as farmers between 1850 and 1875. They

Waco Suspension Bridge.

fiercely defended their log houses from attacks by the Kiowa and Comanche Indians. Many relics and household items used by these early Scandinavian settlers have been collected for display in **Bosque Memorial Museum** (301 S. Avenue Q; tel: 254-675-3845; www.bosquemuseum.org; Tue–Sat 10am–5pm) in **Clifton** ⑪ (pop. 3,420). Clifton's Nordic heritage is also celebrated with the Norse Smorgasbord each November, and the Norwegian County Christmas event the first weekend in December.

WACO

Until they were driven out, the Waco were a Wichita tribe occupying a site by the 840-mile (1,344km) -long Brazos River in Central Texas. When the whites first settled the area 160 years ago, they took **Waco** ⑫ as the name for their town. First came Fort Fisher, then and now a Texas Ranger outpost, but what really brought attention to the town was the construction, in 1870, of a massive suspension bridge across the river.

"That bridge was very important," explains local historian Roger Conger. "The Brazos was a veritable iron curtain across the center of Texas. After the Civil War, many Southerners were going west. They had to come to Waco to cross the river."

Eight bridges span the river within the city today, but the antique suspension bridge (now pedestrian-only) is still the most significant. When the 475ft (145-meter) bridge supplanted the ferry, it was the longest single-span suspension bridge west of the Mississippi River, and the second longest in the world. Supported by wire cables and 2.7 million Waco bricks, it was built by New York engineer Thomas Griffith from the plans of New York's Thomas Roebling, designer of the Brooklyn Bridge. Longhorns and wagon trains bound for the Chisholm Trail traversed it in its earliest days and, until 1889, a toll was charged: "five cents for each loose animal of the cattle kind."

EARLIEST SITE

Start at **Waco Mammoth Site** ⑬ (6220 Steinbeck Bend Drive; tel: 254-750-7946; www.nps.gov/waco/index.htm; daily 9am–5pm), where, beginning in 1978, 24 Columbian mammoths were uncovered along the Brazos River, the first and only recorded discovery of a nursery herd of Pleistocene mammoths. The site was excavated and cared for by Baylor University until 2009, when it was opened to the public as a city park funded by a nonprofit foundation. There is a museum and numerous activities for kids.

Some of the settlers who followed the Texas Rangers to this beautiful valley on the Brazos in the 1840s lived in log cabins on the site of what is now Cameron Park on Rotan Drive. You'll find woods, hiking trails, **Cameron Park Zoo** (1701 N. 4th Street; tel: 254-750-8400; www.cameronparkzoo.com; Mon–Sat 9am–5pm, Sun 11am–5pm), and **Miss Nellie's Pretty Place** (2602 N. University Parks Drive; tel: 254-750-5980), a wildflower preserve donated to the city by a former congressman's mother.

What the earliest settlement probably

Fact

The town of Waco was founded, and initially thrived, on the profits of five "C"s: cattle, cotton, corn, culture, and collegians.

Petrified dinosaur footprints in the Paluxy River, Dinosaur Valley State Park.

Baskets of peaches at a farmers' market in Waco.

looked like can be seen in the nine early buildings located next to the riverside Fort Fisher Campground in **The Governor Bill and Vara Daniel Historic Village** (One Bear Place #97154; tel: 254-710-1110; www.baylor.edu/mayborn; Mon–Sat 10am–5pm, Sun 1–5pm), on the campus of Baylor University. Inside its Mayborn Museum Complex, Baylor – the largest Baptist university in the world – houses the **Strecker's Cabinet of Curiosities** (tel: 254-710-1110; Mon–Sat 10am–5pm, Sun 1–5pm; free), devoted to natural history. Also on campus is the fascinating, marble-columned **Armstrong Browning Library** (710 Speight Avenue; tel: 254-710-3566; www.browninglibrary.org; Mon–Fri 9am–5pm, Sat 10am–2pm; free), which exhibits portraits of, and 4,000 letters written by or to, the Victorian poets Robert and Elizabeth Barrett Browning. The library's collection – assembled by Baylor's late Professor A.J. Armstrong – is supplemented by 50 lovely stained glass windows depicting verses by the poetic pair.

Between the Baylor campus and US 81 is the **Tourist Information Center** (106 Texas Ranger Trail; tel: 254-750-8696; www.wacoheartoftexas.com), adjoining the **First Street Cemetery**, which contains Confederate graves. Other attractions are the **Texas Sports Hall of Fame** (1108 University Parks Drive; tel: 254-756-1633; www.tshof.org; Mon–Sat 9am–5pm), where kids can try on helmets of the Houston Oilers or Dallas Cowboys, and the **Texas Ranger Hall of Fame and Museum** (100 Texas Ranger Trail; tel: 254-750-8631; www.texasranger.org; daily 9am–5pm). Jim Bowie's knife and the rifle he carried at the Alamo are here, as well as a jewel-studded saddle (which cost $5,800 in 1903), novelist James Michener's typewriter, the pistol Pat Garrett used to kill Billy the Kid, and enough of the early Rangers' Colt revolvers to equip an army. If you're interested in Texas history, this is definitely a place you won't want to miss.

SIX-SHOOTER JUNCTION

In its prime, Waco was a rough cowtown. "Next stop, Waco," the train conductors would yell as the train approached, "Get out your six-shooters." The last legal

Inside the Dr Pepper Museum.

DR PEPPER MUSEUM

The fun Dr Pepper Museum (300 S. 5th Street; tel: 254-757-1025; www.drpeppermuseum.com; Mon–Sat 10am–5.30pm, Sun noon–5pm) is dedicated to the famous soft drink, which was invented in Waco's Old Corner Drug Store by pharmacist Charles Alderton in 1885. His boss, Dr Morrison, named it Dr Pepper but the reason remains unclear. The museum is housed in a bottling plant opened in 1906. It covers the history of Dr Pepper and the soft drink industry, including Big Red, a drink that was invented a block away. You can sample traditional sodas and sundaes at the museum's soda fountain; there is no entrance fee if you just go in for a drink. The site is on the National Register of Historic Places, but Dr Pepper has not been produced here since the 1920s.

hanging in Texas occurred here in 1923, witnessed by over 4,000 people, and, in 1955, a Waco television station was the first in the world to broadcast a murder trial. A more genteel era is reflected by the city's group of 19th-century homes, operated from the gingerbread-style Hoffmann House by the **Historic Waco Foundation** (810 S. 4th Street; tel: 254-753-5166; www.historicwaco.org; Mon–Fri 8.30am–5pm, Sat–Sun 1–4pm). The foundation also hosts the annual Brazos River Festival in April.

Two of these Victorian homes lie between I-35 and Waco Drive and can be toured on Tuesday through Sunday. They are the Greek Revival **Earle-Napier-Kinnard House** (814 S. 4th Street), completed in 1869, and the Italianate **East Terrace (100 Mill Street)**, shielded by large elm and pecan trees, with walks down to the river. Home of industrialist John Wesley Mann, *c.*1872, it contains original furniture.

CONFEDERATE SUPPORT

At 1901 N. Fifth Street, the **Earle-Harrison House** (tel: 254-753-2032; www.earleharrison.com; rentals and tours available by appointment), sitting in 5-acre (2-hectare) gardens, is gloriously furnished. Portraits of General Robert E. Lee abound in some of these old homes, a reminder that Waco's men marched off to support Confederate armies in the Civil War.

A total of six Confederate generals hailed from Waco, which has also been home to former Texas Governor Ann Richards and Madison Alexander Cooper Jr, whose 840,000-word novel, *Sironia, Texas* – on view in the public library – is said to be the longest ever written.

Another among Waco's dozen or more museums is the hometown **Helen Marie Taylor Museum of Waco History** (701 Jefferson; tel: 254-752-4774). Just five years after it opened, the museum closed, however, various organizations are working to re-open it. At this time, 10 or more people can take self-guided tours in the museum upon request. It sits on the site of one of the Waco tribe's main villages.

AUSTIN BOUND

Like most towns south of Waco, **Temple** ⓮ and **Belton** ⓯ were originally built around loading pens and general stores about a century ago. Today, the area is known primarily for the commanding presence of **Fort Hood**, the largest military base in the US, which is set on no fewer than 217,000 acres (87,800 hectares), near Lake Benton. The base is one of the primary training grounds for US soldiers dispatched to Iraq and other global assignments. It was also the site of a horrific mass shooting in 2009 that resulted in 13 deaths by a US Army Major and psychiatrist. The main drag of nearby Harker Heights is lined with car dealerships, eating places, and fairly rowdy nightclubs.

Two historic army divisions maintain museums at Fort Hood: the **1st Cavalry Museum** on Headquarters

Tip

For fans of the HGTV program, *Fixer Upper*, the city created the Magnolia Trail (https://wacoheartoftexas.com/magnolia-trail), a self-guided walking tour. Along the tour you'll visit many of the shops, restaurants, and attractions mentioned in the show.

The Waco Hippodrome on Austin Avenue.

Fact

The settlement of Bryan/College Station is actually two towns, not one. Bryan, founded in 1859, was joined, in 1877, by College Station, developed as a railroad stop and a new site for A&M University.

Avenue and the **Third Calvary Museum** on Battalion Avenue (both open daily; free; bring proof of ID). Kids will enjoy sitting atop a tank and learning about soldiers here.

LIFE AND DEATH

There are a number of eateries in the Temple-Killeen area, and, in addition to plenty of hearty Texan specialties, they offer a good opportunity to observe small-town life. In fact, Texan-watching is at its best while sawing a batter-fried corn dog or a chickenfried steak, a cheap cut of hammered beef breaded like fried chicken and served with potatoes and gravy, a country dish invented in Texas.

In towns like Temple, Belton, and **Killeen** ⓰, there is still much pleasure to be taken in daily life. They have their characters, language tricks, and private jokes as anywhere else, possibly more, since the storytelling tradition remains strong in both rural and urban Texas. In this region, times are changing: Temple-Killeen's Standard Metropolitan Statistical Area is one of the 10 fastest-growing in Texas.

Bell Country Courthouse, Belton.

LOCAL HISTORY

I-35 follows the railroad – beside the Chisholm Trail, along which cattle were driven to rail-heads farther north – so busy Temple is a logical place to find the **Temple Railroad and Heritage Museum** (315 W. Avenue B; tel: 254-298-5172; www.templerrhm.org; Tue–Sat 10am–4pm) in the 1910 Santa Fe depot at 31st Street and Avenue H. It houses a steam engine and railroad equipment.

The **Czech Heritage Museum and Genealogy Center** (119 W. French Ave; tel: 254-899-2935; www.czechheritagemuseum.org; Tue–Sat 10am–4pm) exhibits an unusual collection related to Czech immigration. Preserved artifacts include a bible dated 1530. The **Bell County Museum** in Belton (201 N. Main Street; tel: 254-933-5243; www.bellcountymuseum.org; Tue–Fri noon–5pm, Sat 10am–5pm, free), is a local history museum occupying a 1905 Carnegie Library building.

FARMS AND PLANTATIONS

The pretty little town of **Salado** ⓱, once a stage stop on Salado Creek, a few miles south of Killeen, is best known for its popular and picturesque historic **Stagecoach Inn** (416 S. Main Street; tel: 254-947-5111; www.stagecoachsalado.com), a motel with 48 rooms, pool, and a restaurant with mid-19th-century antecedents. Across the street is the **Central Texas Area Museum** (423 S. Main Street; tel: 254-947-5232; www.saladoscottishfestival.com; Mon–Sat 10am–4pm), housed in a lovely old rock building where Sam Houston delivered an anti-secession speech from the balcony. In addition to displaying local memorabilia, it hosts the annual Scottish Clan Gathering and Highland Games in November, a three-day Celtic festival.

Texas's first chapter of the Grange, an important organization of anti-corporate American farmers that flourished during the Progressive era, was founded at Salado in 1873. The related

Farmers' Alliance, which had several million members throughout the country in its most successful days, originated at Lampasas, about 50 miles (80km) west of Fort Hood, in 1875. Together they helped elect the famous Populist James Stephen Hogg, who was governor of Texas 1891–95.

Near the I-35 access road at Salado, the antebellum **Robertson Plantation House** is unusually complete, with outbuildings, slave quarters, and a family cemetery. It was built in 1856 by E.S.C. Robertson, son of Sterling Clack Robertson, who settled 600 families in the Brazos River Basin, northwest of Stephen F. Austin's colony.

The steady character, intelligence, and diligence with which Austin won the respect of his fellow "Texans" were also displayed by E.S.C. Robertson. One of the directors of his "Nashville Company" was Sam Houston, who had already been the governor of Tennessee and later became both president of the Texas Republic and governor of the state of Texas.

The complex, ultimately unsuccessful attempt to turn the early settlers into Mexican citizens makes a long and stirring story. The patriarch Moses Austin, father of Stephen, who did not live to see the Anglo-Southerners enter the Promised Land, had wished to give his name to a great port, Austina, which would rival New Orleans. Instead, a new capital in the wilderness was named for the Father and Grandfather of Texas. The now abandoned town of **Nashville**, one of the principal settlements of Robertson's colony, was also considered for the capital. If Nashville had been made capital of Texas instead of Austin, Robertson would be better known today.

COLLEGE TOWN

Austin, home of the University of Texas (UT), is the state's best-known college town, but the campus of Texas A&M University in the metro area of **Bryan/College Station** 18 (pop. 250,000), northeast of Austin, is even larger – some 69,000 students are now enrolled at A&M, while UT currently enrolls 51,000.

A great rivalry exists between A&M and UT. A&M receives a third of the oil revenue from public lands (endowed before the hidden oil was discovered on them), but UT receives the remaining two-thirds. In the budget wars between the Austin campus and the state government, politicians have depicted UT to rural and poor voters as an arrogant, wasteful, privileged school. Part of this has to do with Austin being a bastion of liberal politics, of course, in contrast to the state's general conservatism.

Texans are fond of Aggies (the nickname for students at the university) – trusting, stalwart, and stupid, as portrayed in the innumerable Aggie jokes. Watching an Aggies football game on the huge **Kyle Field** – at 102,000 capacity, the fourth largest stadium in the US – is an unforgettable experience. The roar of the crowd is absolutely deafening. You'll be caught

Fact

The Fourth of July Celebration and PRCA Rodeo (tel: 254-939-3551) in Belton takes place every Independence Day on Nolan Creek. It's a community picnic and barbecue event as well as a professional rodeo filled with six-second cowboys and thrills and spills.

A sculpture entitled The Day the Wall Came Down outside the George Bush Presidential Library and Museum.

Fact

Notorious bandit Sam Bass was high on the Texas Rangers' wanted list. They finally got their man in 1878, after a tip-off about a planned bank raid in Round Rock. They set an ambush, and Bass was badly injured in the gunfight. He died two days later.

up in the "12th man" tradition, for sure – whereby the entire stadium remains standing for the whole game, a tradition that began in 1922, apparently, during a difficult fixture, when the fans let their team know that they were all ready to serve as the "12th man" to help them out, if need be.

Tours of the enormous A&M campus can be arranged at the **Appelt Aggieland Visitor Center** (tel: 979-845-5851; www.tamu.edu; Mon–Fri 8am–5pm) in the Rudder Tower. Among the attractions on campus are the Sanders-Metzger Gun Collection (free), displaying famous Colt pistols and the George Bush Presidential Library and Museum (1000 George Bush Drive West; tel: 979-691-4000; Mon–Sat 9.30am–5pm, Sun noon–5pm). Bush senior was an A&M student, and the museum houses a record of, and papers from, his presidency.

INDEPENDENCE SITE

Continuing its journey down to the Gulf of Mexico, the Brazos River reflects significant dates in Texas history at many points along its route. Eighty miles (128km) southeast of Waco, at **Washington-on-the-Brazos** ⓳ in 1836, Texas declared its independence from Mexico. Then the river was the lifeblood of the fledgling republic, as can be seen in the **Star of the Republic Museum** (tel: 936-878-2461; www.starmuseum.org; open daily).

INNER SPACE CAVERN

At Temple, you can either proceed down I-35 to Austin through **Jarrell** ⓴, an old Czech community with a stagecoach stop, or head south on State Route 95, a picturesque alternative with interesting small towns. (Note: This highway bypasses Austin, so keep an eye out for west-bound US 79 or US 290, to reach the city.)

Inner Space Cavern ㉑ (tel: 512-931-2283; www.innerspacecavern.com; Mon–Fri 9am–4pm, Sat 10am–5pm, Sun 11am–5pm), on I-35 near Georgetown, is one of Texas's most accessible caves. Its large rooms are unusual in this part of the state, and the tour takes visitors into the most beautiful of them.

A football game at Kyle Field.

These caves, the springs, and the change in topography – especially noticeable between Austin and San Antonio – are due to the geological activity that created the Balcones Fault Zone, which runs alongside I-35 from Mexico up to Oklahoma. The ground rose to the west, producing what the Spanish called *los balcones* (balconies), and the springs, around which early settlements grew, gushed up through fissures in the rock. This important geological formation divides East and West Texas.

ROUND ROCK

In **Round Rock** ㉒, 10 miles (16km) south of Georgetown on Brushy Creek, the eroded round rock, for which the city was named, was used to gauge the depth of the water of Bushy Creek, which was crossed by the old Chisholm Trail. Some of the buildings alongside the stage route were built as early as the 1850s.

Sam Bass, the legendary train and stagecoach robber, who claimed never to have killed a man, was ambushed by Texas Rangers in the 100 block of East Main on July 19, 1878. Businesses and condominium blocks are named after the outlaw, who became more famous after he was killed than he had ever been when alive. His grave is in the northwest corner of **Old Round Rock Cemetery** on Sam Bass Road, west of the intersection with Old Chisholm Trail. Covered with wildflowers in spring, the cemetery is easy to find and has an Anglo section, with crooked and cracked Victorian monuments, and a more colorful, smaller Mexican section, with paper and plastic flowers on the graves.

The **Palm House Museum** (212 E. Main Street; tel: 512-255-5805; Mon–Fri; free) doubles as the Round Rock Chamber of Commerce office and adjoins a pharmacy that still has the pressed-tin ceiling once common in small-town stores. Another famous Round Rock son was Vander Clyde, a renowned aerialist, who had great success in Paris in the 1920s. Clyde made his entrance in an evening dress, completely convincing as a woman, and performed to the music of Wagner and Rimsky-Korsakov.

Round Rock is also home to **Dell Diamond**, where the minor league baseball team Round Rock Express (a farm team of the Houston Astros) plays its games.

SNAKE SACKING

US 79 East is the road to **Taylor** ㉓, famous for its barbecue and annual snake sacking contest. Snake sacking is highly controversial. Have the rattlesnakes been stunned or their mouths sewn up with monofilament? Animal lovers demonstrate outside, while the snake handlers, usually covered with bites, say all that preparation would be too much trouble.

It's something to contemplate as you head to Austin, where the snakepit of politics keeps things lively at the state capitol while the rest of this liberal college town eases on down to the beat of a hundred different bands.

Fact

The armadillo, the State Mammal, is commonly found in rural Central Texas.

Stalactites at the Inner Space Cavern.

View of Congress Avenue and the State Capitol Building.

AUSTIN

The laid-back Texas state capital – home to the University of Texas, live music, and foodies – attracts lovers of high and low culture, and everything in between.

The Texas state capital of Austin (pop. 950,000) – now one of the nation's fastest growing and most attractive cities – has cemented its popularity by making numerous Top 10 lists in the US in recent years: coolest, best for jobs, best college town, best for doing business, fastest-growing tech center, best to retire, best for women, best for LGBTQ, best for live music and culture, best barbecue, best to visit... the list goes on. Suffice it to say: Austin is a very happening place these days.

Fueling a boom in downtown redevelopment; a burgeoning jobs market and skilled workforce, particularly in Austin's "Silicon Hills" high-tech sector; and growth on every front is Austin's double act as both state capital and true cultural capital. These strange bedfellows have helped cement Austin's reputation as one of America's top "creative cities," a term coined by sociologist Richard Florida to describe that unique mix of jobs, culture, services, low cost of living, affordable housing, liveability, and general exuberance that makes a city interesting to creative people. This is the home of Whole Foods, hipsters, South by Southwest, movie stars, localism to "Keep Austin Weird," University of Texas (UT), and the acknowledged "Live Music Capital of the World" – a bastion of liberal politics and environmentalism surrounded by a conservative state whose demographics are rapidly changing in Austin's favor. Just about everything is on the table.

Austin gained both its state capitol and UT campus in the early 1880s, but set at the edge of the ranchlands of rural Hill Country it remained a backwater for decades. It began earning its cultural chops during the 1960s, when it was a hippie mecca. It went on to spearhead the "outlaw country" movement of the 1970s, when country singers like Willie Nelson, Waylon Jennings, and Jerry Jeff Walker first

Main attractions

State Capitol
Bullock Texas State History Museum
Barton Springs Pool in Zilker Park
Driskill Hotel
Lyndon B. Johnson Library and Museum
Lady Bird Johnson Wildflower Center

Map on page 145

Tapas bar on Sixth Street.

> **Fact**
> The Texas State Capitol Building is the largest of all the state capitols in the United States and, on completion, was thought to have been the seventh biggest building in the world.

came to prominence at places like the now-closed Armadillo World Headquarters and other legendary Austin music venues. The music scene has been bolstered for over 40 years by the popular PBS television live concert series, *Austin City Limits*, originally recorded in a small studio on the UT campus and now housed in its own purpose-built theater downtown. The TV series led to an annual Austin City Limits Music Festival, and more recently, the immensely popular South by Southwest (SXSW) Festival, which draws acts from all over the world and has spawned a concurrent film and tech festival.

Yet another boom came in the 1990s, with the arrival of high tech companies attracted by a never-ending crop of highly skilled UT grads who wanted to stay put in Austin, a business-friendly environment, low taxes, and that constant – quality of life. In recent years, the film industry has also taken a shine to Austin, which has served as the location for movies by local directors like Richard Linklater and Terrence Malick. A number of movie stars make their home here, along with various writers, artists, and other creatives who appreciate Austin's easy-going style and attractive mix of Victorian neighborhoods and modern downtown architecture.

WALKING DOWNTOWN

Austin spreads out on either side of Texas's Colorado River, which rises in Lubbock and flows through the state capital. It is dammed in places to form small lakes that offer kayaking, swimming, birding, and a chance to enjoy nature in several riparian nature reserves within sight of downtown. There are lots of places to walk along the river. The **Boardwalk Trail** is next to **Lady Bird Lake**, on the southeast side of town, next to I-35. It is popular for its fabulous views of the changing downtown skyline to the north, lit up at night in a blaze of neon.

Although Austin is growing, its downtown is relatively easy to get around. It is dominated by government buildings, notably the distinctive **State Capitol Building** Ⓐ (1100 Congress Avenue;

City skyline.

tel: 512-463-4630; https://tspb.texas.gov/prop/tc/tc/capitol.html; free guided tours), which, in typically Texas style, is 14 feet (4.2m) higher than its model in Washington, DC. The local version is made of distinctive pink granite. Its white, classical interior focuses on the great rotunda, commemorating the six governments that reigned over Texas: Spain, France, Mexico, the Confederacy, the Republic of Texas, and the United States. Above, at the apex of the dome, is the lone star that is the state's emblem: independence, self-determination, and singularity. Construction began in 1882 but the building was not completed until 1888. A thorough renovation was completed in 1995, and includes an underground extension, its roof landscaped to fit in with the historic wooded grounds.

The **State Capitol Visitors Center** is in the Old Land Office building (112 East 11th St.; tel: 512-305-8400; open daily), a distinctive castle-like building southeast of the capitol. Informative 2-hour walking tours down historic Congress Avenue and along Sixth Street start from the capitol steps at (contact the Austin Visitor Center, 602 E. 4th Street; tel: 866-GO-AUSTIN; open daily).

Across from the capitol is the Greek Revival-style **Governor's Mansion** B (1010 Colorado Street; tel: 512-305-8524; www.txfgm.org; free tours Wed, Thu, Fri 2–4pm). This elegant building was constructed in 1856 by Abner Cook, master builder of many of Austin's most significant 19th-century buildings.

The enjoyable **Bullock Texas State History Museum** C (tel: 512-936-8746; www.thestoryoftexas.com; open daily), behind the capitol on the 357-acre (145-hectare) UT campus, is housed in an attractive modern building constructed from the same pink granite as the capitol. Its soaring Texas-sized atrium contains three floors of well-presented audiovisual exhibits covering the state's American Indian, Spanish, and American history, as well as an IMAX theater. This is the best place in Texas to learn about its history – and there's a lot here for kids to enjoy, too.

Art lovers won't want to miss a visit to the **Blanton Museum of Art** (200 E. Martin Luther King Boulevard; tel: 512-471-7324; www.blantonmuseum.org; Tue–Fri 10am–5pm, Sat 11am–5pm, Sun 1–5pm) across the street from the Bullock Museum. The Blanton houses one of the top university art collections in the US and it is quite wide ranging, with more than 17,000 pieces, including an extensive European art collection and drawings and prints. It's likely to appeal to all tastes.

The UT campus has four excellent museums and takes up a large part of downtown Austin. It has a current enrollment of 51,000 students, somewhat less than Texas A&M, its varsity nemesis. The rivalry between the two schools is on full display during football games in UT's Darrell K. Royal – Texas Memorial Stadium, home to the college's Texas Longhorns team (who play in orange). Guided tours of the campus's landmark **UT Tower** and

State Capitol Building.

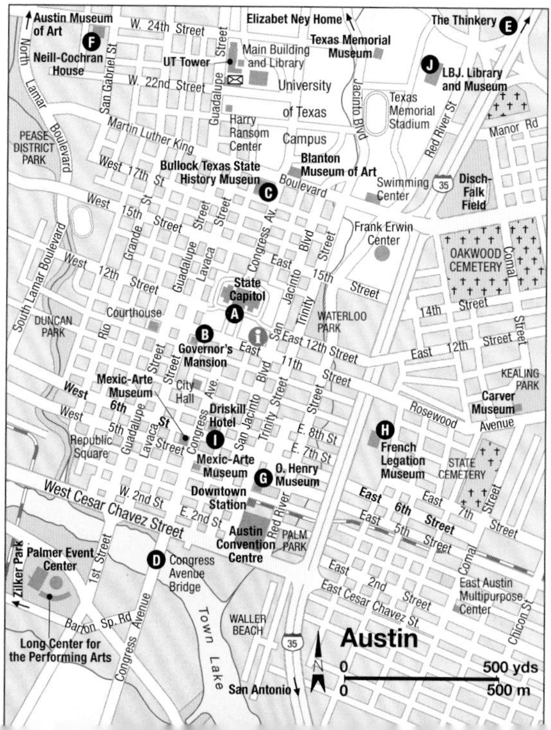

Visitors to the Bullock Texas State History Museum are greeted by a 35ft (11-meter) -tall bronze sculpture of the Lone Star.

observation deck are offered daily (tel: 512-475-6633).

SIXTH STREET VIBES

As the home of the University of Texas (UT), the city melds an air of youthful exuberance with legislative seriousness, but it is primarily a college town with all that that implies. Only a few blocks from the capitol complex – the heart of state government – renowned **Sixth Street** (www.6street.com) reverberates with rock, jazz, blues, country, and reggae until the early hours.

The seven blocks between Congress and I-35, lined with historic buildings that now contain tattoo parlors, clubs, cafés, antiques stores, and art galleries, are a bit touristy now, but you can still catch some good music here. Festivals like South by Southwest, the Pecan Street Festival, and other annual events take place here. This is also the venue for some great food, including Tex-Mex, Cajun, and of course, the famed "Texas Trinity" of barbecue ribs, sausage, and brisket (whose Holy Grail is **Franklin Barbecue** on 11th Street, east of I-35, voted Best Barbecue in America).

SOUTH CONGRESS

Austin's other hip venue is **South Congress**, popularly known as SoCo. Its lively galleries, funky shops, and eclectic cafés come alive during its popular **First Thursday** event every month, when businesses stay open until 10pm. Many Austinites enjoy the monthly see-and-be-seen block party atmosphere during the stroll between Barton Springs Road and Elizabeth Street. The 1938 **Austin Motel** (1220 S. Congress Avenue; tel: 512-441-1157; www.austinmotel.com) is in this area, a fun place for budget travelers who yearn for simple retro digs in the heart of the action. There's even a kidney-shaped pool.

Several award-winning Austin hotels can be found in the gentrifying **Warehouse District**, bordering downtown and Second Street, along with boutiques, bars, clubs, and restaurants. It's also where you'll find most of Austin's best LGBTQ bars, like Highland Lounge. The artist-founded **Mexic-Arte**

Bats over Ann W. Richards Congress Avenue Bridge.

Museum (419 Congress Avenue; tel: 512-480-9373; www.mexic-artemuseum.org; Mon–Thu 10am–6pm, Fri–Sat 10am–5pm, Sun noon–5pm), focusing on traditional and contemporary Mexican and other Latin American art and culture, is well worth a visit.

RAINEY STREET

On either side of Rainey Street are a collection of charming, historic bungalows that have been transformed into commercial businesses, and consequently, one of Austin's most happening neighborhoods. The tightly-packed street is home to a mix of restaurants and boutiques with funky outdoor seating like hammocks on patios and colorful picnic tables. Many visitors opt for snacks and meals from the food trucks found in the Rainey Street Food Truck Lot. At night, the bars come to life with live bands and the beats of local DJs, making Rainey Street a popular nightlife alternative that's just a 15-minute walk from Downtown.

If you'd like to stay on Rainey Street, **Hotel Van Zandt** is a great boutique with a music-themed décor. Nearby is the **Emma S. Barientos Mexican American Cultural Center** (512-974-3772; www.austintexas.gov/esbmacc; Mon–Thu 10am–6pm, Fri 10am–5.30pm, Sat 10am–4pm), from which you can start the **Tejano Walking Trail** (www.austintexas.org/listings/tejano-walking-trail/10104), a 4.9-mile (7.8km) walking trail with 24 sites that focus on Tejano history in Austin in the East Cesar Chavez and Holly neighborhoods.

BAT HEAVEN

Surely one of the city's most unusual tourist attractions must be the colony of more than a million Mexican free-tailed bats that congregate under **Ann W. Richards Congress Avenue Bridge** **D** over Town Lake. At dusk, they set off in search of food. Between spring and fall, crowds gather every evening for a spectacle that can be thrilling.

The Austin–San Antonio area was called "bat heaven" by Dr. Merlin Tuttle, the founder and president of Bat Conservation International. Most of the bats in this part of the country are Brazilian or Mexican free-tails. The largest known bat colony in the world is found in the "nursery cave," Bracken Cave near San Antonio, where experts say there are an estimated 500 baby bats per square foot.

Bats also figure in **The Thinkery** **E** (1830 Simond Avenue; tel: 512-469-6200; http://thinkeryaustin.org; Mon 9am–noon, Tue–Fri, Sun 10am–5pm, Wed until 8pm, Sat 10am–6pm), a fun, hands-on, educational facility in a purpose-designed modern building in Mueller, Austin's important reclamation project in the northeast-central part of the city. Learning how these mammals fly is just one of the experiences they've offered to families, alongside discovering how cities work, learning about health matters, and more. The museum calls it STEAM (science, technology, engineering, art, and math) learning.

Beside Town Lake, on the south side of the bridge, is lovely **Zilker Nature**

Fact

Food trucks are a big deal in Austin and there are over 1,000 of them dotted around the city. Some of the best include Mighty Cone (fried chicken in a cone), Hey, Cupcake (cupcakes), Coat and Thai (Thai food), and Luke's Inside Out (brunch buffet).

Crowds enjoy a brass band on Sixth Street during the South by Southwest festival.

Fact

The Star of Texas Fair and Rodeo (tel: 512-919-3000; www.rodeoaustin.com) takes place in Austin in March.

Preserve, home of **Barton Springs Pool** (tel: 512-974-6300; open daily), generally regarded as the city's crown jewel. Thirty-two million gallons (121 million liters) of water a day flow from Barton Springs into this idyllic swimming hole, which was reinforced as a pool almost as long as a football field in 1930. The water temperature supposedly hovers around 68°F (20°C), but it feels much colder at first splash.

ELEGANT MUSEUMS

Some lovely historic buildings around town have now been converted into museums, and several are worth your time. **The Contemporary Austin** (700 Congress Avenue; tel: 512-453-5312; www.thecontemporaryaustin.org; Tue–Sat 11am–7pm; Sun noon–5pm) has two locations, one of which is in Laguna Gloria (3809 West 35th Street; tel: 512-458-8191), on the shady banks of Lake Austin. It occupies the 1916 estate of Texas legend Clare Driscoll, who donated the property, and includes the Driscoll Villa, the Betty and Edward Marcus Sculpture Park, and an art school. The downtown branch, the **Jones Center** (700 Congress Avenue; tel: 512-453-5312), is in an old drugstore building on the site of the first brick building in Austin, built in 1851, and displays a variety of contemporary artworks.

The 1855 Greek Revival–style **Neill-Cochran House** F (2310 San Gabriel Street; tel: 512-478-2335; www.nchmuseum.org; Wed–Sun 1–4pm), a few blocks west of the UT campus, is considered to be one of Austin's three most important buildings and also built by Abner Cook. It is now the Texas home of the grandly titled National Society of the Colonial Dames of America in the State of Texas and archives various historic documents as well as displaying luxurious period furnishings.

The **O. Henry Museum** G (409 E. 5th Street; tel: 512-974-1398; www.austintexas.gov/department/o-henry-museum; Wed–Sun noon–5pm; free) was the residence of short-story writer William Sydney Porter (who used "O. Henry" as a pen name) from 1893 to 1895 (he also lived in San Antonio). The home displays

STEAM learning at The Thinkery.

Porter's desk and writing materials, as well as some period furniture.

HISTORIC SITES

The oldest frame building in the city is the **French Legation Museum** Ⓗ (802 San Marcos Street, east of I-35; tel: 512-463-7948; www.thc.texas.gov/historic-sites/french-legation-state-historic-site; Tue–Sun 1–5pm), a Creole-style mansion built in 1840 by Comte Alphonse Dubois de Saligny, French chargé d'affaires, who may never actually have lived in it. Saligny served under Maximilian I, the short-lived French-born emperor of Mexico who was executed in 1867, aged 35. It is a tradition in Normandy, where Saligny bought a château after making himself rich in America, for villagers to "dance on the old count's grave."

In the Maximilian Room of Austin's **Driskill Hotel** Ⓘ (604 Brazos Street; tel: 512-439-1234; www.driskillhotel.com), you can see mirrors ordered by the tragic Maximilian for his mad Empress Carlotta. The Driskill, whose second owner is said to have won it in a poker game and swapped it five years later for a California vineyard, is a dramatic building that has stood at the western corner of the historic Sixth Street block since 1886, among other Victorian buildings now doing time as trendy bars and restaurants.

Farther north is the **Elisabet Ney Museum** (304 E. 44th Street; tel: 512-974-1625; www.austintexas.gov/Elisabet-ney; Wed–Sun noon–5pm; free), the former home of German sculptor Elisabet Ney, who immigrated to the state in 1870, and whose marble busts and statues grace many European palaces. Three of her statues are in the State Capitol. Her best-known sculpture is considered to be Lady Macbeth; the original is in the Smithsonian in Washington, DC, but you can see a copy here in her studio, along with many other items from her collection. This is one of Austin's oldest museums.

The Elisabet Ney Museum is close to Austin's increasingly busy **Austin-Bergstrom International Airport** (3600 Presidential Boulevard; tel: 512-530-2242; www.austintexas.gov/airport/), which recently expanded to serve the 12 million passengers who pass through it each year.

TEXAN PRESIDENT

The most famous Texas-born US President is memorialized in the grand **Lyndon B. Johnson Library and Museum** Ⓙ (2313 Red River Street; tel: 512-721-0200; www.lbjlibrary.org; open daily 9am–5pm; free) on the UT campus. The building was renovated recently to include more audiovisual displays (but thankfully, still has the famous animatronic LBJ greeting visitors with stories, a la Disney's Lincoln).

During his presidency (1963–69), Johnson was the recipient of hundreds of gifts from foreign heads of state, and most of them seem to be here, along with his 1968 Lincoln limousine. There is also an interesting gift shop with authentic political memorabilia. Humanizing his life from boyhood onwards, the

Fact

The Lyndon B. Johnson Library and Museum contains a replica of the Oval Office in the White House, as it looked when LBJ was president in the 1960s.

The Driskill Hotel.

exhibitions include a 20-minute multimedia show, as well as a one-hour film about Lady Bird Johnson, who is sometimes regarded with more affection than America's controversial 36th president.

For years, Lady Bird devoted herself to getting the **Lady Bird Johnson Wildflower Center** (4801 La Crosse Avenue; tel: 512-232-0100; www.wildflower.org; open daily 9am–5pm), established on 60 acres (24 hectares), it has since grown to 284 acres (115 hectares) along Texas's Colorado River. About 8 miles (13km) southwest of Austin, it is a fine place for picnics among the flowers and a must-see for gardeners. It has a visitor center, a library, and "Ralph, the talking lawnmower." The focus of the center is to conserve Texas's native plants and promote sustainable native landscaping.

DAY TRIPS FROM AUSTIN

Among the best places to see wildflowers, especially Texas bluebonnets, the state flower, blooming in the spring, is in the rolling Hill Country, which begins just west of Austin. LBJ grew up in these lovely ranchlands and taught school there. His ranch and boyhood home is still a popular destination, and a lake is named for him (see page 157).

To the east and southeast of Austin the land is flat and fertile. In **La Grange**, where the "Best Little Whorehouse in Texas" once stood, you'll find the **Texas Quilt Museum** (140 W. Colorado Street; tel: 979-968-3104; www.texasquiltmuseum.org; Thu–Sat 10am–4pm, Sun noon–4pm), housed in an old mercantile building. The museum grew out of the popular International Quilt Festival in Houston as a permanent venue to display quilts from all over the world, both contemporary and traditional. It has won several awards for the restoration of its building and for its exhibits, and is a must for quilters.

Not far away, **Shiner**, founded by German-Czech farmers in 1909, is home to **Spoetzl Brewery** (603 E. Brewery Street; tel: 361-594-3383; www.shiner.com; gift shop Mon–Sat 9am–5pm, Sun noon–5pm; tours Mon–Fri 11am, 1pm, 4pm, Sat 11am–4pm, Sun 1.30 and 3.30pm; tours and tastings are free), where Texas's famous Shiner Bock beers are brewed.

The wetland pond at the Lady Bird Johnson Wildflower Center.

KEEP AUSTIN WEIRD

The slogan "Keep Austin Weird" can be found on many bumper stickers, mugs, and t-shirts in Austin. It refers to an anti-big business campaign used to promote local Austin businesses and local culture and perfectly sums up Austin's pride in being funky and original. The term originated in comments made on a radio station in 2000 by Red Wassenich, who tried unsuccessfully to copyright the term. Wassenich operates the website www.keepaustinweird.com and has written *Keep Austin Weird: A Guide to the Odd Side of Town*. The weird movement has now become a cultural phenomenon, highlighting the "shop local" concept and the power of the individual. It has spread from Austin to other communities in the West, including Portland, Oregon, and Santa Cruz, California.

Kayaks on Barton Springs.

A colorful display of Texas bluebonnets and Indian paintbrush.

HILL COUNTRY

The Hill Country is a Texas treasure, offering natural beauty, abundant wildlife, an intriguing slice of German culture, and some of the friendliest towns in the state.

One of the most scenic towns in the Hill Country of Central Texas, a gentle area of sheep and cattle raising, is **Bandera** ❶ (the name is Spanish for "flag"), which describes itself as "the cowboy capital of the world". Bordered on three sides by the cypress-lined Medina River its origins date to 1854, when a lumber mill was established. However, in the 1870s, it became a staging area for cattle drives through Bandera Pass, where, in the 1840s, the Texas Rangers beat off a Comanche ambush.

Bandera (pop. 898) is reputed to have once had a school operated by John Wilkes Booth under the name William J. Ryan. The old jail, one block north of the County Courthouse, is now the **Frontier Times Museum** (510 13th Street; tel: 830-796-3864; www.frontiertimesmuseum.org; Mon–Sat 10am–4.30pm), which has 30,000 pieces from early Texas cultures and items of technology from the 19th and 20th centuries. Exhibits include a totem pole, a wooden idol from Easter Island, and a 400-year-old pair of stirrups that once belonged to a conquistador. Bandera's Main Street also has two renowned honky-tonk dancehalls. Between May and Labor Day, there are rodeos once a week on Fridays, and in front of the Bandera Courthouse stands a bronze monument honoring the many national rodeo champions who lived in the town.

PRETEND COWBOYS

Before the close of the 19th century, Bandera was already a popular vacation area for families from Houston. They would be entertained by hard-riding ranch hands from nearby spreads who would ride in on weekends to show off, and gradually the concept of the "dude," or vacation cowboy, developed. Today the Bandera area has dozens of dude ranches, with names like Silver Spur (tel: 830-796-3037; www.silverspur-ranch.com); the Dixie (tel: 830-796-7771; www.dixieduderanch.com); 2E Twin Elm Guest Ranch (tel:

Main attractions

Enchanted Rock State Natural Area
Fredericksburg
Luckenbach
Lyndon B. Johnson National Historical Park
Gruene Hall

Map on page 154

Down on the ranch.

Fact

Southwest of Bandera, Ney Cave was used during World War II for Project X-Ray, a plan to drop thousands of bats, carrying firebombs, on Japan. In a practice run, the bats returned to their home base, "dropping bombs" on US planes; the strategy was scrapped.

830-796-3628; www.twinelmranch.com); the Flying L (tel: 830-796-7745; www.flyingl.com); the West 1077 (tel: 830-796-5675; www.west1077.com); and, on the Medina River, the Mayan (tel: 830-460-3312; www.mayanranch.com), nearly all offering comfortable accommodations, swimming pools, Western cuisine, cowboy-themed entertainment and horseback-riding lessons. Some offer additional attractions such as golf and fishing.

Also of interest is a self-guided tour of the **LH7 Ranch** a 1,200-acre (485-hectare) ranch bought in 1982 by Maudeen Marks, whose family is dedicated to preserving the Texas longhorn. At **Mountain Home** ❷, near Kerrville, the **Y.O. Ranch** (tel: 830-257-4440; www.yoranchhotel.com) welcomes wildlife lovers, who can expect to see white-tail deer, antelope, and a majestic longhorn or two.

At **Kerrville** ❸ itself, music plays a big part in everyday life, with the Kerrville Folk Festival in late spring/early summer (tel: 830-257-3600; www.kerrvillefolkfestival.org). The town's **Museum of Western Art** (1550 Bandera Highway; tel: 830-896-2553; www.museumofwesternart.com) is a treasure house of Western art, most of it executed by artists who have ridden the range, while the **Hill Country Museum** (226 Earl Garrett Street; tel: 830-895-5222; www.caillouxfoundation.org/schreiner-mansion; appointment only), operated by the Hill Country Preservation Society in the restored 1879 Shreiner Mansion, portrays the affluent life of the region's early days. In downtown Kerrville is Old Republic Square, with brick sidewalks, old stone walls, fountains, and cedar-finished buildings shaded by pecan trees.

WILDLIFE

Near the Guadalupe River, at the Town Creek junction, is the **Riverside Nature Center** (150 Francisco Lemos Street; tel: 830-257-4837; www.riversidenaturecenter.org; Mon–Sat 10am–6pm; free), incorporating a wildflower meadow and butterfly garden surrounding a turn-of-the-20th-century house, which has exhibits and displays. It has an arboretum with over 140 species of tree.

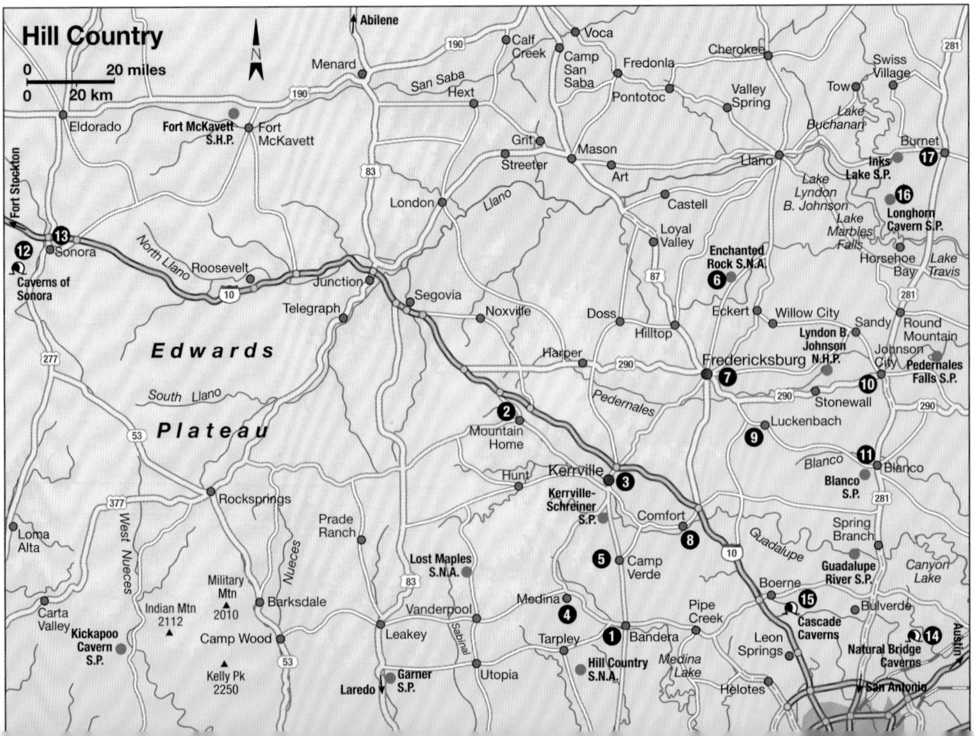

The Texas Hill Country is a bird-watcher's paradise, home to such rare species as the golden-cheek warbler, the green kingfisher, and the zone-tail hawk. Near Kerrville, at **Ingram**, is the Exotic Wildlife Association (tel: 830-315-7761; www.myewa.org), which has helped introduce to the region such animals as the llama, the greater kudu, the Siberian ibex, the sable antelope, the ostrich, the zebra, and many varieties of deer. Completely out of context, in Ingram, is an inexact but intriguing replica of Stonehenge called Stonehenge II.

APPLE CAPITAL

Highway 16 winds for 30 miles (48km) between Kerrville and Medina. This is one of the most scenic roads in the Hill Country, with ancient live oaks and white-flowering yucca plants decorating the roadsides and hairpin bends, while green grasses cling to limestone outcrops. Tiny **Medina** ❹ is known as "the apple capital of Texas." You can pick your own apples at **Love Creek Orchards**, on a former ranch that has been given over to apple growing since the 1980s. The big draw here is the Patio Café, located inside a large barn, which is famous for its hamburgers and superb apple desserts, including a killer apple pie. In 2000, the owners donated a large portion of the original ranch to the Texas Nature Conservancy.

The Medina River is a great place to enjoy a peaceful kayak trip. It is shaded by cypress trees, which were harvested from 1853 in a mill staffed by early Polish immigrants. Local wildlife includes deer, antelope, boar, and wild turkey. Medina Lake is a good fishing spot and also the scene every September of the Medina Lake Cajun Festival (held at Lakehills Civic Center in Lakehills), home of the Great Gumbo Cookoff. Cajun music and history are also celebrated.

CAMEL COUNTRY

Camp Verde ❺, 60 miles (96km) northwest of San Antonio, is where Jefferson Davis conceived the idea of training a US Camel Corps to operate in rough desert terrain during the US War with Mexico. Initially, 33 camels were imported, along with experienced handlers from

Tip

To learn more about the Hill Country, check out the online collection of posts about this area on TexasHillCountry.com (https://texashillcountry.com/tag/enchanted-rock).

Trail ride near Bandera.

The house of Felix van der Stucken (1823–1912), a Belgian immigrant who ran a steam-powered flour mill in Fredericksburg.

North Africa and, although the sight and scent of the unfamiliar beasts frightened horses and mules, they proved capable of transporting loads up to 500 lbs (227kg) without any trouble. The project ultimately failed, however, and, after the Civil War, the camels were sold to individuals and zoos, although a handful continued to roam the hills for many years.

ENCHANTED ROCK

South of Llano and north of Fredericksburg is **Enchanted Rock State Natural Area ❻** (tel: 830-685-3636; https://tpwd.texas.gov/state-parks/enchanted-rock), a popular state park centered around a huge pink granite dome rising 425ft (131 meters) above the ground. Tonkawa Indians believed ghost fires flickered at the top and heard weird creakings and groanings, which geologists explain as the noise of the hot rock contracting in the cool of the night. It's a good, stiff vertical hike to the top.

One of Hill Country's most popular destinations is **Fredericksburg ❼**, founded in 1846 by German settlers. The town retains many traces of its ancestry in its architecture and in the German dialect heard on the streets, as well as place names. Main Street, for example, is called "Hauptstrasse" and is lined with pseudo-Teutonic beer gardens, restaurants, and bakeries that offer a wide variety of cuisines. The town is a magnet for shoppers because of its antiques, gifts, ethnic foods, and local wines.

Wineries abound in Hill Country (there were more than 50 at last count) and wines can be sampled along the highway into town, at numerous German-named farms, such as "Der Peach Garten," which sell wines and liqueurs. If you're passing between May and August, you'll get chance to pick your own peaches in local orchards – a delicious way to while away a summer's day.

Large-scale German immigration continued right up until the Civil War. One notable characteristic is *Fachwerk* – a traditional German building technique consisting of heavy framing and diagonal bracing, with an infill of limestone. Early Germanic homes can be explored at the **Pioneer Museum Complex** (325

Shops in Fredericksburg.

W. Main Street; tel: 830-990-8441; www.pioneermuseum.net; Mon–Sat 10am–5pm, Thu 10am–4pm in Oct and Nov).

Gish's Old West Museum (502 N. Milam Street; tel: 830-997-2794; appointments only) is filled with the saddles, lawmen's badges, guns, and other relics that make up the personal collection of Joe Gish, who will be happy to show them to you.

The **National Museum of the Pacific War** (340 E. Main Street; tel: 830-997-8600; www.pacificwarmuseum.org; daily 9am–5pm), which includes the Admiral Nimitz Museum, is named for the naval officer born in the town and attracts the many visitors with an interest in World War II. Part of it is housed in a "ship-shape" old hostelry and includes a Garden of Peace, donated by the people of Japan.

Nearby **Comfort** ❽, another town settled by German immigrants, has, in addition to numerous century-old stores in the business district, a distinctive 1892 German church.

Tiny **Luckenbach** ❾ (tel: 830-997-3224; www.luckenbachtexas.com; open daily), southeast of Fredericksburg, is a world-famous ghost town. On the banks of South Grape Creek – and easy to miss, so keep your eyes peeled as you wander down this backroad – it was never much more than a store, a post office, and a saloon. But it was bought in its entirety by humorist Hondo Crouch in 1970, and made famous by a No. 1 country-and-western hit, recorded in 1976 by Waylon Jennings and Willie Nelson, that featured the refrain "Let's go to Luckenbach, Texas." After that, people began making pilgrimages here for impromptu Sunday music gatherings, which still take place (often attended by Nelson and other major country-and-western stars) though now as a daily line-up of musical acts. The old bar is a classic spot to stop and listen in on a jam session and buy yourself a famous Frito Pie in the general store.

LBJ TOWN

Johnson City ❿, at the intersection of US 290 and US 281, was named for the ancestors of 1960s President Lyndon B. Johnson, who was raised here.

Tip

Drive carefully when looking for Luckenbach. The little place is not easy to find. After the popularity of the song *Luckenbach, Texas*, so many road signs were stolen that the Texas Highway Department stopped erecting them.

Having a drink at the Luckenbach General Store.

TEXAS BARBECUE TRAIL

No trip to the Hill Country would be complete without a pilgrimage to sample Central Texas's famous "Texan Trinity" – barbecued beef brisket, sausage, and ribs, dry rubbed and slow smoked until the meat is falling off the bone. The Texas Barbecue Trail (www.texasbbqtrails.com) from Taylor through Elgin to Lockhart and ending in Luling, takes in 12 different barbecue joints that are famous for their barbecue and can be driven in about two hours. You'd better come hungry and pace yourself, because this is some serious 'cue – and it's served up in mountainous portions. If you're on a budget, never fear. Prices in beef country are rock bottom and you'll be spoiled for choice.

To sample some of the best barbecue in one location make a beeline for the town of Lockhart, proclaimed by the State of Texas as "the Barbecue Capital of Texas." The barnlike Kreuz Market (650 N. Colorado Street; tel: 512-398-2361; www.kreuzmarket.com; Mon–Sat 10.30am–8pm, Sun 10.30am–6pm) is one of the best known and oldest (since 1900) of the barbecue joints. You can choose from barbecued brisket, sausage, beef shoulder, ribs, or pork chops. All are sold by the pound from the pits and wrapped in paper for carry out, and can be shipped to anywhere in the US.

Free tours of his restored **Boyhood Home** are given every half hour. The home is part of **Lyndon B. Johnson National Historical Park** (tel: 830-644-2252; https://tpwd.texas.gov/state-parks/lyndon-b-johnson; open daily; free) near Stonewall, between Fredericksburg and Johnson City, which displays buffalo, longhorns, and white-tail deer in enclosures and a restored 1908 house on the site of a working farm. From the park, tours can be taken of the LBJ Ranch.

Another of the Hill Country's little towns that retains some of the quiet style of a bygone era is **Blanco** ⓫. Beside the river of the same name, it promotes its friendly atmosphere and the annual Lavender Festival in June that offers lavender-related experiences, live music, and a market.

UNTOUCHED BY CIVILIZATION

What was once a 5,400-acre (2,180-hectare) ranch was donated to Texas Parks and Wildlife in 1976, with the stipulation that it "be kept far removed and untouched by modern civilization, where everything is preserved intact, yet put to a useful purpose." Today it is **Hill Country State Natural Area** (tel: 830-796-4413; www.tpwd.state.tx.us/state-parks/hill-country; daily 8.15am–4.45pm), 45 miles (72km) northwest of San Antonio, a region of rocky limestone hills, flowing springs, oak groves, grasslands, and canyons.

Five miles (8km) north of Vanderpool, off State Route 187, is **Lost Maples State Natural Area** (tel: 830-966-3413; www.tpwd.state.tx.us/state-parks/lost-maples; daily 8am–10pm), spectacularly colorful in November, but an attractive and very popular park year round. It offers camping and picnicking among rugged limestone canyons and bubbling springs.

GOING UNDERGROUND

Over the centuries underground streams have carved out spectacular caverns all through this region. Among the best-known are the **Caverns of Sonora** ⓬ (tel: 325-387-3105; www.cavernsofsonora.com; daily 8am–6pm, 9am–5pm from Sept–Mar), at exit 392 of I-10, 8 miles (13km) south of the

A cow rests in a field of Texan bluebonnets.

TEXAS WILDFLOWERS

The spring wildflowers that dot Central Texas hillsides starting in March and continuing to June each year inspire locals and visitors alike to take to the backroads and admire the Hill Country's Impressionistic displays of primary hues. Indian paintbrush, greenthread, Indian blanket, coreopsis, winecup, black-eyed susans, and sunflowers bloom in waves throughout the season – hardy natives well suited to the limestone soil and warm exposures. None is as eagerly awaited as Texas bluebonnets, the state flower, which carpet the swales in early April, particularly plentiful around Burnet. For more information on what is blooming during your visit, contact the state wildflower hotline (tel: 800-452-9292) or Texas Parks and Wildlife (tel: 800-792-1112). Each has travel counselors available 9am–6pm.

town of that name. With 8 miles (13km) of passages lined with crystalline stalactites and stalagmites, it is one of Texas's longest caves. The temperature inside the cave is a steady 78°F (25°C) but with high humidity it feels about 86°F (29°C); sweaters are not needed. There is also a picnic area and a campground.

Beginning in **Sonora** ⓭, between 1910 and 1921, a 250ft (76-meter) wide, fenced track called Tillman's Lane ran 100 miles (160km) northeast to Brady. Thousands of cattle were driven to the railroad on this track, which was equipped with holding pens, wells, and windmills.

Natural Bridge Caverns ⓮ (26495 Natural Bridge Caverns Rd; tel: 210-651-6101; www.naturalbridgecaverns.com; daily 9am–6pm, tour days and times vary) offers exotic sights carved over thousands of years out of the area's natural limestone. The tourist brochure describes the colors as resembling "35 flavors of ice cream," with rocks "nearly as translucent as china and rooms nearly as large as football fields." Nearby is **Natural Bridge Wildlife Ranch** (26515 Natural Bridge Caverns Rd; tel: 830-438-7400; www.wildliferanchtexas.com; daily 9am–6pm), a game ranch that is home to zebras, wallabies, camels, baboons, and parrots, among other exotics. Similar to Natural Bridge Caverns are the **Cascade Caverns** ⓯ (on I-10 south of Boerne; tel: 830-755-8080; www.cascadecaverns.com; daily 9am–5pm), which include an interior, 100ft (30-meter) waterfall.

One of the oldest commercial caves in Texas is Longhorn Cavern in **Longhorn Cavern State Park** ⓰ (6211 Park Road 4, S. Burnet; tel: 512-715-9000; www.visitlonghorncavern.com; daily 9am–5pm, 6pm on weekends), 6 miles (9.6km) outside Burnet. This has seen a number of uses in the past 100 years but was opened as a tourist cave in 1938 by the Civilian Conservation Corporation. Camping is available in nearby Inks Lake State Park (tel: 512-793-2223; www.tpwd.texas.gov/state-parks/inks-lake).

OLDEST DANCE HALL

In the mid-19th century, several thousand German settlers formed the farming communities of **Gruene, Boerne**, and **New Braunfels** just northwest of San Antonio, and the German heritage survives here in the form of *fachwerk* houses replete with gingerbread trimmings. Gruene is the most interesting historically and is home to the oldest dancehall in Texas, **Gruene Hall** (1878), where dances are still held.

Tubing, or floating down a river in inflatable tubes, is a popular Texas activity in the summer. Large groups of friends don their swimsuits and hats, bring a cooler of alcoholic beverages, and spend the day lazily floating on the river. **New Braunfels** and **San Marcos** are Texas-famous for tubing trips on the Comal River and San Marcos River, both of which are spring-fed rivers that are 72 degrees (22 degrees celsius) year-round. Many opt to tube

Lyndon B. Johnson's Boyhood Home.

Watchdog rock formation in Longhorn Cavern.

the Comal River which joins with the Guadalupe River tubing area. To experience this Texas tradition, book with a tubing company which will provide you with a rental tube, life jackets (usually for free and only if needed), parking, and a shuttle service that will pick you up at the end of your tube ride and return you to your car. **San Marcos** is also known for its outlet malls, and is home to Texas State University. The campus is worth a stop to view the large **Witliff Collections** (tel: 512-245-2313; www.thewittliffcollections.txstate.edu; Mon–Fri 8.30am–4.30pm, Sat noon–5pm, Sun 1–6pm; free) on the seventh floor of the Alkek Library. The collection is the photography archive of screenwriter and photographer Bill Witliff and includes many images from the TV series *Lonesome Dove*.

Not far from San Marcos, on a side road, is **Wimberley**, an out-of-the-way small town filled with artists. It's a popular weekend day trip for Austinites who come to brows the cute shops and galleries, stay in a quaint B&B, and sample a slice of Wimberley's famous homemade fruit pies and olive oil from one of the few commercial olive groves in the state. The first Saturday of each month, from April to November, is Wimberley Market Days (www.shopmarketdays.com), when local shops, artisans, and galleries set up hundreds of booths on Lion's Field; entertainments include live music and food.

FLYING VISIT

For travelers seeking only a taste of Hill Country, a steam excursion train runs from Cedar Park City Hall, near US 183 and FM 1431, about 15 miles (24km) northwest of Austin. The journey takes travelers through the Hill Country to **Burnet** ⓱, on US 281, once a frontier town from whose quarries marble for the state capitol in Austin was mined. Running on weekends only, the 80-year-old Hill Country Flyer (tel: 512-402-3830; https://austinsteamtrain.org) takes just over two hours each way, traveling through beautiful countryside and allowing a short stopover for shopping, museum browsing, and refreshment.

Independence Day Parade, Wimberley.

TEXAS WINERIES

Texas may be dry in places – in every sense of the word – but a flood of wineries in the Hill Country attract millions of visitors.

Many are unaware that Texas is one of the oldest wine-growing regions in the US – older even than California – but wine making began here with the Spanish missions in El Paso in West Texas in the 1650s. Today, the state has eight American Viticultural Areas (AVAs): Mesilla Valley, Texas Davis Mountains, and Escondido Valley, in West Texas; Texas High Plains and Texoma in North Texas; and Bell Mountain, Fredericksburg in the Hill Country, and Texas Hill Country, in Central Texas. Not bad for a state where as of 2018, there were five dry counties (counties where alcoholic beverage sales are illegal) still left in the state.

In all, Texas has 530 wineries producing millions of gallons of wine each year, making the Lone Star state fifth in the US for wine production, behind California, New York, and Washington. West Texas is still the number one growing region when it comes to acres in cultivation, courtesy of the University of Texas System, which has 1,000 acres of vines in Fort Stockton. But the majority of wineries can be found in Texas's rolling Hill Country, west of Austin, with over 50 wineries clustered in the fruit-growing areas around Fredericksburg, where the limestone hills and warm climate favor Chardonnay and Cabernet Sauvignon grapes. The area attracts more than 7 million wine enthusiasts a year.

Most wineries welcome visitors and offer tours and tastings. Pick up a copy of the Texas Wine Trail brochure and map (www.texaswinetrail.com) for details and opening times. Many wineries offer special events throughout the year. The long-running Fredericksburg's Food and Wine Fest takes place in late October in downtown Fredericksburg's Marktplatz. Make reservations well in advance for festival tickets and to be sure of a hotel room.

If you'd rather not drive (a wise option), you could take a wine tour with one of the specialist companies in Fredericksburg, such as Fredericksburg Limo and Wine Tours (tel: 830-997-8687; www.texaswinelimos.com) or 290 Wine Shuttle (tel: 210-724-7217; https://290wineshuttle.com), a hop-on, hop-off wine shuttle that operates every Saturday.

Wineries are coming online regularly in this area, but some to check out are:

Spicewood Vineyards (1419 CO Rd 409, Spicewood; tel: 830-693-5328; www.spicewoodvineyards.com; Wed–Sat 10am–6pm, Sun noon–5pm, Mon–Tue by appointment). Nine award-winning wines, including a rich 2011 Tempranillo that was a 2013 *Texas Monthly* winner.

Becker Vineyards (464 Becker Farms Road; tel: 830-644-2681; www.beckervineyards.com; Mon–Thu 10am–5pm, Fri–Sat 10am–6pm, Sun noon–6pm). Award-winning wines and a lovely stone barn tasting room. The largest wine cellar in the state.

Fall Creek Vineyards (1820 CR 222, Tow, Tx, near Llano; tel: 325-379-5361; www.fcv.com; Mon, Fri–Sat 11am–5pm, Sun noon–5pm). On the shores of Lake Buchanan, and known for German Rieslings and Chenin Blanc.

Dry Comal Creek Winery and Vineyard (1741 Herbelin Road, New Braunfels; tel: 830-885-4076; www.drycomalcreek.com; Thu–Mon 12am–5pm, Tue–Wed by appointment only). An up-and-coming small winery in a unique setting.

Not to be missed – a wine tasting at a Texan vineyard.

San Antonio's River Walk.

SAN ANTONIO

A cultural crossroads, San Antonio is where the United States and Mexico merge, with a splash of German tradition thrown in for good measure.

Main attractions
The River Walk
The Alamo
Spanish Governor's Palace
San Fernando Cathedral
Brackenridge Park
San Antonio Missions National Historical Park

Map on page 164

San Antonio (pop. 1.49 million), now sprawling over 465 sq miles (1,205 sq km) is the second-largest city in Texas and the seventh-largest city in the US. It is overwhelmingly Hispanic – with a Latino population that is now the fourth largest in the United States. It is often called Mexico's northernmost city, and the National Autonomous University of Mexico, the oldest institution of higher learning in this hemisphere, has maintained a campus here since 1972.

San Antonio borders both the South Texas Plains – the high desert flatlands sweeping down to Mexico on the other side of the Rio Grande – and the pretty ranchlands of Hill Country, and is the principal city of both regions. Its location close to Mexico has historically placed it on the frontlines of Spanish, Mexican, early Texan, and American ambitions and military might. Today, these historic links remain an integral part of this city's allure, and interest both historians and cultural tourists alike.

There is plenty to do within the attractive and relatively compact historic downtown – from the enchanting River Walk, diverse museums, and colorful Mexican *mercado*-style markets to the photogenic historic Spanish missions strung along the river. The latter include, of course, the Alamo, the ruins of a small, fortified former mission that looms large in the minds of every Texan – and all who still "remember the Alamo."

A DOWNTOWN FOR TOURISTS

Today, much of the early drama that made San Antonio such a prize for newcomers – including its reputation for being a rowdy, multicultural town whose colorful residents liked to shoot up the place – is lost to the mists of time. Ironically, what attracts Texans and tourists alike today is San Antonio's relaxed *mañana* attitude and celebratory approach to life.

The Alamo.

Tip

For those that prefer to move around on wheels, San Antonio Segway Tours (260 E Houston Street; tel: 210-441-1198; www.nationtours.com/texas/san-antonio-segway-tours) is a popular way to see the area.

The city's main attraction is its delightful 15-mile (24km) **River Walk** **A**, where, 20ft (6 meters) below street level, a romantic sidewalk-lined river that has been channeled and landscaped for 2.5 miles (4km) through the heart of downtown, is bordered by shops, restaurants, hotels, bars, and museums. During busy seasons, the sidewalks can become crowded with tourists, but the River Walk, or Paseo Del Rio, is still well worth the trouble. Watch flat-bottomed *chalupa* boats drift by, or board one of the **GO RIO Cruises** (tel: 210-227-4746; www.goriocruises.com; daily tours) for a 35-minute round-trip boat ride. Tickets are available at kiosks along the River Walk. Private dinner cruises can also be arranged. The River Walk is particularly enchanting at night, when it is all lit up.

CENTRAL AREA

The main river, which runs roughly north to south, makes an almost circular loop between College and Villita streets, with the vast majority of the city's attractions located within those perimeters.

The most convenient starting point for tours of the city is at the **Alamo** **B** (www.thealamo.org; open daily; guided tour $7), originally known as the Mission San Antonio de Valero. Named after the viceroy at the time, it was built as the first of five missions in 1718, during the Spanish Colonial era, but its worldwide fame was established during 13 days in 1836, when the Alamo was besieged by 5,000 Mexican troops.

Early in the 19th century it had served as a presidio (garrison) for a cavalry unit from Alamo de Parras – hence the name. But, by the time General Santa Anna seized the Mexican presidency, the Anglo settlers in San Antonio (the Texians) were claiming the city for their own. It was in the Alamo that they chose to make a stand when Santa Anna came to reclaim the garrison.

A FEW VOLUNTEERS

On February 24, 1836, barricading himself with his small force within the Alamo's thick stone walls, the commander of the Texians, General Travis, sent out a desperate appeal for reinforcements in

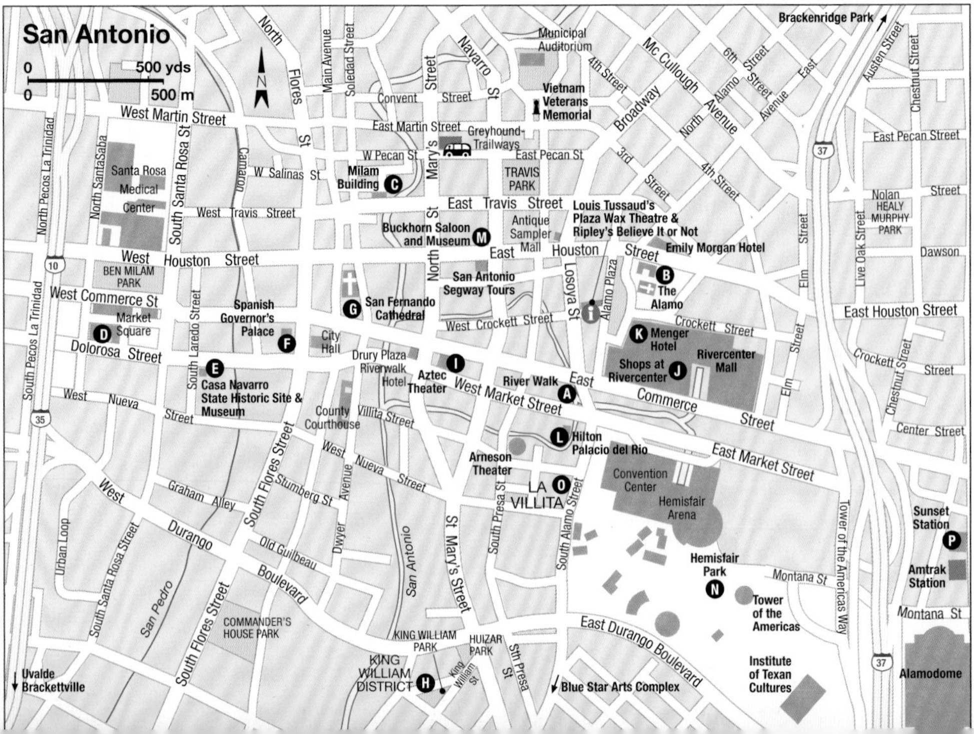

The city's main attraction is its delightful 15-mile River Walk.

a stirring letter. Thirty-two Texans from Gonzales, the Lexington of Texas where the first shot of the Texas Revolution was fired, joined Travis. They were supported in their defense by some notable Tennesseeans. These included Colonel James Bowie, who had disobeyed General Sam Houston's order to destroy the fortress, and the now famous Davy Crockett. However, early on the morning of March 6, Santa Anna's men attacked the Alamo, overran the fortress, and killed all 189 of its defenders.

It turned out to be a Pyhrric victory. Forty-six days later, the cry "Remember the Alamo" served as the inspiration for the Texans who surrounded and decisively beat Santa Anna's men at San Jacinto on April 21. (The date is still celebrated by the city of San Antonio at their annual Fiesta.) Thus, the Republic of Texas was born, and San Antonio came to be known as the "cradle of Texas liberty."

PRESERVED FOREVER

In 1883, the State of Texas bought the familiar chapel with its bullet-riddled walls, but the *convento*, the surrounding area where the beautiful Alamo Gardens are planted, belonged to a liquor dealer who was said to be planning to build a hotel.

Two "Saviors of the Alamo," as they have come to be called, stepped forward: Sam Johnson, the father of President Johnson and a state senator in 1905, arranged the purchase of the Alamo convent, and Clara Driscoll – owner of Laguna Gloria, the lakeside mansion in Austin that is now part of The Contemporary Austin art gallery – advanced $75,000 to complete the purchase (the state repaid the loan two years later). From the beginning, the Daughters of the Republic of Texas, who trace their ancestry to the original citizens of the republic, have been involved in lobbying for preservation, then entrusted with managing the Alamo; they remain the day-to-day managers of the shrine, under the auspices of the Texas General Land Office (GLO).

A plaque on the front door of the graffiti-etched **Alamo Shrine**, originally the Chapel, requests "Be quiet

A statue of Saint Anthony on the River Walk.

Trolley on Houston Street.

Traditional Mexican paper-cut decorations adorning San Antonio's Market Square.

friend, here heroes died to blaze a trail for other men." Most visitors focus on taking photos of the famous exterior of the shrine (which is surprising small and underwhelming in real life, almost like a stage set), then head to the lovely garden, shaded by everything from myrtles to a mescal bean tree, then the all-important souvenir shop.

The display cases in the museum at the Alamo hold surprisingly few artifacts – most have spread far and wide and ended up in private collections. So it's heartening to learn that the famous letter penned by Col. Travis pleading for reinforcements prior to the Alamo seige returned to the Alamo in 2013.

Even more significant, in 2014, musician Phil Collins – a knowledgeable Alamo fan and collector – donated his priceless collection of Alamo artifacts to the state for posterity. It includes hundreds of documents, ranging from a letter Stephen F. Austin wrote from a Mexican prison in January 1834 and Sam Houston's original 1835 land grant for property in East Texas to the signed receipt for 30 beeves that William Travis brought into the Alamo on the day the siege began. Other artifacts include uniforms and Brown Bess muskets that belonged to Mexican soldiers, a sword belt believed to have been worn by Travis when he died atop the northern wall, and a shot pouch that Crockett is thought to have given a Mexican soldier just before he was executed.

These donations significantly help the GLO in its aim of bolstering the Alamo's holdings, improving its status, and better portraying the story of the national historic landmark. A longer-range dream is to expand the Alamo, back to its original size. On **Alamo Plaza**, in front of the Alamo, you will find the Alamo Visitors Center (tel: 210-247-0238; www.thealamo.org; open daily), offering advice and discount coupons for San Antonio attractions. An Alamo Trolley tour (tel: 210-492-4144) provides an excellent history of the city in the shortest amount of time. A horse-drawn carriage from the Yellow Rose Carriage Company (tel: 210-225-6490) can give you a 20 to 60-minute tour. Carriage stands are on either side of the Alamo.

Musician Phil Collins announces the donation of his private collection of Alamo artifacts to the State of Texas.

VICTORY OR DEATH

In 2013, the Alamo saw the return of a Texas treasure. Through a joint project of the Texas General Land Office, The Alamo, and the Texas State Library and Archives Commission, the original "Victory or Death" letter penned by William B. Travis in 1836 was returned for the 177th anniversary of the siege and battle. Over 24,000 people attended the exhibit. The text of the letter is as follows:

"To the People of Texas and All Americans in the World – Fellow Citizens and Compatriots: I am besieged with a thousand or more of the Mexicans under Santa Anna. I have sustained a continual Bombardment and cannonade for 24 hours and have not lost a man. The enemy has demanded surrender at discretion, otherwise, the garrison is to be put to the sword, if the fort is taken. I have answered the demand with a cannon shot, and our flag still waves proudly from the walls. I shall never surrender or retreat. Then, I call upon you in the name of Liberty, of Patriotism, and everything dear to the American character, to come to our aid with all dispatch. The enemy is receiving reinforcements daily and will no doubt increase to three or four thousand in four or five days. If this call is neglected, I am determined to sustain myself as long as possible and die like a soldier who never forgets what is due his honor and that of his country. VICTORY or DEATH." – William Barret Travis Lt. Col. Comdt.

A WALKING TOUR

To get away from the crowds, at least for a while, begin your stroll on the quieter stretch of the River Walk – at 4th Street, for example, behind the Municipal Auditorium. The first major landmark on this route is at Travis Street, where the Art Deco **Milam Building** **C** has been a landmark since the 1920s, when it housed the offices of early oil companies.

The next bridge – there are 35 within the city limits – is at Houston Street. From here, you can take a trolley to visit colorful **Market Square** **D**, also known as "El Mercado," (514 W. Commerce Street), a few blocks to the west. The Market Square is the largest Mexican market in the US and it's where you'll find live music, as well as many souvenir shops, myriad restaurants, weekend celebrations, and full-scale festivals in summer and fall.

The huge **Mi Tierra Café and Panadería** (218 Produce Row; tel: 210-225-1262; www.mitierracafe.com; open 24 hours) has been a landmark here since 1941, and is also where the mariachi bands gather. They will be happy to perform their music tableside for a gratuity.

HISTORIC HOMES

Walking back to the river along Dolorosa Street, you'll pass the square, stuccoed limestone **Casa Navarro State Historic Site and Museum** **E** (228 S. Laredo Street; tel: 210-226-4801; www.thc.texas.gov/historic-sites/casa-navarro-state-historic-site; Tue–Sat 10am–5pm, Sun noon–5pm), which preserves the home of José Antonio Navarro, one of two Texans who signed the Texas Declaration of Independence. Also here is the beautifully restored **Spanish Governor's Palace** **F** (105 Plaza de Armas; tel: 210-224-0601; www.spanishgovernorspalace.org; Tue–Sat 9am–5pm, Sun 10am–5pm). The name is a misnomer, as no governor ever lived here; instead, the building was occupied by the captains of the Presidio de San Antonio de Bexar, between 1722 and the early 19th century. This is all that remains of the presidio.

Overlooking Main Plaza is the limestone Gothic Revival **San Fernando**

Fact

Some historians complain about the presentation of the Alamo site today, that too much emphasis is placed on the famous battle, and not enough on the founding of the mission itself – effectively the founding of the city of San Antonio.

Mi Tierra Café and Panadería.

Fact

The roll call of "Heroes of the Battle of the Alamo" does not only list citizens of American states. Among the countries represented are Ireland, Scotland, Wales, England, Denmark, and Germany.

Cathedral G (tel: 210-227-1297; www.sfcathedral.org; open daily), North America's oldest sanctuary, founded in 1731 and rebuilt in 1873. A plaque stating that the remains of the Alamo dead are located here may be inaccurate, as Santa Anna probably burned the bodies.

Here, writer Graham Greene was reminded of Victorian albums and valentines by the *mantillas* worn by the Hispanic women. He wondered if the San Antonio River wound itself into a heart shape and, in fact, it very nearly does. In 1938, the pecan "shelleries," as Greene called them, still flourished on the West Side, where impoverished pecan shellers worked for a few cents a day.

The plaza fronting the cathedral is the earliest permanently settled spot (by European immigrants) in the state. After the Texas Revolution, it became the liveliest place in town, featuring market stalls and feisty, flirtatious "chili queens," who were ordered to remove their chili stands when San Antonio's new City Hall and the red-sandstone-and-granite Bexar County Courthouse, by James R. Gordon, were completed in the 1890s.

THE GERMAN QUARTER

Soon after the Republic of Texas was established, a sizeable influx of German immigrants established themselves in the historic **King William District** H – named after the Prussian king – between the river and South St Mary's Street. Here, in this 25-block area, many refurbished Victorian homes can be admired on a walking tour conducted by the San Antonio Conservation Society (in the Wulff Building at 107 King William Street; tel: 210-224-6163; www.saconservation.org), which can supply a map of the neighborhood. The Society and **Villa Finale Museum & Gardens** manages the nearby **Edward Steves Homestead** (509 King William Street; tel: 210-223-98000; daily 10am–3.30pm), an impressive 1876 mansion filled with period antiques and surrounded by an exceptional garden and fountain.

Across the river is the **Blue Star Contemporary Art Museum** (116 Blue

San Fernando Cathedral.

Star; tel: 210-227-6960; www.bluestarart.org; Thu–Fri 10am–8pm, Sat–Sun 10am–6pm) in the Blue Stars Arts Complex, a restored warehouse district now housing shops, contemporary art galleries, and studios, as well as a brew pub. Once a month, the museum stays open until 9pm on Friday for the First Fridays Art Walk, the longest running art walk in San Antonio. In addition to the museum, galleries in the Southtown Arts District open their doors for a family-friendly night of art.

Not far from Southtown is **Ruby City** (150 Camp Street; tel: 210-227-8400; www.rubycity.org; Thu 10am–8pm, Fri–Sun 10am–6pm; free), an entirely red-colored museum with a 900-piece collection of contemporary art. The museum was founded by the late Pace salsa sauce-heiress Linda Pace, and is renowned for its angular architecture by architect Sir David Adjaye OBE.

The San Antonio Conservation Society, organized in 1924, primarily to preserve and restore many of the Alamo buildings, later turned its attention to saving a trio of the city's Art Deco movie theaters. The facade is all that remains of the Texas (1926), while the Majestic (1929) is now a performing arts and concert venue. The third is the **Aztec Theater** ❶ (1926), an entertainment center on the River Walk whose architect gained his inspiration from studying Mexico's Mayan and Aztec ruins.

The colonnade at Mitla was the model for the foyer, and each column is decorated with a plaster mask of the Aztec moon goddess. A 2-ton (1.8-metric ton) chandelier is a replica of a sacrificial stone. On the fire curtain, the meeting of Cortez and Montezuma is depicted, and over the proscenium Quetzalcoatl, the plumed serpent god of the Aztecs, appears.

HOTELS OLD AND NEW

Right across from the Alamo lies the neo-gothic Emily Morgan Hotel (705 E. Houston Street; tel: 210-225-5100; www.emilymorganhotel.com). Behind the Alamo, another loop of the river is flanked by two Marriott Hotels (one of the many points you can board a boat for a sightseeing cruise). Here, too, is

Fact

San Fernando Cathedral was founded by settlers from the Canary Islands.

A marching band passes through King William District.

Fact

At 40ft (12m) -tall, the Virgin Mary at the Guadalupe Cultural Arts Center is the largest Mary mosaic in the world.

the **Shops at Rivercenter** **J** (849 E. Commerce Street; tel: 210-225-0000; www.shoprivercenter.com; open daily), with more than 100 shops, and the city's huge Convention Center. The story of the hallowed Alamo is told in appropriately spectacular fashion on the six-story screen of the imax theater (tel: 210-228-0351) in the Rivercenter Mall, between the 1909 Crockett Hotel and the 1859 limestone-and-stucco **Menger Hotel** **K** (204 Alamo Plaza; tel: 210-223-4361; www.mengerhotel.com), the city's first deluxe hostelry.

In the 1850s, William Menger opened a brewery on the grounds of the Battle of the Alamo and, soon after, he and his wife offered rooms to German farmers from Fredericksburg, Seguin, Comfort, and New Braunfels, who periodically rode into San Antonio in ox carts, bringing their prepared meats and produce to sell.

Old German farmers gave way at the Menger to presidents, generals, and writers, including Oscar Wilde and O. Henry, Jenny Lind, Sarah Bernhardt, and consumptive poet Sidney Lanier, who came to San Antonio for his health. At the Menger, the old lobby (the Rotunda) and patio is a good place to savor the local's favorite cocktail, the margarita.

A FEW GOOD MEN

It's said that, just as the Menger had to send all the way to Boston for ice in those days, so Boston sent to Spanish Texas for horses. Accordingly, the horse Paul Revere chose for his famous midnight ride was obtained from a ranch 20 miles (32km) southeast of San Antonio, where the Polish town of Cestohowa is now located.

In a similar vein, in 1898, during the Spanish-American War, Teddy Roosevelt recruited members of the US Volunteer Cavalry (the "Rough Riders") in the Menger Bar (located at the other side of the hotel). "I need a few good men," he is reputed to have said, "who can ride a horse, shoot a gun, and want to serve their country." This elite corps of cowboys and millionaires from the East generated a great deal of attention before they went on to Cuba.

Buckhorn Saloon and Museum.

In contrast, the 21-story **Hilton Palacio del Rio** Ⓛ (200 S. Alamo Street; tel: 210-222-1400; www.hilton.com), which overlooks the river a few blocks to the south, was built in record time in 1968. It was claimed to have been the world's first hotel put together from pre-constructed rooms produced on an "assembly line." As its honeycomb facade suggests, the rooms, completely furnished and ready to assign to guests, were lifted into place by a crane, and then nudged and straightened with the help of a helicopter.

At the other end of the River Walk, the **Drury Plaza Riverwalk Hotel** (105 S. St Mary's Street; tel: 210-270-7799; www.druryhotels.com) occupies the beautifully restored 1925 Alamo National Bank Building. The hotel's Terrace Rooms overlook a portion of the River Walk that was restored by the family-run hotel chain and donated to the city.

FUN AND THRILLS

For some fun, next to the Visitor Information Center on Alamo Plaza you will find **Louis Tussaud's Plaza Wax Theater**, with 200 waxworks of celebrities, and **Ripley's Believe It or Not** (tel: 210-224-9299; www.ripleys.com/sanantonio), where you'll see all kinds of weird and wonderful items. Two blocks away is the historic (1881) **Buckhorn Saloon and Museum** Ⓜ (318 E. Houston; tel: 210-247-4000; www.buckhornmuseum.com; daily from 10am, closing times vary), which contains the world's largest collection of horns and an impressive taxidermy collection. The small Texas Ranger Museum here houses hundreds of Texas Ranger artifacts, including revolvers, automatic handguns, sawn-off shotguns, badges, and photographs, along with a re-creation of San Antonio during its Wild West times.

Don't overlook San Antonio's biggest entertainment attractions like Six Flags Fiesta Texas, (17000 W IH 10; tel: 210-697-5050; www.sixflags.com/fiestatexas) home to gut-wrenching rollercoasters, and Morgan's Wonderland, (5223 David Edwards; tel: 210-495-5888; www.morganswonderland.com) the world's first ultra-accessible amusement park that

Colorful sweet treats on display in a panadería.

La Villita.

Tip

Save a visit to the Shops at Rivercenter for a rainy day. As well as plenty of shops, and the familiar food court, it has the benefit of an IMAX theater, where *The Alamo* movie is just one of a series of daily features.

is free for travelers with disabilities. Even Trader's Village (9333 SW Loop 410; tel: 210-623-8383; http://tradersvillage.com), a 250-acre (101-hectare) outdoor flea market, provides an 11-ride amusement park in addition to over 1,000 vendors.

PANORAMIC VIEW

Farther down Alamo, past the Convention Center, is **Hemisfair Park** N – site of the 1968 World's Fair – dominated by the 750ft (231-meter) **Tower of the Americas** (open daily), which has glass elevators to take you to an observation deck for a panoramic view of the city. Above the observation deck is a restaurant that rotates once each hour. Here also are the **Institute of Texan Cultures** (801 Cesar E. Chavez Boulevard; tel: 210-458-2300; www.texancultures.com; Mon–Sat 9am–5pm, Sun noon–5pm) and the **Mexican Cultural Institute San Antonio** (600 Hemisfair Plaza Way; tel: 210-227-0123; http://icm.sre.gob.mx/culturamexsa;Tue–Fri 10am–5pm, Sat–Sun until 4pm; free), both displaying interesting historical and contemporary exhibits with a multicultural emphasis.

LITTLE VILLAGE

Opposite Hemisfair Park is **La Villita** O ("Little Village"), the old town of Béjar, now spelled "Bexar" and pronounced "bear," from which Santa Anna's troops set up their cannon line for the Alamo siege in 1836. The previous year, Santa Anna's brother-in-law, General Martin Perfecto de Cos, had stayed in a house here while in command of the Mexican forces sent to calm the Texans.

Despite its name, La Villita was not an exclusively Spanish neighborhood, for Germans and others moved here during the Republic (1836–45). When it was restored, the intention was to honor San Antonio's Spanish, German, Mexican, French, American, and Texan heritage, evidence of which is found in La Villita's architectural styles.

Today, the tiny limestone and adobe buildings contain craft shops, art galleries, restaurants, and boutiques. Head down to the River Walk and you will find the grassy steps of the

The Institute of Texan Cultures.

open-air **Arneson River Theatre** (tel: 210-207-8614), which often puts on dance and musical performances in summer and during Fiesta. Bring a blanket or a lawn chair.

To the east of I-37, close to the Alamodome sports and convention hall, is **Sunset Station** Ⓟ (1174 E. Commerce Street; tel: 210-474-7632; www.sunsetstation.com), a distinctive 1902 railroad depot, also known as the "Building of a Thousand Lights," that was refurbished in 1998 and is now part of a 10-acre (4-hectare) historic center and used to host events. Where once the hoots and whistles of steam trains could be heard, today the noise and bustle come from live music and parties.

PEARL

North of downtown San Antonio, next to the San Antonio River is the **Pearl**, one of the newest and most popular destinations in the city. The district obtained its name from the historic Pearl Brewery, which has been transformed into boutique hotel property, **Hotel Emma** (136 E Grayson St; tel: 210-448-8300; www.thehotelemma.com). In addition to a pool and rooms that overlook the River Walk, the hotel maintains some historic structures of the brewery in its tavern and club room. Mixed-use development has risen around the old brewery to include apartment and office buildings, boutiques, bookshops, and stores.

However, what makes Pearl stand out the most is its reputation as a foodie destination. In addition to being home to the third campus of the **Culinary Institute of America** (www.ciachef.edu/cia-texas), the Pearl has some of San Antonio's best restaurants and bars, as well as the **Bottling Dept Food Hall** (312 Pearl Parkway; tel: 210-564-9140; www.bottlingdept.com; Sun–Thu 11am–9pm, Fri–Sat 11am–10pm), a food hall and incubator for chef-driven cuisine. Weekends draw large crowds for the Pearl Weekend Market, which features 45-plus local vendors. You'll discover a producers-only farmers market on Saturday which differs from the artisanal and prepared food vendors featured at the market on Sunday.

Fact

The San Antonio Stock Show and Rodeo (tel: 210-225-5851; www.sarodeo.com) takes place in February each year.

The San Antonio Museum of Art.

Tip

Pick up a copy of the city's own free weekly magazine, *San Antonio Current*, which lists all the local and nearby festivals, as well as music, theater, arts, and nightlife.

HISPANICS AND AMERICAN INDIANS

Hispanic politicians from San Antonio have made major inroads into politics at the national level and are proving a dynamic force. The first Hispanic mayor of a major US city, Henry Cisneros, elected in 1981, reelected in 1985, and tapped as President Bill Clinton's Secretary for Housing and Urban Development (HUD), was a groundbreaker. The dynamic twin brothers Joaquin and Julian Castro have put San Antonio on the map again in recent years – Julian followed in Cisneros's footsteps as mayor of San Antonio (2009–14),served as President Barack Obama's Secretary for Housing and Development (2014–17), and briefly ran for president on the Democrat ticket before pulling out in 2020, while Joaquin is a US Congressional representative for the 20th district that includes San Antonio.

San Antonio's early American Indian history, as well as local history and flora and fauna, is explored in the Art Deco **Witte Museum** (3801 Broadway; tel: 210-357-1900; www.wittemuseum.org; Mon–Sat 10am–5pm, Tue until 8pm, Sun noon–5pm) in Brackenridge Park. San Antonio's original inhabitants, the Payaya Indians, were hunters who supplemented their catches with the fruit of pecan and mesquite trees, and prickly pear cactus. The Payayas cooperated readily with the Europeans, but the Apache, who controlled the plains to the north, took more convincing, and the nomadic Comanche were always a threat.

The Witte Museum also includes the four-story H-E-B Body Adventure multimedia exhibit, which offers kids an interactive way to explore their bodies, take virtual adventures, and learn about Texas. Behind the museum is a complex of historic houses, including one owned by Francisco Ruiz, who was the uncle of José Antonio Navarro and the second of the two native-born Texans who signed the Texas Declaration of Independence.

PARK LIFE

San Antonio has an impressive park system. For instance, **San Pedro Springs Park** is the second-oldest

CREATING THE RIVER WALK

For more than a century, the San Antonio River has been the scene of social clubs, carnivals, rodeos, and circuses. It has had private landings and wide lawns, and the entire city has picnicked on its banks, and swum, fished, and been baptized in it. In *A Journey Through Texas*, landscape architect Frederick Law Olmsted noted: "Few cities have such a luxury... the streets are laid out in such a way that a great number of houses have a garden extending to the bank, and to a bathing-house, which is in constant use."

After disastrous floods in 1921 and 1929 left the business district under 8ft (2.5 meters) of water, a three-block-long river cutoff was created, joining the bends of the river where it loops around a 16-block area. It is inconceivable today, but at one time there were plans to fill in the river, or run it underground so it would, in effect, be used as a sewer. Fortunately, the Conservation Society banded together to protect it and nearby landmarks. In 1938, aid was provided by the Works Progress Administration, FDR's New Deal federal works scheme to cut unemployment. The river was dredged. Dams and rock retaining walls, the pleasant cobblestone and flagstone walks, and stairways from bridges were constructed. More than 11,000 trees were planted along the riverbanks and, when it was complete, spotlights were deployed in the bushes. Thirteen bridges now cross the River Walk.

The Japanese Tea Gardens in Brackenridge Park.

park in the US. Humans have gathered at this site for 12,000 years, drawn by natural springs that have since been replaced by a large outdoor swimming pool. Others are similarly as impressive like **Friedrich Wilderness Park** which has 10 miles (16km) of hiking trails throughout the 600-acre (242-hectare) park, **Comanche Lookout Park**, home to a historic stone tower, and **Confluence Park**, designed as an outdoor scientific classroom for students and adults alike.

Brackenridge Park, which adjoins Fort Sam Houston, lies between US 281 and the Austin Highway, northeast of the city. In its 340 acres (138 hectares) can be found the well-stocked **San Antonio Zoo and Aquarium** (3903 N. St Mary's Street; tel: 210-734-7184; www.sazoo.org; daily 10am–5pm), the Japanese Tea Gardens, the Sunken Gardens Amphitheater, Brackenridge Golf Course, riding stables, a sky ride, and a carousel, as well as a miniature train ride.

To the west, in the original 1880s Lone Star Brewery, is the sensational **San Antonio Museum of Art** (200 W. Jones Avenue; tel: 210-978-8100; Tue–Sun 10am–5pm, until 9pm Tue and Fri). This is a great place to see a wide variety of traditional and modern art from all over the world, but particularly Latin American and Spanish art. The special exhibits here are also a big draw.

Farther north, before the airport, is the **McNay Art Museum** (6000 N. New Braunfels; tel: 210-824-5368; www.mcnayart.org; Wed, Fri 10am–6pm, Thu 10am–9pm, Sat 10am–5pm, Sun noon–5pm), housing the collection of an oil heiress, Marion Koogler McNay, who donated it to the state. Artists showcased include Gaugin, Picasso, Matisse, and Cézanne. This is one of the best art collections in the Southwest.

ON THE TRAIL OF THE MISSIONS

The Witte Museum now stands at the headwaters of the San Antonio River, named by the Spaniards for St Anthony of Padua. It was here that Don Martin de Alcaron and Fra Antonio de San Buenaventura Olivares arrived with settlers, soldiers, and Franciscans in 1718, and most likely encountered

Tip

The Witte Museum is a good place to take children. It depicts the early American Indian history, ecology, and wildlife of Texas through plenty of hands-on exhibits.

A mariachi band performs A Night in Old San Antonio.

Fact

San Antonio is known for its mid-April Fiesta, a 10-day, nonstop celebration revealing the heart and history of San Antonio. There are far too many parades, festivals, and events to list here (over 100 of them), but check the Fiesta website for a schedule (https://fiestasanantonio.org).

Payaya Indians for the first time.

The missionaries, protected by a presidio (garrison), set about building their missions and took it upon themselves to convert the Payaya, and teach them new building techniques, crafts, ranching, and farming. The missions were large, thriving, self-sustaining enterprises on the frontier, which shipped goods back down the Camino Real trade route to the capital of New Spain in Mexico City and received supplies just once a year. It was a difficult life for all concerned, made even more so for the Payaya by the high expectations of their competing Spanish overlords – priests, military, and private landowners.

Mission San Antonio de Valero (now the Alamo) was originally established on the west bank of the river in 1718, but by 1793, it had been relocated to the east bank and secularized, and Mexican troops were transferred there to protect the pueblo that had grown up on the riverbanks. This converted mission, named the Alamo (meaning cottonwood), was a crucial fortification then and much later, when it played its starring role in Texas history.

Four more missions were founded. Today, all except the Alamo are preserved as part of **San Antonio Missions National Historical Park** (tel: 210-932-1001; www.nps.gov/saan; open daily) and are managed by the National Park Service. The missions stretch over a 6-mile (10km) route to the south, next to the river (see page 178).

Exhibit at The Witte Museum.

OUT OF TOWN

Heading out of San Antonio along US 90 will bring you to the border at **Del Rio**, around 150 miles (240km) to the west. As you leave San Antonio, there's a parched quality to roadside grasslands that offers a taste of the dessication ahead toward the border and the Rio Grande. At first, however, agriculture maintains a foothold. Historic **Castroville**, 15 miles (24km) along US 90, proclaims itself as "'the Little Alsace of Texas," and has several Alsation restaurants. **Hondo** feels like the Great Plains, with huge fields of corn and wheat, while **Knippa** – "Go Ahead and Blink, Knippa is Bigger than you Think" is devoted to stone quarrying.

The Great Depression hit South Texas pretty badly, but the town of **Uvalde** fared better than most because it was the birthplace of President Franklin Roosevelt's vice president John Nance Garner ("Cactus Jack"). Garner took care of his hometown with projects like **Garner State Park**, a riverfront park created in 1941 by the Civilian Conservation Corps, and the **Aviation Museum at Garner Field** (tel: 830-278-2552), a World War II training base that displays old bombers and other aircraft. The **Briscoe-Garner Memorial Museum** (333 N. Park Street; tel: 830-278-5018; www.cah.utexas.edu/museums/garner.php; Tue–Sat 9am–4pm) is located in the former Garner home and now run by the University of Texas. Its name honors Garner and former Governor Dolph Briscoe, both Uvalde born, and contains exhibits pertaining to both their lives.

Mission Concepcion, Nuestra Senora de la Purisima Concepcion, is one of five existing missions along the San Antonio River.

THE CRUCIAL ROLE OF THE SPANISH MISSIONS

Some of North America's oldest buildings survive in Texas, built by Spanish missionaries who sought to educate and "civilize"the local Indians.

Across South Texas lies a chain of early Spanish outposts. Established in the 18th century, these missions are evidence of the early efforts made by Spain to colonize the region, but the missions soon found a role in developing the Catholic faith among the local natives, bringing American Indian communities under the Christian banner.

Missions farther east became threatened by French incursions from Louisiana, and their communities relocated to San Antonio. The city is the mission heartland of Texas today, housing four separate complexes (five if you include the Alamo) within its boundaries. The four lie to the south, at 2-mile (3km) intervals along the San Antonio River. The most beautiful is San José y San Miguel de Aguayo, dubbed "Queen of the Missions." Mission Concepción is noted for its handsome twin towers, while Missions San Juan and Espada have distinctive three-bell towers. All can be explored using the San Antonio Mission Trail, with literature from the tourist office.

Each complex presents a different theme about mission life for the visitor. Concepción deals with the religious role of the mission, San José handles the defense and social functions, San Juan focuses on the economic importance, and Espada looks at the educational angle.

The craftsmanship of the builders working on the missions is demonstrated by the Rose Window at San José Mission, San Antonio.

The most famous mission of them all, though not universally known as such, is the bullet-riddled Alamo – or Mission San Antonio de Valero – founded in 1718 and now surrounded by downtown structures.

A shrine to Our Lady of Guadalupe in the San Ysleta Mission, the oldest mission in the state. It was built by the Tigua people who were forced to flee their ancestral home near what is now Albuquerque, New Mexico.

Mission church decor is simple: bare walls and beams, the occasional fresco and a dotting of religious icons.

Socorro Mission, one of the three missions on the El Paso Trail. The original building was destroyed by flooding in 1829.

The mission was more than a church: it was the base for a community, housing animals, workshops, granaries, kilns, and sleeping quarters.

American Indian Influences

In addition to the one in and around San Antonio, Texas has another mission trail beginning in El Paso. Stretching 9 miles (14km) out to the east of the city, it covers three historic sites: Ysleta Mission, Socorro Mission, and San Elizario Presidio Chapel.

These centers differ from the San Antonio missions in that they were established by the Spanish together with the local Pueblo Indian communities. The Pueblo influence is apparent. The oldest is Ysleta, which stands next to the Tigua Indian Cultural Center; it was rebuilt in 1908. Socorro, like Ysleta, dates originally from the late 17th century, though the current structure was completed in 1840. Its foundation by Piro Indians is reflected in the architecture. San Elizario is the chapel of a former presidio (garrison) and was rebuilt in 1877.

The wooden Mission of San Francisco de los Tejas, the first mission in East Texas, was founded in 1690. It has now been fully rebuilt.

Market Square.

HOUSTON

Bustling port, financial hub, and home of Mission Control, Houston is a moneyed metropolis, with a wealth of cultural attractions and a laid-back attitude.

Houston is without doubt a city with fascinating contradictions. In just a few decades, it has turned into a sprawling urban behemoth yet possesses one of the country's first historic planned communities in downtown. It has a subtropical climate with almost junglelike vegetation and sticky air within hailing distance of the white sand beaches of the Gulf of Mexico. It's full of urban cowboys, yet possesses one of the country's largest LGBTQ populations and cutting-edge modern art. And even as oilmen have drilled beneath the ground, NASA's celebrated astronauts have soared to the outer edges of space and explored the moon.

There's money and culture aplenty in this city, which channels a little Austin Weird even as it puts on the Ritz – but you'd be hard pressed to find anyone being snobbish. This is much too large and diverse a city to get away with that anymore.

Virtually a small town as recently as the late 1950s, Houston's population of 2.3 million (a staggering 6.99 million if you include the metro area) is incredibly diverse and international, with people from all over the world making their home here – from British immigrants (the United Kingdom has its main consulate in the US Southwest here) to refugees from the Sudan. Houston's busy international airport serves as an immigration hub for the world.

Houston is now far and away the largest city in Texas and the fourth largest in the US, most of it recently built. The lack of planning has created unchecked urban growth, resulting in a wide-open city overlaid with dizzying intersecting highways and distinct neighborhoods that have a plethora of interesting restaurants, shops, museums, and cultural activities.

Surreal scale and proportion result from the lack of zoning: a small

Main attractions

- Tranquility Park
- Menil Collection
- Rothko Chapel
- Museum of Fine Arts, Houston
- The Galleria
- Johnson Space Center

Map on page 182

Motorized cupcakes at the annual Houston Art Car Parade.

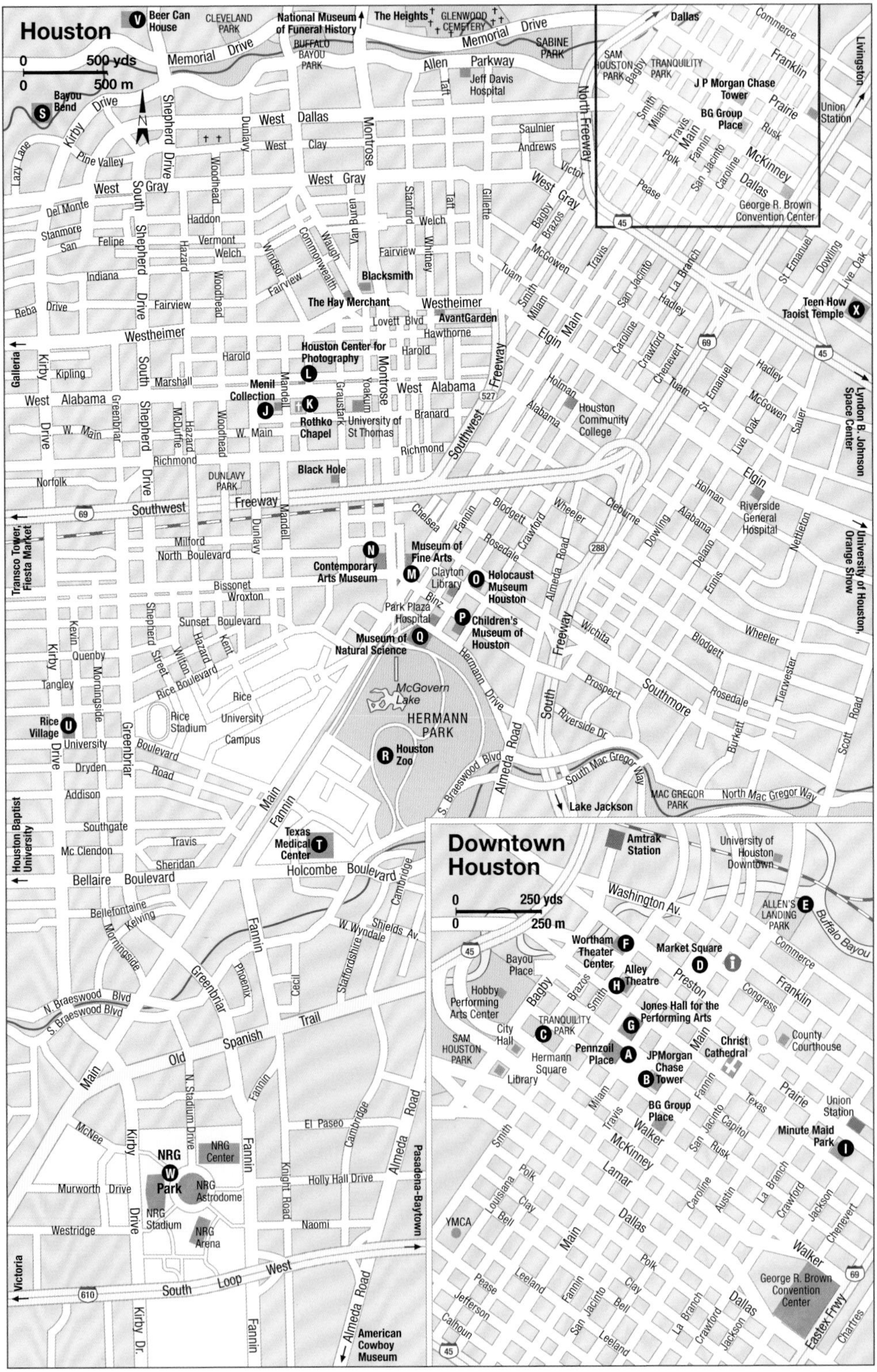
Houston
0 500 yds
0 500 m
Beer Can House
Cleveland Park
National Museum of Funeral History
The Heights
Glenwood Cemetery
Memorial Drive
Buffalo Bayou Park
Sabine Park
Allen Parkway
Jeff Davis Hospital
Bayou Bend
Kirby Drive
Lazy Lane
Pine Valley
Shepherd Drive
Dunlavy
West Dallas
Montrose
West Clay
Saulnier
Andrews
Woodhead
West Gray
Del Monte
Stanmore
San
Felipe
Haddon
Vermont
Welch
Hazard
Van Buren
Stanford
Taft
Gillette
Whitney
Fairview
Windsor
Commonwealth
Waugh
Indiana
Blacksmith
Reba Drive
Westheimer
The Hay Merchant
Lovett Blvd
AvantGarden
Hawthorne
Harold
Houston Center for Photography
Galleria
Kipling
Marshall
Menil Collection
Mandell
Graustark
Yoakum
West Alabama
Rothko Chapel
University of St Thomas
Branard
Greenbriar
McDuffie
W. Main
Richmond
Southwest Freeway
Norfolk
Dunlavy Park
Black Hole
Transco Tower, Fiesta Market
Milford
North Boulevard
Bissonet
Wroxton
Contemporary Arts Museum
Museum of Fine Arts
Clayton Library
Holocaust Museum Houston
Park Plaza Hospital
Children's Museum of Houston
Museum of Natural Science
Sunset Boulevard
Kevin
Quenby
Morningside
Tangley
Kent
Wilton
Rice Boulevard
Rice University Campus
Rice Stadium
Rice Village
McGovern Lake
Hermann Park
Houston Zoo
Hermann Drive
Almeda Road
South Freeway
University Boulevard
Dryden Road
Addison
Southgate
Travis
Mc Clendon
Sheridan
Houston Baptist University
Bellaire Boulevard
Texas Medical Center
Holcombe Boulevard
Main
Fannin
Cambridge
Shields Av.
W. Wyndale
Bellefontaine
Kelving
Phoenix
Cecil
Staffordshire
N. Braeswood Blvd
S. Braeswood Blvd
Old Spanish Trail
N. Stadium Drive
McNee
El Paseo
NRG Center
NRG Park
NRG Astrodome
NRG Stadium
NRG Arena
Murworth Drive
Westridge
Holly Hall Drive
Knight Road
Naomi
Pasadena–Baytown
Victoria
South Loop West
Kirby Dr.
American Cowboy Museum
Lake Jackson
South Mac Gregor Way
Mac Gregor Park
North Mac Gregor Way
Riverside Dr.
Southmore
Prospect
Wichita
Rosedale
Tierwester
Burkett
Scott
Wheeler
Blodgett
Holman
Elgin
Alabama
Ennis
Delano
Dowling
Cleburne
Nettleton
Riverside General Hospital
University of Houston, Orange Show
Lyndon B. Johnson Space Center
Houston Community College
Sauer
Live Oak
McGowen
Hadley
St. Emanuel
Tuam
Chenevert
Crawford
Caroline
San Jacinto
La Branch
Teen How Taoist Temple
St. Emanuel
Dowling
Bagby
Brazos
Smith
Milam
Victor
North Freeway
Dallas
Sam Houston Park
Tranquility Park
J P Morgan Chase Tower
BG Group Place
Commerce
Franklin
Prairie
Rusk
McKinney
Livingston
Union Station
Polk
Pease
George R. Brown Convention Center
Downtown Houston
0 250 yds
0 250 m
Amtrak Station
University of Houston Downtown
Washington Av.
Allen's Landing Park
Buffalo Bayou
Wortham Theater Center
Market Square
Alley Theatre
Preston
Congress
Bayou Place
Hobby Performing Arts Center
Jones Hall for the Performing Arts
City Hall
Hermann Square
Library
Pennzoil Place
JPMorgan Chase Tower
Christ Cathedral
County Courthouse
Texas
Capitol
Minute Maid Park
Walker
Lamar
Louisiana
Bell
Clay
YMCA
Leeland
Jefferson
Calhoun
Austin
Jackson
Eastex Frwy
Chartres

boutique may stand next to a 60-story office building, adjoining a house next to a heliport. Houston, more than anywhere else in Texas, operates according to the wildcatter's philosophy: "Dig a little deeper where others have given up, and maybe you'll bring something in."

RISK-TAKING WILDCATTERS

Its economy is based on black gold, on an oil and gas industry notorious for the eccentrics and risk-takers it spawns. Because of the oil price fluctuation in the 1970s, Houston's fortunes rose more quickly than those of any other Texas city. After the drop in world oil prices and demand for energy supplies, its growth slowed to merely brisk. The boom that had shaped the city for three decades faltered following Enron's spectacular plunge into bankruptcy in 2001. The collapse of the Houston-based energy company left thousands unemployed, accelerating the city's dip into recession.

But Houston's listless economy has rebounded just as spectacularly, following recent big oil discoveries in South Texas and accelerated production. Another legacy of the 1970s is the rich ethnic mix – Hispanics, African-Americans, American Indians, East Indians, Iranians, Chinese, Thais, and Vietnamese. This contributes to Houston's resilience, and is undoubtedly part of the reason that Houston is the most diverse city in the US.

Near this utterly flat city are low hills and pine forests, salt marshes, swamps and steamy bayous (marshy inlets), some of which are infested with alligators. Far to the west, but no more than a day's drive, are real hills, then cactus and the desert. And it is only an hour's drive to the Gulf of Mexico beaches.

FREEWAY LIFE

Because of its size, the only logical way to tour Houston is by car, in which many Houstonians spend more time than at home. The downtown area is enclosed by I-45 on the west and, some way to the east, US 59, with two other much-visited areas – the Museum District and the famed Texas Medical Center – to the southwest. The city yawns between a vast network of busy highways, as a result of which buildings are consciously designed as "freeway architecture." Since there are no changes in elevation, tall buildings function as the only landmarks for the driver.

The I-610 loop that garlands the city also divides it as surely as the Wall once separated Berlin. If there is snobbery here, it's on the part of those who live inside the Loop, where all the desirable neighborhoods and almost all of the tourist attractions are located. Perhaps the best-known downtown structure is Philip Johnson's **Pennzoil Place Ⓐ**, with its two towers that appear to separate and then come together as one drives around the city. One block from Pennzoil Place is I.M. Pei's distinctive **JPMorgan Chase Tower Ⓑ**, formerly the Texas Commerce Bank Tower, a cool, gray slab nicknamed "the Texas Tombstone." A

Statue of General Sam Houston, the Texan hero who gave his name to the city.

Shops in Midtown.

Tip

To get a feel for the diversity of lifestyles in the Montrose area, grab a drink at one of the sidewalk cafés and watch a colorful parade of college kids and trendy singles cruise by on foot and in cars.

few blocks north, Market Square Tower is home to the state's highest swimming pool, which protrudes from the top of the building allowing swimmers to look through a transparent floor at the street 40 floors below.

Tranquility Park C, at Bagby and Walker streets, near Sam Houston Park, and its restored century-old structures, including an 1878 general store, is named for the moon base Tranquility. It is landscaped to look like Tranquility Base, with craters and mounds, fountains, reflecting pools, and copper tubes representing the rockets taking off. The Houston Welcome Center (1001 Avenida de las Americas 77010; tel: 713-853-8100; www.visithoustontexas.com; Tue–Fri 8am–5pm, Sat–Sun 10am–5pm) is near here, just a 20-minute walk away.

The oldest part of the original city is **Market Square Park D**, but more significant is **Allen's Landing Park E**, a few blocks north, beside the bayou. Here is where Houston's founders, Augustus and John Allen, first came ashore in 1836.

Among the best downtown parks is **Discovery Green Park**, a 12-acre (5-hectare) urban park with a small lake, jogging trails, event spaces, gardens, restaurants, and a playground. It's a favorite among Houstonians for many reasons. Not only can they cool off in various fountains and a giant artsy mister when the Houston heat wave hits, but the park encourages activities like bocce and golfing with a putting green and kayak rentals on the lake. Others just like grabbing a drink or meal at Discovery Green's restaurants like The Grove and The Lake House before admiring some of the park's great public art with their dog in hand or catching a free concert on one of the stages.

A 6-mile (10km) system of **underground tunnels** connects 55 buildings and 95 city blocks in Houston's downtown area, making it possible to visit more than 100 shops and some small restaurants without surfacing into the heat. This subterranean city is open from 6am to 6.30pm weekdays, and maps are available at banks along the route.

Part of Houston's 6-mile (10km) underground tunnel system.

ENTERTAINMENT AREAS

Downtown Houston is also the upscale entertainment district, home of the **Wortham Theater Center** F, (501 Texas Avenue; tel: 832-487-7000; www.houstonfirsttheaters.com), hosting the Houston Grand Operaand Houston Balletcompanies. The Houston Symphonybunks down in **Jones Hall for the Performing Arts** G (615 Louisiana Street; tel: 832-487-7050; www.houstonfirsttheaters.com) along with Houston Society for the Performing Arts. These and other venues operate under the aegis of Houston First Corporation, which has recently joined forces with the Houston Convention and Visitors Bureau to promote arts and culture in Houston. Drama has its main home at the acclaimed **Alley Theatre** H (615 Texas Avenue; tel: 713-220-5700; www.alleytheatre.org).

Minute Maid Park I (501 Crawford Street; tel: 713-259-8000; http://houston.astros.mlb.com/hou/ballpark) has a capacity of 41,000 and houses the Houston Astros baseball team. It features a full-size vintage locomotive along one side and has a retractable roof to cater to all aspects of the Texan climate. Tours are available daily.

HIPSTER MONTROSE

Heading south on Montrose Boulevard, west of downtown, brings you to the **Montrose** district, established in 1911, a major entertainment area whose center is the intersection of Westheimer and Montrose. This attractive area has been called "the Heart of Houston," and named one of America's great neighborhoods. Driving from downtown along Gray Street takes you through the old Fourth Ward, a tough neighborhood of single-corridor houses. Montrose is the home of the largest LGBTQ community in Texas, as well as of artists, designers, museum personnel, and trendy young singles, and, as you might imagine, it has gentrified into an attractive mix of renovated bungalows with wide porches, cute cottages, and updated mansions.

In its back streets, LGBTQ bars cater to every taste; on the main drag, Westheimer, entertainment is directed to a

Eat

For a proper hipster cup of coffee head to Blacksmith (1018 Westheimer Road; tel: 832-360-7470; www.blacksmithhouston.com) or Black Hole (4504 Graustark Street; tel: 713-528-0653). For something a little stronger than coffee head over to The Hay Merchant (1100 Westheimer Road; tel: 713-528-9805; www.haymerchant.com) or Avant Garden (411 Westheimer Road; tel: 832-287-5577; www.avantgardenhouston.com).

Fashionable Montrose boutique.

Fact

The huge Houston Livestock Show and Rodeo (tel: 832-667-1000; www.rodeohouston.com) takes place in March.

broader spectrum and boutiques display vintage clothing, erotic birthday cakes, neon hair ornaments, and punk garb. In the 5,000–6,000 blocks is The Galleria, the largest mall in Texas with 30 million visitors each year. East of the intersection is a string of restaurants and bars, characterized by Tex-Mex cuisine, lasers, videos, and neon.

ART AND INTERFAITH

As Montrose Boulevard heads south, it becomes more elegant prior to crossing US 59 and heading into the grassy purlieus of the **Museum District**. A few blocks west, in a specially designed building, is the terrific **Menil Collection** J (1533 Sul Ross Street; tel: 713-525-9400; www.menil.org; Wed–Sun 11am–7pm; free), Houston's premier art museum. The collection is a legacy of the de Menil family, with exhibits ranging from medieval and Byzantine art to contemporary works, including the world's largest private collection of Surrealist art.

Across the street is a Greek Orthodox church offering a collection of icons for public viewing, and facing it is the celebrated **Rothko Chapel** K (3900 Yupon Street; tel: 713-524-9839; www.rothkochapel.org; daily 10am–6pm; free), commissioned by John and Dominique de Menil to house 14 paintings by the abstract expressionist Mark Rothko. This interfaith chapel, its entrance flanked by the Broken Obelisk – a memorial to Dr Martin Luther King – is a remarkable space, a hushed temple to art with a meditational aura. The completion of its renovation in 2020 means the Rothko Chapel now has a Visitor Welcome House across the street and a new lighting design around Rothko's work.

Near here can be found the **Houston Center for Photography** L (1441 W. Alabama; tel: 713-529-4755; www.hcponline.org; Wed, Thu 11am–9pm, Fri 11am–5pm, Sat–Sun 11am–7pm; free), a worthwhile destination if you enjoy photography.

Where Montrose Boulevard crosses Bissonnet Street, heavy culture sets in. The **Museum of Fine Arts, Houston** M (1001 Bissonnet; tel: 713-639-7300;

Children's Museum of Houston.

THE ORANGE SHOW

The Orange Show Center for Visionary Art (2401 Munger Street; tel: 713-926-6368; www.orangeshow.org; Wed–Sun 9am–1pm in summer and Sat–Sun 11.30am–5pm in spring and fall; call for off-season hours) is a remarkable piece of folk art in Houston. It's a labyrinth of passages, murals, antiques, and a tiny museum, otherwise impossible to describe. The life's work of mail carrier Jeff McKissack, who built it over 26 years out of junkyard scraps between 1956 and his death in 1980, it promotes the life-giving qualities of the orange. "Be smart; eat oranges" is spelled out in mosaic tiles. When McKissack died, it was bought by a Houston nonprofit organization of donors, including Texas rockers ZZ Top, restored, and opened to the public.

www.mfah.org; Tue–Wed 10am–5pm, Thu until 9pm, Fri–Sat until 7pm, Sun 12.15–7pm; free) and the **Contemporary Arts Museum** N (5216 Montrose; tel: 713-284-8250; www.camh.org; Tue, Wed, and Fri 10am–7pm, Thu until 9pm, Sat 10am–6pm, Sun noon–6pm; free) sit across the street from one other. MFAH, whose modern addition was the work of the renowned architect Ludwig Mies Van der Rohe, houses a large permanent collection from all periods, with strong holdings of French Impressionists and 20th-century Americans. Across the street, the museum's Cullen Sculpture Garden, designed by Isamu Noguchi and displaying sculptures by Matisse, Miro, and Giacometti, among others, is open until 10pm. The CAM does not have a permanent collection, but is a stainless-steel kunsthalle staging nine exhibitions each year, featuring the latest wrinkles in new art.

A more somber experience is offered at the **Holocaust Museum Houston** O (5401 Caroline Street; tel: 713-942-8000; www.hmh.org; Mon–Fri 9am–5pm, Sat 10am–5pm, Sun noon–5pm; free; tours available), an educational facility aimed at eliminating prejudice and hatred through poignant permanent and visiting exhibitions.

SCIENCE AND NATURE

Four blocks down Binz Street is the **Children's Museum of Houston** P (1500 Binz Street; tel: 713-522-1138; www.cmhouston.org; Tue–Sat 10am–6pm, Thu until 8pm, Sun noon–6pm; free), with hands-on exhibits.

In nearby Hermann Park, you'll find the **Houston Museum of Natural Science** Q (tel: 713-639-4629; www.hmns.org; daily 9am–5pm) home to a Space Age museum and the Burke Baker Planetarium, and one of the top ten attended museums in the US. Part of the complex houses the Cullen Hall of Gems and Minerals, containing more minerals and gemstone varieties than you knew existed, the Wortham IMAX Theater, which projects movies hourly onto a six-story screen (tel: 713-639-4629 for schedule), and the recently donated Gordon W. Smith North American Collection, which displays a stellar 600-piece collection of tribal headdresses and other paraphernalia acquired from American Indian friends of Smith starting in the 1920s.

As you enter the park, be sure to stop and smell the roses at the Garden Center (open daily; free) and wander through the six-story glass cone that houses the recently renovated and expanded **Cockrell Butterfly Center**, in which thousands of brightly colored lepidoptera flutter around a waterfall in a tropical garden.

Also in the park is the **Houston Zoo** R (tel: 713-533-6500; www.houstonzoo.org; daily 9am–6pm) has a Tropical Bird House, which takes the form of an Asian jungle.

MORE MUSEUMS

There are more museums and art galleries in Houston than in any other

Fact

Hermann Park covers some 455 acres (185 hectares) of wooded land and, as well as museums and gardens, includes facilities for sports such as golf, tennis, cycling, and hiking.

The Museum of Fine Arts.

> **Fact**
>
> The Galleria is home to nearly 400 stores, in three sections and on three levels. Deluxe department stores like Neiman Marcus grab the headlines but even the cheapest goods can be bought in the center.

Texas city, and plenty of money to support world-class exhibits. The Museum of Fine Arts Houston, for example, also owns **Bayou Bend Collection and Gardens** ❺ (6003 Memorial Drive; tel: 713-639-7750; www.mfah.org/visit/bayou-bend-collection-and-gardens; Tue–Sat 10am–5pm, Sun 1–5pm; free), just before Memorial Park. This stunning 24-room mansion, designed by Houston architect John F. Staub, is filled with decorative American art from colonial times to the early part of the 20th century. The collection was left to the museum by Houston philanthropist Ima Hogg (yes, it was her real name), daughter of the state's first Texas-born governor, James Stephen Hogg. The 14 acres (6 hectares) of landscaped grounds are open to the public every day except Sunday and Monday.

Also not to be overlooked is the **Blaffer Art Museum** (4173 Elgin Street; tel: 713-743-9521; Tue–Sat 10am–5pm, Thu until 8pm; www.blafferartmuseum.org) – described as a "laboratory for the visual arts and contemporary culture" – located in the Arts District of the campus of the University of Houston. Echoes of the Old West are preserved in the **American Cowboy Museum** (11822 Almeda; tel: 713-478-9677; appointment only), and proof that Houston can be as weird as the best of them, the **National Museum of Funeral History** (415 Barren Springs Drive; tel: 281-876-3063; www.nmfh.org; Tue–Fri 10am–4pm, Sat until 5pm, Sun noon–5pm), which has a collection of hearses, sarcophagi, and coffins, and memorabilia from the funerals of Michael Jackson, JFK, and others, always evokes curiosity from macabre-minded visitors.

> **NEIGHBORHOOD DINING**
>
> Houstonians are said to eat out more than any other US community, and there are over 10,000 restaurants in the Houston area from which to choose. Reflecting the city's multicultural background, you'll find every cuisine here, from Chinese, Vietnamese, and Indian to Cajun, Italian, and Tex-Mex, plenty of casual fare, and some of the most inventive gourmet dining around. Neighborhood restaurants are constantly springing up, as Houston grows and new areas become hot destinations. In the West University/Rice area, **Goode Company Texas Bar-B-Q** (tel: 713-522-2530; www.goodecompany.com), is a nationally recognized Texas barbecue mecca. In the Museum District, **Green Seed Vegan** (tel: 844-365-8346; www.greenseedvegan.com) is considered to be one of the best vegan restaurants in the US. Award-winning chef-owner Hugo Ortega's **Hugo's** (tel: 713-524-7744; www.hugosrestaurant.net) in a beautiful dining space in Montrose is the place to push the boat. In the Galleria, you'll find popular **RDG + Bar Annie** (tel: 713-804-1800; www.cafeanniehouston.com), a great place for inventive Southwest food. Meanwhile, in the Upper Kirby/Greenway Plaza neighborhood of Central Houston, you can enjoy casual Indian dining at **Pondicheri** (tel: 713-522-2022; www.pondichericafe.com), a sister restaurant to **Indika** (tel: 713-524-2170; www.indikausa.com) in Montrose. You'll eat well in Houston. Bring a big appetite.

OAK-SHADED CAMPUS

The gentle Victorian Romanesque campus of **Rice University**, surrounded by giant oaks, abuts Hermann Park to the west. Beyond is the immense and highly regarded **Texas Medical Center** ❼, whose 700-acre (283-hectare) complex, renowned for its cancer treatments. The center's former cardiac surgeons include Michael deBakey, who was awarded the US Congressional Gold Medal for his work. Kings, world leaders, and presidents have come here for treatment. Rice, a pleasant retreat from the sterile towers of the Medical Center, has set up a monumental sculpture by Michael Heizer – three 70-ton (63.5-metric ton) blocks of pink Texas granite.

ECCENTRIC ARCHITECTURE

The area around Rice is the most beautiful in Houston. **Rice Village** ❽, at Kirby and University, was Houston's first upscale shopping center and its 325 stores are still a major attraction today. Two stately streets, North and South boulevards, set the local standard for majestic oak tree canopies, and, behind Georgian Revival facades live the old moneyed classes of Houston eccentricity, as seen in a totally pink house at the corner of Hazard and

Sunset streets. Everything, including the fence and garage, is painted tropical flamingo pink.

A comprehensive tour of Houston architecture would also have to include the unbelievable folk art building **Beer Can House** Ⓥ (222 Malone Street, off Memorial Drive; tel: 719-926-6368; www.orangeshow.org/beer-can-house; Sat–Sun noon–5pm in spring and fall, Wed–Sun noon–5pm in the summer), constructed from 50,000 cans by John Milkovisch, a retired upholsterer for the Southern Pacific Railroad, near the extensive and lovely Memorial Park.

ART DECO TOWER

Heading out from the city center, US 59, also called the Southwest Freeway, carries a river of commuters every day, with rush hours lasting 6–9am and 2–8pm. At the point where it intersects with Loop 610 stands the ultimate in freeway architecture, the **Williams Tower**, formerly the Transco Tower, designed by Philip Johnson and John Burgee. The facade, inspired in part by the San Jacinto Monument, is the same on all four sides, in order to be admired from any direction, and its Art Deco lines can easily be taken in while driving at 55mph (88kmph). A beautiful nearby fountain rewards those who see it on foot.

UPSCALE SHOPPING

Williams Tower is right next to the famous upscale **Galleria** shopping center, centered around Post Oak Road and Westheimer Road, near the West Loop (I-610). Here can be found a Who's Who of retailing – Neiman Marcus, Saks Fifth Avenue, Gucci, Tiffany, Cartier, and Versace, to name but a few. The area is marked by glamorous buildings designed by Cesar Pelli and Johnson and Burgee, and the enclosed Galleria itself is modeled on Milan's Galleria, but blown up to immense size. Every luxury store under the sun is represented, as well as an ice-skating rink and a jogging track around the roof.

In its early years, the Galleria was supported by the well-heeled from sections like River Oaks, around the

The Houston Gay Pride Parade has been held annually since 1979.

Rice Village.

Fact

With its increased Asian population, Houston is no longer just known for its Cajun or Tex-Mex cooking. Here you can eat Chinese, Vietnamese, Thai, Japanese, Indian, and many other exotic cuisines.

610 Loop, between Uptown and Downtown, one of America's first planned communities and a model for beautifully integrated homes and landscaping. River Oaks was established around a country club in the 1920s by brothers William and Michael Hogg (brothers of Ima Hogg) and is now the most expensive subdivision in Texas, with mansions costing between $1 million and $20 million. The mansions along streets like River Oaks Boulevard, Lazy Lane, and Inwood belong to captains of industry, oil and cattle barons, their descendants, and a few Arab sheiks. First-run foreign and independent movies can be seen at the 1939 vintage River Oaks Theatre (2009 W. Gray Street, near Shepherd; tel: 713-524-2175, www.landmarktheatres.com/houston/river-oaks-theatre).

FIESTA MARKET

If you exit the Southwest Freeway at Hillcroft and head south toward the Bellaire intersection, you will come to the **Fiesta Market**, the ultimate ethnic grocery store. Advertising is in Spanish, Vietnamese, Chinese, Hindi, and English. Fiesta sells everything from cowboy boots to goat's milk. It is always jammed with shoppers, and the interior is ablaze with huge neon signs. It is an astonishing and hilarious store, now replicated at other locations. In another display of pure Texas culture – the culture of bigness – a huge piano on the Southwest Freeway alerts drivers to the presence of a piano store.

HEADING NORTH

Just north of the center of the city, and slightly west, is a mixed residential and industrial neighborhood called **The Heights**. The houses are older and more graceful, but one of the highlights of The Heights is the grave of Texas billionaire Howard Hughes in **Glenwood Cemetery**, off Washington Boulevard. Hughes's grave is as simply marked as those of his parents nearby. All three are completely overshadowed by the dramatic figure of a weeping angel embellishing an adjacent grave. This flamboyant monument was prepared by a local interior designer for himself.

Goode Company Texas Bar-B-Q.

DOWN SOUTH

In the southern part of the city is **NRG Park** Ⓦ (tel: 832-667-1400; www.nrgpark.com), which includes the famous Astrodome, built in 1968 and once nicknamed "The Eighth Wonder of the World." It is vast – large enough to fit an 18-story building inside. After the building was shuttered in 2008 due to numerous occupancy code violations, it fell into disuse. Plans to convert the Astrodome into a luxury hotel, movie production studio, or convention center were rejected by voters. The Astrodome was added to the National Register of Historic Places in January 2014 but remains empty.

Nearby is NRG Stadium, home of the NFL American football team the Houston Texans, along with NRG Center (with 706,000 sq ft/7,061 sq meters of exhibit space) and NRG Arena, another event center. NRG Stadium has a retractable roof and seats nearly 70,000 spectators. In 2017, it hosted one of the most spectacular Super Bowls in history which saw the New England Patriots defeat the Atlanta Falcons 34-28 in overtime. NRG Park hosts the huge Houston Livestock Show and Rodeo, the world's largest event of its kind, featuring Western contests from bronco-busting to chuckwagon-racing, as well as soccer matches, an increasingly popular sport in the US.

HOUSTON'S ORIENT

Many of Houston's attractions are in East Downtown, also known as EaDo or the East End, beginning, on the other side of US 59. The area that was once known as **Old Chinatown** is anchored by the landmark **Teen How Taoist Temple** Ⓧ (1507 Delano Street). Here visitors can determine their fortune by shaking out numbered reeds. Be sure to visit the nearby **Kim Son** (2001 Jefferson Street; tel: 713-222-2461; www.kimson.com), a Vietnamese landmark and the largest Asian restaurant in the state. Across town, there's a burgeoning Vietnamese community operating other restaurants on Milam Street, just south of downtown, while Chinese immigrants and their descendants

Fact

At the base of the San Jacinto Monument is a free museum dedicated to the history of the region, covering events from the American Indian period through to the Civil War and beyond.

Ice rink at the Galleria shopping center.

Fact

In 2005, the Astrodome served as the main relief center for refugees from Hurricane Katrina. Many of those refugees, welcomed to Houston, have stayed in the city.

shop and eat in **New Chinatown**, located in Southwest Houston along Bellaire Boulevard, between Gessner and Wilcrest. New Chinatown is sometimes referred to as Asiatown, the Bellaire Corridor, or the Diho Area, after the **Diho Square**, a large Asian shopping center.

SHIPS AND SPACESHIPS

The wealth Houston enjoys today derives not only from oil discovered elsewhere but the 50-mile (80km) **Ship Channel** that turned it into an inland port. Houston businessmen persuaded the government to pay for the shipping channel, which developed their city into one of the three busiest ports in the US, stealing the glory (and the trade) from coastal Galveston, after an apocalyptic storm wrecked the latter city's harbor in 1900. The channel's turning basin, off US 90A near Navigation Boulevard, is the site of free harbor tours, but a more rewarding trip is to visit the other end of the channel, where it enters Burnett Bay and ends its journey to the sea.

Historic Queen Anne building on Heights Boulevard.

The way there, however, takes one through the **Pasadena–Baytown Industrial Corridor**, a district filled with every kind of petrochemical processing plant. The air smells like floor cleaner and plays havoc with the sinuses, although at night the industrial landscape assumes a beautiful, otherworldly quality. Pasadena also has a landmark: the vast **Armand Bayou Nature Center** (8500 Bay Area Boulevard; tel: 281-474-2551; www.abnc.org; Wed–Sat 9am–5pm, Sun noon–5pm). You can visit the center's Martyn Farm, which will take you back to farm life in the late 1800s.

There are two attractions at this end of the channel, in La Porte: the World War I dreadnought Battleship Texas **State Historic Site**, which served as General Eisenhower's flagship during the 1944 D-Day invasion, and the 1,200-acre (486-hectare) San Jacinto Battleground State Historic Site (3523 Independence Parkway; tel: 281-479-2431; www.tpwd.texas.gov/state-parks/san-jacinto-battleground; daily 9am–6pm, self-guided tours). The latter commemorates the Battle of San Jacinto on April 21, 1836, making it arguably the most significant monument in the state, as it marks the date on which Texas won its freedom from Mexico with General Sam Houston's defeat of Mexico's Santa Anna. Only weeks after the ignominy of the Alamo, revenge must have been sweet. The Art Deco monument offers an elevator ride 570ft (174 meters) to the top for a view of downtown Houston on one side and a spaghetti bowl of pipelines on the other.

Notwithstanding its varied other attractions, what has brought Houston to worldwide attention in recent decades has been the **Johnson Space Center** (see page 194), 25 miles (40km) southeast of downtown (take I-45, then NASA Road 1; tel: 281-483-0123; www.nasa.gov/centers/johnson/home/index.html; open daily).

TEX-MEX

Tex-Mex is a homestyle border cuisine that emphasizes inexpensive spiced meats such as hot chili, beans and tortillas, salsa picante, guacamole, and cheese.

Visitors to Texas are guaranteed to encounter Mexican food – and plenty of it. But it's not exactly Mexican. What you will find is a Texan version of it called "Tex-Mex." These dishes are quite a bit hotter than California-Mex or Arizona-Mex, so keep plenty of beans or rice handy.

Discussing what precisely constitutes Tex-Mex is a state pastime – so don't expect to discover any definitive answers. However, most Texans would probably agree that, in its most elemental form, Tex-Mex food consists of some preparation of flat corn-meal tortillas, beans, and tomatoes, onions, and chili peppers, the latter three items frequently chopped together in a picante (hot) sauce. They'd possibly also accept by definition cheese and chili meat sauce, but beyond that they're likely to disagree.

Texans are more unified in their definition of what Tex-Mex isn't. Any part of the States with a Mexican heritage will have its own related version of "Mex" cooking, but the cuisine of Mexico is not Tex-Mex. Neither is New Mexico-Mex, with its refined green *chile* (note the Spanish spelling) sauces and distinctive blue cornmeal; neither is California-Mex, rich with sour cream and lavish produce.

Tex-Mex food is not fancy. The meat it includes is usually inexpensive and tough, chopped or marinated into submission. The most famous, of course, is chili, which in Tex-Mex is a spicy meat stew without beans. Tex-Mex food is home fare, the food of the common people. But, most importantly, it is the supreme expression of the noble chili pepper, and as such it must be as hot as the hinges of Hell's Front Door.

Where to find the best Tex-Mex is a bigger debate than what it contains. Serious devotees contend that real Tex-Mex food can't be found north of Waco (mid-state), but all Texans agree it doesn't exist outside the state.

Most Tex-Mex is eaten as Mexican restaurant fare. The menu traditionally consists of the following: baskets of fried tortilla chips and bowls of *salsa picante and queso*, melted bowls of cheese, accompanied by beer or sweet tea, are offered while the order is prepared. Shortly afterward, a hot plate of several different specialties arrives.

These might include *enchiladas* – tortillas wrapped around cheese and onions and covered with meat or a spicy tomato sauce; *tacos* – tortillas folded, fried, and stuffed with ground meat, beans, cheese, and the above-mentioned vegetables; a guacamole salad of spiced mashed avocados; and *fajitas* – marinated and grilled bits of steak. The meal is served with rice and beans, hot tortillas, and, of course, several more bowls of *salsa picante* to spoon over everything. Dessert may be *sopapillas* which are fried dough pockets covered in cinnamon sugar and usually eaten with honey.

Tex-Mex cooking has recently absorbed some refinements – using better cuts of meat than its beloved *cabrito* (roast kid) and *menudo* (tripe stew) for example; and the "Tex-Mex cuisine" gaining popularity in the eastern US and Europe is a considerably cooled-down version of it. The more accessible it becomes, the less it resembles real Tex-Mex. To a certain extent this is necessary: every ethnic food has ingredients that appeal only to those who have been raised on them.

Colorful, spicy, authentic Tex-Mex dishes can only be truly savored in Texas itself.

HOUSTON'S SPACE CENTER

Houston, home base for NASA's Apollo lunar missions, was the most important and recognized city on Earth during the early era of space travel.

In the future, should aliens look back on man's first tentative steps beyond Earth, the name Houston will be on the tips of their tongues, tentacles, or whatever it is they use for speaking. Texas's biggest city never actually launched a man into orbit during the heyday of the space program, but US-manned space flights relied upon ground staff here to guide them on their way. Houston, or Mission Control, is the focus of all earthly activity when an astronaut is up there in the deep blue yonder. As well as guiding spacecraft during their missions, Houston is also the selection and training base for NASA astronauts, where they are put through their paces, physically and mentally, before being sent into orbit.

The Manned Space Center, renamed the Johnson Space Center, was opened by the National Aeronautics and Space Administration (NASA) in 1962, as part of President John F. Kennedy's declared intention for America to land a man on the moon and return him safely to Earth before the decade was out. The center played its part to perfection, and "Houston" was the first word spoken from the surface of the moon, by Apollo XI commander Neil Armstrong.

In 1981, NASA launched the Space Shuttle, the first reusable space exploration vehicle, and Houston was again central to its success. Much of NASA's current work revolves around the International Space Station – a cooperative venture between the US and Russia – the Mars Rover program.

Space Center Houston, at the Johnson Space Center, has a fascinating collection of artifacts, including moon rocks, space capsules and an impressive collection of space suits.

From the air, the size of the Space Center's 1,625-acre (660-hectare) site is immediately apparent.

The men who made history – the crew of Apollo XI, the first mission to land on the moon: Neil Armstrong, Michael Collins, and Edwin "Buzz" Aldrin.

The Prebreathe Reduction Program is a research study program at the JSC that is currently being developed to improve the safety and efficiency of space walks from the International Space Station.

In 1995, NASA opened a new Mission Control Center at the site. Costing around $250 million, it replaced the old Mission Control, which had monitored the Apollo and Space Shuttle crews.

Originally known as the Manned Space Center, NASA's Houston site was later renamed to honor Texan-born President Lyndon B. Johnson.

Space-age Fun For All

NASA was established in 1958 as a US Government agency for research into aeronautics and space flight. Throughout the 1960s, it enjoyed substantial funding and plenty of glory, but times have become harder since, with both politicians and the public losing interest in the agency's work.

The fatal 2003 space-shuttle explosion cast further doubt on NASA, which has had to publicly justify every mission.

Part of the PR exercise has been the opening up to the general public of bases like the Kennedy Space Center in Florida and the Johnson Space Center in Houston.

With the help of the Walt Disney Corporation's creative genius, NASA developed a fascinating entertainment and educational exhibit. Now 1 million visitors a year come to see IMAX films, moon rocks, spacecraft, including a replica of Space Shuttle *Independence,* and other memorabilia, and to take tram tours of previously off-limits areas. Interactive exhibits allow them to simulate landing a space shuttle or retrieving a satellite.

One of the Center's biggest attractions is the 363ft (110-meter) long Saturn V rocket. The most powerful rocket of its day, it lifted the Apollo craft into space.

Sunrise over a Texas swamp.

EAST TEXAS

Dense woodlands, stunning lakes, and historic towns make this often ignored part of Texas a discovery; even the oil-producing cities of the "Golden Triangle" have much to interest the traveler.

There's a whole section of Texas that is larger than New England – and has more trees – and its un-Texas topography is certain to confuse most newcomers. **Piney Woods**, the timber country of East Texas, lies between Louisiana and Central Texas, the state's economic launch pad. It was here that industrial interests first wrestled with Mother Nature, raking timber off the land and squeezing oil from beneath it. A lot of scars remain, but this region is known as much for its natural beauty as for its oil and timber industries.

The economic significance of the Gulf of Mexico and the salt dome geological formations along the relatively unsettled coast mean that the region's largest metropolitan area is found at its southeastern corner, specifically around Beaumont, Port Arthur, and Orange. Practically located in Louisiana, and flanking I-10, the three cities, dubbed the "Golden Triangle," now have a metropolitan population approaching 387,711.

GOOD GUESS

Founded in 1835, **Beaumont ❶**, the state's first oil boomtown, sits 21 miles (32km) up from the Gulf of Mexico on a deep-water ship channel dredged from the Neches River. Geologists of the late 19th century had scoffed at the theory that oil reservoirs might be tucked inside the salt domes, but a local real estate developer, Patillo Higgins, suspected the gaseous vapors and sulfurous water at nearby Spindletop Hill indicated a pool of the valuable liquid. Along with an Austrian immigrant, Anthony F. Lucas, he drilled several unsuccessful wells in 1900, before hitting the Lucas Gusher. After the Spindletop oil discovery on January 10, 1901, Texas was transformed from an agriculturally dominated economy into one that could tap very fast-flowing pockets of wealth.

Main attractions

- Texas Energy Museum, Beaumont
- Caddo Mounds State Historic Site
- Sam Rayburn House Museum, Bonham
- Eisenhower Birthplace State Historic Site, Denison
- Big Thicket National Preserve

Map on page 198

McFaddin-Ward House Museum.

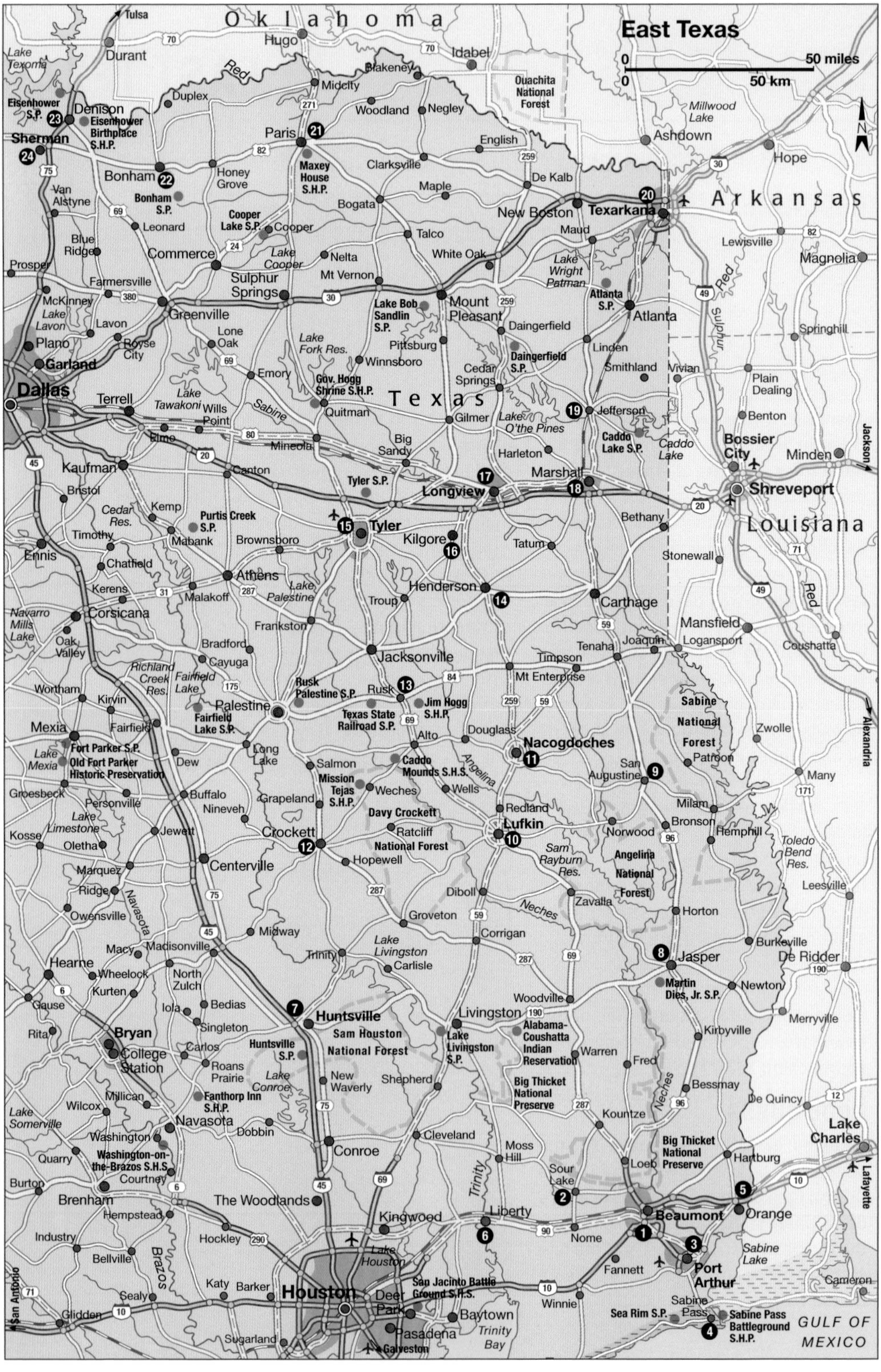
East Texas
0 50 miles
0 50 km
Oklahoma
Texas
Arkansas
Louisiana
GULF OF MEXICO
Dallas
Houston
Tyler
Longview
Texarkana
Shreveport
Beaumont
Port Arthur
Nacogdoches
Lufkin
Huntsville
Palestine
Paris
Sherman
Denison
Bonham
Marshall
Jefferson
Kilgore
Henderson
Crockett
San Augustine
Jasper
Orange
Liberty
Sabine National Forest
Angelina National Forest
Davy Crockett National Forest
Sam Houston National Forest
Big Thicket National Preserve
Ouachita National Forest
Sam Rayburn Res.
Toledo Bend Res.
Lake Livingston
Lake Texoma
Caddo Lake
Sabine Lake
Sabine Pass Battleground S.H.P.
Sea Rim S.P.
San Jacinto Battle Ground S.H.S.
Caddo Mounds S.H.S.
Mission Tejas S.H.P.
Texas State Railroad S.P.
Jim Hogg S.H.P.
Fort Parker S.P.
Eisenhower Birthplace S.H.P.
Eisenhower S.P.
Alabama-Coushatta Indian Reservation

In the space of two years, Beaumont's population swelled from 9,000 to 50,000, as East Texas became a get-rich-quick magnet. Oil derricks sprouted here as thick as the pines, and their furious pumping of the salt domes took its toll. At the appropriately named **Sour Lake** ❷, about 20 miles (32km) west of Beaumont on State Route 105, visitors can still survey the damage in the form of a 10-acre (4-hectare) sinkhole created in 1929 by three decades of drilling.

Among the many museums devoted to the industry's fascinating history are Beaumont's reconstructed **Spindletop-Gladys City Boomtown Museum** (5550 Jimmy Simmons Boulevard; tel: 409-880-1750; www.lamar.edu/spindletop-gladys-city/index.html; Tue–Sat 10am–5pm, Sun 1–5pm) on the Lamar University campus, and the **Texas Energy Museum** (600 Main Street; tel: 409-833-5100; www.texasenergymuseum.org; Tue–Sat 9am–5pm, Sun 1–5pm).

The city's oldest home, the **John Jay French Museum** (3025 French Road; tel: 409-898-0348; https://beaumontheritage.org/john-jay-french-house; Tue–Fri 10am–3pm, Sat 10am–2pm), depicts the life of the Connecticut-born trader, who settled here in 1845, while the elegant **McFaddin-Ward House Museum** (1906 Calder Avenue; tel: 409-832-2134; www.mcfaddin-ward.org; Tue–Fri 10am–3.30pm, Sat 10.30am–3.30pm, Sun 1–3.30pm) is a 17-room mansion owned by an early 20th-century oilman.

Among the city's other sights are the **Edison Museum** (350 Pine Street; tel: 409-981-3089; http://edisonmuseum.americommerce.com; Tue–Fri 9am–2pm, Sat 10am–2pm; free), housed, appropriately, in a converted power station and devoted to the life of the great inventor; the **Fire Museum of Texas** (400 Walnut Street; tel: 409-880-3927; www.fmotassn.com; Mon–Fri 8am–4.30pm; free), and the **Babe Didrikson Zaharias Memorial** (1750 I-10 East; tel: 409-833-4622; www.babedidriksonzaharias.org; Mon–Sat 9am–5pm; free), which commemorates the state's most famous athlete, the Beaumont-born triple winner of track and field events at the 1932 Los Angeles Olympics and only woman to qualify for a men's golf tournament, the Los Angeles Open in 1938.

LIVELY CAJUNS

Beaumont's sister city to the southeast is **Port Arthur** ❸. Home of one of the world's largest petrochemical complex, it is noted for its fleet of shrimp boats, its superlative seafood, and its Cajun nightclubs, with their fiddle music and rowdy atmosphere. *"Laissez les bon temps rouler!"* – Let the good times roll! – is a much-quoted Cajun saying, which the tourist board never tires of pointing out.

Port Arthur was the birthplace of the late rock singer Janis Joplin, whose birthday is celebrated every January 19, and is the kind of place where tourists can attend a genuine, music-filled Cajun wedding – of two alligators.

The city was founded in 1895 as the seaport terminus of his Gulf Coast Railroad by Arthur Stilwell, who ran out of money and lost ownership to a famous

Port Arthur is home to the world's largest petrochemical complex.

Caddo Lake State Park.

speculator, John "Bet-a-Million" Gates. But the glamorous mansions of what was once "Stilwells' Dream City" still remain along the white sandy shores of **Lake Sabine**, some 9 miles (14km) long and 7.5 miles (12km) across, and joined to the ocean by the Sabine–Neches Ship Channel, which flows right through the city.

The little town of **Sabine Pass** ❹, laid out by Sam Houston himself in 1836, was the site of a famous 1863 Civil War battle; today it is part of Port Arthur. **Sabine Pass Battleground State Historic Site** (6100 Dowling Road; tel: 512-463-7948; www.thc.texas.gov/historic-sites/sabine-pass-battleground-state-historic-site; daily 8am–5pm, until 8pm May–Aug) honors the 46 Confederates, led by a barkeep named Dick Dowling, who deployed half a dozen cannons to drive off a Union force at least a hundred times as large. The site features a stately bronze statue of Confederate Lt. Richard "Dick" Dowling, who led the men to victory, and an interpretive pavilion illustrating the story of the battle. Nearby **Sea Rim State Park** (19335 South Gulfway Drive; tel: 409-971-2559; http://tpwd.texas.gov/state-parks/sea-rim; open daily), along the gulf, is a great place to do some birdwatching.

The most famous house in Port Arthur is **Pompeiian Villa** (1953 Lakeshore Drive; tel: 409-983-5977; www.museumofthegulfcoast.org/pompeiian-villa; Mon, Wed and Fri 1–5pm, Tue and Thu 10am–2pm), built in 1900 for barbed wire inventor Isaac Ellwood. He sold it to a fellow tycoon, Diamond Match Company president James Hopkins. When Hopkins's wife arrived to discover Port Arthur's oppressive heat, mosquitoes, and muddy streets she turned right around and returned to St Louis, so Hopkins traded the mansion to banker George Craig for 10 percent of the stock in the newly formed Texas Oil Company (which became Texaco). When teased later about why he'd given up his stock for what became known as "the billion dollar house," Craig replied: "Oil companies were a dime a dozen then. How did I know the Texas Oil Company would survive?"

Two other old Lakeshore mansions are worth visiting: **Rose Hill Manor**

The marshy areas of East Texas are alligator country – beware!

(100 Woodworth Boulevard; tel: 409-985-7292; www.woodworth-ancestors.com/woodworth-places/wdwrth-port-arthur/index.htm; Tue–Fri 11am–5pm, Sat by appointment only; donation) and **White Haven** (2545 Lakeshore Drive; tel: 409-984-6101; free guided tours by appointment). Port Arthur's heritage is further displayed in its **Museum of the Gulf Coast** (700 Procter Street; tel: 409-982-7000; www.museumofthegulfcoast.org; Mon–Sat 9am–5pm), where such celebrated locals as Janis Joplin, the Big Bopper, Harry James, Babe Didrikson Zaharias, and artist Robert Rauschenberg are honored.

OVER THE RAINBOW

Rainbow Bridge, a 1.5-mile (2.5km) graceful arc over the Neches River, at a clearance height of 177ft (56 meters), is the tallest on the coast and joins Port Arthur with the city of **Orange** ❺. Here Farmer's Mercantile on Division Street, a funky store that opened in 1928, is not only still in business but carries some of the same items as when it began.

On Green Avenue, the **Stark Museum of Art** (712 Green Avenue; tel: 409-886-2787; http://starkculturalvenues.org/starkmuseum; Tue–Sat 9am–5pm) and nearby **W.H. Stark House** (610 W Main Avenue; tel: 409-883-0871; http://starkculturalvenues.org/whstarkhouse; open every second Friday and Saturday of the month) are eye-popping structures whose exteriors are almost as interesting as the furniture and artworks that they contain.

From Orange, fascinating airboat tours can be taken (Swamp and River Tours, 813 East Lutcher Drive; tel: 409-883-0856; http://swampandrivertours.com) of the alligator-infested swamps, salt marshes, and bayous that surround the area. The rice fields and marshlands, with their moss-laden trees and tropical palms, are a refuge for hundreds of thousands of migrating waterfowl, attractive alike to the birdwatcher and, alas, the hunter.

FARTHER NORTH

Liberty ❻, on US 90 near the Trinity River, between Beaumont and Houston, traces its history back to the Spanish mission erected nearby and its downtown area created by the Mexican government in 1831. **Huntsville** ❼, 70 miles (113km) north of Houston, on US 75 and I-45 – which marks the western boundary of the East Texas pioneer region – was founded in 1830 by settlers from Huntsville, Alabama. It has the state prison and Sam Houston State University, and claims added significance as the town where Sam Houston lived his later life. The site of Houston's grave is also here, along with a 67ft (20-meter) -tall statue of Houston as you approach Huntsville from the south on I-45. **Jasper** ❽, 100 miles (160km) to the east, where US 190 meets US 96 (which runs part of the way alongside Sabine National Forest), offers visitors another chance to view historic sites. Founded in 1824 beside the Angelina River, Jasper was the home of the Tavern Oak, a 250-year-old giant pine oak (connected to a tavern there in 1839 but

Fact

Mission Señora de los Dolores de los Ais (also known as the Dolores Mission) was founded in 1716 and abandoned in 1773. Nothing remains of the historic structure, but there is a museum with informative displays and archaeological artifacts and a walking trail at the site.

W.H. Stark House.

unfortunately destroyed by a tornado in 1996). Several old historic houses, from around the middle of the 19th century, do, however, exist.

Almost in Louisiana, **San Augustine** ❾ is a town where, at one time or another, nearly every famous Texan in those early days walked the streets, including Davy Crockett who was given a feast here on the way to the Alamo. Historic places include Cullen House (205 S. Congress Street; tel: 936-275-5110; www.drtinfo.org/preservation/chapter-owned-properties/ezekiel-cullen-house; open Thu–Sat 1–4 pm from February-December), the 1839 house of the famous Texas judge; the site of the 18th-century Mission Señora de los Dolores de los Ais; and the Old Town Well in the old Stripling's Drug Store, dug to a depth of 27ft (8 meters) by slaves in 1860 to serve travelers.

WOOD WEALTH

After the political turmoil of the early 19th-century had been quelled, a new wave of boomtowns grew up in East Texas, built on another economic base: timber. **Lufkin** ❿, on US 69, southeast of San Augustine, was founded in 1882 and was the home of the South's first paper mill. It remains the center of the state's timber industry. One main attraction in this city of 36,000 people is the **Texas Forestry Museum** (1905 Atkinson Drive; tel: 936-632-9535; www.treetexas.com; Mon–Sat 10am–5pm; free), built in a grove of Texas pines, with large glass windows bringing the forest right inside. A moonshiner's still and a blacksmith's forge are among the exhibits. Lufkin also stages an annual Forest Festival every September.

Nacogdoches ⓫, 20 miles (32km) farther north on US 259, was originally settled by the Nacogdoche branch of Caddo Indians, with evidence of settlement dating back 10,000 years ago. It claims to be the first incorporated town in Texas. Now a modern city of 33,000, with a solid economic base of manufacturing, agriculture, retail trade, and tourism, Nacogdoches, almost midway between Houston and Texarkana, makes a fine base for exploring the rest of East Texas.

Nacogdoches and the surrounding area have numerous historic sites, of which the most interesting, 26 miles (42km) west of town, in Alto, is **Caddo Mounds State Historic Site** (1649 US 21 West; tel: 936-858-3218; www.thc.texas.gov/historic-sites/caddo-mounds-state-historic-site; daily 8.30am–4.30pm), the only significant prehistoric American Indian site in Texas. Built by the Hasinai branch of the Caddo Indians 1,200 years ago, the 397-acre (160-hectare) site was the southwesternmost ceremonial center for the powerful Mississippian Mound Builder culture, which spanned the Eastern Woodlands for 2,500 years. The site preserves two temple mounds and a burial mound as well as much of the village. A trail loops around this lovely site, and takes about 45 minutes to walk.

Just north of Nacogdoches is **Millard's Crossing Historic Village** (6020

Nacogdoches.

North Street; tel: 936-564-6631; www.mchvnac.com; Mon–Sat 9am–4pm, Sun 1–4pm). It comprises a dozen or more structures, including a church and schoolhouse, some dating back as far as 1820 and many stocked with original artifacts. **La Calle del Norte** (presently North Street) once linked the original American Indian settlement to villages in the north, and is said to be the oldest public thoroughfare in the United States.

At Pilar and Lanana streets is the **Sterne-Hoya House Museum and Library** (211 S. Lanana Street; tel: 936-560-5426; www.ci.nacogdoches.tx.us/696/Sterne-Hoya-House-Museum-and-Library; Tue–Sat 10am–4pm; free), built in 1828 by a pioneer merchant who helped found the state, and now occupied by a library. Here too, is the **Stone Fort Museum** (1808 Alumni Drive; tel: 936-468-2408; www.sfasu.edu/stonefort; Tue–Sat 9am–5pm, Sun 1–5pm; free), a 1779 Spanish trading post reconstructed on the campus of Stephen F. Austin State University. The fort marks the site of four unsuccessful rebellions, and the museum features tribal artifacts alongside memorabilia from the eras of the eight flags that have flown above the fort – Spain, Magee-Gutierrez Expedition, Long Republic, Fredonian Republic, Mexico, Republic of Texas, Confederacy, and US.

EL CAMINO REAL

Nacogdoches is on one of the most historic routes in America: **El Camino Real de Tejas**, blazed by the Spanish as "The King's Highway," or the Old San Antonio Road. Travelers can follow that path today by taking US 21 out of Nacogdoches in either direction. El Camino Real de Tejas (now a designated National Historical Trail managed by the National Park Service) linked Spanish Colonial Mexico with settlements in Texas and Louisiana by following American Indian trails, shallow fords, or rivers. Incorporated into the state highway system in 1929 as US 21, El Camino Real connects innumerable other historical sites. Not far to the west, for example, is **Crockett** ⓬, founded in 1837 on the spot where Davy Crockett camped en route to

Fact

The town of Nacogdoches has one further claim to fame: it was here that Texas's first newspaper, the *Gaceta de Tejas*, was published.

Farmland near Rusk.

The Kilgore College Rangerettes have performed at 64 consecutive Cotton Bowl games since 1951.

martyrdom at the Alamo. Davy Crockett Memorial Park's 60 wooded acres (24 hectares) are ideal for picnics and relaxing.

TRAINS AND CONFEDERATE GUNS

Rusk ⓭, at the intersection of US 84 and US 69, between Lufkin and Tyler, was founded in 1846 and is home of the **Texas State Railroad State Historical Park** (tel: 855-632-7729; www.texasstaterr.com; trains depart 11am and return at 3.30pm Mar–May Sat–Sun, May–Nov Fri–Sun), a train track that forms the nation's longest and narrowest state park. Visitors can climb aboard for an enjoyable 50-mile (80km) round-trip journey through the Piney Woods and across over 24 bridges, one a 1,000ft (300-meter) crossing of the Neches River.

Historic Fifth Street features old homes and what is claimed to be the nation's longest footbridge, a 547ft (168-meter) span built in 1861, separating the business district from the old residential area. As an important Confederate Army conscription center, Rusk figured prominently in the Civil War. Look for the historical marker that denotes the Confederate Gun Factory. Two miles (3km) west of town is the **Jim Hogg State Historical Park**, 178 acres (72 hectares) dedicated as the birthplace of the state's first Texas-born governor (1891–95).

Henderson ⓮, on US 259 in the center of Rusk County, is another find for visitors in search of old houses, with 44 historic properties on the National Register. Founded in 1843 on land owned by the Cherokee Indians, Henderson's attractions include **The Depot** (514 N. High Street; tel: 903-657-4303; www.depotmuseum.com; Mon–Fri 9am–4pm), an old railroad depot restored as a museum and children's learning center.

METROPOLITAN CENTERS

Three other metropolitan centers – Tyler, Longview, and Marshall – are representative of East Texan urban life, with their oil and timber economic foundations.

Tyler Municipal Rose Garden.

Tyler ⓯ (pop. 105,000), the largest, is located about 100 miles (160km) east of Dallas on I-20 and is a petroleum production center. Also known as the "Rose Capital of America," the town markets more than 50 percent of the nation's rose bushes, maintaining a 14-acre (6-hectare) **Municipal Rose Garden** (420 Rose Park Drive; tel: 903-531-1212), containing over 35,000 bushes and more than 500 varieties. The garden is at its best from May through October.

The oil boom of 1900 at Beaumont proved a harbinger of things to come for the entire region, as wildcatters scattered throughout the Piney Woods prospecting for oil. The frenzy peaked in 1930 with the discovery of the biggest well of all, in Rusk County. This well, known as the Great East Texas Oil Field, was a discovery that held the state's economic spotlight until the fields of West Texas surfaced after World War II.

The boom town associated more than any other with the 1930 strike is **Kilgore** ⓰, just off US 259, 25 miles (40km) east of Tyler. At the peak of its oil boom, more than 1,000 oil-producing wells sat next to local homes and buildings. The "world's richest acre" was the description for a downtown block of Kilgore, where 24 oil wells once produced simultaneously. The town's **East Texas Oil Museum** (1201 S. Henderson Boulevard; tel: 903-983-8295; https://easttexasoilmuseum.kilgore.edu; Wed–Sat 10am–5pm) tells the story. Another attraction is the **Rangerette Showcase** (1100 Broadway Boulevard; tel: 903-983-8265; www.kilgore.edu/campus-life/rangerette-showcase-and-museum; Wed–Fri 10am–3pm) at Kilgore College, which pays tribute to the college's high-kicking precision dance team, formed in 1940 to provide half-time entertainment at football games.

On I-20 is **Longview** ⓱ (pop. 82,000), 10 miles (16km) northeast of Kilgore, which enjoyed explosive growth in the oil-crazed 1930s. Thanks to a dynamic industrialization program begun after World War II, Longview considers its location – among the tall pines, near several well-stocked bass lakes – a magnet for industry as well as recreation. The town's **R.G. Le Tourneau Museum** (2100 S. Mobberly Avenue; tel: 903-233-3260; www.letu.edu/library/rg-museum.html; daily 8am–5pm; free), on the Le Tourneau University campus, displays patents and objects related to the man who became the world's foremost inventor of heavy earth-moving equipment.

CONFEDERATE BASE

Continuing east on I-20, next comes **Marshall** ⓲ (pop. 23,500), a once-wealthy city that supplied gunpowder and ammunition to the Confederacy, for which it became an administrative center. Originally a stagecoach stop, it achieved its prosperity after the arrival of the Texas and Pacific Railroad. A reminder of those early days is provided by the venerable **Ginocchio Hotel** (1896), now a restaurant, which anchors the town's three-block historic district.

Tip

Driving remains the best way to explore the scattered East Texas cities and towns, and the Longview Visitors Bureau can suggest several routes.

The House of the Seasons, in Jefferson, built by Benjamin Epperson.

Replica Eiffel Tower, Paris, Texas.

HISTORIC HOMES

There's always debate about which town in East Texas has the best old homes. San Augustine usually wins great praise, but **Jefferson** ⓳ (pop. 2,000) on US 59, just 58 miles (93km) south of Texarkana, is high on the list, too. It is a living museum of antebellum houses.

Laid out in 1842 as a river landing on Big Cypress Bayou, Jefferson grew into early Texas's primary river port, as steamboats from New Orleans brought settlers westward. With them came the plantation culture and architecture of the Old South. But decline began when the city refused a rail depot.

Many of the city's fine old homes are open during the Annual Historical Pilgrimage on the first weekend in May. Highlights include the **Freeman Plantation** (Highway 49 West; tours by appointment), built in 1850 in Greek Revival style and embodying the grandeur of Louisiana plantation life.

FAMOUS PATRONS

Jefferson's **Excelsior House Hotel** (211 W. Austin; tel: 903-665-2513; www.theexcelsiorhouse.com), dating from 1858, claims to be the oldest hotel in continuous operation in Texas, a place patronized by US Presidents Rutherford B. Hayes and Ulysses S. Grant, as well as Irish playwright and novelist Oscar Wilde and the famous 19th-century industrialist Jay Gould. Still in operation today, it offers guests a chance to relax amid period furnishings, many of them acquired when the hotel first opened more than a century ago – and rumor has it some of the rooms are haunted.

Nearby is Jay Gould's well-preserved luxury railroad car, named the Atalanta (call Excelsior House Hotel for tours). From **Jefferson Landing**, across the bridge from downtown Jefferson, visitors have the chance to take a 45-minute river tour along the old steamboat channel in 20ft (6-meter) handcrafted river boats.

TWICE AS NICE

In the northeastern corner of the region is **Texarkana** ⓴ (pop. 37,000), perched on the Texas-Arkansas state line and thus half in each state. Texarkana is an

Draughon-Moore Ace of Clubs House, Texarkana.

ALABAMA-COUSHATTA

There are few signs in modern times of Texas's once-thriving American Indian population. The small Alabama-Coushatta Indian Reservation has existed since 1854, when Sam Houston established it as a reward to the two tribes for their neutrality during the war for Texan independence. The Alabama-Coushatta trace their ancestors to the historic Muscogee or Creek Confederacy in Alabama, east of the Mississippi, who were removed to this area in the late 18th century. They are one of six federally recognized tribes whose members are descended from the Creek Confederacy. The tribe is known for its annual powwow, which takes place in late May/early June. It also runs a pleasant campground with tent sites, RV hookups, and cabins at Lake Tombigbee (tel: 936-563-1220 for reservations).

agribusiness center for farming, livestock, and timber interests in Arkansas, Louisiana, and Texas. Its slogan is "Twice as Nice," a phrase to describe the city's unique status, which is best illustrated by one of its most unusual landmarks – the Post Office Building, which straddles the state line.

In addition to the town's **Museum of Regional History** (219 State Line Avenue; tel: 903-793-4831; www.texarkanamuseums.org; Tue–Sat 10am–4pm; free), depicting 19th-century life in the region, there is the multi-faceted **Draughon-Moore Ace of Clubs House** (420 Pine Street; tel: 903-793-4831; www.texarkanamuseums.org; open Tue–Sat for tours at 10am, 1pm, and 3.30pm, Sun 1pm and 3.30pm), built over a century ago by the winner of a poker game and still containing the original furnishings.

PIONEER TOWNS

Another notable pioneer town is **Paris** ㉑ (pop. 25,000), on US 82 near the Oklahoma border. Founded in 1839, Paris became home to a notorious list of frontiersmen, including retired outlaw Frank James (brother of Jesse James) and bandit queen Belle Starr. Here (by appointment) visitors can tour the **Sam Bell Maxey House State Historic Site** (812 S. Church Street; tel: 903-785-5716; www.thc.texas.gov/historic-sites/sam-bell-maxey-house-state-historic-site; Tue–Sun 9am–4pm), an exquisite Victorian home built in 1868 by a Confederate general.

A lesser-known victim of the Alamo siege in 1836, James B. Bonham, had a town named after him the following year. It can be found on Highway 82 in the northern part of the state. **Bonham** ㉒ (pop. 10,200) was the home of Sam Rayburn, the Texas politician who served as Speaker of the US House of Representatives for longer than anyone else. The enjoyable homestead that comprises **Sam Rayburn House Museum** (890 W. State Highway 56; tel: 903-583-5558; www.thc.texas.gov/historic-sites/sam-rayburn-house-state-historic-site; Tue–Sun 10am–4pm), with the nearby Library, contains papers of the farmer's son from Fannin County who was House Speaker from 1940 until his death in 1961, apart from two brief interludes.

The **Fannin County Museum of History** (1 N. Main Street; tel: 903-583-8042; www.fannincountymuseum.org; Tue–Sat noon–4pm; free), in a restored railroad depot, is an absorbing collection of pioneer artifacts, ranging from ancient costumes to railroad tools. **Fort Inglish Village** (W. Sam Rayburn Drive; tel: 903-583-3943; http://visitbonham.com/things-to-see/fort-inglish-village; Apr–Sept Thu–Sat 11am–3pm) displays replicas of the blockhouse and stockade built by Bailey Inglish in 1837.

EISENHOWER COUNTRY

Denison ㉓ and **Sherman** ㉔ on the Oklahoma border near Lake Texoma – an impoundment of the Red River – are rich from farming and livestock industries. While it is well known that Texas produced President Lyndon Johnson, another president also came from the Lone Star State, and Denison takes

Tip

When visiting any of the East Texas natural areas, don't forget your insect repellent. The mosquitoes can be ferocious!

Eisenhower Birthplace State Historic Site.

pride in honoring that favorite son: Dwight D. Eisenhower. The **Eisenhower Birthplace State Historic Site** (609 S. Lamar Avenue; tel: 903-465-8908; www.thc.texas.gov/historic-sites/eisenhower-birthplace-state-historic-site; Tue–Sat 9am–5pm, Sun 1–5pm), a two-story frame house, has been restored to its appearance in 1890, the year Ike was born. The adjoining visitor center depicts life during the years when he was president.

DIVERSE ECOSYSTEM

Big Thicket National Preserve (tel: 409-951-6800; www.nps.gov/bith; open daily; free) in East Texas is a fabulous counterpoint to West Texas's massive desert of Big Bend National Park. A dense and mysterious forest, it blankets much of southeast Texas and is bounded by the Neches and San Jacinto rivers and Pine Island Bayou.

Set aside during the Great Depression, when the federal government bought the area from hard-pressed timber companies, Big Thicket withstood challenges from the oil and timber industries for decades and finally, in 1974, environmentalists persuaded Congress to establish the preserve. Its 113,100 acres (45,769 hectares) protect nine different ecosystems, including forests of longleaf pine growing near yucca and cacti, and bald cypress-lined bayous next to southern magnolia trees. Since 1981, it has been a Unesco International Biosphere Reserve, and, in 2001, the American Bird Conservancy designated it a Globally Important Birding Area.

The preserve has 40 miles (64km) of hiking trails, from short boardwalk trails to longer hikes, but no campgrounds; however, primitive camping is allowed with a permit. Boating and kayaking are popular on the **Neches River and Village Creek**. Wildlife watching is the big draw. The preserve lies beneath two major bird migratory routes, and some 300 species of bird can be found living in or migrating through the preserve. Watch for the red-cockaded woodpecker and the brown-headed nuthatch on the Sundew Trail, two birds on most life lists.

For an orientation, stop at **Big Thicket Visitor Center** (6102 FM 420; tel: 409-951-6700; daily 9am–5pm; free), located 8 miles (13km) north of Kountze, or 30 miles (48km) north of Beaumont via US 69/287. Park rangers can help with trip planning and also offer talks and guided hikes daily.

Caddo Lake State Park offers one of the most unique state park experiences in all of Texas. Located right on the border of Texas and Louisiana, Caddo Lake State Park is home to the 26,810-acre (10,849 hectares) Caddo Lake, a maze of bayous, ponds, and waterways lined in bald cypress trees covered in Spanish moss. Explore 50 miles (80km) of paddling trails in this alligator-infested lake by renting one of the park's canoes or fish among 70 species without a state fishing license off the fishing pier or in your own boat. The park offers campgrounds and historic cabins, built by the CCC between 1933–1937, for rent.

Native fungi, Big Thicket National Preserve.

Trail in Caddo Lake State Park.

Galveston Island.

THE GULF COAST

The sea border of Texas runs from Louisiana in the east to Mexico in the south. Its sweeping arc encompasses countless unspoiled beaches, several wildlife sanctuaries, and two historic cities.

It's been called a lot of different things – "funky," "scruffy," oddly even "Byzantine" – but one label has rarely been pinned on the Texas Gulf Coast: "chic." It just does not fit. It's not the Riviera, and it isn't Rio. Even Daytona and Malibu are very distant American cousins. But, from South Padre Island north to Bolivar Peninsula, the Gulf Coast ranks as one of Texas's most powerful magnets for travelers. It exudes history.

When the European explorers arrived, its shores were home to coastal tribes, some with a reputation for cannibalism. In keeping with its faded, once rather barbaric image, the coast sheltered early 19th-century pirates seeking refuge from the early US Navy, which established strongholds along the Gulf. From such a heritage sprang a prosperous trading culture in the late 19th century. The inheritors of that legacy are the present-day developers who have ventured cautiously onto its shores in order to build condominiums and professional buildings. They tread lightly with good reason because, within that legacy, lies a pattern of destruction that visits with clockwork regularity.

NATURE'S FURY

Here on the Texas coast, nature has demonstrated its powers as it has nowhere else. Galveston is the site of the most celebrated catastrophe in US history – the 1900 hurricane, which destroyed the city and killed thousands of people. The area was once again battered by a destructive hurricane in September 2008, when Hurricane Ike, a Category 2 storm with winds up to 110mph (178kph), made a direct hit on East Galveston, creating a massive storm surge that inundated Galveston and the nearby Bolivar Peninsula. The destruction on Bolivar was almost total, flattening 3,000 homes and businesses, destroying the historic lighthouse, and blowing debris

Main attractions

High Island, Bolivar Peninsula
Texas Seaport Museum, Galveston
Bishop's Palace, Galveston
Moody Mansion, Galveston
Art Museum of South Texas, Corpus Christi
Padre Island National Seashore
King Ranch

Maps on pages 21[illegible]16, 221

Galveston harbor.

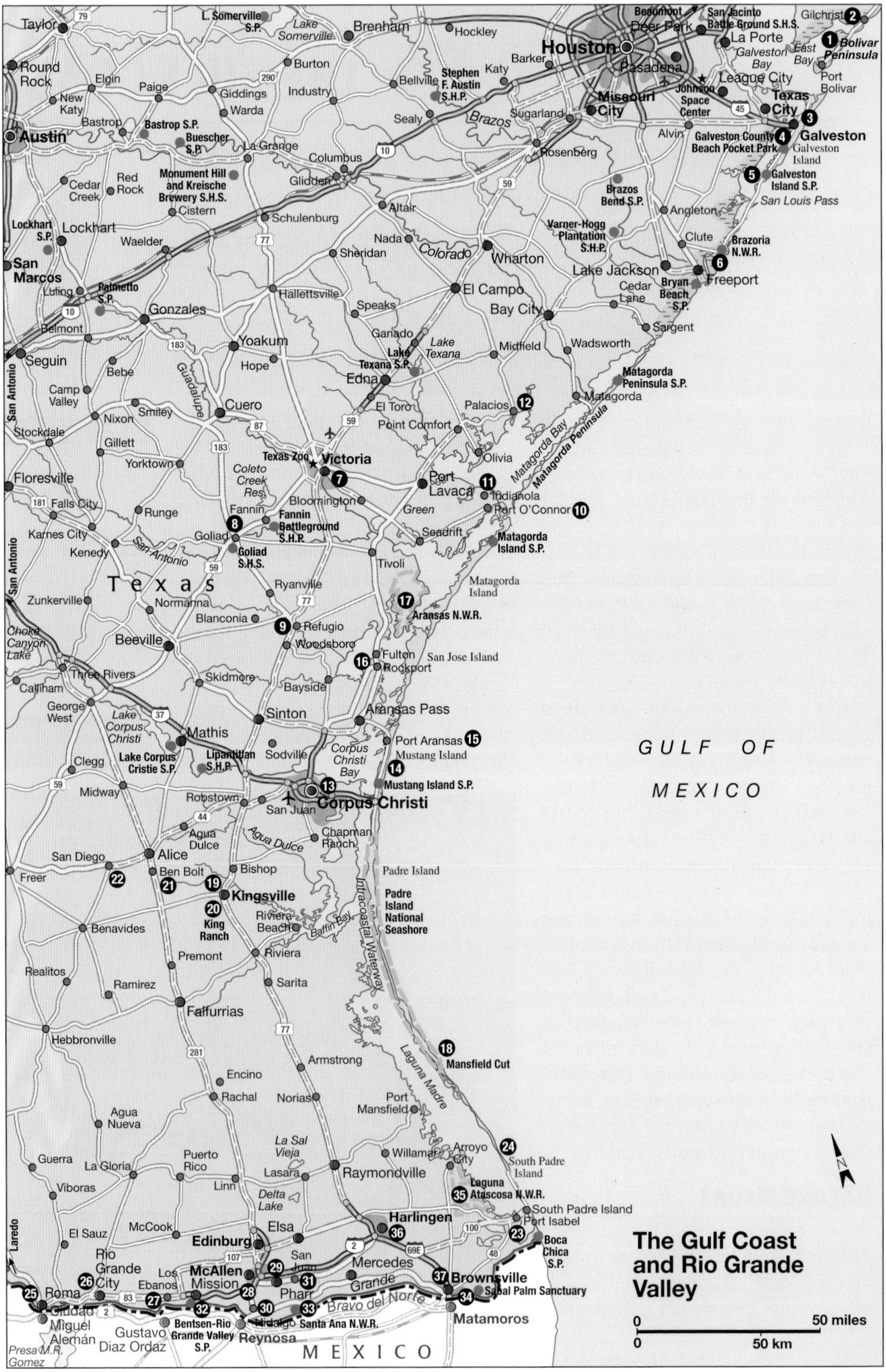
The Gulf Coast and Rio Grande Valley
GULF OF MEXICO
Texas
MEXICO
Houston
Austin
San Marcos
Victoria
Corpus Christi
Kingsville
Harlingen
Brownsville
McAllen
Edinburg
Galveston
Matamoros
Reynosa
0 50 miles
0 50 km

into Galveston Bay. It took many years, but the devastation of Ike is fading and the Bolivar Peninsula is welcoming visitors once again. A new visitors center at Crystal Beach Plaza supplies brochures and beach parking stickers.

THE GREAT ESCAPE

Whether or not the wind and rain are pounding from above, the Gulf of Mexico is always pulling from below, eating at the shoreline, and claiming the land. Engineers have predicted the eventual reclamation of beach homes at many points during the 21st century. Still, developers take their risks and beach visitors continue to seek that special relationship with the sea. Between storms, and in spite of their fears, coastal Texans have created an enchanting domain. The Gulf of Mexico in summertime is as warm as bathwater, and the hour's drive from Houston to nearby tranquil Galveston provides a contrast that can be felt as well as seen.

Less cluttered by neon and glitz than most modern coastlines, Texas's Gulf shore is a welcome escape hatch for city refugees. Visitors won't find the world's best surf, but they will find isolated beaches and sleepy villages with a lifestyle that is as surprising as it is charming.

The Texas coastline runs 367 miles (590km) in a great arc that forms the southeastern corner of the state. The land here does not end in the abrupt cliffs and rocky shores to be found in other parts of America. In Texas, the land surrenders gradually to the water, drifting from the region of rolling hills and pine forests known as the Coastal Plains into a grassy marshland called the Coastal Prairie. The Coastal Plains includes East Texas and the Rio Grande Valley; the Coastal Prairie is, more precisely, the Texas coast.

Starting at Bolivar Peninsula, just north of Galveston, the Texas shore forms one of the world's longest chain of barrier islands as it slips toward Mexico: 624 miles (1,000km) of tidewater coast, when you add the bays, lagoons, and swamps between the bayou marshland in the north and coastal brush in the south. The region includes two cities – Galveston to the north and Corpus Christi to the south.

BOLIVAR PENINSULA

Unspoiled South Padre Island, to the south, is generally considered the tourist's best chance for a Caribbean resort-style vacation in this state. Compared with South Padre, **Bolivar Peninsula ❶**, a wild barrier island that has been developed, is a diamond in the rough, to the north. But it can be a true gem for those who appreciate a holiday uncluttered with glitz.

Extending like a long finger down the Texas Coast from Louisiana, the peninsula was named in 1815 to honor the Latin American revolutionary Simon Bolivar, during an era when the Gulf Coast and the Caribbean were aflame with anti-Spanish sentiment. A free 20-minute ferry carries cars and their passengers from Galveston's east end

Fact

If you're looking for something fancy, you might be disappointed by the Bolivar Peninsula. But it is its simplicity that many find most appealing, and it still stands as one of the best reasons to venture anywhere along Texas's Gulf Coast.

Reddish egret, Bolivar Peninsula.

Fact

Juneteenth, or Emancipation Day, is celebrated by African-Americans in cities all over Texas, with marching bands, music (especially gospel) and dance.

to State Route 87 on the peninsula, which provides the only convenient access to Bolivar's beaches. The route operates 365 days a year, weather permitting. But this very remoteness has guaranteed splendid isolation for Bolivar's beachgoers, who go birding (334 species), crabbing, and camping near the surf. Beach houses – many on stilts and rebuilt following Hurricane Ike – can be rented at the main residential community on the west end of Bolivar, Crystal Beach. Reservations should be made in advance through one of Galveston's real estate companies.

Gilchrist ❷ is a small town about 20 miles (32km) north on State Route 87, and its main attraction was **Rollover Pass**, a channel that sliced through the center of town, serving up some of the best bankside fishing in the state. However, starting at the end of 2019, Rollover Pass was shut down for a project that will fill in the channel and create a park with a fishing pier. Elsewhere along the peninsula, visitors will find an unpretentious montage of honky-tonk taverns, hamburger joints, and convenience stores.

The narrow Bolivar Peninsula runs for 27 miles (43km) along the shore and on its east end crosses bayous, marshes, barrier islands, and the Intracoastal Waterway as it heads north on State Route 124. **High Island** is celebrated for its birding. Its unique salt dome geography allows trees to grow that offer resting places for thousands of neotropical migrating birds during spring migrations. There are no less than four bird sanctuaries run by Texas Audubon here, including Smith Oaks Sanctuary on High Island, and on the other side of the Intracoastal Waterway, on East Galveston Bay, **Anahuac National Wildlife Refuge**, one of several national wildlife refuges along this section of the coast.

HISTORIC GALVESTON

This island city of 50,000 residents has been described as the only part of the coast you'd want to visit on a rainy day. Visitors who head directly for the beach will miss plenty, because, in addition to the sea, recreational attractions and good shopping, **Galveston** ❸ offers a unique historical perspective.

Tall ship Elissa, Texas Seaport Museum.

But for that 1900 hurricane, Galveston might have been today *the* industrial heavyweight, instead of its neighbor, Houston. After a roguish beginning as a seaport haven for the pirate clan of Jean Lafitte, Galveston was one of the South's most significant cities by the end of the 19th century.

The French-born Jean Lafitte and his brother, Pierre, were already legendary smugglers in nearby New Orleans, when, in 1817, they founded a town called Campeachy on Galveston Island. Their fort, Maison Rouge, attracted a "navy" of over 1,000 men, who continually disrupted Spanish shipping in the Gulf of Mexico. Lafitte's pirate "den," as it has been called, was a wicked place: slaving, gaming, drunkenness, and whoring abounded. He sold all the black people of Galveston, including freed slaves, in New Orleans. To some a romantic figure, Lafitte was the last of the pirates on the Gulf, until the US Navy forced him out of the area in the early 1820s. He sailed away to Mujeres Island off the Yucatan Peninsula in Mexico.

Galveston was then developed as a seaport during the Republic, and soon became the state's largest city. Blockaded during the Civil War, the city remained in Confederate hands, except for a few months in 1862. The Union Navy entered the harbor in October, landed on Christmas morning, and was expelled on New Year's Day 1863. They were back on June 19, 1865, to take over the city and proclaim the freedom of the slaves. "Juneteenth" has been celebrated by African-Americans in Texas ever since.

A HURRICANE FOR THE AGES

Galveston continued to grow, but its population was eventually surpassed by San Antonio and Houston. Much of Texas's cotton was exported through the city – ancient cotton warehouses and grain elevators survive today – and the water of the bay is still yellow from the shipping of sulfur. A hub of commercial activity between the 1870s and 1900, Galveston had Texas's first telegraph, electric lights, brewery, and medical college. Splendid mansions were erected, paid for with the profits from all the city's commerce.

The 1900 hurricane on September 8 and 9 dimmed Galveston's glow in a matter of hours. Winds sometimes in excess of 100 mph (160kmh) swept tides of 4–6ft (1–2 meters) across the island to produce one of the nation's worst natural disasters. There was nothing to break the hurricane's force: Galveston's highest elevation was a mere 8ft (2.5 meters). At one point the water rose 4ft (just over a meter) in four seconds: 1,500 acres (600 hectares) of houses were completely destroyed. Death estimates have ranged from 5,000 to 8,000. So complete was the devastation that many wanted to abandon the place, but, stubbornly, Galveston refused to surrender. The people resurrected their demolished homes and constructed a 17ft (5-meter) seawall, protection against future ravaging by the waters of the Gulf. The present seawall is 10 miles

Fact

Galveston is an anglicized version of Galvez, the original Spanish name for the island settlement. It was named for Bernardo de Galvez, the Spanish Governor of Louisiana.

Aerial view of Galveston.

Sculpture carved from one of the thousands of trees felled by Hurricane Ike.

(16km) long, 16ft (5 meters) wide at its base and 5ft (1.5 meters) wide at the top. Hurricane Ike also created damage in Galveston, too, but nothing compared to the great 1900 storm.

Meanwhile, its big rival, Houston, with more people and better rail connections, seized its opportunity and, with federal money, began dredging a ship channel in the Buffalo Bayou to the San Jacinto River and, from there, into the Gulf. So, Houston – 50 miles (80km) inland – became a port city while Galveston, although remaining a port, became less important and was frequently referred to as "that island city south of Houston."

ONTO THE ISLAND

Primary access to the island city is via I-45, a freeway that stretches from Dallas, through Houston, and over a bridge into Galveston. Once on the island, it becomes **Broadway** Ⓐ, Galveston's main street, which carries you through the oldest part of the city to **Stewart Beach** Ⓑ. A right turn on to 61st Street, before I-45 becomes Broadway, bypasses the central city and takes you to the island's most popular beach district, **West Beach**, on the south shore.

In Galveston, all other roads seem to lead eventually to **Seawall Boulevard** Ⓒ, a broad avenue along the waterline above the city's dramatic seawall, with an array of shops, restaurants, motels, bicycle rentals, arcades, and the **Galveston Island Historic Pleasure Pier** (2501 Seawall Blvd; tel: 855-789-7437; www.pleasurepier.com), and the Gulf of Mexico pleasantly filling the horizon on the other. The island's visitor information center is at 2328 Broadway Street (tel: 888-425-4753; www.galveston.com). Popular seafood restaurants on Seawall Boulevard include Gaido's, founded in 1911 and a good place to find gumbo, and the adjoining Nick's Kitchen and Beach Bar.

BUILDINGS RESTORED

There's a lot for families to do in Galveston. Start with a stroll along the **Strand Historic District** Ⓓ, a 12-block area that parallels Broadway between 20th and 25th streets, which was once part of the city's warehouse district.

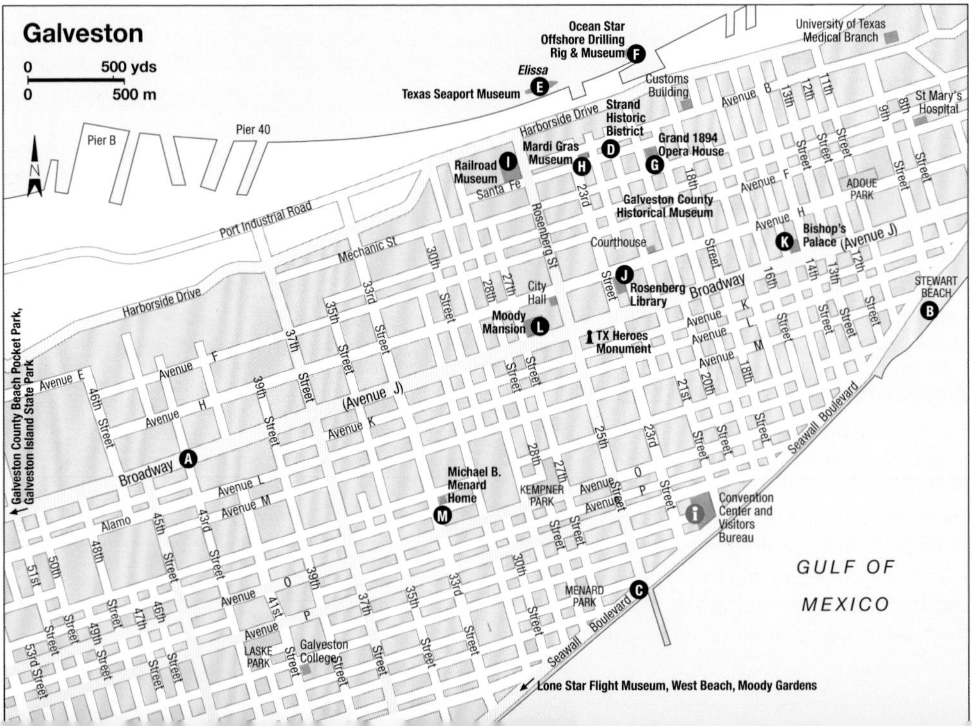

Named for the street in London with all the famous shops, thanks to its profusion of great commercial houses, it was once renowned as "The Wall Street of the West."

The solid, iron-fronted Victorian structures have been refurbished with more than 90 shops and restaurants. Some highlights in the area include La King's Confectionery, home of old-fashioned ice-cream and candies such as saltwater taffy, Hendley Market (Victorian clothing, antique postcards), and the restored square-rigged tall ship Elissa at the **Texas Seaport Museum** **E** (Pier 21, 2200 Harborside Drive; tel: 409-765-7834; www.galvestonhistory.org/attractions/maritime-heritage/texas-seaport-museum; daily 10am–5pm). The museum also offers harbor tours with dolphin watching, a documentary on the 1900 hurricane, and a database of immigrants who disembarked in Galveston between 1846 and 1948. On board the **Ocean Star Offshore Drilling Rig and Museum** **F** (Pier 21, 2002 Wharf Road; tel: 409-766-7827; www.oceanstaroec.com; daily 10am–5pm, summer till 6pm), three decks of equipment, exhibits, and interactive displays detail offshore oil and gas exploration, drilling, and oil production. Housed in a retired jackup drilling rig, the museum offers the rare opportunity to explore the rig floor and pipe deck of a massive, seagoing structure.

Another historic structure is the spectacular **Grand 1894 Opera House** **G** (2020 Post Office Street; tel: 409-765-1894; www.thegrand.com) where contemporary Broadway musicals are performed. The Grand Kids Festival, held every Mar/Apr is a fun-filled day of performances designed to introduce children and their families to the arts.

MARDI GRAS IN GALVESTON

The Strand's ambiance is reminiscent of Bourbon Street in New Orleans's French Quarter, and, like that colorful Louisiana city, Galveston makes a big thing of the Mardi Gras. The entire city turns out for the parade that marks Fat Tuesday. Beads and token coins fill the air as the Strand celebrates and rejoices. The **Mardi Gras Museum** **H** (23rd and Strand streets; tel: 409-763-1133; Mon–Fri 10am–8pm, Sat 10am–10pm, Sun 10am–6pm; free) is devoted to the subject, displaying costumes and other historic memorabilia. Two blocks farther, you will find the **Railroad Museum** **I** (2602 Santa Fe Place; tel: 409-765-5700; www.galvestonrrmuseum.com; daily 10am–5pm, closed mid-Oct to mid-Jan), with audiovisual displays and a collection of 35 old rail cars. It is in a looming early 20th-century skyscraper, the former home of the American National Insurance Company, founded by wealthy Galvestonian William Moody, Jr. Sculpted life-like figures sit optimistically in the waiting room.

The **Rosenberg Library** **J** (2310 Sealy Street; tel: 409-763-8854; www.rosenberg-library.org; Mon–Thu 9am–9pm, Fri–Sat 9am–6pm), opened in 1902, was the first library in the state. The library's history center holds a large collection of historic maps and materials relating

Fact

The stage of the Grand 1894 Opera House has, in its time, played host to the likes of actress Sarah Bernhardt, singer Al Jolson, and the Marx Brothers.

Seawall Boulevard, Galveston.

to Galveston's early businesses, and is a useful archive for historians. The Rosenberg Library Museum on the fourth floor contains displays relating to Galveston's past, from archive photography to rare books and historic quilts.

HISTORIC HOMES

Galveston offers the pleasures of the seaside but is also enthralling for anyone interested in history. The best place to see some of the city's wealth of old mansions is in the delightful **East End Historical District**, bounded roughly by Broadway, Mechanic, 19th and 11th streets. Here, Victorian homes are intermixed with buildings that betray neoclassical, Renaissance, and Italianate influences. Bungalows rest in the shade cast by oleanders, oaks, maples, and palms, and are slightly raised from the ground out of respect for the Gulf. Post Office and Church streets are particularly lovely. Several of the town's best eateries are on 14th Street.

On the corner of Broadway and 14th Street is the pink granite, turreted Gothic fantasy that is the **Bishop's Palace** **K** (1402 Broadway; tel: 409-762-2475; www.galvestonhistory.org/attractions/architectural-heritage/bishops-palace; daily 10am–5pm, Sat until 6pm), also known as Gresham House, is the only building in Texas on the American Institute of Architecture's list of 100 outstanding structures in the US. It was built for the wealthy Gresham family from 1887–92, by famed Galveston architect Nicholas Clayton. Owned since 1923 by the Galveston-Houston diocese of the Roman Catholic Church, it served as the bishop's official residence until it was opened to the public in 1963.

The elaborate, four-story 1895 **Moody Mansion** **L** (2618 Broadway; tel: 409-762-7668; www.moodymansion.org; daily 10am–5pm) is the former home of powerful Galveston financier William L. Moody, who bought the home from the original owners following the 1900 hurricane. Moody made his money in cotton, then later ranching, banking, and insurance. The home remained in the Moody family until 1986, when it was donated to the city along with its contents. Today, visitors can tour 20 rooms of the

Moody Gardens, near Galveston.

restored home and view many 19th- and early 20th-century antiques and furnishings that belonged to the family and tell their history. Special "All-Access" tours (Fri–Sun) show visitors parts of the home that are usually off limits.

The oldest mansion in Galveston is the **Michel B. Menard Home** Ⓜ (1605 33rd Street; tel: 409-765-7834), built in 1838 in the elegant Greek Revival style. French-Canadian fur trader and land speculator Michel B. Menard was one of the founders of Galveston during the time of the Republic of Texas. His mansion has now been restored and is a museum housing remarkable period furnishings and other antiques.

COASTAL MIX

Between Galveston and Houston is the Kemah-Seabrook area, a region where visitors are certain to find a real mixture of Texas coastal dwellers, ranging from space scientists on their day off from NASA to old seadogs and fishermen swapping yarns at popular hangouts like Jimmy Walker's and Maribelle's. In the west, **Galveston County Beach Pocket Park** ❹ and **Galveston Island State Park** ❺ provide beach access with parking, for picnics, swimming, and sunbathing. Out here, just south of I-45, you will also find the sprawling **Moody Gardens** (One Hope Blvd; tel: 409-744-4673; www.moodygardens.com), Galveston's major tourist attraction. Among the highlights in the 242-acre (98-hectare) educational complex are a 10-story glass rainforest pyramid packed with exotic flora and fauna, which thrive among waterfalls, cliffs, caverns, and forests; a Bat Cave; golf-couse; an MG 3D theater; an authentic reproduction of a 19th-century paddlewheel, which offers cruises along the bayou; and an aquarium. Other attractions are a rainforest pyramid and a Special FX MG 4D theater, for a truly multi-sensory experience. There is also a 300-room convention hotel. The **Lone Star Flight Museum** (11551 Aerospace Avenue; tel: 888-359-5736 www.lonestarflight.org; Tue–Sat 9am–5pm, Sun noon–5pm), is a magnet for fans of vintage aircraft, with more than 40 restored planes on display.

DOWN THE COAST

Just down the coast, at the point where the Brazos River empties into the Gulf, is the **Brazoria National Wildlife Refuge** ❻. It was near here that Stephen F. Austin and his colonists first landed and also where the new government of the Republic of Texas held its first session. Today, it's a great place to view large flocks of snow geese and other migratory birds.

Between the cities of Galveston and Corpus Christi, on US 59, the **Texas Zoo** (110 Memorial Drive; tel: 361-573-7681; www.texaszoo.org; daily 9am–4.30pm) at **Victoria** ❼ features 100 species found in Texas, plus lions, tigers, and Texas black bears.

Another place of interest is historic **Goliad** ❽, at the crossroads of US 59 and US 77. Here, not far from the Fannin Battlefield, are the graves of Col. James Fannin and the 342 men who, in 1836, were massacred after surrendering to

Tip

Make a point of visiting Goliad State Park, just south of Goliad, off US 183. The huge park includes the reconstructed Mission Espiritu Santo, which was established in 1749. You can also camp, picnic, and fish.

Galveston's East End Historical District.

The Padre Island National Seashore offers some fantastic opportunities for horseback riding.

Mexican general Santa Anna. "Remember Goliad!" became a battle cry of the Texas Revolution. At **Refugio** ❾, visitors can take haywagon rides and watch cowboys at work at the Dos Vaqueros Ranch Resort (tel: 361-543-4905).

SEASHORE TOWNS

There are a number of relatively unspoiled little seashore towns close to State Route 35, among them **Port O'Connor** ❿, a focal point for serious fishermen and duck hunters. **Indianola** ⓫, now reduced to just a few fishing families living among stone foundations at the water's edge, rivaled Galveston as the top Texas port until September 17, 1875, when a hurricane literally blew the place away. Farther up the coast, **Palacios** ⓬, with its down-home and charming Luther Hotel (408 S. Bay Boulevard; tel: 361-972-2312; www.lutherhotelpalacios.com), is worthy of note, as are Freeport and Surfside.

CORPUS CHRISTI

For fans of sparkling seaside development, **Corpus Christi** ⓭ has the flavor of a young Miami Beach. With a population of 325,000, it is the state's eighth-largest city, yet its semitropical climate and reputation as a recreation capital have created the image of tranquility. "The isles of Texas" is the tourist department's description, and those visitors who experience the offshore beaches, deep-sea fishing, catamaran trips, and the sailboarding and jetskiing might well remember it that way.

Corpus Christi's 2-mile (3km) **Seawall** Ⓐ, 14ft (4 meters) high and 20ft (6 meters) wide, is an attraction in itself, having been designed by the famous sculptor Gutzon Borglum, who went on to carve the presidential heads on Mount Rushmore. Steps from the seawall down to the beach provide a popular resting place, while joggers, strollers and cyclists populate the top.

Driving in Corpus Christi requires a good map. Because it follows the curve of the bay, few of its streets run straight. The focal point for activity is the **Bayfront Science Park** Ⓑ, beside the water at the north end of Shoreline Drive. In addition to a convention center

Texas State Aquarium, Corpus Christi.

and auditorium, the Harbor Playhouse, and a marina, the complex contains the 1972 **Art Museum of South Texas** (1902 N. Shoreline Boulevard; tel: 361-825-3500; www.artmuseumofsouthtexas.org; Tue–Sat 10am–5pm, Sun 1–5pm), designed by Philip Johnson. Near here is the **Corpus Christi Museum of Science and History** **C** (1900 N. Chaparral Street; tel: 361-826-4667; www.ccmuseum.com; Tue–Sat 10am–5pm, Sun noon–5pm), which includes a fascinating display of shipwreck artifacts. The McGregor Gallery has over 250,000 black-and-white photographs depicting the history of Corpus Christi.

Another site worth viewing is the surprising **Texas State Museum of Asian Cultures** **D** (1809 N. Chaparral Street; tel: 361-881-8827; www.texasasianculturesmuseum.org; Thu–Sat noon–5pm), home of a prize collection of treasures from Japan acquired by a Corpus native, Billie Trimble Chandler, during her 17 years as a teacher there.

Fans of the late Tejana singer Selena Quintanilla should stop by the **Selena Museum** (5410 Leopard St.; tel: 361-289-9013; https://q-productions.com; Mon–Fri 10am–4pm). The museum showcases different memorabilia from the singer's life like her awards, notable outfits, and even her car. For those who don't have time to stop by the museum, the **Selena Memorial Statue** (600 N Shoreline Blvd) can be found along the seawall. It features a life-size bronze statue of the singer, as well as voice narration in Spanish and English detailing the singer's life.

After visiting the museums head over to **Lamar Park** (3850 S. Alameda Street; tel: 361-880-5870; www.lamarpark.com; Mon–Sat 10am–7pm, Sun noon–5pm) and spend a few hours browsing its one-of-a-kind specialty shops, popular since 1955.

NORTH BEACH

Corpus Christi first came to life as a tent city and shipping point for the US Army, when the annexation of Texas sparked a war with Mexico. In the 1920s, the US government sent in the dredgers to create what became the deepest port on the coast and one that has retained its

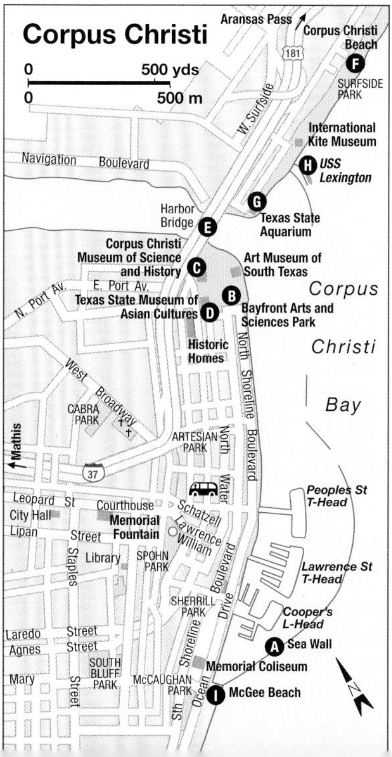

Corpus Christi.

> **Fact**
>
> The USS Lexington was the longest-serving carrier in the US Navy. It saw action in the waters around Japan during World War II. Self-guided tours take in most areas of the ship, including the massive flight deck. There is also a 3D Mega theatre on the Hangar Deck.

military ties, with half of the US Navy's air training bases located in the area.

The **Harbor Bridge** E is an iconic structure in Corpus Christi, that was once 620ft (191-meter)-long and – at 250ft (77 meters) above the water, making it the state's second highest bridge. However, as of 2020, the bridge was undergoing a renovation to make it the tallest point in South Texas and lengthen it to over 6 miles long which would make it the longest cable stay bridge in the US. Once complete, it will also have a shared biking/hiking path, plaza, and LED lighting at night.

Just across Harbor Bridge is **Corpus Christi Beach** F. This area was famous for its casinos and amusement parks in the 1930s, but fell out of favor until a revival in the 1970s. Natives call it "North Beach," and it offers the city's most challenging surf. Also here are the **Texas State Aquarium** G (2710 N. Shoreline Boulevard; tel: 361-881-1230; www.texasstateaquarium.org; daily 10am–5pm), and the World War II aircraft carrier **USS *Lexington*** H (2914 N Shoreline Drive; tel: 361-888-4873; www.usslexington.com; daily 9am–5pm, until 6pm from Memorial Day through Labor Day and Spring Break). About 4 miles (6.4km) to the south is the much shorter **McGee Beach** I, attracting families with small children because of its calm and shallow bay waters.

North Beach.

WILD HORSES

From the crook of Corpus Christi Bay, the city allows excellent access northeast to Mustang Island, Port Aransas, and Aransas Pass, known as the "Shrimp Capital of Texas." **Mustang Island** 14, earning its name from the wild mustang ponies left behind by the Spaniards several hundred years ago, is a barrier between the bay and the Gulf of Mexico. It protects the city to some extent from hurricanes. Visitors will find one of the state's finest beaches at Mustang Island State Park, and, at the northern end of the island, they'll find one of the state's best fishing ports.

A (free) 24-hour ferry runs across from where US 361 ends to **Port Aransas** 15, home for hundreds of shrimp boats moored in Conn Brown Harbor. Among numerous places offering accommodations is the landmark Tarpon Inn (200 E. Cotter Avenue; tel: 361-749-5555; www.thetarponinn.com), an 1895 hotel once favored by President Franklin Roosevelt. Its lobby walls are covered with tarpon scales autographed by successful fishermen.

WHOOPING CRANES

This whole seashore is a big draw for bird-watchers, who come to view the nearly 400 species of birds that either reside or migrate through here. The **Rockport-Fulton** 16 area attracts thousands of hummingbirds, which rest over for their 500-mile (800km) flight across the Gulf of Mexico on the return trip to Mexico each fall. Nearby, famous for the November migration of whooping cranes, is **Aransas National Wildlife Refuge** 17 (tel: 361-349-1181; www.fws.gov/refuge/aransas; daily 9am to 4pm).

These protected birds arrive from Canada for the winter and evoke admiration in thousands of tourists on account of their 7ft (2-meter) wingspans, long black legs, and voracious appetites. The rescue of the whooping cranes from near extinction is a real success story. In 1941, there were only 16 known whoopers left in the US; now an estimated 304 birds turn up at Aransas. This is the only known wild flock of whooping cranes. They can be viewed through binoculars from an observation tower, or seen closer up on one of the frequent boat tours, many of which feature talks by professional ornithologists.

PADRE ISLAND

Farther south, **Padre Island National Seashore**, divided from South Padre Island by **Mansfield Cut** ⑱, and preserved from developers, is the finest stretch of natural beach in America. It was named for Padre Nicolas Balli, who bought it from the Spanish Crown for 400 pesos. In 1844, the last of the Balli family moved away and three years later John Singer and his family were shipwrecked on the island. They chose to build a home and stay here. Singer became rich from his shares in his brother's sewing machine company and reputedly buried treasure on the island before leaving. It has never been found and, after a century of storms disrupting the island's landscape, it is doubtful if it ever will be.

RANCH COUNTRY

Inland, the closest you can get to the coast is along US 77 through ranch country and **Kingsville** ⑲. From here, make a diversion westward along US 141 to reach the visitor center of the famous **King Ranch** ⑳ (2205 W. Highway 141; tel: 361-592-8055; www.king-ranch.com; open daily; tours Mon–Sat 10am and 2pm, Sun 12.30pm and 2.30pm). Visitors can watch a video and then take a 1-hour guided tour along a 12-mile (19km) loop of the immense ranch, known for its wealth – worldwide holdings once covered almost 11 million acres (over 4 million hectares) in seven countries. It also developed a stable of Kentucky Derby winners and its own breed of Santa Gertrudis cattle.

Port Isabel Lighthouse.

TEXAS CITY Y SPILL

On March 22, 2014, Matagorda Island, part of Aransas National Wildlife Refuge was stricken by an oil spill when a ship collided with an oil tanker in Galveston Bay. The refuge is a winter home to many rare birds, including 11 pairs of nesting aplomado falcons and the only wild flock of whooping cranes in the country, as well as Kemp's Ridley sea turtles, which nest on the white sand beaches in spring. The Texas City Y Spill released 168,000 gallons of oil and affected 90 miles (145km) of Gulf coastline. Two million pounds of oily sand were removed, and 331 oiled birds, 39 dolphins, and 17 turtles were cleaned by volunteers. There are at least 275 oil spills in Galveston Bay annually, affecting vulnerable wildlife in the coastal areas.

Freshly caught red snapper, Padre Island.

Tip

The first 10 miles (16km) of Padre Island have a paved roadway and another 60 miles (96.5km) can be driven by car, but demand four-wheel drive. For beachcombers and shell collectors, however, this trip is mandatory.

The annual Ranch Hand Breakfast gives visitors the opportunity to enjoy an authentic cowboy breakfast accompanied by team-roping demonstrations and musical entertainment.

Nearby, on State Route 281, is **Ben Bolt ㉑** (a tiny place with about 361 inhabitants), where a legendary Headless Horseman is buried. This phantom-like figure, who terrorized the region in the mid-19th century with a head dangling from his saddlehorn, was actually a rustler who had been killed by a Texas Ranger, his head tied to a wild mustang as a warning to others.

Northwest of Kingsville, the town of **San Diego ㉒**, on State Route 44, was an important cattle shipping center that became so rowdy a special detachment of Texas Rangers was stationed there. Their task was to deal with the bands of rustlers who infested the backcountry.

SOUTH TO THE BORDER

Between the coast and Padre Island, the Intracoastal Waterway continues all the way down to **Port Isabel ㉓**. Port Isabel Lighthouse (421 E. Queen Isabella Blvd; tel: 956-943-2262; www.portisabellighthouse.com; open daily 9am–5pm) on US 100 is irresistible to photographers. It was built in 1852 on a site used by General Zachary Taylor's army in the US War with Mexico. In summer the lighthouse serves as a movie screen for the Port Isabel weekly movie night.

The most unusual wildlife refuge around is **Sea Turtle, Inc.** (6617 Padre Boulevard, South Padre Island; tel: 956-761-4511; https://seaturtleinc.org; Tue–Sun 10am–4pm), a nonprofit organization that is helping restore the population of the endangered Kemp's Ridley turtle by protecting their nests and hatchlings on South Padre Island beaches. Through rehabilitation, research, and education, the group is actively involved in the survival of all sea turtle species threatened by harvest of their eggs and by hunting. Baby and adult sea turtles, either in rehabilitation or nonreleasable, are on view in large tanks.

South Padre Island ㉔, a 34-mile (54km) section of what is really just a 100-mile (160km) sandbar, or barrier island, is nowhere more than half a mile (0.8km) wide, yet it has become the state's premier beach resort, thanks to its windswept dunes, gorgeous beaches, and balmy tropical temperatures. Discovered by Spanish explorers in 1519, it was first named Isla Blanca for white sands whose purity has been preserved despite extensive development.

Only one paved road, Padre Boulevard, running up the center of the island, carries on beyond the city limits, but it peters out after a few miles amidst sand dunes, marshes, and birdlife.

Even after the island was joined to the mainland by a causeway in 1974, development barely took off, but, later, a real estate boom began when the causeway was widened and the Texas legislature passed laws forcing the insurance industry to provide coverage to coastal areas. The nearest airports are at Harlingen and the border town of Brownsville.

View from Port Isabel Lighthouse.

Oyster boat, Laguna Madre.

White-tailed deer.

RIO GRANDE VALLEY

Drab and downbeat to some, a warm winter haven for others, the Rio Grande Valley looks set to diversify from its citrus-growing past and may well become the new Florida.

Along the river, from the dusty Tex-Mex town of Roma to the sultry fishing village of Port Isabel, lies the Rio Grande Valley, a region packed with the history of border wars, steamboat navigation, and nomadic tribes who have long since disappeared. There are 38 communities scattered along 110 miles (177km) of alluvial plain, but most of the towns situated between Falcon Lake and the lower Rio Grande Valley are nothing but caution lights and an extra lane along the highway.

Roma **25**, founded in 1765, might be considered the beginning of the Rio Grande Valley. Marlon Brando came to Roma in the early 1950s to film several scenes for *Viva Zapata*, a movie about the most romantic hero of the Mexican Revolution, Emiliano Zapata. (Much of the film was shot in the sleepy – and more picturesque – village of **San Ygnacio** farther up the river. The 1830 Jose Trevino house here was chosen because of its typical Mexican design.)

Roma is a border town in economic and architectural decline. There is some interesting old architecture, but the place is so dreary that one South Texas newspaperman declared sarcastically after Falcon Dam was built that a real opportunity had been passed up when Roma wasn't relocated to its middle. The 5-mile (8km) -long dam, constructed in 1953 to control irrigation, was built jointly by the US and Mexico and bears the seals of both countries at the international border line.

Joined by a suspension bridge across the river from Roma is **Ciudad Miguel Alemán**, a clean, modern, and uninteresting Mexican city named after a former president. Eleven miles (18km) northwest of Ciudad Alemán is the forgettable Mexican town of **Mier**. Mier was the site of the capture, in 1842, of the renegade Republic of Texas soldiers involved in the "black bean incident." After capturing Mier, the Texans had to surrender to the

Main attractions

La Borde House, Rio Grande City
Oblate Mission, McAllen
Santa Ana National Wildlife Refuge, Alamo
Laguna Atascosa National Wildlife Refuge, Hondo
Gladys Porter Zoo, Brownsville

Map on page 212

Bentsen-Rio Grande Valley State Park.

Fact

Americans and Canadians fleeing the bitter winters of the North are known familiarly here as "Winter Texans," but their economic contribution to the valley is never underestimated.

Mexican army. They were marched farther into Mexico to Saltillo where 17 of the 176 were executed. A lottery determined who was to die; those who drew one of the black beans from a pot were shot by a firing squad.

ROMAN HILLS

Along this stretch of the Rio Grande there are some tenuous connections with continental culture. Until the 1830s, Roma was called Garcia's Ranch. A visiting priest convinced himself, and the locals, that the hills here were like those of Rome. It still looks like Garcia's Ranch. In **Rio Grande City** ㉖, a Catholic priest built a replica of the Grotto at Lourdes in France called Our Lady of Lourdes Grotto, while, in the same town, a nostalgic François La Borde, in 1899, commissioned a Paris architect to design the family residence. Now the **La Borde House** (601 E. Main Street; tel: 956-487-5101; www.labordehouse.com), it has been restored as an inn.

Until the arrival of the railroads, the river was the valley's principal avenue of commerce, and Rio Grande City, complete with Victorian-era buildings, was an important riverboat terminal. The buildings are still there, but the river has retreated to the south, leaving the town high and dry.

THE MAGIC VALLEY

The region was nicknamed the "Magic Valley" by land developers in the early 1900s to entice farmers to the fertile irrigated fields, which are capable of producing two or three crops a year. The Magic Valley also lures about 130,000 "Winter Texans" annually. These fugitives from the mid-continental weather of Minnesota, Michigan, Canada, and Ohio head south in recreational vehicles to bask in the sun and eat just-picked oranges. Years ago, it was not uncommon to see citrus orchards doubling as seasonal trailer parks, but catering to Winter Texans is now big business. As with other farmers, citrus growers experience boom and bust years. While citrus acreage is shrinking, farm stands still sell fresh, fragrant fruit.

Food stall, Rio Grande City.

RICH SOILS

Centuries of flooding have deposited layers of rich alluvial soil along the Rio Grande's banks, helping to make Hidalgo County one of the state's richest agricultural regions, with sugar cane, cotton, and vegetables – especially onions – grown year-round. The land produces numerous varieties of fruit and vegetables as well as most of the aloe vera grown in the US. But a series of unprecedented cold snaps has occasionally frozen not only the winter citrus crops but many of the trees themselves. Some of the growers of the famous Texas Ruby Red grapefruit have sold up rather than replant.

The valley's disastrous lockstep with the Mexican economy and peso has loosened in recent years. While more and more valley companies are supplying components and logistics for the dozens of brand-name automotive, electronic, and appliance manufacturers just across the border, the region's economic base has diversified. The healthcare, tourism, agriculture, and service industries have expanded enough to bring unemployment levels down. The University of Texas Rio Grande Valley (29,619 students) are graduating educated adults; a lack of education in older generations and remnants of systems that hurt Texans of color, means a high percent of valley residents have incomes below the poverty level.

The Rio Grande Valley now ranks among the fastest-growing regions in the nation, with a construction boom seen in new houses, businesses, and roads, propelled by a relatively young population and a lower than average cost of living. The overwhelming majority of the population is ethnically Latino. Although a significant number of the people whose families have lived here for generations do not speak Spanish at all, first-generation immigrants tend to speak only Spanish. But, like the three-car, hand-drawn ferry at **Los Ebanos** 27 – the last of its kind, running since 1954 – some things still move at a slow pace.

BIGGER AND BETTER

Many consider **McAllen** 28 one of the livelier places in the valley. It is bigger

Our Lady of Lourdes Grotto, Rio Grande City.

Hand-drawn ferry at Los Ebanos.

Tip

For detailed advice about crossing the border into Mexico – even just for a few hours – and all the formalities involved, see Travel Tips at the back of this book.

(pop. 142,696), tidier, and a little more upbeat than most surrounding cities. There are adequate hotels and restaurants, though these are usually full during the September white wing dove hunting season. The city also has large shopping centers and chain restaurants. The ancient La Lomita Mission is where the fathers planted the region's first citrus orchards, but the valley's vast citrus industry began with the McAllen estate of John Shary. Although his estate is still privately owned, the lush orchards can be observed from the road, and, in spring, the air is heavy with the fragrance of orange and grapefruit blossoms.

HOT SPOT

The Mexican border is a political hot spot. Farm workers and growers here will continue to square off across picket lines. Mexicans and Central Americans will continue to slip across the river to work in a country where the streets may not be paved with gold, but are at least paved.

The river is 8 miles (13km) to the south and here the International Bridge connects the American settlement of **Hidalgo** ㉚ – a cluster of freight-forwarding houses – with **Reynosa**, a Mexican city of 612,183. Parking is available on the American side of the bridge.

Within walking distance of the bridge is Reynosa's Plaza Hidalgo and an open shopping mall in the town's *zona rosa* ("pink zone"). In addition to housing tourist-oriented stalls, shops, and restaurants, the zone features bars, clubs, and hotels. Most of the men in khaki uniforms are not policemen, but *cuidadores*, public parking attendants who, for a reasonable fee, will watch your car and attend to the parking meter while you roam.

BORDER TROUBLE

This muddy stretch of the Rio Grande, called the Río Bravo by Mexicans, is shallow enough that undocumented immigrants can tie their belongings around their necks and hazard an illegal entry into the US. Sometimes they hire a "mule," or "coyote," who will carry passengers on his back. When the river is high, inner tubes or small boats shuttle

A Border Patrol agent at Rio Grande River.

the illegal immigrants – usually young men, hoping to find work – to the American side. US Border Patrol officers – *la Migra* – each year apprehend over half a million undocumented immigrants in the US most of whom crossed here, and many of whom are young children traveling unaccompanied to escape persecution in their home countries. What discourages illegals from crossing farther north is the brutal, unforgiving desert, but, from here, Corpus Christi, San Antonio, or Austin can be reached within days. And once within a large American community, undocumented arrivals from Mexico and Central American can easily disappear into the largely Latino population.

MIRACULOUS MEDICINE

East of McAllen at **San Juan** ㉛, on I-83, the reconstructed Basilica of Our Lady of San Juan de Valle houses a replica of a Mexican statue of the *Virgen de Los Lagos*. This local statue won an identity of its own in 1970 when it survived a plane crash that destroyed the original. *Curanderas*, or traditional healers, often invoke the Virgin Mary and are a popular alternative to mainstream medication within the Latino community, particularly among elders. On the Mexican side of the river, Mexican doctors have established clinics that offer treatments not yet approved by the Food and Drug Administration (FDA). Even more popular are Mexican dentists and pharmacists, who offer goods and services at a fraction of US prices. Tiny Nuevo Progreso, south of Weslaco, has over 300 dentists.

WILDLIFE

The Rio Grande Valley is a bird-lover's paradise. Some 360 species are sighted in **Bentsen-Rio Grande Valley State Park** ㉜. The subtropical woodland near Mission has been preserved as a wildlife habitat. Other wildlife can be observed at **Santa Ana National Wildlife Refuge** ㉝ (3325 Green Jay, Alamo; tel: 956-784-7500; www.fws.gov/refuge/santa_ana; daily 8am–4pm), south of Alamo, which includes more than 400 bird species, in addition to bobcats, coyotes, ocelots, and jaguarundis. Nature trails run through the preserve, and a tram takes

Fact

The Rio Grande is the 20th longest river in the world, traveling 1,885 miles (3,030km) from its source in Colorado to its estuary on the Gulf of Mexico.

Basilica of Our Lady of San Juan.

CROSSING INTO MEXICO

Over 150,000 people safely cross the border (La Frontera) to visit Mexico each day – about 9.5 million a year – either traveling by car or walking across the pedestrian bridges over the Rio Grande linking the two countries. All citizens of other countries, including US citizens, need to have valid identity documents: a passport or proof of citizenship with photo, and a green card to reenter the US, if necessary. If you stay in Mexico more than 72 hours, or travel beyond the border zone, you'll need a Tourist Card, available at the border. You will also need auto insurance to cover any car travel in Mexico; US insurance policies do not cover travel south of the border. At this time, travel in the border area of Mexico remains potentially dangerous, as a result of narcotic smuggling, gang violence, hostage taking, rapes, theft, and crossfire from gun fights. The US State Department has an advisory in place warning against travel in the border area. You are advised to be very cautious if you do cross into Mexico. Stay in tourist areas, travel in daylight hours, travel with others, and be low-key in your attire, jewelry, and attitude. Avoid using credit and debit cards, if at all possible, and ask your bank to limit amounts on spending when traveling over the border.

The painted bunting is often described as the most beautiful bird in North America.

Spanish moss draped over trees in Santa Ana National Wildlife Refuge.

visitors on tours with a skilled guide.

On FM 1419, south of Brownsville, is **Sabal Palm Sanctuary** ❸❹ (tel: 956-541-8034; www.sabalpalmsanctuary.org; daily 7am–5pm), an attractive preserve with self-guided trails. Also open to the public is **Laguna Atascosa National Wildlife Refuge** ❸❺ (tel: 956-748-3607; www.fws.gov/refuge/laguna_atascosa; open daily). The refuge of open water, marshes, coastal prairie, cropland, and brushland in Rio Hondo is a sanctuary for deer, bobcat, and migrating birds, located on the coast south of Port Mansfield. And remember if you see an ocelot, report it immediately. It is essential that biologists learn more about their habitat. Half an hour's drive west of the refuge is **Harlingen** ❸❻, noted for its original working model of the famous Iwo Jima War Memorial (320 Iwo Jima Boulevard; Mon–Sat 10am–4pm; free) at Arlington National Cemetery. It depicts the raising of the flag in World War II. At Hugh **Ramsey Nature Park**, native plants have transformed a former landfill into a refuge for animals and people.

BROWNSVILLE

To the south, **Brownsville** ❸❼, connected to the Gulf of Mexico by a 17-mile (27km) ship canal, is the largest American city on the lower border. Here, the **Gladys Porter Zoo** (500 E. Ringgold Street; tel: 956-546-7187; www.gpz.org; Mon–Fri 9am–5pm, Sat–Sun until 5.30pm) is a cageless habitat allowing endangered and other species to reside on mini islands; visitors can wander along ingenious water-fringed walkways. Nearby, the museum **Costumes of the Americas** (5 Dean Porter Park; tel: 956-547-6890; www.costumesoftheamericasmuseum.org; Tue–Sat 10am–5pm, Sun noon–4pm) displays an extensive collection of native garb of North and South American tribes and settlers.

North of Brownsville, near the intersection of FM 1847 and 511, is where an artillery duel opened the US War with Mexico on May 8, 1846. At the Palmito Ranch, south of the city, on May 12–13, 1865, the last battle of the American Civil War took place, although Lee had surrendered at Appomatox a month earlier. Illustrations of such battles can be inspected in the **Historic Brownsville Museum** (641 E. Madison Street; tel: 956-548-1313; https://mitteculturaldistrict.org/historic-brownsville-museum; Tue–Sat 10am–4pm) in the old Southern Pacific Railroad Depot, and at **Brownsville Heritage Complex** (1325 E. Washington Street; tel: 956-541-5560; www.brownsvillehistory.org; Tue–Sat 10am–4pm).

CROSSING THE BORDER

Thousands of people cross every day over the border between Brownsville and Matamoros on the Mexican side. Because of the need for Mexican automobile insurance, many visitors choose to park their cars near the Brownsville Civic Center on International Boulevard, or across from the Chamber of Commerce on Elizabeth Street, both of which are close to the Gateway International Bridge.

Gladys Porter Zoo, Brownsville.

Hiking in Seminole Canyon State Park.

DEL RIO TO LAREDO

This well-watered stretch of the Rio Grande Valley has long been a magnet for colorful characters, attracted by the ease of crossing into Mexico and the trade the border region encourages.

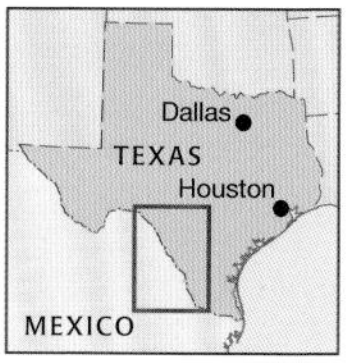

Main attractions

- Amistad National Recreation Area
- Seminole Canyon State Park
- Langtry
- San Agustín Plaza, Laredo
- Lake Casa Blanca International State Park

Map on page 236

Water has been the moving force in Del Rio's history, as in the history of all the Texas border towns. Around 1870, there was considerable development of San Felipe Springs, whose 90 million gallons (over 340 million liters) of water a day attracted farmers and ranchers, and provided agricultural and drinking water for the region. In more recent times, the damming of the Rio Grande and the Devils and Pecos rivers has created a massive lake with huge recreational potential.

FRIENDSHIP LAKE

Amistad National Recreation Area 1 (tel: 830-775-7491; www.nps.gov/amis/index.htm; open daily; free) – *amistad* means "friendship" in Spanish – protects Lake Amistad, a reservoir with more than 1,000 miles (1,600km) of shoreline created by damming the Rio Grande in 1969. It is now managed for recreation by the National Park Service, and boat rentals and scuba diving are available here in what is reputedly the state's best lake for bass fishing and also good for underwater visibility. Hunting licenses for deer, turkey, dove, quail, and the more exotic game found here are available on a daily or seasonal basis. American Indian cave paintings, some dating back 8,000 years, are also found along the shores of Lake Amistad and, although many are inaccessible, others such as Panther Cave can be reached by boat if lake levels are high enough.

Sadly, hundreds of caves were inundated when the Amistad Dam was built, and many of the more accessible ones have been defaced by vandals. However, some of the better paintings are now protected by the State of Texas at **Seminole Canyon State Park and Historic Site 2** (tel: 432-292-4464; www.tpwd.texas.gov/state-parks/seminole-canyon; open daily), on the northern extension of the lake. Camping is permitted in

La Posada Hotel, Laredo.

The Jersey Lilly Saloon, where the self-proclaimed Judge Roy Bean held court.

The Val Verde Winery.

the national recreation area and in the state park. All 400 or so archeological sites on the lakeshore are owned jointly by the United States and Mexico.

WINE AND RODEOS

Del Rio ❸ (pop. 36,006), 13 miles (21km) south of the lake, remains free of the herds of tourists that frequent the towns of the Lower Rio Grande Valley. San Felipe Springs feeds the Horseshoe Park swimming hole and has kept the Qualia family prospering at the **Val Verde Winery** (100 Qualia Drive; tel: 830-775-9714; www.valverdewinery.com; open daily for free tours and tastings) for more than 135 years. Texas's oldest vintner offers free tours and wine-tasting every day.

Del Rio's downtown area has a fine variety of 19th-century architecture. A taste of the cowboy past appears at the **George Paul Memorial Xtreme Bull Riding event** (tel: 830-775-9595; www.georgepaulmemorialbullriding.com), the nation's largest bull riding event in April that salutes a champion bull rider from Del Rio.

The city's **Whitehead Memorial Museum** (1308 S. Main Street; tel: 830-774-7568; www.whiteheadmuseum.org; Tue–Sat 10am–6pm, Sun 1–5pm) houses a collection of reconstructed pioneer buildings put together by a local ranching family. Exhibits include a replica of the famous saloon and courtroom of the notorious Judge Roy Bean who, along with his son, is buried in the grounds.

BORDER CROSSING

Across the river from Del Rio is the city named after the romantic, but ultimately suicidal, Manuel Acuña (1849–73), one of Mexico's most widely read poets. In order to reach **Ciudad Acuña** (pop. 181,426), drive out of Hudson or Las Vacas to the International Bridge. There is ample parking on the American side, and most of the shops offering typical souvenirs are clustered together on Hidalgo Street near the bridge. There is a second international bridge to Mexico at Amistad Dam.

Thousands of visitors cross into Mexico annually. However, the US

State Department warns you to be very cautious about travel in Mexico due to gang violence and crime. Be sure to have valid identity documents with you (see page 310). You will need Mexican auto insurance if you drive over the border into Mexico, so many people simply walk across for the day on the pedestrian international bridges in Del Rio and other towns along the border.

LANGTRY

Judge Roy Bean's original Jersey Lilly Saloon, named after Lily Langtry, the English actress whom he admired from a distance, still stands now as the Judge Roy Bean Museum in tiny **Langtry** ❹ (pop. 12), northwest on US 90, near the Pecos River. Proclaiming himself the "Law West of the Pecos," the illiterate Judge Bean doffed his bar apron in favor of a waistcoat whenever court was in session, drafting a jury from drinkers at the bar. One example of his unconventional justice came during an inquest, when $40 and a pistol were found on the corpse. Fining the corpse $40 for having a concealed weapon, Bean pocketed the money.

Strangers from the east would drop off the train to drink beer at the saloon and buy a round for the judge's pet bear, Bruno. In 1904, the year after the 78-year-old Bean died after a drunken outing, Lily Langtry made her first visit to the town, admired her portrait (which still hangs in the saloon) and was given one of Bean's six-shooters. Today, 85,000 visitors a year call in on the Judge Roy Bean Visitor Center (tel: 432-291-3340) in the tiny hamlet to watch a video about the old judge. If you're headed west, take advantage of the store here to buy snacks and coffee as this is the only available sustenance in the 120 empty miles (193km) between Langtry and Marathon.

Farther downstream is the small town of **Comstock**, before the river runs into Lake Amistad and joins the Rio Grande.

MILITARY TIMES

56 miles (90km) south of Del Rio is **Eagle Pass** ❺ (pop. 27,000) and its Mexican neighbor, Piedras Negras (pop. 29,487,000). Other than Mexican political unrest that closed the International Bridge on several occasions in 1985, not much had happened here since **Fort Duncan** was closed for the second and last time after World War I. That is until 2019, when 1,500 Central Americans arrived at Eagle Pass seeking asylum in the US, which prompted worldwide news coverage and discussion of border politics, human rights, and immigration.

As for Fort Duncan, it had been established by the US Army in 1849, and a detachment of mixed-race American Indian scouts, descended from runaway black slaves, served there after the Civil War. Many of the original buildings, now restored, comprise the **Fort Duncan Museum** (400 Bliss Street; tel: 830-758-1445; Tue–Sat 11am–5pm), featuring military memorabilia and relics of mid-19th-century Texas.

Military history buffs may also want to hazard a guess as to the precise

Fact

A humble storekeeper by profession, Roy Bean was created a Justice of the Peace by the Texas Rangers when the new town, which Bean named Langtry, was founded in 1880. His novel law-keeping methods have been described as "creative," but suitable for the times.

The Pecos River near Comstock.

Fact

The town of Piedras Negras (or "Black Rocks") was named for a seam of coal that had been uncovered by the effects of erosion.

spot along the Rio Grande from which Confederate General Joseph O. Shelby, on July 4, 1865, ordered his Confederate flag weighted and lowered into the river. Shelby, in the romantic tradition of the South, also tore the plume from his hat and cast it into the water.

BLACK ROCKS AND NACHOS

Eagle Pass is the seat of Maverick County, named after early rancher and signer of the Texas Declaration of Independence Samuel Maverick (see page 74). In October each year, the town makes their way to their Mexican border neighbor, Piedras Negras ("black rocks"), where nachos were first created, for Nacho Fest. Piedras Negras ("black rocks") and Eagle Pass (paso de águila) are regular stops for Kickapoo Indians who, under a US-Mexican agreement, are free to reside in either country. The Kickapoo sell handcrafted goods at the border, and at the **Kickapoo Lucky Eagle Casino** (794 Lucky Eagle Drive; tel: 888-255-8259; www.luckyeagletexas.com), Texas's only casino. The flashing lights and bells of slot machines vie for attention with games of Texas hold 'em poker and roulette.

Piedras Negras remains a stop-and-shop Mexican town with a few good restaurants. Although it is now sadly closed, the most famous building in the area is the **Restaurant Bar Moderno** (Allende 407 Oriente), which, in its former guise of the Victory Club, claims to have invented nachos.

TWIN LAREDOS

Laredo ❻ and its Mexican neighbor, Nuevo Laredo, together form a city of some 636,516, with 95 percent of the residents on the Texas side Latino, creating a great destination to practice the Spanish language, eat Mexican-American cuisine, and admire Latino-influenced art. The cities were outposts in what was once the backwater of Spain's American colony, and retain little of what colonial charm they may once have had. Most of the culture here is commercial. Residents from each side of the border once lined for bargains on the other. Nuevo Laredo's current reputation for violence,

Hidalgo Street, Laredo.

reflecting drug gangs' heavy presence in the city, has destroyed its appeal for visitors unwilling to be targets of kidnapping or stray bullets.

Downtown Laredo caters to shoppers with everything from Mexican-import shops to boutiques, art galleries, and the new Outlet Shoppes at Laredo. Dubbed "Main Street," it has been developed over the years, quickly becoming an important part of the city for locals to enjoy the museums and restaurants in the Arts & Entertainment District, craft beer in the Cultura Beer Garden, and the Farmers Market every third Saturday. Downtown Laredo also hosts popular festivals like the music and dance-extravaganza, the UETA Jamboozie Festival in November, and some of the 28 events of Washington's Birthday Celebration, a four-week event with 400,000 attendees who celebrate George Washington's birthday.

San Agustín Plaza, where the Texas city began as a Spanish settlement in 1755, is flanked by **San Agustín Cathedral** (built 1872); the attractive **La Posada Hotel** (1000 Zaragoza Street; tel: 800-444-2099; www.laposada.com), now one of the top hotels in Texas; and the **Republic of the Rio Grande Museum** (1005 Zaragoza Street; tel: 956-727-3480; www.webbheritage.org/museums/republic-of-the-rio-grande-museum; Tue–Sat 9am–4pm). The Republic was a short-lived revolt led by disenchanted Mexican federalists who met in convention in what was still a Mexican city in 1840. Somewhere between the rapidly expanding Manifest Destiny of the United States and the rapidly receding border of Mexico, the Republic of the Rio Grande was lost. The museum's exhibits explain some of this history.

Two blocks north, at San Bernardo and Washington streets, is Bruni Plaza, named for Antonio Mateo Bruni, an Italian immigrant who died a politician and wealthy rancher in 1931. Engraved on a plaque here is part of his philosophy: "God has given us political power to be used for the welfare of the people."

San Bernardo Street shops overflow with Mexican pottery, clothing, leatherwork, colonial-style furniture and

Fact

Laredo was often seen as a "no man's land," abandoned between Texas and Mexico. Only when the Rio Grande was formally recognized as the international frontier in 1848 did Laredo finally settle north of the border.

DJ Wolfman Jack.

RADIO HEALING

Driving at night, you may hear – even as far away as the Canadian border – the broadcast from XERF, one of the last Mexican border-blaster radio stations. In the 1960s, famed DJ Wolfman Jack worked at a border-blaster station and introduced a generation of Americans to rock 'n' roll. Nowadays, the standard radio fare is popular Mexican music and news stories.

The American Medical Association had its reservations about the authenticity of the pills and elixir marketed by one early Del Rio citizen. The proximity of the Mexican border probably made Del Rio seem a favorable business climate to Dr Johnny Brinkley of Kansas, who made a career of peddling exotic cures. In 1933, Brinkley used his own border radio station, KFKB (Kansas First, Kansas Best) – on which he cranked the power up to 1 million watts – to sell goat-gland pills and extended virility to thousands of Americans. Despite spending time in jail for practicing medicine without a license, he became wealthy and built the Dr John R. Brinkley Mansion, which still stands at 512 Qualia Drive in Del Rio. He died penniless, however, following a slew of lawsuits from former patients.

Where

Summer can be blisteringly hot in these parts and the ideal month to visit Laredo is February when many festivals, including the four-week celebration of George Washington's birthday, take place.

curios mixed with the work of artisans. Texas A&M University's TAMIU **Lamar Bruni Vergara Planetarium** (5201 University Boulevard; tel: 956-326-2463; www.tamiu.edu/planetarium) brings the wide Texas skies into focus at sky shows and telescope nights.

Native plants and animals, such as alligators, cacti, and wildflowers, can be seen at the **Lamar Bruni Vergara Environmental Science Center** at Laredo Community College (1 West End Washington; tel: 956-764-5701; Mon–Thu 8am–6pm, Fri 8am–noon), a living laboratory containing representations of the Rio Grande ecosystem.

About two-thirds of the US trade with Mexico crosses the border here, a volume that has only increased since the passage of the NAFTA agreements. Laredo is now the nation's largest port in the country. Immigration and Customs Enforcement offices are open 24 hours daily. On the US side, customs agents collect hundreds of millions of dollars in duties each year. *Casas de cambio,* or currency exchange houses, on both sides of the bridge, usually offer a fair exchange rate for pesos and dollars, and they are convenient. Check the banks (Mexican banks are generally open Mon–Fri 9am–1.30pm) before changing large amounts.

Falcon Reservoir.

ACROSS THE BORDER

Nuevo Laredo, a short walk across the old International Bridge, is something of a Texas Tijuana, with the usual plethora of tacky tourist souvenir shops. Nuevo ("new") Laredo is old, but not attractive. It is also very dangerous as drug cartels fight for power with shootouts on city streets, day and night. You may want to consider visiting other border towns rather than this one.

Surrounding Laredo are miles of the Texas one sees in movies. Ranches are enormous, since making a living on arid scrubland requires a enormous spread. When oil and gas were discovered, most of the region's wealth, although greatly increased, remained concentrated in the hands of a few people. Poverty is still the norm here, and many of the streets of Laredo remain unpaved.

Lake Casa Blanca International State Park ❼ (5102 Bob Bullock Loop; tel: 956-725-3826; www.tpwd.state.tx.us/lake-casa-blanca), off Highway 59, at the eastern edge of Laredo, offers swimming, boating, fishing, and camping. The park has a lovely lake and is home to abundant wildlife, including whitetail deer and ground squirrels. Some 78 miles (125km) south of Laredo is **Falcon State Park** ❽ (tel: 956-848-5327; http://tpwd.texas.gov/state-parks/falcon; open daily), protecting Falcon Reservoir, a jointly owned American-Mexican impoundment.

This massive reservoir covers 84,000 acres (34,000 hectares) and has an international reputation for black bass and catfish, as well as deer and dove hunting in the surrounding countryside. Downriver, the landscape gradually changes from semi-arid, scrubby hills to the lush delta of the Lower Rio Grande Valley.

The Maker of the Peace statue, Seminole Canyon State Park.

Pioneer Plaza.

EL PASO

Thanks to its American Indian roots, its proximity to Mexico, and its distance from other major towns, El Paso – the former haunt of Wild West outlaws – is quite unlike any other Texas city.

Main attractions
El Paso Mission Trail
Magoffin House
El Paso Museum of Art
Franklin Mountains State Park
El Museo de Arte e Historia, Juárez

Maps on pages 244, 254

For some 1,200 miles (1,930km), the Rio Grande twists and turns, widens, then roars through tight places, all the while uniting Texas with the Mexican states of Chihuahua, Coahuila, Nuevo León, and Tamaulipas. In Spanish, it is known as *la frontera* – the border. The US–Mexico border is a place where two contrasting worlds meet. On the Mexican side, *maquiladoras* – American-owned assembly plants – enjoy proximity to the border combined with low operating costs. American retail businesses sell Mexicans what their country can't or won't manufacture: TVs, stereos, medical instruments, and designer jeans.

THE FINAL BARRIER

For Central Americans, the Rio Grande represents the last geographical obstacle in their struggle toward a better life here in *el Norte*. Some of them enter the US illegally. For the fortunate few who find their way to the sanctuary cities, the chances of remaining in the country usually improve. Nevertheless, many will spend their first, and last, night in the US in one of the border detention facilities operated by the US Immigration and Customs Enforcement (ICE), before being forcibly deported.

Despite the Rio Grande's length, fewer than 10 international cities straddle the river. In and around them has gathered a unique mixture of Texans and Mexicans, including a motley crew of international hucksters of low culture and high commerce. If you're looking for the cosmopolitan culture of Mexico City, or the quiet charm of San Antonio, it's unlikely that you'll find it here. But this place is worth a closer look: *la frontera*, if nothing else, is unique.

Much of what this border is about is people standing in line on one side to cross over for something on the other. Border regulars start lining up before dawn: Mexican agricultural laborers

Chamizal Memorial mural.

⊙ Fact

The pictographs at Hueco Tanks are sacred to the Tigua Indians. One of the most revered sites is Speaking Rock – hence the name of the tribe's entertainment center at Ysleta del Sur Pueblo.

wait for the contractor's bus to take them to their day's work. The American day trippers are here – tourists, out for an afternoon in the market, and dinner. Almost all will be home before dark, with a bottle of José Cuervo tequila, crepe flowers, and something for the kids. Then there are the locals, visiting family or friends on the other side, occasionally seeking out better or cheaper medical facilities. And so it goes. Dollars to pesos, pesos to dollars. You can usually spend both on either side.

CASH FLOW

Much of the history of the border in the late 20th century was tied to the exchange rate of the two currencies. For some 30 years, the peso was at a positive 12.5 to the dollar, which allowed most border towns to slouch toward prosperity. But with the first devaluation in 1976, then another devaluation in the early 1990s, the value of the peso fell precipitously and the economic climate on both sides of the river was, at best, cloudy. Mexican workers, with or without papers, found the lure of the dollar irresistible. And why shouldn't they? The federally fixed *daily* wage on the Mexican side is much less than the *hourly* rate on the American side. For the American tourist, the lure has always been well-priced Mexican goods south of the border.

Although things are improving economically in Mexico – and, in theory, the border region – La Frontera has

been beset by an even greater problem: a dangerous drug war operated by competing drug cartels, which has led to horrific violence, from shootouts with guns and grenades to rapes, hostage taking, and high levels of crime. Even though murders and crime figures are now lower for Mexico as a whole, and despite the best efforts of Mexican tourism officials to reassure travelers and promote their cities, La Frontera remains volatile, and Americans are advised by the State Department to either avoid the region or be cautious traveling there. (see page 310 for advice on traveling into Mexico).

A FAR-OUT TEXAS CITY

It has to be said: to get to **El Paso ❶** in extreme West Texas from most Texas cities requires driving from dawn to dusk. Politicians and cartographers claim that El Paso is part of Texas. Most Texans know better. About halfway between Houston and San Diego, California, El Paso's heart belongs to New Mexico, which borders the city, and speaks fluent Spanish.

Sprawling across the Valley of El Paso del Norte, **El Paso-Juárez** is an international city of 2.7 million people, regarded by some as the most diverse city on the border, with its mix of three cultures. The Tigua (or Tiwa) Indians were here first, followed by Norteño Mexicans and Southwestern Americans. Related to the Pueblo Indians of New Mexico, the Tiguas moved to the Spanish mission of San Antonio (later San Augustín) de la Isleta del Sur in 1680, during the Pueblo Revolt, when the Pueblos threw out their cruel Spanish overlords and took back New Mexico for native people until the Reconquest of New Mexico by Spaniard De Vargas in 1692.

Today, the Tiguas are farmers and live in **Ysleta del Sur Pueblo ❷** (an archaic Spanish spelling of "little island"), the oldest community in Texas (1681) and one of the oldest continuously occupied pueblos in the Southwest (Taos and Zuni Pueblos in New Mexico also claim this title). The tribe operates the 850-seat Speaking Rock Entertainment (tel: 915-860-7777), just behind the mission. Ysleta is part of Tigua Indian Reservation, one of only three reservations in Texas.

Signs of an even earlier culture can be seen at **Hueco Tanks State Park and Historic Site ❸** (6900 Hueco Tanks Road No. 1; tel: 915-857-1135; www.tpwd.state.tx.us/state-parks/hueco-tanks; Oct–Apr daily 8am–6pm, May–Sept Mon–Thu 8am–6pm and Fri–Sun 7am–7pm), 32 miles (51km) to the northeast, in the Franklin Mountains. With its thousands of prehistoric colorful and engaging pictographs of human, animal, and mythological figures, the site (also popular with climbers) is spiritually significant to the Mescalero Apache, the Kiowa, and Pueblos like the Hopi who trace their ancestors to the site.

EL PASO MISSION TRAIL

The Ysleta mission is still in use, as is the **Socorro Mission ❹** (tel: 915-859-7718),

The Ysleta Mission, in Ysleta del Sur Pueblo on the Tigua Indian Reservation, was built in 1681 and is the oldest mission in Texas.

Guided tour of Hueco Tanks State Park and Historic Site.

which was built in the same decade, the 1680s, and is the oldest continuously active parish in the US. El Camino Real, the royal highway that once linked El Norte to the capital of New Spain in Mexico, is today a quiet farm road that connects the Ysleta and Socorro missions with the **Presidio Chapel of San Elizario** ❺. The presidio chapel was built in 1789, using a mixture of Spanish Colonial and native architectural styles, as a fortified base for the army. It was reconstructed in 1877.

El Paso Mission Trail Association (tel: 915-851-9997) offers information on self-guided tours and tours by appointment of El Paso's two restored Spanish missions and presidio chapel. They are located 9 miles (14km) apart.

Across the border, in Ciudad Juárez, the even older (1668) **Guadalupe Mission**, also known as the Misión de Nuestra Señora de Guadalupe de los Indios Mansos del Paso del Norte, is famous for the legend that its shadows point to the Lost Padre Mine in El Paso's Franklin Mountains, where Spanish gold is said to be hidden.

A SLAP-LEATHER TOWN

Ever since the Spanish explorer Juan de Oñate laid claim to El Paso del Rio Grande del Norte – a self-explanatory name – this city has been Hispanic, as are most of its residents. Far removed from the events of the Texas Revolution, El Paso for a long time shared a common religion, language, and history with Juárez, becoming a part of Texas a full five years after Texas became a state.

The overall impression of El Paso – at 683,577 souls, Texas's sixth largest city – is of "beige" – from the largely adobe buildings that are made from, and cling to, the pale caliche hills of this part of the Chihuahuan Desert.

The Old West lives on in this dusty and unprepossessing city. El Paso retains something of the ambiance of the slap-leather town it was in 1896, when gunman John Wesley Hardin was shot dead in the Acme Saloon. Hardin had been pardoned, reformed, and was practicing law in El Paso when a local constable ended his life. Along with other notorious gunslingers, he is buried in **Concordia Cemetery** Ⓐ, east

Wall mural on a Seventh Avenue store.

of downtown. Years after his death, the city remained a convenient place for outlaws to cross the river.

CAMPUS ASIAN INFLUENCES

El Paso has a small Chinese community – descendants of the those who laid the tracks for the railroad that reached here in 1881. It grew with Mexican revolutionary Pancho Villa's 1910 attacks on the Chinese living in the neighboring Mexican states of Chihuahua and Coahuila. You won't see too much evidence of this Chinese community, but one unusual Asian feature in El Paso is the Bhutanese architecture on display at the **University of Texas at El Paso (UTEP)** **B** campus.

It's not exactly what you would expect here, but the story is that Katherine Worrell, the wife of the dean at a time when UTEP was known as the Texas State School of Mines and Metallurgy, lifted the design from *National Geographic* after a 1916 fire destroyed almost half of the campus. The three oldest buildings are pure Bhutanese Eclectic, copied from a Tibetan monastery and fortress at Grag-Gye-Jong in the Himalayas. Most later buildings are variations on this style. While you are visiting the campus, check out the university's **Centennial Museum and Chihuahuan Desert Gardens** **C** (tel: 915-747-5565; Mon–Sat 10am–4.30pm; free), where displays include ancient pottery, dinosaur bones, and relics from the Ice Age.

UTEP, in the foothills of the Franklin Mountains, is a large four-year state university with 25,151 students that began life in 1914. Its 51,500-capacity stadium hosts college football on weekends during the season and is the site of the **Sun Bowl**, an annual football classic, second only in age to Pasadena's Rose Bowl. The game is usually played in late December, but the weather is invariably fine: El Paso has more sunny days than almost every other city in the country. Occasional music events are also staged at the stadium. North of UTEP, **McKelligon Canyon**, popular with hikers, is the site of the summer-long outdoor dance extravaganza *¡Viva El Paso!* (tel: 915-231-1100; https://vivaelpaso.org) in a 1,500-seat amphitheater.

Tip

If you can't acquire tickets for the Sun Bowl, pack your binoculars and drag a blanket up the side of the mountain along with the locals and students.

View of downtown El Paso.

A unique feature of El Paso is "The Star on the Mountain" – a 460-by-280ft (140-by-85-meter) star erected by the local electrical utility in 1940. Illuminated by 459 white light bulbs, it can be dedicated by anybody to a friend or relative by the night, week, or month. The *El Paso Times* publishes the dedications daily, and sponsors get a star-shaped pin and certificate.

DOWNTOWN

San Jacinto Plaza marks the original city square and is the starting point for bus routes. Around here is what remains of the El Paso that has been documented, along with downtown Juárez, by Elroy Bode, the city's master of the *bosquejo*, or literary sketch. The city was once called Magoffinville, after one of its founding fathers, and until the 1960s, alligators were kept in the plaza.

El Paso Convention and Performing Art Center D (1 Civic Center Plaza; tel: 915-534-0609; http://elpasolive.com; open daily) should be your first stop to pick up a walking tour brochure of downtown El Paso. Among the sights on the tour are the 1952 **El Paso Museum of Art** E (1 Arts Festival Plaza; tel: 915-212-0300; https://epma.art; Tue–Sat 9am–5pm, Thu until 9pm, Sun noon–5pm; free), which, in addition to its European collection and contemporary American works, possesses an unusually impressive collection of Mexican Colonial art and is well worth a visit. Nearby is the **El Paso Museum of History** (510 N. Santa Fe Street; tel: 915-212-0320; history.elpasotexas.gov; Tue–Sat 9am–5pm, Thu until 9pm, Sun noon–5pm; free), which has exhibits on the city's history, including a massive touchscreen wall (40 by 6ft/12 by 1.8 meters) known as Digie, the first of its kind in the US. The most surprising museum downtown is the **El Paso Holocaust Museum** (715 N. Oregon Street; tel: 915-351-0048; www.elpasoholocaustmuseum.org; Tue–Fri 9am–5pm, Sat–Sun 1–5pm; free), which seems a bit out of place in this heavily Hispanic city, but offers some moving exhibits about the Holocaust in both Spanish and English.

While you are walking around the area, be sure to stop in at the

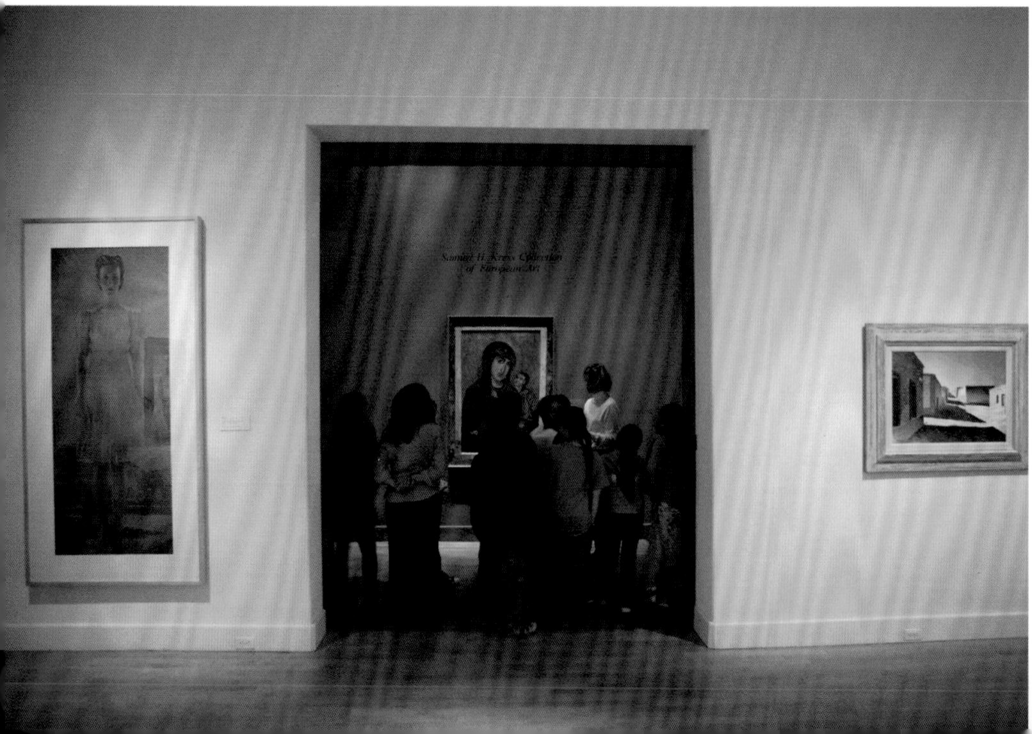

Museo de Arte e Historia.

spectacular historic Hotel Paso Del Norte, Autograph Collection (10 Sheldon Court; tel: 915-534-3000; www.marriott.com/hotels/travel/elpak-hotel-paso-del-norte-autograph-collection). Reason enough to spend the night in El Paso, this handsome and sophisticated hotel has parts dating to 1912, including a simply amazing Tiffany glass-domed lobby, on a par with anything you might enjoy in Texas. At the very least, enjoy a drink at the bar or a gourmet meal in the elegant restaurant under the dome.

Another historic building in downtown El Paso that you should not miss is the **Magoffin Home State Historic Site** **F** (1120 Magoffin Avenue; tel: 915-533-5147; www.thc.texas.gov/historic-sites/magoffin-home-state-historic-site; Tue–Sun 9am–5pm), an elegant 1875 adobe mansion, with walls 2.5ft (76cm) thick, that contains many of the original family furnishings and paintings.

FRANKLIN MOUNTAINS

Northeast of downtown, off US 54, is Fort Bliss Military Reservation, the site of the largest air defense school in the free world. One curiosity here is the **Old Fort Bliss Replica Museum** **G** (tel: 915-588-8482; Mon–Fri 9am–4pm; free), where history buffs can wander through the adobe pre-Civil War army outpost. It is a re-creation of what a frontier fort of the late 19th century would have looked like. Near here, in the Franklin Mountains, is Wilderness Park, home to **El Paso Museum of Archaeology**, Wilderness Park (4301 Transmountain Road; tel: 915-212-0421; http://archaeology.elpasotexas.gov; Tue–Sat 9am–5pm, Sun noon–5pm), which interprets American Indian culture, from prehistoric times to the present and offers hiking on trails into canyons. Next door is the **Border Patrol Museum** (4315 Woodrow Bean Trans Mt Rd; tel: 915-759-6060; www.borderpatrol-museum.com; Tue–Sat 9am–5pm; free), which chronicles the heritage of the Border Patrol force since its inception in 1924.

At almost 27,000 (10,926 hectares), **Franklin Mountains State Park** (1331 McKelligon Canyon Road; tel: 915-566-6441; https://tpwd.texas.gov/state-parks/franklin-mountains), home to North

The El Paso county symbol above the entrance to the city courthouse.

The Sun Bowl stadium.

Franklin Peak, at 7,192ft (2,192 meters), the highest peak in El Paso, is the largest urban city park in the US, home to ringtail cats, coyotes, and other wildlife, and offers numerous places to explore, picnic, and relax. Ride the **Wyler Aerial Tramway** Ⓗ (1700 McKinley Avenue; tel: 915-566-6622; https://tpwd.texas.gov/state-parks/wyler-aerial-tramway) to Ranger Peak (5,632ft/1,716 meters) for views of Mexico and New Mexico. Northwest of the city, scenic drives across the Franklin Mountains, and especially along **Transmountain Road** (exit off I-10 West), provide spectacular views.

ACROSS THE BORDER

Back in 1911, El Pasoans were able to gather on the flat roofs of their houses for "battle teas" and watch the Mexican Revolution unfold in **Ciudad Juárez** across the Rio Grande. For a while, Pancho Villa took refuge north of the border, acquiring a taste for ice cream and learning to ride a motorcycle here.

Political geography, as well as climate, shaped the character of this Mexican city. It was named for Benito Juárez, who fled here in the 1860s when Napoleon III made the Austrian Archduke Maximilian the Emperor of Mexico. Juárez, a Zapotecan Indian, fought as President to make Mexico a secular state.

MEXICAN BARGAINS

Like most border towns, Juárez offers something for almost everyone. The **Museo de Arte de Ciudad Juarez**, on Avenida Lincoln, exhibits Mexican art by period, from pre-Hispanic to the present. The building's design is modern, unique and certainly worth a look. The museum is in a tourist-oriented commercial center that includes the government-sponsored FONART artisans' market. This is not as fecund as the *mercado central*, and there is no haggling with vendors, but it is interesting nonetheless. Along Lincoln, between FONART and the intersection of Avenida de las Americas, are a number of artisans' and curio shops, providing a good walking tour for shoppers.

Shopping is a popular pastime on both sides of the border. In El Paso, the fly-and-buy tourist will find the boutiques of

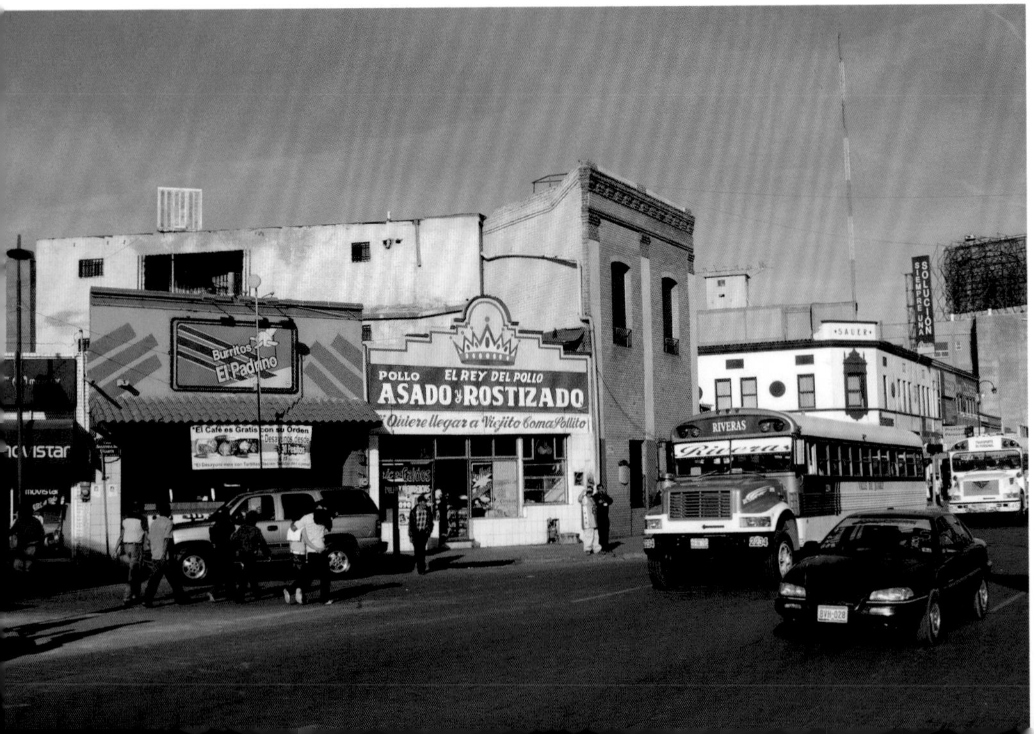

A busy intersection in Ciudad Juárez.

La Placita conveniently located near the airport, and, at I-10 and Hawkins is the Cielo Vista Mall.

Around El Paso, great bargains can be found at factory outlets for cowboy boots and Western wear. On the other side of the river, in the central *mercado*, Avenida 16 de Septiembre, you'll discover a variety of regionally manufactured goods – generally leather and textiles – and local produce.

Pedestrians can enter Mexico over the downtown **Stanton Street Bridge** ❶, which is the closest approach to the Mexican Tourist Center, and walk back across the river by the **Santa Fe Bridge or Paso del Norte International Bridge** ❷. Most automobile traffic crosses via the **Cordova Bridge of the Americas** Ⓚ, off I-10, the largest bridge – and best avoided at rush hours.

Close to the bridge terminals, on both sides of the border, are parks named **Chamizal Park** Ⓛ, which memorialize the victims of the border war of a century ago and mark its peaceful settlement. Here the **Chamizal Memorial** (800 South San Marcial; tel: 915-532-7273; www.nps.gov/cham; open daily; free) records how the border has been surveyed over the centuries. Park entertainments – which take place in an art gallery, an indoor theater, and an al fresco amphitheater – vary from displays of local artworks and musical performances to films and temporary exhibitions. A fourth bridge, the **Ysleta-Zaragoza Bridge**, can be found on the far eastern side of El Paso.

Much of Juárez can be seen on foot, and most cab drivers speak English (but you should agree on a price before closing the door). Spanish and English are spoken in both towns.

The atmosphere in Juárez is a little more *picante* – spicy – than in El Paso, and so is the food (but don't drink the water here, or consume ice cream or ice cubes). There are lots of good and bad bars, and equally good and bad restaurants. Women are discouraged from visiting – and in some cases turned away from – *cantinas*, the traditional "men's bars." In fact, several working-class *cantinas* in downtown Juárez are best avoided by all tourists: size things up before you decide to hang around.

Fact

The Sunland Derby (https://sunlandderby.com; tel: 575-874-5200) takes place in March in El Paso.

IMPROVED SECURITY

El Paso and its sister city Juárez have been particularly hard hit by their reputation as being on the front lines of the drug war. A staggering 106,831 people died in drug-related violence during Mexican President Felipe Calderon's time in office from 2006 to 2014. In some ways, things have improved in the last decade, at least in popular tourist areas of Mexico which continue to see surges in tourism. However, that doesn't negate the fact that in 2018 there were 35,964 reported homicides, a 12 percent increase from 2017. While not all the homicides are linked to drug violence, there are definite areas throughout the country where violence from the drug wars are impacting citizens significantly.

Pedestrians queue at the Cordova Bridge of Americas crossing.

An old movie set in Big Bend Ranch State Park.

BIG BEND COUNTRY

This arid region is as tough as it gets, a land dominated by unforgiving desert and a lack of drinkable water, but a land rich in minerals and natural beauty, with the highest peaks in the state.

Main attractions

Marfa
Museum of the Big Bend, Alpine
Fort Davis National Historic Site
McDonald Observatory
Guadalupe Mountains National Park

Map on page 254

In his classic novel, *West of the Pecos*, Zane Grey described this part of western Texas as "desolate, gray and lonely, an utter solitude uninhabited even by beasts of the hills or fowls of the air." The Spanish conquistadors who discovered it in the 16th century named the region *el despoblado*, the uninhabited place, and 300 years later a pioneer cattleman, Charles Goodnight, cursed it as "the graveyard of the cowman's hopes." General Sheridan summed up his impressions by saying that, if he owned Texas, he would "rent it out and live in hell."

THE PECOS RIVER

Beginning as a clear stream in the Sangre de Cristo Mountains north of Santa Fe, the Pecos flows 900 miles (1,440km) southward to the Rio Grande, entering "a flat, hellish desert of mesquite and greasewood" even before it reaches Texas. "Buzzards soar above the flat, torrid land," wrote Bryan Wooley in the Dallas Morning News about the Pecos region, "Dust devils dance across the plain like small brown tornadoes. Oil well pump jacks dot the landscape, many of them leaking. Quicksand forms below the river's banks and its water turns too salty for man or beast to drink." It was a major hazard to all who had to cross it, from the American Indian fighters marching to their West Texas forts to the early 1850s immigrants on their way to search for gold in California.

The mythical Pecos Bill, legendarily reared by coyotes and who fed his horse barbed wire, stems from this region of tall tales and great accomplishments. Such an accomplishment was featured in Larry McMurtry's *Lonesome Dove*, which was inspired by the way that Goodnight and Oliver Loving expanded the range of the longhorn hundreds of miles north, driving a quarter of a million cattle across the Pecos. In that era – the 1860s – the river was 50–100ft

The Big Bend Saddlery store, Alpine.

(15–30 meters) wide, spreading to a mile (1.6km) after floods and leaving deadly lakes of poisonous alkaline water behind when the floods receded.

Spanish gold is said to be buried in the desert, though it would take unimaginable endurance to search for it. In the 1930s, Hollywood struck a rich vein of its own with a raft of titles such as *The Pecos Kid*, *The Stranger from Pecos*, *King of the Pecos* (starring John Wayne) and *Robin Hood of the Pecos* (Roy Rogers). "The Pecos river holds a fascination for people," Paul Patterson, a 90-year-old cowboy who has lived along the river most of his life, told the *Dallas Morning News*, "unless they have to stop and camp and drink the water." A local joke maintains that when a coyote drinks the water he immediately licks his behind to get the bad taste out of his mouth.

THE FOSSIL CLOCK

Like the Grand Canyon, the history of the earth can be read clearly in arid West Texas, where vegetation has not scrawled its graffiti of decay. Nature's first attempts at complex creatures can still be seen in the 600-million-year-old remains of algal colonies in pre-Cambrian limestone, 2.5 miles (4km) north of Allamoore, 10 miles (16km) northwest of **Van Horn** ❻ (pop. 1,919). Van Horn is an historic crossroads of the old Bankhead Highway and the Old Spanish Trail, 150 miles (240km) southeast of El Paso, an area of West Texas dubbed Big Bend Country. US 90 and I-10 cross here today, and it's a good jumping-off point for explorations to this remote southwestern section of Texas.

It's worth stopping in Van Horn to view the ancient pictographs on dark red precambrian rocks and pink and purple cambrian formations on **Red Rock Ranch** (305 Broadway; tel: 432-284-1284; tours by reservation, with at least one week's notice), north of town. The 3.5-hour tours take in the rock art, an 1880 ranch house, and an old movie set.

West of here, I-10 crosses the foothills of the Sierra Diablo Mountains before passing through **Sierra Blanca** ❼, with dramatic views of 6,891ft (2,100-meter) Sierra Blanca Mountain and "forests" of Spanish dagger yucca

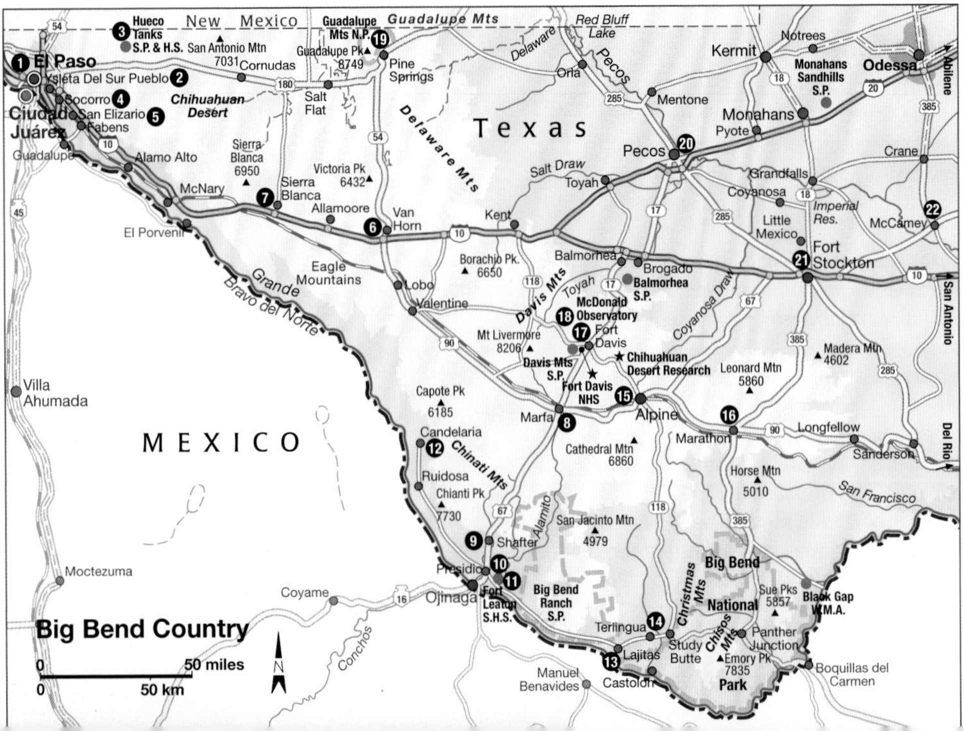

plants. This is where Chinese railroad workers from the west met Irish laborers from the east to complete the second transcontinental railroad.

MARFA

Beginning life in 1883 as a water stop and freight headquarters for the Galveston, Harrisburg, and San Antonio Railway, **Marfa** 8 (pop. 1,772), 75 miles (120km) south of Van Horn, was reportedly named for a character in Fyodor Dostoevski's *The Brothers Karamazov*. The book was being read at the time by the wife of the chief railroad engineer. By 1885, when the impressive courthouse was built, poker bets in the saloons were being made with town lots. At 4,830ft (1,472 meters), in a semi-arid region, Marfa boasts a superb climate and, in summer, is one of the coolest places in Texas.

Marfa is celebrated as the location for the 1956 movie *Giant*, starring Rock Hudson, Elizabeth Taylor, James Dean, and other Hollywood stars who took over downtown's charming 1930 **Hotel Paisano** (207 Highland Street; tel: 432-729-3669; www.hotelpaisano.com) as a headquarters. The Pueblo Deco hotel, designed by Trost and Trost, has been updated to reflect an air of Western glamor; the lobby, courtyard, restaurant, and store are all worth a visit. You can still stay in one of the historic rooms the stars occupied, including the Rock Hudson Suite.

THE CHINATI FOUNDATION

Spain had practically abandoned West Texas by the time it became a part of independent Mexico in 1821. As the Anglo frontier moved westward, the fierce mounted Comanche war parties began to prey on wagon trains and Mexican and Anglo settlements along the Comanche War Trail, especially during the late summer and early fall harvest season. To counter these depredations, a line of cavalry forts was established soon after the Republic of Texas joined the United States in 1846. The old fort, just north of Marfa, has today been transformed into the **Chinati Foundation** (1 Cavalry Row; tel: 432-729-4362; www.chinati.org; Wed–Sun 9am–5pm; tours by reservation), a contemporary art museum founded by artist Donald Judd specifically designed to exhibit large-scale installations by a range of artists.

The New York sculptor Don Judd fathered the $4 million project, with Houston oil heiress Philippa de Menil Pelizzi Friedrich as reluctant mother. Judd needed isolation for himself and open spaces for his work, both of which Marfa offers in abundance. His variously permutated groups of large rectangular concrete structures are rhythmically arranged in an endless progression toward the far horizon; some 100 aluminum pieces are housed in a glass-walled gun shed. There are also works by other prominent contemporary artists on display in the fort, such as the crushed auto-body sculptures of John Chamberlain and the fluorescent sculptures of Dan Flavin.

The Prada Marfa art installation, north of Marfa.

Eastbound freight train.

Fact

Big Bend Ranch State Park should not be confused with Big Bend National Park, although it is equally stunning in many ways. The land was acquired by Texas Parks and Wildlife Department in 1988.

UNLIKELY ART AND FOOD OASIS

Countless artists followed Judd to Marfa, and the town is now a haven for hip East Coast urban artists, many of whom have sensitively restored historic buildings as homes, art galleries, restaurants, a great hometown independent bookstore (with books on art, of course), and next door, a popular local public radio station. The wail of locomotives flying through town is often the only sound in this quiet West Texas backwater.

For its size, Marfa is spoiled for enjoyable places to stay and eat out on top of its novel attractions – it boasts a double-take fake Prada Marfa store beside the highway northwest of town, actually an art installation, and is also known for its Marfa Lights, nightly illuminations in the sky that can be viewed out beside the highway. Next to the train tracks, visit the small weekly farmer's market and line up for tasty Mediterranean food at the popular **Food Shark** food truck (or visit its brick-and-mortar cafeteria-style eatery in downtown). For dinner, **Cochineal** (107 W. San Antonio Street; tel: 432-729-3300; www.cochinealmarfa.com; reservations recommended), owned by seasoned restaurateurs from New York City, is a chic eatery that gives any fine dining establishment in New York a run for its money.

DOWN TO THE BORDER

From Marfa, US 67 heads southwest to **Shafter** ❾, a ghost town in the Chinati Mountains, where millions of dollars of silver were mined and where stories persist about treasure buried in caves. Farther south, on the banks of the Rio Grande, is **Presidio** ❿ (pop. 4,099), described in the WPA guidebook to Texas in 1940 as "an old town of sun-baked adobe houses, squatting like an ancient hombre in the shade of giant cottonwoods." The town, which was founded by Franciscan missionaries in 1683, is a bit different today. Check out the mural of a woman looking across the border on the town's water tower – a gift from Mexico – as well as outdoor concerts during their Bluebonnet Music Series and local cuisine at the Bean Café and El Patio Restaurant.

Fort Leaton State Historic Site ⓫ (tel: 432-229-3613; http://tpwd.texas.gov/state-parks/fort-leaton; daily 8am–4.30pm), an interesting example of native adobe construction, southeast of town, was not a military outpost but a trading post operated in the mid-19th century by a certain Ben Leaton. Leaton had been among the first Anglo settlers to arrive in Presidio. In their fortified trading post, he and his wife outfitted and accommodated travelers who were somehow drawn to this backwater of civilization. The Texas Rangers had a base here when Pancho Villa was rampaging south of the border, but the post was abandoned in 1926. Most of the old outpost has now been restored.

Across the river from Presidio is **Ojinaga** ("o-hee-NAH-ga"), which lacks the touristy feel of most border towns. There are a few good restaurants (some that Anthony Bourdain visited in 2018),

Marfa attracts many visitors.

and at least one good hotel. Cautions for travel in Mexico apply here, as elsewhere along La Frontera; be sure to have your passport.

The highest waterfall in Texas is on a private ranch near the tiny settlement of **Candelaria** ⓬, northwest of Presidio. Capote Falls crashes 175ft (54 meters) on to the rocks below. Inquire locally about making a visit.

El Camino del Rio (Farm Road 170) follows the Rio Grande southeast from Presidio down to the tiny village of **Lajitas** ⓭, a spectacular drive with sharp curves, steep grades, and occasional wandering livestock. After quicksilver was discovered in the nearby town of Terlingua, an influx of settlers settled in Lajitas, and by 1900, the town became a port of entry to Mexico. In 1915, a US Army base was established to protect settlers against Pancho Villa's border raids, and it is from here that General Jack Pershing mounted his "punitive expedition" against Villa. This unsuccessful foray demonstrated the army's lack of experience in fighting on foreign terrain. A young lieutenant by the name of George Patton saw his first action here, as a member of Pershing's expedition, and killed two men and a horse. There are a range of hotels and motels in Lajitas, including the four-star Lajitas Golf Resort & Spa (21701 FM 170; tel:1-877-LAJITAS; www.lajitasgolfresort.com) which has an 18-hole golf course, a pool, spa, movie theater, outdoor activities like shooting, and an equestrian center.

Several companies licensed by the National Park Service in nearby Big Bend National Park offer raft trips of 1–9 days' duration on the Rio Grande, through narrow 1,500ft (460-meter) deep canyons, or farther down in challenging rapids. Among them is the **Far Flung Outdoor Center** (tel: 432-371-2633; www.bigbendfarflung.com) in Terlingua. Just east of Lajitas, on FM 170, is **Barton Warnock Environmental Educational Center** (tel: 432-424-3327; http://tpwd.texas.gov/state-parks/barton-warnock; daily 8am–4.30pm), named after a local botanist. The center sits at the eastern entrance to **Big Bend Ranch State Park** (tel: 432-358-4444; http://tpwd.texas.gov/state-parks/big-bend-ranch; daily 8am–6pm), a state park adjoining the national park to the east; the western entrance is at Fort Leaton State Historic Site.

GEM HUNTING

FM 170 continues onward to **Terlingua** ⓮ (pop. 58), a prosperous mining town of 2,000 inhabitants at the turn of the 20th century. Here red cinnabar ore was mined and cooked to yield millions of dollars' worth of mercury. The 27 miles (43km) of tunnels and shafts – some as much as 900ft (275 meters) deep – of the abandoned mercury mines have yielded a treasure trove of rocks, fossils and mineral specimens cast aside by miners, as well as abundant specimens of cinnabar. This looks much like lipstick smears on the fissured surfaces of igneous rocks.

Today, the Terlingua mining town is a collection of mostly abandoned stone and adobe ruins, though some have been renovated into coffee shops and

Terlingua's historic cemetery.

A section of the Cleburne history mural, Alpine, by award-winning artist Stylle Read.

glampsites, of which there are many in town. Travelers have discovered that Terlingua is as fascinating as its neighbour, Big Bend National Park. The town watches the sunset over the park's mountains every day from the patio of the Terlingua Trading Company, which is often full of locals and visitors jamming out on a variety of instruments. Popular restaurants include Long Draw Pizza and La Kiva Restaurant and Bar, a subterranean spot with rock walls, great barbecue, dinosaur décor, and sometimes live music. Most tourists, grab a Texas-sized dinner and margaritas at the historic Starlight Theatre Restaurant, set in an old movie theater and decorated in Texas-themed murals.

Views of the nearby peaks of the Chisos Mountains in Big Bend National Park (see page 265), and multicolored badlands on every side, form a surreal backdrop for rock hounds and cactus collectors, who can run amok here. Amber, the hard golden resin of prehistoric plants, is occasionally collected from cretaceous coal outcrops along Terlingua Creek, just west of Big Bend.

Guests at the Holland Hotel, Alpine.

The mountains in this region were once the hideout of outlaws, renegades, and the like – especially the little settlement of **Valentine** (pop. 126) on US 90, northwest of Marfa. They now attract rockhounds, on account of the numerous minerals and gems they yield. An outstanding example is the famous Texas plumed agate, in which red flames and black feather shapes are captured in a translucent white matrix. It is most easily found near Marfa and Alpine.

ALPINE

An attractive college town with a lot of art galleries, restaurants, and lodging options, **Alpine** ⓯ (pop. 6,065), the northeastern corner of the triangle made up of Marfa and Presidio, is the main center of activity in Big Bend Country. To someone arriving from the broiling flatlands, the town's 4,500ft (1,370-meter) altitude can indeed seem alpine. In the heart of cattle country, Alpine is a stop on AMTRAK's Sunset Limited, between New Orleans and Los Angeles. Many people choose the town for their vacation headquarters and enjoy summer theater productions and museums at **Sul Ross State University**, which stages the annual Cowboy Poetry Gathering every February for a week-long celebration of culture and art. Also on campus is the excellent **Museum of the Big Bend** (tel: 432-837-8143; www.museumofthebigbend.com; Tue–Sat 9am–5pm, Sun 1–5pm), which interprets the natural and cultural history of Big Bend.

MARATHON

Less than one hour to the south of Alpine, at the junction of US 385 and US 90, the turnoff for Big Bend National Park, you'll find tiny **Marathon** ⓰ (pop. 470). Geologists are delighted by the diversity of rocks and minerals in the vicinity, while rugged nature photographers use Marathon as a jumping-off point for trips to **Black Gap Wildlife Management Area**, 58 miles (93km) away. Though 80 miles

(129km) distant, Big Bend National Park is the next sign of civilization toward the south. If you're driving west along the Rio Grande route along the border, Marathon is the first main town after leaving Langtry and a good place to spend a night before heading down to Big Bend National Park. While in Marathon, visit Brick Vault Brewery and Barbecue for beers and good grub, catch an event in the downtown square, and admire art in the Klepper Gallery.

The beautifully renovated **Gage Hotel** (tel: 432-386-4205; www.gagehotel.com), a national historical landmark, is just the ticket for weary travelers with a taste for backcountry luxury and the Old West. It was built as a private lodge by rancher Alfred Gage in 1927 and is set around a lovely courtyard and fountain, hacienda style. All rooms are furnished with antiques, American Indian artifacts, and Mexican furniture. The restaurant is an oasis for foodies, offering delicious New West dishes in a memorable setting. It is alone worth the trip.

FORT DAVIS

To the north of Alpine, at the intersection of highways 17 and 118, is **Fort Davis** ⓱, named after the much-honored Jefferson Davis, who was president of the Confederate States of America but is remembered locally as the man who, as US Secretary of War, introduced camels to West Texas. The fort stands dramatically with its back to a wall of volcanic rock named Sleeping Lion Mountain. At 5,000ft (1,540 meters), the community is the highest in Texas and has some lovely artisan stores and lodging options.

At **Fort Davis National Historic Site** (tel: 432-426-3224; www.nps.gov/foda; daily), the life of the late 19th-century frontier soldier has been recreated. Actual buildings survive from the days when such soldiers mounted up to escort wagon trains on the Chihuahuan Trail, or stagecoaches on the Butterfield Overland Mail Route. This is considered the best-preserved US fort in the West. The fort adjoins **Davis Mountains State Park** (tel: 432-426-3337; http://tpwd.texas.gov/state-parks/davis-mountains; open daily), a pretty valley that is a lovely place to hike and relax, with oak-shaded campsites in its campground.

The **Chihuahuan Desert Research Institute** (tel: 432-364-2499; Mon–Sat 9–5pm, Sun 12.30–5.30pm), on Highway 118 a few miles south of Fort Davis, is a popular port of call for those fascinated by native desert plants. Among its attractions is a cactus greenhouse. Visitors can also, in two hours, drive a scenic winding loop on highways 166 and 118 through the Davis Mountains, where gentle, weathered slopes belie their violent volcanic origins. From Wild Rose Pass on, one has the same view of Limpia Brook, as it runs between high cliffs, that the Apache and Comanche raiding parties had as they lay in ambush.

In this area, **McDonald Observatory** ⓲ (3640 Dark Sky Drive; tel: 432-426-3640; www.mcdonaldobservatory.org; daily 10am–5.30pm), perched atop Mount Lock, houses one of the largest astronomical telescopes in the world, the giant 433in

Fact

Davis Mountains State Park attracts more than 150,000 visitors each year. Facilities include camping sites, hiking trails, and fishing.

Desert highway near Marathon.

DESERT PLANTLIFE

Hardy survivors of the scorched earth, desert plants endure through cunning, thrift, and clever adaptations, and emerge in spectacular springtime displays after wet winters.

The flowering plants of the Chihuahuan Desert perform a spectacular, although brief, extravaganza after the spring rains; but most of the rest of the year they are occupied with vegetative survival rather than reproductive exhibitionism. If you see a *lechuguilla* plant, you'll know where you are, since the habitat of this member of the amarillis family coincides perfectly with the boundaries of the Chihuahuan Desert.

Lechuguilla, which means "little lettuce" in Spanish, is easily recognized by its rosette of succulent bluish-green, spine-tipped leaves about 2ft (67cm) long and 1.5 inches (4cm) wide. In true desert plant fashion, it can inflict a painful wound on the unwary.

The yucca species are somewhat similar to agave but are actually members of the lily family. They have narrower, more flexible, and less succulent leaves, and flower annually. The torrey yucca grows almost to the height of a tree north and west of Van Horn, forming the only "forest" in the desert lowlands.

There are over 100 native species of cactus in Texas.

The cactus family, that classic form of desert life, originated in the southwestern US and Mexico and has attained its greatest diversity there. Over 100 species of cactus are Texas residents.

Ocotillo is a cactus prevalent in the Far West. It looks like a naked spider on its back and its long 6–20ft (2–6-meter) legs, protected by stiff spines, are used as living fences by goat raisers. This cautious species puts out leaves only after rainfall and discards them as soon as drought returns.

Greasewood, or creosote bush, is, along with cactus, ubiquitous in North American deserts, taking its name from the thick resin on its small yellowish-green paired leaflets. Usually only around a meter in height, it has been used as fuel by the desert cultures for thousands of years. Its wide, even spacing and the general absence of competing species are the result of special adaptation to the limited availability of water, for greasewood secretes a poison that kills even its own seedlings.

Another plant particularly common on mesas and hillsides is sotol, or "bear grass," so called for its 4ft (1.25-meter) long, arching, narrow leaves with small claw-like spines along the margins. Its slender, 4–15ft (1.25–4.5-meter) brush-like, flowering stalk may persist for several seasons.

All of these large plants were important to the American Indians who inhabited the area. Their leaves provided fiber for clothing and utensils, as well as soap, and the thick basal stems were baked in stone-lined fireplaces, of which the scattered remains can be seen.

The pea family is also well represented by thorny shrubs like the infamous cat claw acacia, or "wait-a-minute bush," from the automatic cry of "Wait a minute!" as hikers try to extricate themselves from this vegetable's clutches.

Devil's head cactus is an interesting plant about a foot (31cm) in diameter. It lurks, partially buried, ready to snare a hoof, paw, or sneaker with its four-pronged spines. On the whole, desert plants are best admired from a safe distance.

(9.2-meter) HET optical telescope. The observatory posts regular updates about what will be visible in the night sky on their website, and offers two-hour long Star Party nights on Tuesdays, Fridays, and Saturdays.

THE MOUNTAINS

Interstates I-10 (which runs through Fort Stockton) and I-20 (through Pecos) meet to the west, on the edge of the Davis Mountains. This vast range (under different names) runs from the New Mexico border – aside from a gap between Fort Davis and Alpine – all the way south to Big Bend National Park on the Rio Grande. Islands of green – the forests and meadows of the high mountains – rise in the sea of brown.

Six of them soar to over 8,000ft (2,400 meters), including **Mount Livermore** at 8,378ft (2,553 meters). In these enclaves of pine, fir, maple, and oak, there are small populations of elk, black bear, bighorn sheep, and mountain lions, the reminders of better, wetter grazing times. A drying trend over the past 100 years, coupled with overgrazing by livestock, has depleted the grass and the steppe has become a desert hell.

The youngest ranges are the Franklin Mountains at El Paso and the Delaware Mountains north of Kent, which are part of the Rocky Mountain system and still rise at an average rate of more than quarter of an inch (0.65cm) per year. Many of the ranges in the basin-and-range area of Texas were formed during the tumultuous Tertiary period, approximately 60 million years ago. Massive uplifting and faulting led to intrusions of molten rock, like those in the Chisos Mountains of Big Bend National Park, and extensive lava flows that created the Davis Mountains.

These volcanic formations cover mountains from earlier periods, as well as marine sediments and coral reefs. Folding and overthrust faulting have left young rock strata covered by a layer 150 million years older in places – a picture puzzle complex enough to delight the most jaded structural geologist.

Texas's highest and most majestic mountains, the Guadalupes, at the Texas–New Mexico border, began as a massive coral reef, the Permian Reef, some 250 million years ago. Two periods of uplift have raised the reef to its current elevation of over 8,000ft (2,440 meters) – Carlsbad Caverns, just over the border in New Mexico, meanwhile, protects decorated caves in that same formation beneath ground. The dominant feature in **Guadalupe Mountains National Park** ⓳ (tel: 915-828-3251; www.nps.gov/gumo/index.htm; open daily) is 8,751ft (2,667-meter) Guadalupe Peak, the highest point in Texas. Approached from the west on US 62/180, this giant wedge of limestone resembles an enormous ship moving over the desert. The cliffs of El Capitan Peak form the prow, towering above a white sea of salt. McKittrick Canyon is a major draw in fall foliage season, when its maples display brilliant hues. The park's small campground is a nice spot to relax, hike, and enjoy the desert, and is convenient for

Fact

Romantics can still send out their Valentine's cards with a Valentine, Texas, postmark. If you can't get there in person, you can mail your card, with the recipient's address marked and the appropriate postage affixed, inside a larger envelope to: Valentine's Day Postmark, Postmaster, 311 W. California Avenue, Valentine TX 79854-9998 and the good people at the tiny post office will stamp it and send it on.

Fort Davis National Historic Site.

Fact

West of the Pecos Rodeo (http://pecosrodeo.com), touted as the World's First Rodeo – a couple of other rodeos compete for that moniker – is a classic Western event with bucking broncos, team roping, calf roping, and steer wrangling competitions.

visiting nearby Carlsbad Caverns. Get there early to secure a spot.

CANTALOUPES AND RODEOS

Pecos ⓴ (pop. 9,922) is the largest town along the river of the same name and famous for its cantaloupes. In 1883, the world's first rodeo (supposedly) took place. The tradition is carried on, with a major rodeo here at the end of June each year. The **West of the Pecos Museum** (120 E. Dot Stafford Street; tel: 432-445-5076; www.westofthepecos-museum.com; Mon–Sat 9am–5pm, Sun 1–4pm) displays a century-old saloon in one of its 50 rooms.

Bordering New Mexico, is **Loving**, one of the most sparsely populated counties with 152 people. Four hundred oil leases have been registered, but there is no water – it has to be trucked in.

The only reservoir in Texas along the Pecos River is Red Bluff in Loving County, but it has only once been full in the past 60 years. New Mexico defended itself in court for 16 years against Texan charges that it was taking too much water out of the river. Finally, in 1988, the US Supreme Court ruled in Texas's favor and its neighbor was forced to pay $14 million in damages.

The first place of any size along the river south of Pecos is **Fort Stockton** ㉑ (pop. 8,356). By the mid-1880s, with no enemies left to fight, the fort was abandoned, but it has been restored to its earlier appearance. Four of the original fort's buildings, constructed in 1867, can be visited and a museum and visitor center (tel: 800-336-2166; www.historicfortstocktontx.com; open daily) has been established in Barracks 1. Burrowing owls pop out of the parade grounds during the day. Other sights, include the world's biggest roadrunner, are included on the self-guided tour map.

At the junction of US 67 and US 385, is **McCamey** ㉒, an "instant town" on November 16, 1925, when the No. 1 Baker oil well blew in. After, there were 10,000 people in town and the solitary Texas Ranger – lacking a jail – had to chain prisoners to a post. One group uprooted it and took it to the nearest saloon. In 1936, McCamey was the scene of the world's first Rattlesnake Derby.

Rider at the West of the Pecos PRCA rodeo.

CHILI COOKOFF

If you're a fan of hot food, Terlingua is the place to make for on the first Saturday in November every year. Since 1967, this dusty little hamlet on the Rio Grande, west of Big Bend National Park, has been the venue for the Terlingua International Chili Cookoff. The cookoff attracts over 10,000 "chiliheads" for two annual chili cookoffs: the Chili Appreciation Society International and the Frank X. Tolbert/Wick Fowler World Chili Championships. Among the founders of the first chili cookoff in 1967 was car manufacturer Carroll Shelby, who owned a 220,000-acre (89,000-hectare) ranch nearby. Expect hotels to be full. For more information, visit www.abowlofred.com.

THE MARFA LIGHTS

Alien spacecraft, atmospheric mirages, burning gases, desert reflections – no one knows what causes the famous nightly lights in the sky near Marfa.

Robert Reed Ellison, a young cowhand, was the first to report the Marfa Lights. Looking across to the Chinati Mountains in West Texas he saw them twinkling in the night and figured they must have been the campfires of Apache Indians. But when he went searching the next day he found no Apaches – nor even the ashes of any fires. This was 114 years ago and people have been watching the lights ever since, but still without being able to explain what they are and where they're coming from. As elusive as rainbows, they disappear as soon as you think you're getting up close.

According to one guidebook the lights "move about, split apart, melt together, disappear and reappear." They have become such a tourist attraction that the Texas State Highways Department has built a special parking area from which to view them along US 90, about 10 miles (16km) east of town.

FOLLOWING THE LIGHTS

During World War II, pilots training at the nearby army base conducted an aerial search but were no more successful than previous investigators: the lights remained a mystery. Superstitious locals tend to reflect the views of a Mrs W.T. Giddings who claims they are a friendly source that once saved her father from a blizzard by leading him to a cave. Other explanations have included: electrostatic discharge, St Elmo's Fire, swamp gas or other natural gases igniting, moonlight reflecting on veins of mica, and even the ghosts of conquistadors in search of gold. *A New Handbook of Texas* says the most likely explanation is that the lights are a mirage caused by atmospheric conditions, produced by the interaction of cold and warm layers of air that bend light so that it can be seen from a distance but not up close.

ENOUGH THEORIES FOR A BOOK

The Desert Candle, the former local newspaper, which during its years of publication ran numerous reports of sightings, some of which were compiled in a book by editor Judith M. Brueske, suggested that the spaciousness of the Big Bend region and "the relatively low light contaminant," compared to more heavily populated areas, might make such lights easier to see. In the chapter titled *"The Marfa Light"* she offers several explanations, ranging from the phenomenon known as *ignis fatuus* (the spontaneous combustion of natural gases) or static electricity to the combination of moisture with bat guano phosphates (there are many bat caves in the mountains). And she, too, brings up the possibility that many of the sightings could be mirages, pointing out that, especially at sea, people have conjured up the vision of islands or villages.

What argues against this theory is the sheer ubiquity of the sightings. Usually they are small and seen at a distance, but occasionally lights as big as footballs have come close to people's cars. Nobody has ever reported being harmed.

Marfa Lights are visible every clear night between Marfa and Paisano Pass, in the direction of the Chinati Mountains.

Spectators gather to watch the Marfa Lights.

Santa Elena Canyon.

BIG BEND NATIONAL PARK

Beautiful Big Bend, where the Rio Grande lurches to the northeast, has canyons, waterfalls, and hiking trails galore, but with far fewer visitors than you'll find at Yosemite or the Grand Canyon.

The state's largest park, Big Bend National Park, is most challenging to backpackers and nature lovers. The Chisos Mountains, the wide desert, the Rio Grande, and the magnificent canyons combine to form a true wilderness, sections of which are still relatively unexplored.

Big Bend National Park (tel: 432-477-2251; www.nps.gov/bibe; open daily) is one of those places you have to be going to in order to get there. The closest town is Alpine, about 65 miles (105km) to the northwest of the northernmost tip. The park encompasses a vast area of 801,163 acres (324,219 hectares) and varies in altitude from 1,800ft (548 meters) all the way up to 7,832ft (2,387 meters). It has hundreds of trails, 100 miles (160km) of paved roads, and 160 miles (257km) of dirt roads. There is a campground with hookups and shelters, a post office, and a gas station. **Panther Junction ❶** has the park headquarters and visitor center (daily 8.30am–5pm), which should be your first stop on arrival. Year-round, Chisos Mountains Lodge (tel: 432-447-2291), at **Chisos Basin ❷**, provides camping and motel accommodations. RV and tent campsites are also available at **Rio Grande Village ❸** (tel: 432-477-2251), near Boquillas, and at Cottonwood, near Castolon. Permits ($12) are required for backcountry camping.

Cacti on an arid hillside.

WILD COUNTRY

King of the air around here is the endangered peregrine falcon, whose concentration of aeries is the largest in the contiguous 48 states. Golden eagles are frequently seen in winter, near the mountains and over the high grasslands, but, as the clouds move across this desolate land, you may be reminded of the gargantuan pterosaur whose 51ft (15.5-meter) reptilian wings cast terrifying shadows on the lesser dinosaurs below. The remains of these cretaceous

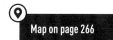

Main attractions
- Chisos Basin
- Chisos Basin Trail
- Rio Grande Village Nature Trail
- Santa Elena Canyon
- Castolon

Map on page 266

> **Quote**
>
> "In 1902, the Big Bend was pretty wild country. The stage brought mail and passengers once a week from Marfa and that was the only connection there was... the area at the time was a favorite hangout for cattle rustlers. It was easy to run cattle from one side of the Rio Grande to the other. Texas Rangers were scarce and didn't get to that part of the country very often."
>
> Topographical surveyor Stuart T. Penick.

creatures, the largest animals ever to fly, were found in the Big Bend area in the early 1970s.

THE GREAT OUTDOORS

The real Big Bend is best seen from its hiking trails, or from a kayak trip on the Rio Grande. Extensive information about getting the best out of your visit through hiking, camping, kayaking, scenic hikes, and river rafting trips is available from the National Park Service. But Big Bend is wild country, and should be respected as such.

HIT THE TRAIL

Some of the 36 marked hiking trails are strenuous and treacherous; others are easy. Many are interpreted by self-guiding leaflets and trail signs. A number of trails take off from near Chisos Basin.

During the summer, park naturalists lead hikes down the easy, 1.8-mile (2.8km) **Chisos Basin Trail**, though check the schedule as this could change year to year. At the overlook about halfway along the trail, the major features of the Chisos Basin stand out against the sky: towering Emory Peak, at 7,825ft (2,385 meters) the highest in the park; Ward Mountain; Carter Peak and The Window; Vernon Bailey Peak and Pulliam Ridge; Casa Grande and Toll Mountain. This trail provides a good introduction to the major features of the Big Bend park.

Halfway between The Basin and Panther Junction, the **Pine Canyon Trail** explores a wooded canyon for 4 miles (6km). At trail's end, a waterfall pours down the 200ft (60-meter) cliff after a heavy rain.

Just north of The Basin, the moderately difficult 5-mile (8km) Lost Mine Trail follows the north slope of Casa Grande and leads to a point high on the west side of Lost Mine Peak. It affords beautiful views of the surrounding mountains and canyons. A very difficult trek up the 7,500ft (2,300-meter) Casa Grande Peak takes off from the Juniper Canyon Overlook along the Lost Mine Trail.

The 5-mile (8km) **Chimneys Trail** lies southwest of The Basin and leads to a group of high rock outcroppings, or "chimneys," the southernmost of which contains ancient American Indian pictographs.

Two groups of trails into the Chisos lie south of The Basin: the High Chisos Complex trails and the Outer Mountain Loop trails. The High Chisos trails are some of the most beautiful, but they require serious hiking and climbing. The panorama from the South Rim Trail includes Santa Elena Canyon 20 miles (30km) to the west, Emory Peak to the north, and the mountains in Mexico to the south. Various trails branch off from this one and, for instance, lead up Emory Peak into Boot Canyon – the summer home of the Colima Warbler, found nowhere else in the United States.

While the High Chisos trails are strenuous, they are, at least, well marked. The Outer Mountain Loop trails, on the other hand, are not so well marked and hardly flat at all. Among these, Blue Creek Trail is known for its colorful balanced rocks and pinnacles. However, these two series of trails can be combined for a lengthier expedition into the Big Bend wilderness.

SPECTACULAR CANYONS

Another popular trailhead is the Rio Grande Village area, near the river in the eastern part of the park. The very easy **Rio Grande Village Nature Trail**,

Tip

Water can be a real problem on both long and short hikes. Dehydration comes on quickly in Big Bend's dry air, and springs and streams are not reliable for drinking. Make sure you bring at least a gallon of water per person per day and drink it frequently, along with salty, nutritious foods that help balance electrolytes in the body.

One of the 36 marked hiking trails in the park.

Fact

Big Bend's first cattleman, Don Milton Faver, had a herd of longhorns and burro-riding cowboys. Many of the cattle were unbranded and were stolen. His cattle drives were the subject of TV's *Rawhide* series.

just under a mile (1.2km) long, interprets several plant habitats, including the lush river floodplain and the arid desert. An overlook at trail's end gives breathtaking views of Mexico, the river, the Chisos Mountains, and Boquillas Canyon.

Boquillas, the longest and deepest canyon in the park, is also accessible along the 1.5-mile (2.5km) **Boquillas Canyon Trail**. For the more adventurous, a three-day trip covering 17 miles (27km) in the canyon and 8 miles (13km) on the Rio Grande can be a wonderful experience, with all the side canyons there are to explore on both banks, in Texas and Mexico.

The most spectacular of the Big Bend canyons, **Santa Elena**, can be seen on an easy 1.5-mile (2.5km) trail that crosses Terlingua Creek and wanders through the magnificent 17-mile (27km) canyon to the river.

If you decide to run the waters, bear in mind that the river is very tricky, especially in high or low water. Eleven miles (18km) of scenic river precede the canyon entrance, but watch for strong currents over hidden rocks. The most dangerous part of the canyon is the rockslide about a mile (1.6km) beyond the entrance. Running the slide is always difficult, and downright dangerous at high and low water levels. Portaging it is socially acceptable and no blemish whatsoever on anyone's manhood. After the slide, navigation is more tranquil and boaters can enjoy colorful canyon walls and also explore the jewel-like Fern Canyon.

Mariscal Canyon, the most isolated of the three major canyons, is accessible on a strenuous, unshaded 6.5-mile (10km) hike. The rim affords a wide view of the canyon 1,500ft (460 meters) below, to reward the persevering hiker.

Relaxing in the Hot Springs bathing pool, along the Rio Grande in the south part of the park.

BY CAR

Even from a car, Big Bend visitors can see the wild country. The River Road traverses the 51 miles (82km) between the Boquillas–Rio Grande Village road and Castolon. The road can be traveled by most high-clearance vehicles, but its side roads usually require four-wheel-drive. Old ranches and fishing camps occasionally appear along the road, and it passes the ruins of Mariscal Mine, an old mercury working at the foot of Mariscal Mountain. The ruins are fun to explore, but beware of open, unmarked mine shafts. Farther west lie the remains of the Johnson Ranch House, probably the largest adobe ruin in the park. The road ends at **Castolon** ❹, a 19th-century farming settlement and early 20th-century US Cavalry and Texas Ranger post.

Big Bend has amenities and adventures for everyone – from automobile tours to rugged mountain trails and river running, in moderate mountain temperatures or hot-as-Texas sun. But the visitor does well to remember that it's still wild country and must be enjoyed on its own terms.

Boquillas Canyon.

WILDLIFE IN TEXAS

You don't need to venture deep into the Texas countryside to discover the state's weird and wonderful wildlife. But, if you do, take care.

As you wander the civilized streets of Dallas or Houston, catching your reflection in a glass skyscraper, it's easy to forget that this is still the Wild West – "wild" in the sense that the animals that call Texas their home remain as unfazed by progress as they were in the days of the frontier pioneers.

The scurrying armadillo is a familiar sight in many parts of the state. Other creatures are more regionalized, preferring the marshy wetness of East Texas or the unrelenting dryness and heat of West Texas. Some Texas wildlife is continually on the move – winging, crawling, or grubbing its way into new corners of the state.

The comical antics of the prairie dog, the elegance of deer grazing in the Hill Country, or the smiling dolphins off the Gulf Coast should not lead visitors into a false sense of security. Like the prickly desert plants, native Texan beasts must be met on their own terms, if met at all. They can bite, they can sting. They can annoy, they can maim. The rule is: Don't mess with them. If you leave the animals to themselves, the chances are they'll keep well away from you. Be sensible. Follow all warning signs and don't tempt danger. But, for all the cougars, black bears, rattlesnakes, alligators, and coyotes, there are also stunning birds, majestic buffalo, thriving longhorns, languid sea turtles, and exotic fish you won't find anywhere else.

And with scores of natural wildlife refuges for safe viewing, the beautiful creatures of Texas can still charm and enthrall.

The prairie dog, a member of the squirrel family, lives in colonies of thousands. Its name is derived from its cry, or "bark."

In the marshy bayous of East Texas lurk some 200,000 alligators, the state's largest reptile. They feed on fish and other small animals, and seldom attack humans – but don't push it!

The caves of Central Texas are the breeding grounds for a variety of bat species. The adults here are all female, the males being left in South America.

A western diamondback rattlesnake ready to strike.

Snakes in the Grass

The statistics tell the truth: there is more chance of being killed by a lightning strike in Texas than from a snake bite. Nevertheless, the thought of a venomous rattler is enough to panic many Texas visitors.

The state is home to 115 species and subspecies of snake, but only 15 percent are a danger to humans. The rattlesnake (10 varieties in Texas) is the most feared. It can be found in most parts of Texas, but is prevalent in the Big Bend region. The coral snake is also a nasty little wriggler and may be encountered in areas from Central Texas south. The same territory is inhabited by the copperhead, equally dangerous if provoked, while the cottonmouth is semi-aquatic and lives mostly around rivers in Central and East Texas.

Cougars are found in the mountains of Big Bend Country. They can be aggressive towards humans and should not be approached. Smaller cats live elsewhere in the state: lynx-like bobcats in East Texas and ocelots in South Texas. Look out for wild dogs, too, particularly coyotes and wolves.

The prickly looking horned lizard, often mistakenly referred to as the "horny toad," can shoot a stream of blood from its eyes.

Despite being armed with tusks and musk, the near-sighted javelina, a cousin of the South American tapir, is not dangerous.

The Big Texan Steak Ranch, Amarillo, home of the "free" 72-oz steak.

WEST TEXAS

Dusty West Texas has ridden coal and oil booms and boasts a tough, independent character that has fostered ranchers, presidents, and early rock and roll.

West Texas, as a geographic region, takes in the whole western part of the state. It's a huge area, not easily defined except by generally being in the Chihuahuan Desert. People in the far western desert portions of Texas, from El Paso and Big Bend Country to Amarillo and the Panhandle Plains, call themselves West Texans, but so, interestingly enough, do the people of the southern parts of North Central Texas.

The latter do so not out of geographical ignorance, but out of a sense of history and place. After the Civil War, their ancestors from southern states, knowing no place else to go to begin a new life, headed west, where they encountered a foe more relentless than General Sherman: the slow-yielding, tightfisted land itself, ruled by distance, drought, and the most ferocious aboriginal army ever to ride horseback: the Comanche. Thus, mile after uncertain mile was conquered by people who were not searching for wealth, but for a place to survive. They did survive, and left their descendants with the knowledge that anything is possible if one is self-reliant and looks toward the horizon.

Travel in this relatively featureless landscape can become an agonizingly slow unfolding of geography, if you expect to be constantly entertained by the fluff and fanfare of tourist extravaganzas. However, if you adopt the easy-going friendliness of its people, and attune yourself to the voices of its heroic past, West Texas will be an unforgettable experience.

FORT WORTH TO EL PASO

West of Fort Worth, where I-20 drops down from rough-cut juniper- and oak-covered hills on to the fitful beginning of the Panhandle Plains, are the ruins of **Thurber ❶**, a coal-mining town better suited to northeastern Pennsylvania or the Ruhr Valley than post-frontier Texas. Where 10,000 people

Main attractions

Old Jail Art Center, Albany
Permian Basin Petroleum Museum, Midland
Palo Duro Canyon State Park, Canyon
National Ranching Heritage Center, Lubbock
Buddy Holly Center, Lubbock

Map on page 274

A Texas icon: the oil pump.

from 17 countries lived between 1880 and 1922 – making it the biggest coal mining town in Texas at the time – there now exist only 8 residents, a tall brick smoke stack, a restaurant-museum, the remains of a great brick factory, and a service station. The rest of the town has been sold brick by brick, down to the last utility pole.

As one looks across the now empty valley to the conical piles of black coal spoil and "red dog" cinders, it is difficult to imagine the wealthy, cosmopolitan city that stood here on the near side of frontier times. Thurber is where the Metropolitan Opera of New York performed, where Miss Wallis "Wildcat" Warfield (later the Duchess of Windsor) grew up in one of the mansions along Silk Stocking Road on New York Hill, and where a World War I clothing drive netted no fewer than four dozen mink coats.

In 1895, Thurber was one of the first completely electrified cities in the world. After a long, bitter strike presided over by Texas Rangers, Thurber became the first and perhaps the only 100-percent unionized town in America. The 100 million tonnes of coal mined here powered the belching locomotives of Jay Gould's Texas and Pacific Railroad as they trundled across the prairie. In 1881, the last 595 miles (958km) of the T&P mainline were completed between Fort Worth and Sierra Blanca in a phenomenal 11 months, by a crew of 300 hard-drinking Irishmen.

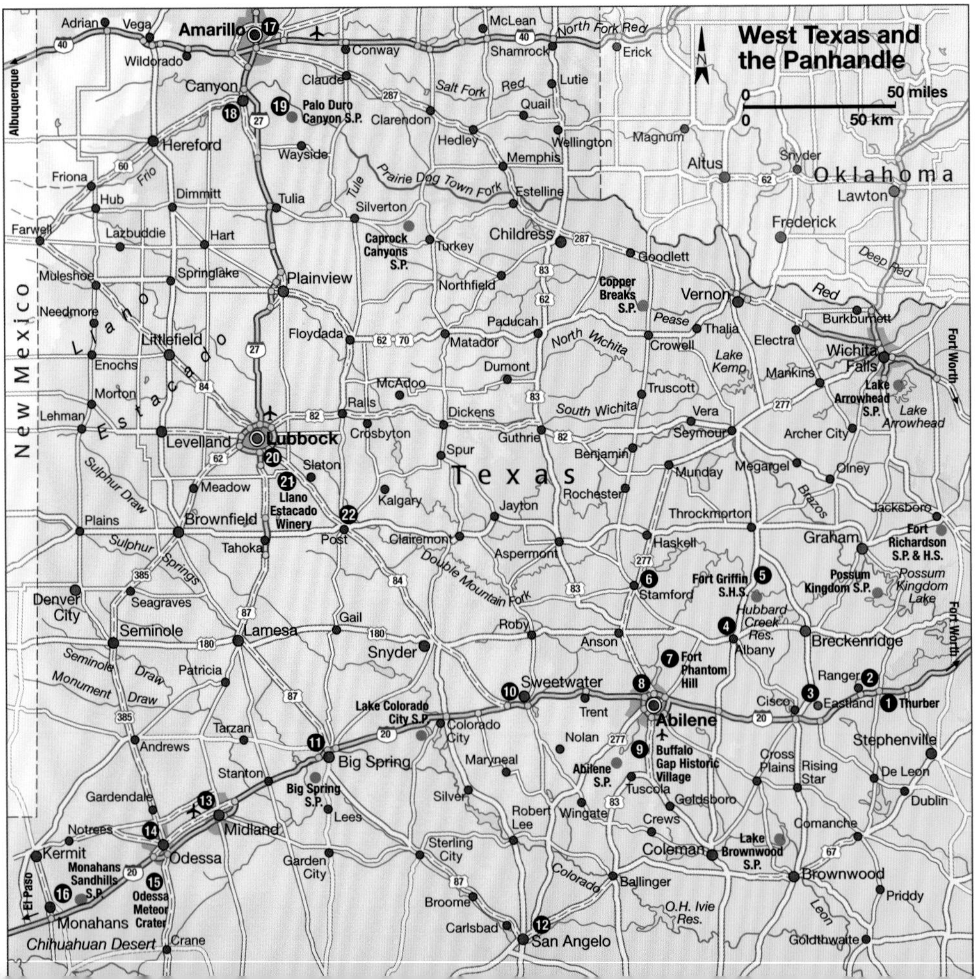

The railroad's role in the rapid demise of the frontier is dramatically demonstrated by the almost simultaneous founding of Abilene, Big Spring, Midland, Odessa, and the other major cities of the region. They were shipping points for cattle, eliminating the long trail drives to Dodge City and Abilene in Kansas. The change from coal- to oil-powered locomotives led to the dismantling of Thurber and helped set the stage for the meteoric emergence of **Ranger ❷**, 13 miles (21km) to the west and the most rip-snorting boomtown of all.

OIL BOOM DOOM

Derricks and pump jacks are still in evidence, but the quiet streets of modern Ranger fail to suggest the frenzy of the weeks in 1917, after oil rig McClesky No. 1 blew in with 1,700 barrels a day. At World War I prices, a good well yielded $250,000 a week. The 10 trains that rolled into Ranger every day were filled with speculators, jacklegs, riffraff and ruffians, ambitious men and loose women. The town exploded from a village of 1,000 to a seething city of 40,000 in a matter of months. Streets turned into a sea of mud, traversed on sleds or the backs of men in hip boots. Guests in those days paid luxury hotel rates to sleep in armchairs. The evangelist Billy Sunday went in search of souls to saloons called the Grizzly Bear, the Blue Moose, and Oklahoma, where as many as five people a day met their oil boom doom. Small wonder there was violence when, for example, one lease changed hands three times on a Friday, increasing in value from $150 to $15,000. Everyone in the trade but the middle man must have felt taken. Talk to some of the old-timers for more details of the years when Ranger's oil produced more wealth than the California gold rush at its peak.

REST IN PEACE

A few miles west lies **Eastland ❸**, another boomtown gone bust. Today its principal claims to fame are the Post Office mural, a montage of 11,217 stamps, which depicts the history of the communications service; the restored 1920s Majestic Theatre; Outdoor Art's reproductions of 42 masterpieces, such

Shackelford Country Courthouse, Albany.

Remote farmhouse.

Fact

Horned toads like Old Rip, an Eastland celebrity, are not actually amphibians but lizards. Although the little critters are unable to cause warts, they do shoot a thin stream of blood out of the corners of their eyes, to a distance of up to 4ft (1.2 meters).

as Andy Warhol's Campbell's soup can, on a round building; and a horned toad named Old Rip (Rest in Peace), which was sealed into the cornerstone of the old courthouse in 1897 and found to be alive when the new courthouse was built some 28 years later. The creature died a year later, after achieving national fame. His stuffed body was then placed in a glass case in the new building. In his miniature coffin, he resembles a rather flat and very prickly pin-cushion, about the size of a child's hand.

Today, one approaches **Albany** ❹, northwest of Cisco, over the same rolling red plains the cowboys covered on the trail to Dodge City in the 1870s. Due to overgrazing, however, the lush prairie grasses they found here are gone. There is only the eroded soil and lacy-leaved mesquite trees. Although mesquite steals precious moisture from the soil, it puts back nitrogen, because it is a leguminous plant. Its protein-rich beans were ground into a flour by the nomadic Plains Indians and are still eaten today by cattle in times of drought. More importantly, its wood is considered by many Texans to be without parallel for cooking barbecue.

ONLY IN ALBANY

At first sight, Albany is as unimposing as the mesquite "forests" that surround it, but this prairie town of about 2,000 possesses an exceptional collection of 20th-century art, displayed in the **Old Jail Art Center** (201 S. Second Street; tel: 325-762-2269; www.theojac.org; Tue–Sat 10am–5pm; free), a place where drunken cowboys and assorted desperados were once detained. The limestone building itself (*c.*1878) is a good example of frontier architecture, with its decoratively routed and scored casements and cistern out front. Alongside pre-Columbian displays, among the many artists represented in the large permanent collection are Matisse, Rouault, Picasso, Modigliani, Miró, Henry Moore, and Giacometti. In the Center's Marshall R Young Sculpture Courtyard you'll find more than 20 important works by famous North American and European sculptors. The center aims to be the primary cultural resource for the region.

The restored St. Barbara's Catholic Church, Thurber.

Albany's **Fort Griffin Fandangle** (tel: 325-762-3838; www.fortgriffinfandangle.org) is the oldest outdoor musical in Texas. The historical pageant is staged during the last two weeks in June. The roles of American Indians, cowboys, buffalo hunters, soldiers, bandits, and settlers are sung and acted, as they have been since 1938, by the descendants of those who originally occupied the Texas frontier.

Stop at the **Albany Visitor Center** (2 Railroad Street; tel: 325-762-2525; www.albanytexas.com; Tue–Fri 10am–4pm), in the depot at the corner of Railroad and Main, to pick up a walking tour map of Albany's historic buildings. One to look out for is the **Ledbetter Picket House** (24 S. Main Street; hours vary; free), a restored "dog run cabin" 1880s frontier ranch house with many authentic furnishings that was built near Fort Griffin and moved to this location in the 1950s. A similar ranch house served as the commandant's headquarters in the early days of what is now **Fort Griffin State Historic Site** ❺ (1701 N US 283; tel: 325-762-3592; www.thc.texas.gov/historic-sites/fort-griffin-state-historic-site; daily 8am–4.30pm), 15 miles (24km) north of Albany. Established in 1867, Fort Griffin belonged to the outer line of frontier defense. The first line, which swung in a wide arc southwest from Fort Worth to San Antonio, was established in the late 1840s on the edge of Comanche territory. Its line of forts was a buffer between the Plains Indians and white colonies. The renovated fort has one of the state herds of longhorns, managed by Texas Parks and Wildlife and now numbering 250 head in several parks, and also a campground.

THE ROUGHEST TOWN IN TEXAS

From its hilltop, the stone ruins and partially reconstructed wooden remains of the fort look down on what was possibly the roughest, most brawling and iniquitous town in the history of Texas: "The Flats." Never has a lustier mixture of manhood been stirred in one pot. Imagine them bellied up to the same bar: bitter, defeated southern veterans of the Civil War alongside the

Tip

Take advantage of the fact that Palo Duro is one of America's more accessible canyons. A spectacular 10-mile (16km) drive by car can be made year-round across the canyon floor.

Replica frontier cabin, Fort Griffin.

A scissor-tailed flycatcher, also known as the Texas Bird of Paradise.

blue-jacketed conquerors and the Buffalo Soldiers, as the American Indians called freed slaves who were part of the US Army. As if they were not enough, add buffalo hunters flush from selling hides, plus the professional gamblers and bandits who preyed on them, and the bounty hunters who, in turn, preyed on them. Ironically, one of the few original buildings remaining in "The Flats" was far more respectable: it served as the church, school, and Masonic lodge.

Cowboys still exist here. You can find them at the Texas Cowboy Reunion (www.texascowboyreunion.com) in **Stamford** ❻ on the Fourth of July. This is no slick, professional production in an air-conditioned coliseum. This is where "good ol' boys" risk their necks, not for love of money – or even the love of their girls, who perch on the top rail of the arena fence – but for love of their favorite activity: roping horses.

Farther west, 14 miles (22km) north of Abilene, is **Fort Phantom Hill** ❼. The very name has the chill of desolation to it. Loneliness still lingers about the tall, solitary chimneys, the empty commissary, guardhouse, and powder magazine, especially in the dim red light of dusk. From its founding in 1850, to protect the region from hostile Comanche Indians, there were frequent desertions from this post, where boredom alternated with the raids. After its abandonment in 1854, the hated fort was burned by one of the withdrawing soldiers. Later, it became an overnight stop for mail coaches on the Butterfield Trail.

In making your way through the scrub oak and mesquite to Abilene, you will probably see the silver-and-salmon flash of the scissor-tailed flycatcher. In excited flight, the graceful tails, which are twice as long as the bodies, almost seem to flitter like a carnival bird on a stick.

GOD'S GLORIOUS CITY

Abilene ❽ (pop. 117,000) likes to promote itself as "The Defining City of West Texas" but might more aptly be described as the "Glorious City of God," being the home of three religiously affiliated institutions of learning – McMurry University, Abilene Christian University,

Buffalo Gap Historic Village.

and the Southern Baptists' Hardin-Simmons. Round-the-clock prayer meetings for rain didn't bring an end to the drought of the early 1950s, but they must have made an impression: the region has been blessed with oil discoveries ever since. A rig was set up on the **Taylor County Expo Center** (1700 Highway 36 at 11th Street; tel: 325-677-4376; www.taylorcountyexpocenter.com) grounds here for demonstration and, of course, it struck oil. Rodeos are held here each spring and fall along with horse shows, circuses, and many other events.

The extensive **Grace Museum** (102 Cypress Street; tel: 325-673-4587; www.thegracemuseum.org; Tue–Sat 10am–5pm, Thu until 8pm) has history exhibits relating to Camp Barkeley, the World War II army base and prison camp, whose ruins can still be seen on US 277, south of town. There are other sections in this attractive complex that are devoted to children and fine arts. The sizeable art collection focuses on American art with a Texas connection with works by Ansel Adams, Andy Warhol, and Charles Taylor Bowling, amongst others.

BUFFALO GAP

An authentic taste of the Old West is to be had 10 miles (16km) southwest of town, where the low, dark juniper-covered hills of the Calahan Divide are broken abruptly at **Buffalo Gap Historic Village** ❾ (133 N. William Street: tel: 325-572-3365; Tue–Sat 10am–5pm). A mix of authentic frontier buildings and tourist attractions is found at this site operated by the Texas Frontier Heritage Cultural Center. An old courthouse, jail and log cabins are among the old buildings. A doctor's office, a barber shop and a print shop are modern reconstructions.

Twice a year, in the 19th century, buffalo passed through the mountain gap here, indelibly etching a permanent trail. When this brown, woolly group flowed between these ancient hills, Tonkawa and Comanche Indians still camped in the cool shade of the native pecan groves and made arrowheads, traces of which can still be found. Charles Goodnight, one of the most celebrated of early longhorn ranchers out west, described the main buffalo herd as being 125 miles (200km) long and 25 miles (40km) wide. The trail they blazed was later the one he used to drive his own cattle to the Kansas railheads.

When the area was settled by whites in the 1870s, this natural funnel through the hills continued to be a focus for the region. Today, over 20 of the original buildings have been restored, including the limestone courthouse and jail. In the Buffalo Gap Cemetery, gravestones of Civil War veterans and others tell the history of the settling of West Texas in a few poignant words.

Frontier Texas (625 N. First Street; tel: 325-437-2800; www.frontiertexas.com; Mon–Sat 9am–6pm, Sun 1–5pm) is a hands-on, multimedia immersion in early Texas, with buffalo stampedes and saloon shootouts, alongside exhibits on the Comanche peoples, the frontier economy, and weapons that shaped the frontier lands.

Fact

The Texas High School Rodeo Finals take place in Abilene in June. Tel: 936-590-4447.

A cowboy snake-handler at the World's Largest Rattlesnake Roundup in Sweetwater.

Fact

The Texan town of Abilene, founded by cattlemen in 1881, was named for Abilene in Kansas, which was the final stop on the Chisholm Trail.

GYPSUM DEPOSITS

The town of **Sweetwater** ⑩, 40 miles (64km) west of Abilene on I-20, was well named in an area where so many of the streams are tainted with gypsum. Gypsum, otherwise known as Epsom salts, is fine for soaking tired feet but, as a drink, keeps one on the run. The rich, local gypsum deposits have been put to constructive use in the manufacture of wallboard by two large factories.

One of the few towns in West Texas to predate the coming of the railroad, Sweetwater began in 1877 as a general store for buffalo hunters, dug into the banks of Sweetwater Creek. The world's largest rattlesnake roundup is held here during the second weekend in March, at the Nolan County Coliseum (tel: 325-235-3484; www.nolancc.com). It is a bring-em-back-alive affair in which the snakes are milked for their venom and prizes are given for the longest, shortest and heaviest (by the pound). A record 14,000 lbs (6,350kg) were delivered in 1985. If you have ever had a hankering to eat a fried 6ft (2-meter) long western diamondback, or buy a transparent toilet seat with a rattler coiled in it, here is such an opportunity.

A few moments on the weed-broken tarmac of the Old Sweetwater Army Airfield will resurrect memories of the 1940s, when the Women's Airforce Service Pilots (WASPS) received their flight training here. Farther west, past Colorado City (locally pronounced Cah-la Ray-da Ciddy), is the town of **Big Spring** ⑪, a site important in another war. American Indian occupation of this natural oasis goes back to Folsom Indian times, 10,000 years ago, and it served as a major rest stop for the tribes on the Comanche War Trail, halfway between their home on the High Plains to the north and the white settlements in Texas and Mexico to the south. They shared its precious water with antelope, buffalo, and wild mustangs. This ancient oasis is still very appealing in late afternoon among the trees of Comanche Trail Park or at **Big Spring State Park** (tel: 432-263-4931; www.tpwd.state.tx.us/state-parks/big-spring; daily 8am–sunset), which provides a

Downtown Midland.

view of the entire area from a 200ft (60-meter) mesa within the city limits.

Southbound travelers along US 87 from Big Spring will pass through **San Angelo** ⓬, a modern city of lakes and rivers on the edge of the Texas Hill Country. Like San Antonio, it has a River Walk, winding its way past landscaped gardens, parks, and beautiful homes by the Concho River. **Fort Concho National Historic Landmark** (630 S. Oakes Street; tel: 325-657-4444; www.fortconcho.com; Mon–Sat 9am–5pm, Sun 1–5pm), the best preserved of the Indian War stockades, is filled with exhibits from frontier times. Events are held throughout the year; check the website for details.

THE PERMIAN BASIN OIL FIELD

At the midway point of the 600-mile (965km) drive from Fort Worth to El Paso, a mirage of civilization rises out of the endless illusion of water over the highway ahead. The small city of **Midland** ⓭ (pop. 134,000), the hometown of President George W. Bush, is dominated by glass-and-steel towers, containing the offices of companies dedicated to coaxing crude oil from the bottom of a 250-million-year-old inland sea, now buried tens of thousands of feet below the desert sand. The city is a vibrant, modern haven with an active cultural scene. It has weathered the roughest historic and economic storms, and since 2017, has been one of Texas's fastest growing metropolitans.

The city was in the thick of battles between Comanches and settlers when the oil boom arrived and prosperity flooded the region. Consequently, when Texas oil went bad, the city faced rough times. The **Permian Basin Oil Field** is the world's top oil producer, and the price of a barrel of Texas Permian Intermediate Weight Crude is the standard against which the prices of all other US oils are determined. The nodding, hobbyhorse-like pump jacks seem to repeat as they suck at the earth: "Fiftydollars, fiftydollars, fiftydollars..." Not only have their rhythms enriched many a slouch-hatted rancher, but the University of Texas as well. In the 19th century, having virtually no funds to offer the fledgling institution, the state legislature apologetically proffered 2.2 million acres (890,000 hectares) of sand and desert scrubland. That these holdings coincide with the outlines of the Permian Basin is a happy coincidence that has bequeathed the University around $2.5 billion.

The science and technology of oil are brilliantly explained in the **Permian Basin Petroleum Museum** (1500 W. I-20, exit 136; tel: 432-683-4403; www.petroleummuseum.org; Mon–Sat 10am–5pm, Sun 2–5pm), where visitors can stroll along the bottom of the ancient sea where deposits eventually trapped oil for later wealth. Another educational site is the **Midland Army Air Field Museum** (9612 Wright Drive; tel: 432-254-6182; http://highskywing.org; Sat 10am–3pm), a museum dedicated to the history of the Midland Army Air Field, as well as offering aircraft ride opportunities.

Fact

Alibates Flint Quarries National Monument, north of Amarillo, near Lake Meredith, protects an ancient flint quarry on the red bluffs above the Canadian River that was used by local tribes as a source of flint for arrow-making for thousands of years. Managed by the National Park Service, it is one of three national monuments in Texas.

A crew working at an oil rig in the Permian Basin.

⊙ Fact

It was the sheer abundance of rattlesnakes, which were troubling local ranchers and farmers, that led the town of Sweetwater to organize the first rattlesnake roundup.

Midland's other claim to fame is that it is the "Tumbleweed Capital of the World." In the scorching 100+°F (38+°C) days of summer, when all else turns brown, legions of prickly green tumbleweeds (in actual fact Russian thistle, an introduced species) crowd the roadside and abandoned fields. These tumbleweeds resist the heat as they grow up to 8ft (2.5 meters) tall, awaiting the moment in the fall when they break free of the earth to rush pell-mell down the road. Since Bob Nolan and the Sons of the Pioneers immortalized this common nuisance in the song Tumbling Tumbleweed, the plant has become a symbol for the spirit of movement that led to the development of the West Texas frontier, especially in the person of the drifting cowboy.

ODESSA

Traveling on to **Odessa** ⓮, expect to encounter the authentic West Texas "redneck." Midland is the business center of the Permian Basin, and Odessa is the home of the oil field worker or "roughneck." "Oil field trash and proud of it," say bumper stickers often seen on huge pickup trucks, with loaded rifles hung in racks across the back window. No need to search farther for the modern counterpart of the frontier cowboy.

Odessa does hold a few surprises, though – none of which have anything to do with oil. For example, on the Odessa College campus you will find the **Globe of the Great Southwest Theatre** (2308 Shakespeare Road; tel: 432-335-6818; https://odessa.edu/community/GlobeTheateratOdessaCollege; tours available by reservation), a replica of Shakespeare's Globe Theatre in London, plus a replica of Anne Hathaway's Cottage, complete with a Shakespeare library. A professional repertory company produces the classics and an annual Shakespeare Festival. There is also a Permian Playhouse Theater and a symphony orchestra.

At 622 N. Lee Street is the **Presidential Archives and Leadership Library** (tel: 432-552-2850; https://shepperdinstitute.com/presidential-archives; Mon–Fri 8am–5pm; free), an interesting but

Monahans Sandhills State Park.

blaringly patriotic museum dedicated to the US Presidency, including campaigning memorabilia and First Lady dolls. The restored homes of Presidents George H.W. and George W. Bush, who lived in Odessa for a while, are on the grounds here.

To visit a natural wonder, take a drive out to the **Odessa Meteor Crater** ⓯, just west of town, off Farm Road 1936. The nation's second largest meteor crater, it has a diameter of 500ft (152 meters). The crater was formed when some 2 million lbs (907,200kg) of extraterrestrial iron crashed into the earth during the last Ice Age.

West of Odessa, at the western edge of "West Texas," the great Chihuahuan Desert begins and continues across Big Bend Country into Mexico. The best vantage point for an eyeful of sandy "desertscape" is **Monahans Sandhills State Park** ⓰ (2500 E. I-20, exit Park Road 41; tel: 432-943-2092; www.tpwd.state.tx.us/state-parks/monahans-sandhills; daily 8am–10pm), 24 miles (38km) west of Odessa, where naked dunes tower up to 70ft (21 meters) high and stretch north and south for 200 miles (320km). Camping is available in the park but space is limited so reserve ahead of time.

America's most bizarre forest grows along the margin of this desolation. The Havard oak forms a dense, at times almost impenetrable growth that is easily overlooked, because the mature trees stand only about 3ft (1 meter) tall. West Texans call the trees "shin oak" and the forest the "shinnery." These plants are marvelously well adapted to drought, with roots that can reach a depth of 90ft (27 meters).

AMARILLO

In the northern Panhandle sections of West Texas, the landscape stretches in an unbroken line, with perhaps an occasional pump jack or farmhouse on the horizon. The sunsets can be breathtaking: with nothing to obscure the view, the sky blazes with oranges, yellows, and reds, and fades to soft pinks and purples. Driving at night, you can see the lights of many small towns in all directions. Because of the relatively high altitude, the air is very clear and

Tip

For a taste of old fort life, visit Fort Concho on the first weekend in December, when an 1880s-style celebration is held, reenacting a Christmas holiday from that era.

Presidential Archives and Leadership Library, Odessa.

A Route 66 sign on Fifth Street, Amarillo.

dry. And, after the sun sets in the summer, the evening brings cool breezes.

Amarillo ⓱ (pop. 195,250), which means "yellow" in Spanish, is a major center for cattle distribution. This dusty town claims to have one of the largest private cattle auctions in Texas, and it certainly smells that way as you near it. Enormous feedlots of cattle are destined for market – the **Amarillo Livestock Auction** (100 S. Manhattan Street; tel: 806-373-7464; www.amarillolivestockauction.com; tours daily, auctions Monday; free) sells over 100,000 head a year. At the eye-catching **American Quarter Horse Hall of Fame and Museum** (2601 E. I-40; tel: 806-376-5181; www.aqha.com/museum; Mon–Sat 9am–5pm), perched roadside along one of the major cross-country routes in the US, visitors learn why this particular breed was the cowboys' favorite mount. Amarillo is headquarters for the Working Ranch Cowboys Association, which organizes the World Championship Ranch Rodeo every November.

Visitors to the **Don Harrington Discovery Center** (1200 Streit Drive; tel: 806-355-9547; www.discoverycenteramarillo.org; Tue–Sat 9.30am–4.30pm, Sun noon–4.30pm) can enjoy the experience of an interactive science and technology attraction, as well as daily laser and planetarium shows. Children under 6 will enjoy the Kinderstudio, an imaginative space for interactive play, with hands-on science activities.

ROUTE 66 AND STEAKS

The city's one-way system can be a bit confusing to travelers. But if you follow signs for the US Route 66–Sixth Street Historic District, west of Amarillo's central business district, you'll encounter a section of historic Route 66 that is still very much alive, with antiques stores, gift shops, and great little eateries in restored historic buildings. On Sixth, look for the Natatorium (604 S. Georgia), built as an indoor swimming pool in 1922 and later converted into a ballroom, Taylor's Sixth Street or "Texaco" Gas Station, built in 1937; and the Golden Light Café, a landmark that has been serving homestyle food since 1946 and now offers live music in its cantina.

The **Big Texan Steak Ranch** (7701 E. I-40; tel: 806-372-6000; www.bigtexan.com; daily 7am–10.30pm), now located near the Quarter Horse Hall of Fame just north of I-40, used to be located on Route 66 and, with its famous beckoning cowboy, was one of its most distinctive landmarks. After the interstate was built in the 1970s and Route 66 fell by the wayside for most travelers, the owners decided to relocate the kitschy restaurant and adjoining hotel, famous for its Texas-shaped pool, along the freeway. This roadside attraction is a lot of fun and worth a stop to enjoy a good steak (they even serve bison and rattlesnake). Its famous 72oz (2kg) steak is free if you can down the whole thing, along with all the trimmings, in an hour. Fans of barbecue will be delighted to know that some of the best mesquite-smoked ribs and brisket in the state can be found at Tyler's

Big Texan Steak Ranch chef.

Barbecue (3301 Olsen Boulevard; tel: 806-331-2271; www.tylersbarbeque.com, Tue–Fri 11am–7.30pm, Sat 11am–6pm or until they sell out), a regular entry on the *Texas Monthly* 50 Best BBQ Joints list. Expect a line at both these restaurants; they are hugely popular.

TEXAS'S O'KEEFFE COUNTRY

South of Amarillo is the town of **Canyon** ⓲, home of West Texas A&M University and the sprawling Panhandle-Plains Historical Museum (2503 4th Avenue; tel: 806-651-2244; www.panhandleplains.org; Mon–Sat 9am–5pm, June–Aug, open until 6pm and Sun 1–6pm). This state history museum contains an art collection, geological exhibits, and a reconstructed pioneer town of a century ago. One wing is devoted to the oil-boom years of the Texas Panhandle during the 1920s and '30s, displaying equipment from that period. One exhibit, People of the Plains, relates 14,000 years of man's occupation of the Southern Great Plains.

Canyon is also notable for the tenure from 1912–18 of Georgia O'Keeffe. As a young woman, the celebrated artist came to teach art in Amarillo, then at West Texas State Normal College in Canyon. While there, she produced a striking series of watercolors of the plains, sunrises, and night skies. She said, "Texas is my spiritual home."

SEARCH FOR GOLD

Here at Canyon, 16 miles (29km) south of Amarillo, the flat plains come to a dead halt. What lies ahead is a vast chasm. At 120 miles (193km) long, up to 20 miles (32km) wide, and 800ft (245-meter) deep, Palo Duro Canyon gives the Grand Canyon a run for its money. Spanish conquistador Francisco Vasquez de Coronado, head of the first Spanish expedition to make an entrada into El Norte from New Spain, is believed to have come upon Palo Duro in 1541 while searching for Quivira, the richest of the mythical cities of gold – a tall tale told by survivors of an earlier Spanish expedition who shipwrecked in the Gulf of Mexico and wandered west, eventually returning to Mexico City.

In the 19th century, the canyon was a Comanche stronghold. The Comanche

Palo Duro Canyon State Park.

suffered their final defeat in 1874, when they were surprised by a cavalry force commanded by General Ranald Mackenzie, who drove 1,500 horses and mules out of Palo Duro and slaughtered them. Without their horses, the Comanche were helpless. They were removed from their homelands to reservations in Oklahoma. Geologists say over 240 million years of erosion by creeks and streams, abetted by incessant wind, formed this majestic canyon. Palo duro means "hard wood" in Spanish, and refers to the juniper trees found in the area.

Enchanting **Palo Duro Canyon State Park** ⓳ (11450 Park Road 5; tel: 806-488-2227; http://tpwd.texas.gov/state-parks/palo-duro-canyon; daily 7am–10pm). The state park covers over 28,000 acres (11,300 hectares) and offers hiking and horse trails, scenic overlooks, and camping options that range from primitive to developed; you can also book one of several extremely rustic Civilian Conservation Corps (CCC) cabins right on the rim or nearby. In summertime, there are nightly (except Mondays) performances of the spectacular, rousing musical drama Texas (reservations tel: 806-655-2181 or visit https://tickets.texas-show.com). With a canyon wall as a backdrop, a cast of 60 brings to life Pulitzer Prize winner Paul Green's play about the settling of West Texas.

THE GREAT RANCHES

The legendary figure of Charles Goodnight, the first rancher to move into the Panhandle in 1876, is closely associated with Palo Duro Canyon and with the beginning of the cattle drives. Goodnight designed the first chuckwagon. Backed by the British financier John Adair (their cattle were branded with "JA" and the ranch was christened "The JA"), Goodnight built up his herd to as many as 100,000 head in 1889. For a while in the 1880s, theirs was the largest ranch in Texas – more than 1,325,000 acres (536,000 hectares). Then in 1885, the XIT Ranch was established in the far northern Panhandle on over 3 million acres (1.25 million hectares), which the State of Texas

The Buddy Holly Center.

had traded for the new State Capitol building in Austin. In order to stock the XIT Ranch, British and Midwestern investors were again brought in. An XIT reunion is held at Dalhart, 80 miles (130km) north of Amarillo every year, in the first full week of August. The amateur rodeo and enormous barbecue attract thousands.

Horse and jeep tours at the working cattle ranch of Palo Duro Creek Ranch (tel: 806-488-2100; www.paloduroranch.com; Mon–Sun; reservations required) always draw plenty of dudes. Keep an eye out for their upcoming helicopter tours.

LUBBOCK

Even though singer Mac Davis claims "Happiness is Lubbock, Texas, in my rear-view mirror," most residents of **Lubbock** 20 (pop. 253,000) would live nowhere else. Even Mac concedes at the end of his song that now "Happiness is Lubbock, Texas, getting nearer and dearer." A center for cotton growing that also ships grain and livestock, Lubbock is on the South Plains, at one of the southernmost tips of the Llano Estacado, or "Staked Plains." The Staked Plains, from the name early Spanish explorers gave the immense plains that sweep for 1,600 miles (2,560km) through America's center, all the way up to Canada, produce a substantial proportion of the country's grain, meat, and fiber. A plaque marking the Llano Estacado's eastern boundary sits on US 84, southeast of town.

Texas Tech University, at 4th Street and Indiana Avenue, is one of Lubbock's main attractions. Its full sports agenda entices enthusiastic crowds. The university's teams are known as the Red Raiders and are members of the Big 12 Conference.

The university has established the Museum of Texas Tech University (3301 4th Street; tel: 806-742-2490; www.depts.ttu.edu/museumttu; Tue–Sat 10am–5pm, Sun 1–5pm; free) and the **National Ranching Heritage Center** (3121 4th Street; tel: 806-742-0498; www.depts.ttu.edu/nrhc; Tue–Sat 10am–5pm, Sun 1–5pm; free),

The famous Cadillac Ranch.

CADILLAC RANCH

Millionaire rancher Stanley Marsh 3 (never III) once said that he envisioned art as "a series of unanticipated rewards." If so, then his Cadillac Ranch, alongside I-40, west of Amarillo, is art of the highest order. Who, after all, could anticipate a row of 10 long-finned luxury cars (dating from 1949–63) buried nose down in a field in the plains at, it is said, the exact same angle as the Great Pyramid of Cheops? A San Francisco art collective called The Ant Farm, which specialized in art as public spectacle, built the 1974 creation at Marsh's behest.

Marsh, the proverbial eccentric Texas tycoon, made his money in television stations and decided to spend it having some fun. The much-photographed and graffiti-adorned Cadillac Ranch is his love letter to the promise of the open road. Be sure to stop and bring with you a can of spray paint to add your own graffiti to what is already there. Due to westward sprawl from burgeoning Amarillo, Cadillac Ranch has already had to be relocated once, and will probably have to be relocated again soon. But be sure to stop: this is a modern American roadside attraction – a counterpoint to the Big Texan Steak Ranch, the old Route 66 roadside attraction on the northside of I-40, east of Amarillo. Cadillac Ranch is on the south side of I-40, between exits 60 and 62 (daily during daylight hours; free).

a 19-acre (8-hectare) area through which winds a trail past more than 50 buildings, including a schoolhouse, a blacksmith's shop, homes, barns, and windmills, representing ranching's early days. The museum offers a mixed bag of paintings of the American West, along with European art, sculpture, ceramics, and lithographs. Changing exhibitions narrate the story of the region from prehistoric times through the Spanish explorations and the settling of the region by ranchers and farmers.

The museum also contains the **Moody Planetarium** and operates an archeological site beside Lubbock Lake Landmark (2401 Landmark Drive; tel: 806-742-1116; www.depts.ttu.edu/museumttu/lll; Tue–Sat 9am–5pm, Sun 1–5pm) northwest of the city, near US 84 and Loop 289. This site has yielded artifacts and tools from all known cultural groups who once lived in the Southwest, from the mammoth hunters 10,000 years ago to the Comanches of the 19th century. No other New World site houses such a complete chronological record.

A museum dedicated to Lubbock's most celebrated musical son is housed in the Historic Depot District. The **Buddy Holly Center** (1801 Crickets Avenue; tel: 806-775-3560; www.buddyhollycenter.org; Tue–Sat 10am–5pm, Sun 1–5pm) honors the rock 'n' roll pioneer.

An offbeat monument to another Lubbock musical icon lies on East Broadway across from the South Plains Fair grounds. A larger-than-life bronze of the late C.B. Stubblefield stands on the site of his former Stubb's BBQ restaurant and club. "Stubbs" was a mentor and friend of many of the 1970s generation of Lubbock musicians, including Terry Allen, Joe Ely, and Butch Hancock.

Off University Avenue, 3 miles (5km) south of town, is **Science Spectrum & Omni Theater** (2579 S. Loop 289, No. 250; tel: 806-745-2525; www.sciencespectrum.org; Mon–Fri 10am–5pm, Sat 10am–6pm, Sun 1–5pm), a hands-on science, nature, and technology museum. It has an OMNI theater and a movie theater with a 58ft (18-meter) domed screen. At the Lubbock

BUDDY HOLLY

Charles Hardin Holley, better known as Buddy Holly, was born in Lubbock, Texas, on September 7, 1936. As a child he played piano, then accompanied himself with guitar on favorite country songs, particularly those of Hank Williams who, along with Bill Monroe was to influence his early singing style. But seeing Elvis Presley perform changed Buddy's style forever, prompting him to distill a blend of pop, blues, and country.

In 1955, a Nashville recording agent saw Buddy and his group and, the following year, invited him to Nashville, where he recorded "Blue Days, Black Nights," his first single release. With a country melody, but a blues inflection, the track was difficult for some reviewers to categorize. In February 1957, Buddy, along with Jerry Allison, Niki Sullivan, and Larry Welborn as The Crickets, recorded *"That'll Be the Day"* at Norman Petty's studios in Clovis, New Mexico. *"That'll Be the Day"* topped the charts in September 1957, followed by "Peggy Sue." Its innovative "Holly sound" included steady guitar strumming, rapid, accented drumming, and his famous vocal "hiccup." With *"Words of Love"* (also recorded in 1957) Buddy introduced another innovation – overdubbing.

In 1958, the same year the Crickets released *"Not Fade Away"* and *"Oh Boy!,"* they released *"Rave On," Think It Over,"* and *"It's So Easy."* They toured widely, appearing for the second time on the top-rated Ed Sullivan Show. On February 3, 1959, a few weeks into a tour with singers Ritchie Valens and J.P. Richardson (the "Big Bopper"), Holly's plane crashed in a snowstorm near Clear Lake, Iowa, killing all on board.

It's hard to overstate Holly's and the Crickets' importance to the development of rock 'n' roll. Holly was among the first – if not the first – to use his own band in the studio. They were among the first to generate their own material for release as singles; among the first to work outside the established studio system and to use overdubbing and other soon-to-be-common effects in their recordings. Holly cast a long shadow over The Beatles, The Rolling Stones, Bob Dylan, Bruce Springsteen, and generations of other rock performers.

Holly's statue stands in the Buddy and Maria Elena Holly Plaza across the street from the museum in his honor. Visitors from all over the world pay homage at his grave in the City of Lubbock Cemetery on East 31st Street.

Children's Museum on the ground floor, children under 5 can experience science and craft projects (Mon and Thu 10:30–11.30am) under the museum's Tot Come-and-Go programming.

The **Canyon Lakes Project** is a string of five lakes in Lubbock's Yellowhouse Canyon, where man-made waterfalls, fishing piers, camping and picnicking areas, and hike and bike trails, attract fans of the outdoors. Part of the canyon is devoted to Mackenzie Park, where one of the few remaining colonies of prairie dogs resides. These amusing, squirrel-like creatures proved such a pest at one time that farmers did their best to exterminate them. Living in giant underground colonies, their "towns" covered thousands of square miles under the prairie grass before civilization overtook them.

The region's soil and climatic conditions have proved to be excellent for most of the California-type wines. There are several vineyards, among them the **Llano Estacado Winery** ㉑, 3 miles (5km) east of US 87, on FM 1585. Here, free daily tours and wine tastings are offered (3426 East FM 1585; tel: 800-634-3854; www.llanowine.com; Tue–Fri noon–5pm, Sat 11am–5pm, Sun noon–5pm; free).

POST

Fifteen miles (24km) southeast of Lubbock, at the foot of the dramatic Caprock escarpment on US 84, is **Post** ㉒ (pop. 5,400), named for cereal magnate Charles W. Post. He founded it in 1907, after an extended stay in the Kellogg brothers' Battle Creek sanitarium for his health. Noting that the Kelloggs had devised for their patients food substitutes made from grain, Post blended wheat, bran, and molasses to create a coffee substitute called Postum. In the decade beginning in 1902, he spent $60 million to advertise Postum and such other products as Grape Nuts and Toasties. Long after his death in 1914, the Postum cereal company became General Foods Corporation which was later acquired by American multinational Philip Morris Companies. A spin-off company was created called Post Foods.

The National Ranching Heritage Center.

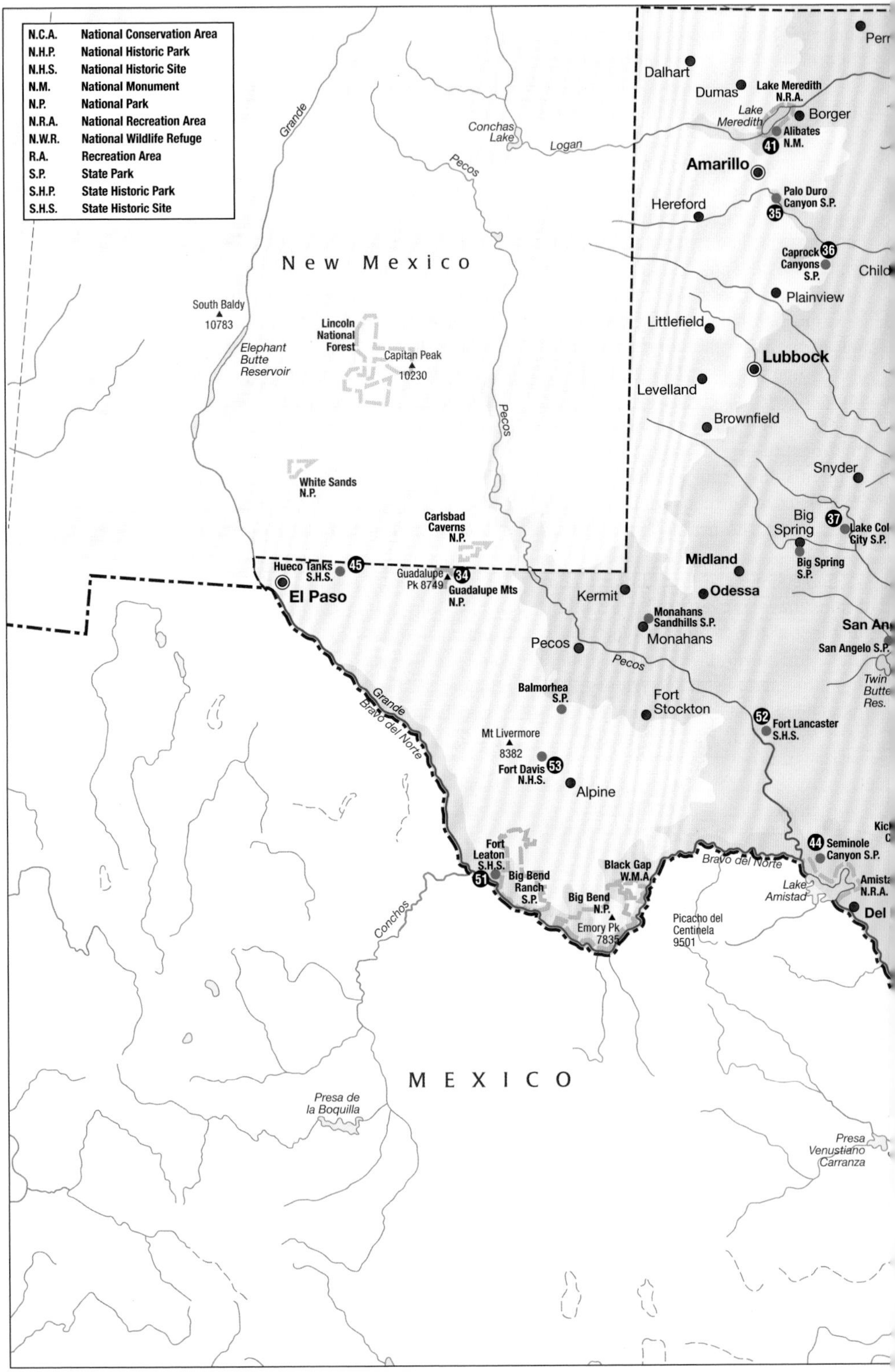

N.C.A. National Conservation Area
N.H.P. National Historic Park
N.H.S. National Historic Site
N.M. National Monument
N.P. National Park
N.R.A. National Recreation Area
N.W.R. National Wildlife Refuge
R.A. Recreation Area
S.P. State Park
S.H.P. State Historic Park
S.H.S. State Historic Site
New Mexico
MEXICO
Grande
Conchas Lake
Logan
Pecos
South Baldy 10783
Elephant Butte Reservoir
Lincoln National Forest
Capitan Peak 10230
White Sands N.P.
Carlsbad Caverns N.P.
Hueco Tanks S.H.S.
45
El Paso
Guadalupe Pk 8749
34
Guadalupe Mts N.P.
Dalhart
Dumas
Lake Meredith N.R.A.
Lake Meredith
Borger
Alibates N.M.
41
Amarillo
Palo Duro Canyon S.P.
35
Hereford
Caprock Canyons S.P.
36
Childress
Plainview
Littlefield
Lubbock
Levelland
Brownfield
Snyder
Big Spring
37
Lake Colorado City S.P.
Big Spring S.P.
Midland
Odessa
Kermit
Monahans Sandhills S.P.
Monahans
San Angelo
San Angelo S.P.
Twin Buttes Res.
Pecos
Balmorhea S.P.
Fort Stockton
52
Fort Lancaster S.H.S.
Grande
Bravo del Norte
Mt Livermore 8382
53
Fort Davis N.H.S.
Alpine
44
Seminole Canyon S.P.
Fort Leaton S.H.S.
51
Big Bend Ranch S.P.
Black Gap W.M.A.
Big Bend N.P.
Emory Pk 7835
Bravo del Norte
Lake Amistad
Amistad N.R.A.
Del Rio
Picacho del Centinela 9501
Conchos
Presa de la Boquilla
Presa Venustiano Carranza

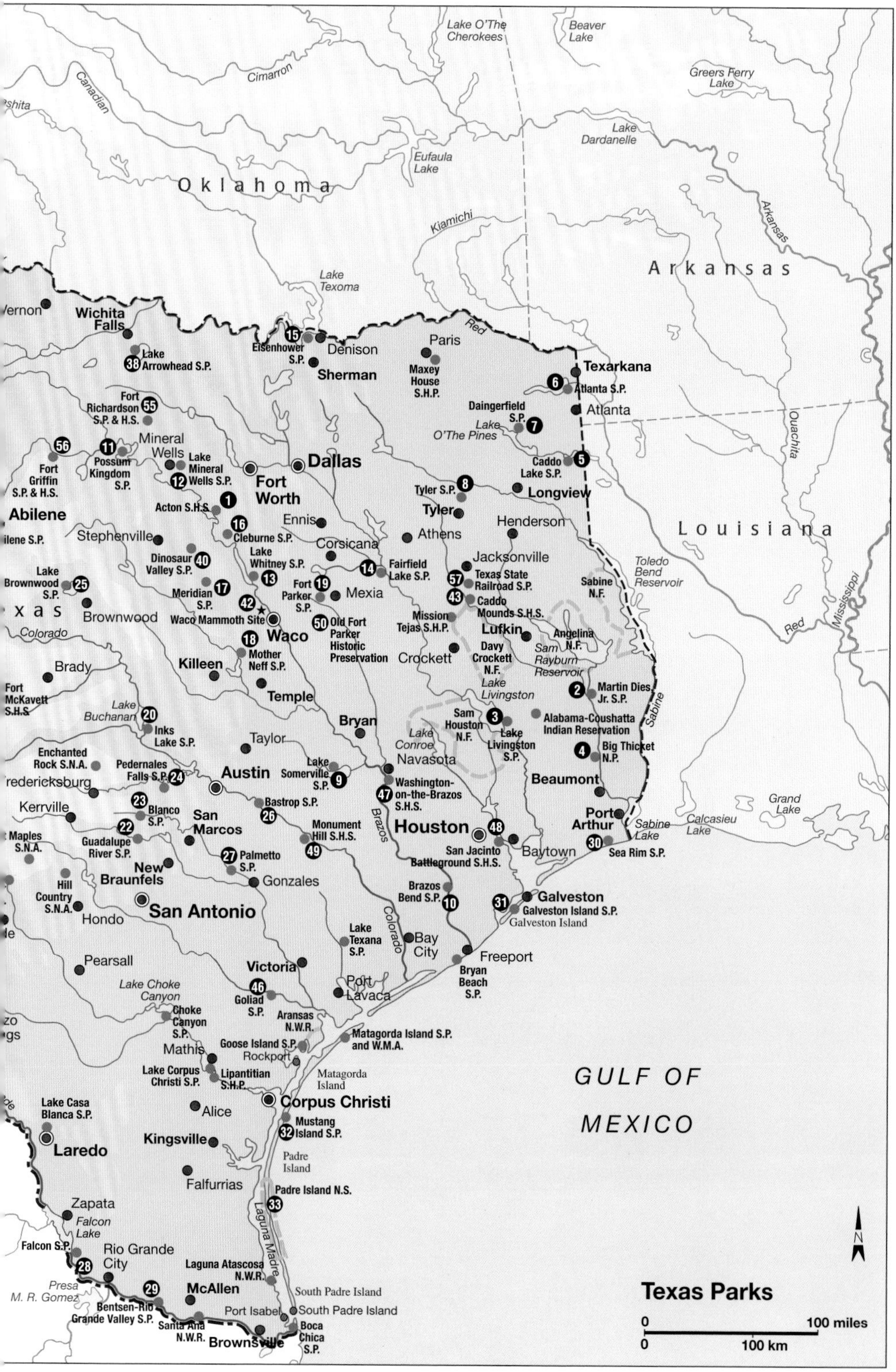
Lake O'The Cherokees
Beaver Lake
Cimarron
Canadian
Greers Ferry Lake
Lake Dardanelle
Eufaula Lake
Oklahoma
Kiamichi
Arkansas
Arkansas
Lake Texoma
Red
Vernon
Wichita Falls
15
Eisenhower S.P.
Denison
Paris
Lake Arrowhead S.P.
38
Sherman
Maxey House S.H.P.
Texarkana
6
Atlanta S.P.
Atlanta
Ouachita
Fort Richardson S.P. & H.S.
55
Daingerfield S.P.
7
Lake O'The Pines
Mineral Wells
56
11
Possum Kingdom S.P.
Lake Mineral Wells S.P.
12
Fort Griffin S.P. & H.S.
Dallas
Fort Worth
Caddo Lake S.P.
5
Tyler S.P.
8
Longview
Acton S.H.S.
1
Abilene
Ennis
Tyler
Henderson
Louisiana
Abilene S.P.
Stephenville
16
Cleburne S.P.
Corsicana
Athens
Lake Whitney S.P.
Dinosaur Valley S.P.
40
13
Jacksonville
Fairfield Lake S.P.
14
Toledo Bend Reservoir
Lake Brownwood S.P.
25
Meridian S.P.
17
Fort Parker S.P.
19
Mexia
57
Texas State Railroad S.P.
43
Caddo Mounds S.H.S.
Sabine N.F.
Texas
42
Waco Mammoth Site
Brownwood
Colorado
18
Waco
50
Old Fort Parker Historic Preservation
Mission Tejas S.H.P.
Lufkin
Angelina N.F.
Red
Mississippi
Mother Neff S.P.
Sam Rayburn Reservoir
Davy Crockett N.F.
Crockett
Brady
Killeen
Temple
Lake Livingston
2
Martin Dies, Jr. S.P.
Fort McKavett S.H.S.
Lake Buchanan
20
Inks Lake S.P.
Bryan
Sam Houston N.F.
3
Lake Livingston S.P.
Alabama-Coushatta Indian Reservation
Sabine
Taylor
Lake Conroe
Enchanted Rock S.N.A.
Navasota
4
Big Thicket N.P.
Fredericksburg
Pedernales Falls S.P.
24
Austin
Lake Somerville S.P.
9
47
Washington-on-the-Brazos S.H.S.
Beaumont
Kerrville
23
Blanco S.P.
San Marcos
Bastrop S.P.
26
Brazos
Port Arthur
Grand Lake
Lost Maples S.N.A.
22
Guadalupe River S.P.
Monument Hill S.H.S.
49
Houston
48
Sabine Lake
Calcasieu Lake
30
Sea Rim S.P.
27
Palmetto S.P.
New Braunfels
San Jacinto Battleground S.H.S.
Baytown
Hill Country S.N.A.
Gonzales
Brazos Bend S.P.
10
31
Galveston
Galveston Island S.P.
Galveston Island
San Antonio
Hondo
Colorado
Lake Texana S.P.
Bay City
Pearsall
Victoria
Freeport
Bryan Beach S.P.
Lake Choke Canyon
46
Goliad S.P.
Port Lavaca
Choke Canyon S.P.
Aransas N.W.R.
Matagorda Island S.P. and W.M.A.
Mathis
Goose Island S.P.
Rockport
Lake Corpus Christi S.P.
Lipantitlan S.H.P.
Matagorda Island
GULF OF MEXICO
Corpus Christi
Lake Casa Blanca S.P.
Alice
Mustang Island S.P.
32
Laredo
Kingsville
Padre Island
Falfurrias
Padre Island N.S.
33
Zapata
Falcon Lake
Laguna Madre
Falcon S.P.
Rio Grande City
28
Laguna Atascosa N.W.R.
Presa M. R. Gomez
29
McAllen
South Padre Island
Bentsen-Rio Grande Valley S.P.
Port Isabel
South Padre Island
Santa Ana N.W.R.
Brownsville
Boca Chica S.P.
N
Texas Parks
0
100 miles
0
100 km

Texas bluebonnets along a path by Inks Lake.

TEXAS PARKS

Camping, fishing, and water sports are major attractions in the state's many parks, but these well-tended sites also provide fascinating lessons in geography, history, and natural science.

Parks in Texas are as varied as the people and the landscape. There are very large areas, like massive Big Bend National Park (see page 265), while, at the opposite extreme, the most intimate one is probably the grave of Davy Crockett's wife in **Acton State Historic Site ❶**, near Granbury, in the heart of the Cross Timbers region. Parks planned around lakes and rivers are especially plentiful, testifying to the Texan love affair with water, historically a rare, almost mystical commodity in much of the state.

Tent and trailer camping, hiking, picnicking, birdwatching, horseback riding, golf, and all manner of zoos are found in parks throughout the state. Best of all, Texas parks showcase the natural features of their region, whether they are the moss-laden cypresses of Caddo Lake in East Texas, the cliffs of Palo Duro Canyon in the Panhandle, or the lonely shell-strewn beaches of Padre Island.

Thirteen parks are managed by the National Park Service as part of the National Park System, over 90 are state-owned, and there are countless roadside parks. At least one park is found in every Texas town or county and beside every lake. Amenities and standards of maintenance vary, but all these parks exist because of Texans' strong attachment to the outdoors. Many parks were developed by the Civilian Conservation Corps (CCC) in the 1930s, as part of Roosevelt's New Deal program.

Many Texas parks are built around water. Large lakes are found in various parts of the state. Although mainly for power generation and flood and drought control, they are the basis of some of the best park fun in the Lone Star State, and especially sports such as waterskiing, boating, and fishing. While most lakes are artificial, the parks on Texas rivers are notable for their natural scenery and features. And

Main attractions

- Big Thicket National Preserve
- Lost Maples State Natural Area
- Aransas National Wildlife Refuge
- Guadalupe Mountains National Park
- Palo Duro Canyon State Park
- Big Bend National Park

Map on page 290

Palo Duro Canyon State Park.

Tip

Spring and fall are the prettiest times of the year to visit parks in East Texas; summertime, as in the deep South, is hot, humid, and bug-ridden. Remember to bring a good insect repellent.

the many miles of Texas beaches are just plain fun-in-the-sun.

NATIONAL FORESTS

Angelina National Forest, one of four national forests in Texas, lies on both sides of the Sam Rayburn Reservoir, a 115,000-acre (47,000-hectare) lake east of Lufkin, 160 miles (256km) northeast of Houston. This is Texas's largest reservoir, and its surrounding recreation areas provide a wide variety of boating, hiking, and camping activities in the towering pine forest and along the lake branches. Backpacking and primitive camping are permitted throughout the 153,000-acre (62,000-hectare) forest, unless otherwise posted.

West of Angelina, **Davy Crockett National Forest** covers more than 160,000 acres (65,000 hectares) along the Neches River. A second-growth forest, it has made a remarkable comeback since logging stopped in the 1920s. The 4-C Trail, a scenic 20-mile (32km) trek, connects Ratcliff Lake Recreation Area with Neches Bluff. It is best to travel along it in the fall, winter, or spring, when the climate is more hospitable and the bugs are less numerous. Basic camping is allowed along the 4-C Trail, but be suspicious of the water. Carry your own or use water purifiers.

Sabine National Forest, with 160,000 acres (65,000 hectares), stretches along the Texas side of the Toledo Bend Reservoir on the Louisiana border. It includes a historic battleground where a 47-strong band of Confederates prevented a Union invasion of Texas. There are amenities for hikers, campers, boaters, and anglers. Catfish, bass, and crappie are the major fish to be found in the smaller lakes, but be sure to have a current fishing license and observe all bag limits.

HIKING IN THE EAST

In East Texas, **Sam Houston National Forest** offers excellent hiking and camping between Huntsville and Lake Livingston. Its highlight is **Lone Star Trail**, the longest developed hiking route in the state, at 128 miles (208km). The forest's Double Lake and Stubblefield recreation areas have extensive

Great Blue Heron, Caddo Lake State Park.

camping and picnicking, and serve well as trailheads. Camping is also permitted along the trail and in designated areas. Hikers are advised to tote their own water in and garbage out. But beware: from early-November until mid-January, hiking can be dangerous, because the hunting season is open.

ON THE WATER

Martin Dies, Jr. State Park ❷, on Steinhagen Reservoir, lies 15 miles (24km) east of the town of Woodville. The trees are gorgeous in the fall and, in addition to water sports, there is a wide variety of birdlife along its trail.

Lake Livingston State Park ❸, 75 miles (120km) northeast of Houston, occupies the east shore of the 85,000-acre (34,000-hectare) lake. Ninety-eight species of birds have been spotted along its 5.8 miles (9.3km) of trails.

Just 15 miles (24km) east is the **Alabama-Coushatta Indian Reservation**, established in 1854, when the state legislature gave 1,110 acres (449 hectares) to the Alabama Indians, who had moved into East Texas in the 1780s. Additional land has since been added to this densely forested region. An area along the Neches River, to the east of the reservation, has been set aside as **Big Thicket National Preserve ❹**, a unit of the National Park System, protecting an area of immense biodiversity, where desert and swamp sit cheek by jowel. Gourd dancing predominates at the tribe's annual powwow held the first weekend in June.

MOSSY CYPRESSES

Caddo Lake State Park ❺, near Marshall to the northeast of here, is the largest natural lake in the state. Spanish moss drapes its ancient cypress trees. Waterskiing is possible on sections of the lake, but drifting along in a canoe is better suited to its peaceful nature.

In the northeast corner of Texas, **Atlanta State Park ❻** sits on the banks of Wright Patman Lake, in a forest of oak, pine, and dogwood. Near the town of Daingerfield, 30 miles (50km) to the southeast, **Daingerfield State Park ❼** surrounds a small lake often filled with blooming water lilies. Its trails reward hikers with glimpses of wildlife, including deer and raccoons.

Tyler State Park ❽, just north of the city of Tyler, is a large park where swimming areas and a good fishing lake can be found. When the dogwood blooms in spring, Tyler Park is at its best.

Lake Somerville State Park and Trailway ❾, on the western edge of East Texas near Brenham, 85 miles (135km) northwest of Houston, consists of two units on either side of the lake. They are connected by a 13-mile (21km) trail, along which some of the campgrounds are especially for equestrians. There is also a wildlife management area in the park.

On the Brazos River, less than 70 miles (110km) south of Houston, **Brazos Bend State Park ❿** has 3.2 miles (5km) of river frontage. The alligator and hundreds of bird species are stars here, and migrating waterfowl lure so many

Fact

About 600 tribal members live on the Alabama-Coushatta Indian Reservation. Their homes are now made of brick, or are wood-framed. They only wear traditional dress for ceremonies, and many work in the timber industry.

Canoeing on Caddo Lake.

Tip

If you plan to visit several Texas state parks, invest $70 in an annual Texas State Parks Pass, which allows unlimited admission to the state's more than 90 parks. Contact Texas Parks and Wildlife Department at 512-389-8900.

visitors in the fall that reservations are necessary for its overnight facilities.

NEW LAKES

Drought and flood control projects of the 1950s and '60s created a multitude of new lakes in the central and western parts of Texas. There are no pine forests surrounding these lakes, but they often have their own special appeal.

About 100 miles (160km) west of Fort Worth is **Possum Kingdom State Park** ⓫, its 300 miles (482km) of shoreline shaded by deciduous oaks and juniper trees, which many westerners call "cedar." Waterskiing and scuba diving are popular here. About 55 miles (89km) southeast, **Lake Mineral Wells State Park** ⓬ sits in a pretty valley with an equestrian trail and small boats for rent.

Down the road, **Lake Whitney State Park** ⓭, 75 miles (120km) south of Fort Worth, is excellent for waterskiing and bass fishing. Its numerous facilities include an airfield for campers who fly in with the herons and geese.

Anglers in search of a good fishing lake with a lot of variety will enjoy **Fairfield Lake State Park** ⓮, 90 miles (145km) southeast of Dallas, noted for large-mouth bass and catfish.

On the Red River border separating Texas and Oklahoma, Lake Texoma is popular with sailboaters and water skiers. Anglers go after crappie, bluegill, large-mouth bass, the native Red River white bass, and the black and striped bass. There are campgrounds along the lake's 15-mile (24km) Cross Timbers Trail, but water is not available, except in the developed areas, and the presence of snakes requires caution. **Eisenhower State Park** ⓯ lies on the cliffs above Lake Texoma, offering plenty of room for campers, fishermen, and boaters, and even a protected cove for swimmers. Five miles (8km) southeast, in Denison, is the restored two-story birthplace of President Dwight D. Eisenhower.

LESS CROWDED

Four parks in North Central Texas, more or less along the Fort Worth–Waco corridor, are very pleasant, have good amenities, and are not often crowded. **Cleburne State Park** ⓰,

Preparations for a cliff-diving competition on Possum Kingdom Lake.

near the town of the same name, was built around a small lake, while **Meridian State Park ⑰**, 70 miles (110km) southwest of Fort Worth, also has a small lake with a hiking trail around.

Mother Neff State Park ⑱, 128 miles (206km) south of Fort Worth, was the first Texas state park, the first 6 acres (2.5 hectares) being donated by Governor Pat Neff's mother. The governor gave an additional 250 acres (100 hectares) in 1933. Developed by the CCC in the 1930s, it is a fitting tribute to early park pioneers. **Fort Parker State Park ⑲**, on Fort Parker Lake, near Mexia, provides waterskiing and fishing; the grounds incorporate the now-dead town of Springfield – only its cemetery remains.

HILL COUNTRY

Large lakes and cypress-shaded rivers in the Hill Country, between Austin and San Antonio, host a wide array of water activities. There are six large lakes on the lower section of Texas's Colorado River alone, all dotted with informal camping and fishing areas, and with private marinas and resorts, while the Guadalupe River feeds Canyon Lake, about 40 miles (65km) southwest of Austin, as well as six smaller lakes. The most popular lake park is probably **Inks Lake State Park ⑳** near Burnet, offering waterskiing, scuba diving, fishing, and 9.3 miles (15km) of hiking trail. Reservations are essential.

Garner State Park ㉑, on the Frio River, 30 miles (50km) north of Uvalde, although now enlarged, still tends to be crowded, with reservations necessary year-round for the picturesque cabins. Frio means cold in Spanish, and this river usually is. The scenery is at its best when the spring wildflowers make their show. One of the best ways to see the beautiful river canyon is from a rented pedal boat or inner tube.

Guadalupe River State Park ㉒ is a favorite spot for canoeing, which is a growing sport in Texas. Thirty miles (50km) north of San Antonio, the park's rapids have excited enthusiasts of all skill levels. Deer, coyotes, raccoons, and gray foxes can often be spied directly from the hiking trails, and birdwatching

Alligator, Brazos Bend State Park.

The Lighthouse Rock, Palo Duro Canyon State Park.

enthusiasts will find golden-cheeked warblers nesting in a stand of Ashe juniper from March to late summer.

Within an hour's drive north of San Antonio, **Blanco State Park ㉓** straddles 1mile (1.6km) of the Blanco River, near its namesake town. Its small size seems to discourage crowds. The park's main activities are swimming, fishing, and watching the river go by.

The diversity of the Hill Country is especially evident at **Pedernales Falls State Park ㉔**, about 45 miles (70km) west of Austin. Along parts of the Pedernales River, one finds lush vegetation and armadillos among the scrub cedar. The Pedernales, like a lot of Texas rivers, floods when it rains, but is otherwise a peaceful stream running over a rock bed into calm pools. Watch out for flash floods and an occasional treacherous waterfall or whirlpool, especially when the river is rising. The 7-mile (11km) Wolf Mountain Trail is rewarding to skilled backpackers and hardy novices alike.

Lake Brownwood State Park ㉕ is 22 miles (35km) west of Brownwood, where the Hill Country segues into West Texas. Its many facilities include picturesquely situated stone cabins. The 7,300-acre (3,000-hectare) lake imposes no limit on boat size.

Blanco State Park.

GRANITE AND COOL FORESTS

Several parks within easy reach of Austin are very popular. **Enchanted Rock State Natural Area**, 18 miles (30km) north of Fredericksburg, centers around a billion-year-old granite mountain. Its prominence in the landscape has made it a source of American Indian legends and a traveler's landmark. While most trails around the rock are taxing, one trail to the top is manageable by most healthy hikers.

A large stand of big-tooth maples, 45 miles (72km) southwest of Kerrville, is the focus of **Lost Maples State Natural Area**. One of the few remnants of the large maple forests of a less arid time in Texas, these trees provide glorious color in October. Most of the trails here are challenging, but a short one along the Sabinal River is easy. The park is pleasant at all times and is particularly popular with birders. Golden and bald eagles can often be seen in winter.

Less than 30 miles (45km) southeast of Austin, the rustic **Bastrop State Park ㉖** gives another glimpse of an earlier Texas. Made famous by its relic pine forest, or the 'Lost Pines,' the park suffered a major loss in a 2011 fire that tore through 96 percent of the park's 6,500 acres. Over the years a lot of effort has been put into rebuilding the forest, protecting the remaining pines, and making way for new ones. Its picturesque cabins were built by the CCC. Reservations are necessary for these and for the park's campgrounds.

Farther south, **Palmetto State Park ㉗**, 60 miles (95km) east of San Antonio, near Gonzales, has hiking trails that show off the plant and animal life and the extensive bird population. Its Ottine Swamp contains a tropical forest of palmettos (low-growing palms native to Texas) and other exotic flora. Rumor has it that a Big Foot creature locally-known as the "Swamp Thing" has also made its home in the Ottine Swamp. Spring and fall are the best times to visit; summer can be humid and stifling.

KEEPING COOL

Perhaps nowhere in the state are water sports more appreciated than in South Texas, a pretty dry place that can get very hot in summer. Spring and fall are the most enjoyable seasons for both locals and visitors. **Lake Texana State Park** is well stocked with catfish, large-mouth bass, and striped bass, with early spring being the best time for fishing. Additional campsites are available at the nearby Lavaca-Navidad River Authority's Brackenridge Campground.

Although **Lake Corpus Christi State Park** was developed by the CCC in the 1930s, most of its amenities are more modern. Fishing, especially for catfish, is good. Because of its mild climate and proximity to Corpus Christi, 35 miles (55km) to the south, the park is popular all year round and can be crowded.

Up the Rio Grande, near Del Rio, **Amistad National Recreation Area** provides facilities all along the American side of Lake Amistad for watersports. Scuba diving is especially good because the water is so clear. Deer and feral hog hunting with bow and arrow and shotgun hunting for dove, quail, duck, and rabbit are only allowed in certain areas during the season.

One of the largest lakes in Texas, Falcon Lake, is also on the US–Mexican border. **Falcon State Park** ㉘, 15 miles (24km) north of the historic border town of Roma, has comfortable accommodations. Birders here are rewarded with a variety of rare species, including the green kingfisher.

Bentsen-Rio Grande Valley State Park ㉙, on the river near Mission, is most popular in the winter, when its subtropical climate attracts many wintering tourists. As part of the World Birding Center, its nature trail

Tip

On the Guadalupe and other rivers in the state, the water levels are unpredictable and are subject to rapid rises and falls. Be forewarned.

Lake Amistad.

Tip

The most popular time to visit Lost Maples is late October/early November, when the leaves turn stunning colors. If you want to visit at this time, make it a weekday, when the crowds aren't so pervasive.

interprets the hundreds of rare birds, animals, and plants in the area.

WILDLIFE REFUGES

Aransas National Wildlife Refuge, on San Antonio Bay near Rockport, has a visitor center and miles of trails for viewing the refuge wildlife, including the rare and endangered whooping cranes that winter here. Sixteen miles (26km) of roads give glimpses of the many deer, alligators, and javelinas, as well as other birds that live here year round. Probably the surest way to see the whoopers is to take the boat that goes out from the Sea Gun Inn, near Fulton, from October to early April. Campgrounds are handy at nearby **Goose Island State Park**.

Laguna Atascosa National Wildlife Refuge is just north of Port Isabel on the Laguna Madre. When ducks and geese fly south for the winter, this is where many of them come. Camping is not allowed, but there are trails for and biking. The auto trail is suspended to vehicles as the park undergoes some construction, so consider the tram tour, an accessible vehicle tour through the refuge.

Santa Ana National Wildlife Refuge, on the Rio Grande near McAllen, has 12 miles (19km) of hiking trails through its 2,000-acre (800-hectare) subtropical forest. It is the northern limit of many Mexican birds' migration.

Riding along Padre Island beach.

AT THE BEACH

The beaches of the Gulf of Mexico are the site of some of the state's best-developed and most popular parks. **Sea Rim State Park** 30, on the coast near the Louisiana border, is one of the more tranquil. The greater part of the large park is an extensive marsh inhabited by a multitude of alligators, nutria, mink, raccoons, and wintering waterfowl.

Galveston Island State Park 31, on the west end of the island, has well-located beach campgrounds and picnicking areas. Occupying 5.5 miles (9km) of Gulf beach, down the coast, is **Mustang Island State Park** 32, with hundreds of campsites and picnic sites. About half of the beachfront is undeveloped. At both parks, reservations are advisable, especially in the summer.

Fourteen miles (23km) farther south is **Padre Island National Seashore** 33, the world's longest undeveloped stretch of barrier island. Its camping facilities stretch along a 64-mile (102km) white sand beach strewn with seashells – the prettiest beach in Texas.

The most remote beach park has to be **Matagorda Island State Park and Wildlife Management Area**. Accessible only by private or charter boat across Aransas Bay, the park has no drinking water, no electricity, and no telephones. Whooping cranes winter on the island. Make sure you contact park headquarters in Bay City prior to a visit.

TO THE MOUNTAINS

Guadalupe Mountains National Park 34 straddles the New Mexico–Texas border, about 100 miles (160km) due east of El Paso. These mountains are actually an uplifted Permian era fossil reef, the largest in the world (and also home to all that Texas oil). Over the border, in New Mexico, an underground section of the reef has been eroded by groundwater into the famous stalactites and stalagmites protected in Carlsbad Caverns National Park. In this lovely location, the Chihuahuan Desert rises to spectacular evergreen forests more reminiscent of the Rocky Mountains in Colorado than flat and dusty West Texas. The highest point in Texas, Guadalupe Peak, at 8,751ft (2,667 meters) can be found here, along with the sheer cliffs of El Capitán, which tower over 3,600ft (1,097 meters) high. The varied landscape supports a great deal of flora and fauna. Greasewood and lechuguilla give way to lush ferns in the protected canyons, and more than 289 species of bird and over 55 different reptiles and amphibians live in the park, as well as elk, mule deer, gray foxes, coyotes, and a mountain lion and black bear or two.

McKittrick Canyon, with its historic cabins and famous maple fall foliage, is one of the highlights of Guadalupe Mountains National Park. The canyon displays a rare and varied collection of vegetation. High sheltering walls and year-round streams ensure the right conditions for ferns, big-tooth maples, and little-leaf walnuts to grow. The marked trail into it is not difficult, but stay on the trail to avoid disturbing the fragile ecological system. Permits are required for backcountry camping; the park's lovely little campground is a popular spot. Get there early to secure a spot – the nearest lodging is in Carlsbad, New Mexico.

Rugged landscapes also characterize **Palo Duro Canyon State Park** ㉟, in the Panhandle, spectacular from every angle. Smaller canyons can be found at **Caprock Canyons State Park** ㊱, 35 miles (56km) southeast of Palo Duro.

HUNTING AND BOATING

As in South Texas, where large lakes make summer more acceptable, way

A rare sight: whooping crane in Aransas National Wildlife Refuge.

Guadalupe Mountains National Park.

A pictograph of Tlaloc, a rain deity, in Hueco Tanks State Historic Site. The Jornada Mogollon people (450–1400 AD) drew many symbols associated with water, which was vital for growing corn in the desert.

up in West Texas's Panhandle Plains, 35 miles (56km) east of Amarillo, **Lake Meredith National Recreation Area** cools the arid Llano Estacado. Deer and bird hunting is permitted in certain parts of this park during the season. There is usually a good wind for sailing, but storms are unpredictable and boaters of all types should always be very cautious on this stretch of water.

Not as heavily developed as Lake Meredith, other West Texas lakes still give welcome recreational relief to many Texans and tourists. **Lake Colorado City State Park** ❸❼, between Big Spring and Abilene, and **Lake Arrowhead State Park** ❸❽ near Wichita Falls, are both on good-sized lakes and are popular with motor boaters and waterskiers.

Abilene State Park ❸❾ about 20 miles (30km) southwest of town, is just across the road from Lake Abilene, and not far from an area once rife with wild buffalo. The park's campgrounds and swimming pool are set in a historic pecan tree grove.

Freshly caught bass.

CULTURAL PAST

A large and growing class of parks protect and display the cultural heritage of the state. The historical and recreational are often combined in these parks, providing fun flavored with a little education.

Dinosaur Valley State Park ❹⓿ exhibits the tracks made by the Sauroposeidon proteles and Acrocanthosaurus dinosaurs, prehistoric reptiles that walked around in the mud of a shallow sea that covered Central Texas during the Cretaceous era, more than 100 millions years ago. The interpretive center explains the tracks, and a trail leads right to them. Camping, hiking, and picnicking are also provided in this park, which is 60 miles (95km) southwest of Fort Worth, near Glen Rose.

Remnants of other prehistoric Texas cultures are preserved in several parks. **Alibates Flint Quarries National Monument** ❹❶, on the red bluffs above the Canadian River north of Amarillo, in the Panhandle of West Texas, was the source of flint used by prehistoric tribes for thousands of years. Of particular interest is the **Waco Mammoth Site** ❹❷, in Central Texas, where paleontologists have uncovered the fossils of 22 Columbian mammoths and other mammals from the Pleistocene Epoch.

Caddo Mounds State Historic Site ❹❸ clear across the state in East Texas, 30 miles (50km) west of Nacogdoches, protects three ceremonial mounds built by the Caddo, the westernmost branch of the Missippian Mound Building culture, a branch of the eastern Woodland culture. The site was inhabited from the end of the eighth to the beginning of the 15th centuries and is the best-preserved ceremonial site in Texas. Interpretive exhibits and a self-guided tour explain as much as is known about the early Caddo people. During summer, archeological digs sometimes take place, and visitors are invited to watch.

Recreational and camping facilities are convenient at **Mission Tejas State Park**, 8 miles (13km) down the road.

PICTOGRAPHS

Close to Del Rio, on the border in South Texas, is another site with striking evidence of inhabitants 7,000–12,000 years ago. These ancient nomadic people painted the walls and ceilings of their cave dwellings, in what is today **Seminole Canyon State Park and Historic Site** ㊹, with fanciful animals and other images whose meaning is now lost. One pictograph-covered shelter is open to visitors on a guided tour. The trail leading to it takes stamina, particularly in the summer heat. An award-winning exhibit at the visitor center interprets the prehistory and history of the park. Campsites with water are available.

Rock art is also found at **Hueco Tanks State Historic Site** ㊺, 37 miles (60km) northeast of El Paso in West Texas. Tribes may have come through the area as long as 10,000 years ago. Water held in the depressions of the rocks made it a popular place for travelers in the surrounding desert. Pueblo rock art dating from as early as 6,000 BC and Mescalero Apache images from the 19th century can be seen on a self-guiding tour. Wildlife watching is also fruitful here, and campsites and picnic areas are both available.

SPANISH COLONIAL

The first colonizers of Texas, the Spanish, have left substantial reminders of their presence. **San Antonio Missions National Historical Park** (see page 178) includes four 18th-century mission churches, a dam, and an aqueduct along the San Antonio River. All are managed by the National Park Service; the remains of a fifth mission, the Alamo Chapel in downtown San Antonio, is owned by the state of Texas.

The Spanish mission of Nuestra Señora Espiritu Santo de Zuniga is the centerpiece of **Goliad State Park** ㊻, just south of the historic town of Goliad. The mission was reconstructed by the CCC on the ruins of the 1722 church. The park has a scenic campground on the river and exhibits in the church and granary. The nearby Presidio La Bahia gained notoriety in 1836 when it was the site of Santa Anna's execution of Fannin's men during the Texas Revolution – hence "Remember Goliad!" The old presidio (garrison) has been reconstructed and is open to the public.

INDEPENDENT TEXAS

Washington-on-the-Brazos State Historic Site ㊼ is the site of the proclamation of the Texas Declaration of Independence on March 2, 1836. Nothing much remains of the bustling 1850s town, but a replica of Texas's Independence Hall and the home of the Republic's last president have been reconstructed. Reenactors bring 19th-century life to present-day visitors at the Barrington Plantation State Historic Site. The Star of the Republic Museum, operated by Blinn College, sits in the park grounds and has a

Fact

Alibates flint, found in Alibates Flint Quarries National Monument, north of Amarillo, was named for Allie Bates, a one-time local cowboy.

LOCAL HERITAGE

Like much of the rest of the United States, Texas has gradually become more aware of its cultural heritage over the past 40 years, particularly the Victorian period after Texas became part of the United States and new communities were founded.

Almost every city and town has at least one historic house museum that local folks point to with pride. Some are large groupings of houses with a paid staff and long opening hours, like **Sam Houston Memorial Museum** in Huntsville, which has assembled buildings associated with Sam Houston, hero of the Texas revolution, including two homes, a gazebo, and a blacksmith's shop.

Others are smaller and either run by the city or privately, and often manned by dedicated volunteers. They include places like French's Trading Post, now the **John Jay French Museum**, in Beaumont, the city's first two-story house; the **Annie Riggs Memorial Museum**, a former hotel in Fort Stockton that once accommodated passengers on the Butterfield Overland Mail stage coaches; the gothic **Bishop's Palace** in Galveston (listed as one of the top 100 significant historic buildings in the US), which was built for the Gresham family and later used as the bishop's official residence; and the **Stillman House Museum** in Brownsville, built in 1850 by Charles Stillman, founder of the city.

number of good exhibits about life in early Texas. The park's riverside picnic area is on a bluff above the Brazos.

Six weeks after the declaration of Texas Independence, Sam Houston's small band of Texans routed Santa Anna in the marshes of Buffalo Bayou, now commemorated by **San Jacinto Battleground State Historic Site ㊽**. In La Porte, just east of Houston, San Jacinto Monument rises in the midst of the battleground and houses a museum. The park provides picnic areas but no campgrounds.

Although the Texas Republic was established by the April 1836 battle at San Jacinto, it struggled against continued Mexican incursions for the next 10 years. **Monument Hill State Historic Site ㊾**, in La Grange, 70 miles (115km) east of Austin, honors the Texans who died in two responses to such attacks, the Dawson and Mier expeditions. **Kreische Brewery State Historic Site** is contiguous and contains the ruins of a mid-19th-century brewery, at one time the third largest in the state. The sites share a well-developed picnic area and grand views of Texas's Colorado River. No camping is available.

FRONTIER FORTS

Fortifications of many types are scattered around the state and represent battles of various sorts fought on Texas soil. The most famous of all, of course, is the Alamo in San Antonio. **Old Fort Parker Historic Preservation ㊿**, about 40 miles (65km) east of Waco and now owned by the City of Groesbeck, commemorates another famous battle of 1836, a Native America attack on Parker's Fort and the capture of little Cynthia Ann Parker.

After annexation by the United States in 1845, the Texas frontier stretched long and wide and was poorly protected. Settlers in the most remote areas had to create their own defense systems. **Fort Leaton State Historic Site ㉛**, on the Rio Grande near present-day Presidio, was built by a border trader (some called him a smuggler), Ben Leaton who traded with the Comanche and Apache. The federal government also built forts to cope with American Indian threats

Battleship Texas, San Jacinto Battleground State Historic Site.

to the advancing settlers, and a group of fort parks represents the initiatives. **Fort Lancaster State Historic Site 52**, **Fort Davis National Historic Site 53**, and **Fort McKavett State Historic Site 54** were all built before the Civil War.

Fort Lancaster's adobe ruins lie about 80 miles (120km) east of Fort Stockton, and are interpreted in the visitors' center and via a self-guided tour of the old parade field. At Fort McKavett, about 40 miles (65km) northwest of Junction, and Fort Davis, in the Davis Mountains 25 miles (40km) north of Alpine, little is left of their earliest incarnations, but they have been restored to their post-Civil War state. More forts were built after the war, when American Indian hostilities reached their height. **Fort Richardson State Park and Historic Site 55** in Jacksboro, 100 miles (160km) northwest of Fort Worth, and **Fort Griffin State Park and Historic Site 56**, 50 miles (80km) north of Abilene, have been developed with pleasant camping and picnicking adjuncts. Highlights of visits to all the forts are occasional military reenactments: check individual parks for details.

PARKS OF ANOTHER KIND

Some parks defy the usual categories. **Texas State Railroad State 57** runs for 25 miles (40km) between Rusk and Palestine, and is one of the most popular parks in East Texas. The turn-of-the-20th-century rolling stock gives an authentic flavor to the scenic ride along the historic route. The round trip takes three hours. There are picnic sites at both ends to round off the journey.

Battleship *Texas* State Historic Site, a memorial to Texans who fought in World War II, is moored at San Jacinto Battleground State Historic Site in La Porte. Commissioned in 1914, it is the only surviving Navy ship that served in both wars, notably in D-Day operations off the coast of Normandy in 1944 and in the Pacific at Iwo Jima and Okinawa in 1945. The ship has been undergoing a lengthy construction project since 2019, so check to make sure the ship is accessible to visitors before visiting. Generally, it is open to the public seven days a week, and features a self-guided tour and interesting displays about ship life.

It is not the only warship to be named after Texas. In the 1980s, a nuclear submarine was named after the city of Corpus Christi, which is the home of a naval air station. The name had to be changed when complaints about the implications of its Latin meaning (Body of Christ) were voiced.

BEYOND WORDS AND PICTURES

There are, of course, many excellent parks in the state that have not been mentioned here, through lack of space. But the list is also incomplete in that no words or pictures can ever fully capture the beauty and spirit of the Texas landscape like a campout in the East Texas Piney Woods, a hike through a dusty, rugged canyon, or a quiet afternoon's sailing on a placid lake on a late fall afternoon.

Fact

It's hard to believe that the little village of Washington-on-the-Brazos was once capital of the independent Republic of Texas. Today, it has only 265 inhabitants.

Hiking through McKittrick Canyon.

The Armadillo Palace, Houston.

TEXAS

TRAVEL TIPS

TRANSPORTATION

A – Z

FURTHER READING

TRANSPORTATION

GETTING THERE

By Air

There are four airports in Texas classified as international: Dallas–Fort Worth, George Bush Intercontinental in Houston, Austin-Bergstrom in Austin, and San Antonio. Air passengers to Texas usually arrive at Dallas–Fort Worth Airport or George Bush Intercontinental Airport in Houston, but direct flights from London to Austin with British Airways mean that airport is also popular. Many flights touch down in El Paso for passengers to board or change planes.

A network of smaller airports serves the state, with scheduled flights to over 30 cities. Connections are easy to arrange, even between different carriers, and there are frequent shuttles between major cities all day.

Airline Companies

More than two dozen airlines fly in and out of Texas airports, including major carriers such as Fort Worth-based American Airlines (and its regional off-shoot, American Eagle) and Dallas-based Southwest Airlines, as well as United, Continental, British Airways, and Delta.

Air fares change frequently, as do schedules and discount rates. Check the internet regularly for specials, or contact airlines directly by telephone for information and reservations. Local or toll-free central numbers can be obtained either from directory assistance (in Texas, dial 1-411) or the Yellow Pages of the local telephone directory.

By Train

Two Amtrak lines run through Texas: the Texas Eagle from Chicago to San Antonio, with a Dallas–Austin connection; and the Sunset Limited from Los Angeles to New Orleans with a Houston stop. The trains stop at 19 passenger terminals in the state: Alpine, Austin, Beaumont, Cleburne, Dallas, Del Rio, El Paso, Fort Worth, Houston, Longview, Marshall, McGregor, Mineola, San Antonio, Sanderson, San Marcos, Taylor, Temple, and Texarkana. Accommodations include coach and sleeping facilities. There are lounge and dining cars. Outside North America, you can purchase a USA Rail Pass from travel agencies, which allows unlimited rail travel within specified dates.

For reservations and information inside the US, call 1-800-USA-RAIL or 1-800-872-7245 toll-free, international visitors can use 1-215-856-7924 or visit www.amtrak.com.

By Bus

Greyhound buses (US tel: 800-231-2222; international tel: 1-214-849-8100; www.greyhound.com) connect Texas with all major US cities. Buses are always air-conditioned, with toilets on board and free Wi-fi.

GETTING AROUND

On Arrival

Dallas–Fort Worth Airport

The airport (tel: 972-973-3112; www.dfwairport.com) is 18 miles (29km) northwest of Dallas and within four hours of most cities in the US. DFW International Airport is the fifteenth busiest airport in the world in terms of passengers and fourth busiest in the world in terms of operations.

The Trinity Railway Express (TRE; www.trinityrailwayexpress.org), a train system that connects Fort Worth to Dallas, stops near the airport (you must take a Remote South bus to reach it) at least once an hour on weekdays; one zone costs $2.50. Allow at least an hour's travel time. A taxi ride downtown takes around 35 minutes and costs about $45. A shared ride service like Lyft or Uber costs to downtown costs anywhere from $28–$80 depending on what type of service you book (Economy to Luxury), traffic, time of day, and number of available drivers.

Love Field Airport

The hub for Southwest Airlines, Love Field (tel: 214-670-LOVE; www.dallas-lovefield.com) is 7 miles (11km) northwest of downtown Dallas, but within the city limits. The DART Love Link 524 bus runs between Dallas Love Field and the Inwood/Love Field DART train station, which allows travellers to use the DART Rail Green or Orange Line to reach their destination or connect to the TRE in downtown Dallas.

A taxi takes about 20 minutes to get downtown and costs about $18. Shared ride services can cost as low as $15 and as high as $50 to downtown Dallas depending on a variety of factors.

George Bush Intercontinental

Located 23 miles (37km) north of downtown Houston, Bush Intercontinental (tel: 281-230-3100; www.airport-houston.com) has daily services to over 180 cities worldwide, and is a hub for United Airlines.

Houston's METRO bus system has a route that runs from Intercontinental Airport to downtown Houston every 15–30 minutes, from 5am to 1am Mon–Sun for $1.25. Taxis to downtown cost about $62 and take around 30 minutes. Expect shared rides services like Lyft and Uber to cost between $30–$100 to downtown Houston depending on whether you book a Luxury or Economy car, time of day, etc.

William P. Hobby Airport

Serving as a hub for Southwest Airlines, Hobby (tel: 713-640-3000; www.fly2houston.com/hou/overview/) is 7 miles (11km) southeast of downtown Houston.

The METRO bus system goes from Hobby to downtown Houston every 30minutes from 6am to 1.30am Mon–Fri and every 30 minutes from 7am to 2am on weekends for $1.25. Taxis downtown cost about $30 and take around 20 minutes. Rates for shared service rides like Lyft and Uber to downtown Houston can start as low as $15 for Economy rides and can go as high as $70 for Luxury car rides.

Austin-Bergstrom International Airport

ABIA (tel: 512-530-ABIA; www.austintexas.gov/airport) is 8 miles (13km) from downtown Austin.

The METRO bus from ABIA to downtown Austin takes 35 minutes and operates every 15 minutes from 5am to midnight Mon–Fri and 6am to midnight on weekends,; fare $1.25. Taxis downtown cost a minimum rate of $13.30 plus mileage and take around 20 minutes. The SuperShuttle shared van service (tel: 800-258-3826) is approximately $20 but takes an hour or more, depending on destination.

Public Transportation

By Air

Within Texas, Southwest Airlines has the largest number of flights and usually the lowest fares; Express Jet and Alaska Airlines offer other affordable flights between Texas cities.

By Bus

All cities and most towns have some form of local bus service at very low rates. Contact the local tourist office for listings (see page 317) or call the main office of the bus company listed in the telephone directory. Major cities like Dallas, Fort Worth, Austin, San Antonio, and Houston offer other bus and transportation services well suited to visitors, such as Molley the Trolley in Fort Worth and the D-Link in Downtown Dallas.

By Train

There are over 100 stations on the popular light-rail DART system (Dallas Area Rapid Transit) (tel: 214-979-1111; www.dart.org) serving downtown Dallas and 12 surrounding cities. The DFW Airport Station has greatly improved access to the metroplex for travelers who do not wish to rent a car. Each station has ticket machines with clear instructions for use. There are also special services for people with disabilities. For further information, tel: 214-979-1111. An AM/PM pass costs $2.50/$6 for a day pass.

DART stops at Union Station, from which Amtrak trains connect Dallas with Chicago and Houston. The station is connected by pedestrian tunnel to the Hyatt Regency Hotel (beside Reunion Tower). See page 308 for information on Amtrak services.

Houston's METRORail (tel: 713-635-4000; www.ridemetro.org) connects downtown, midtown, the Museum District, the Texas Medical Center, Reliant Park, and the South Fannin Park & Ride lot.

By Taxi

Taxis can be a convenient way to get around cities. However, unlike those in major cities like New York and London, Texas taxis do not cruise around looking for people hailing them from the curb. To get a taxi, you must call the cab company (look under Taxicabs in the Yellow Pages of the local telephone directory). Ask what the rates are, as they vary from city to city (but not from cab to cab). A 15 percent tip is appreciated if you are satisfied with the service provided, and especially if you need help with luggage.

Driving

The size and climate of Texas are good reasons to drive, since walking between attractions, even in a city, requires more time than most people have while on their vacations; for much of the year, it is simply too hot to walk around.

Interstate highways 10, 20, 27, 30, 35, 37, 40, and 45 crisscross Texas, providing direct and relatively hazard-free routes to major cities. For anyone interested in a closer look, however, there is a variety of US highways, state routes, and backroads (marked on the maps as FM or "Farm to Market", RM or "Ranch to Market", and RR or "Ranch Road") intertwined between all the major cities, smaller communities, and even ghost towns. Buy a map and plan a tour, but allow plenty of time to reach your destination since some of these Texas roads get quite winding and pot-holed.

Be aware, as well, that leaving the main track means fewer gas stations and convenience stores. However, if you remember to fill the tank and allow plenty of time to get where you're going, especially after dark, these secondary roads (dubbed "blue highways") may prove the most enjoyable way to travel since you'll be able to enjoy the countryside without having to worry about heavy traffic.

The Texas Department of Transportation (TDOT) runs 12 information centers offering advice on trip planning, road conditions, and other travel matters. For information call 800-452-9292; www.txdot.gov.

Anyone spending a significant amount of time driving US highways is strongly advised to join the **Automobile Association of America** (tel: 800-765-0766; www.aaa.com). Benefits include emergency breakdown service, excellent road maps, travel literature, and personalized trip planning, as well as discounts at motels like Best Western and other chains. Premier level offers towing up to 200 miles (320km) from breakdown site – important if you are in the middle of nowhere – and lock-out, refueling, and jumpstart service. Insurance is also available through the association, which has a reciprocal arrangement with some of the automobile associations in other countries.

Car Rental

Cars can be rented in most cities. This is often done at the local airport since much of the rental business is with customers who have arrived by air. Choose the best rate available from one of the side-by-side booths or better, book a car in advance as, quite often, certain levels of vehicle are unavailable.

You must be at least 21 years of age to rent a car. Most companies require a credit card or debit card, although some do not accept debit cards, so be sure to inquire ahead of time. Be sure to arrange auto insurance if you do not have US coverage of your own. Even with your own coverage, you may be required to cover any damages upfront and be reimbursed later.

Some rental agencies expect the car to be returned to them. If you want to drive to another city and fly on from there, inform the rental agent at the time you arrange the terms. There are branches of the main rental companies across the state. There may be a charge to drop the car at their branch in another city. Check ahead because the cost can be prohibitive.

Interstates

Interstates (motorways) bypass most towns. They do get you to your destination fast, but when you are driving from Austin to Dallas or from San Antonio to El Paso, even fast can mean 4–10 hours. Along the interstates there are rest stops with restrooms and picnic areas, as well as restaurants and gas stations.

Highway Patrol and Hitchhiking

The Highway Patrol cruises these highways, not just monitoring speed limits but also looking for drivers in trouble. If you have any emergency that won't allow you to continue the trip, signal your distress by raising the hood and putting on the emergency lights. Be sure to keep a current driver's license and a certificate proving you have liability insurance with you at all times because you will be required to show them to the law enforcement officer who stops your car for any reason. It is illegal to drive in Texas without these items.

Motorists are often warned that they are safer staying in the car with the doors locked until a patrol car stops to help, rather than leaving it and trying to hitchhike. Hitchhiking is not considered safe, whether you are on the giving or the receiving end.

Rules of the Road

Speed limits for roads and highways are posted on white signs to the right, as are all other road signs. Some roads are for one-way traffic only and are identified by a black and white sign with an arrow pointing in the permitted direction of travel. At an intersection where each corner has a red stop sign with a smaller sign below it that says "4-Way" or "All-Way," motorists must stop and then proceed across the intersection following the order in which they arrived at the stop.

The official highway speed limit is 70mph (112kph); some highways are 75mph (121kph). Although everyone passes you, resist the temptation to accelerate. If caught in a "speed trap" by the Highway Patrol, whose black-and-white cruisers have radar, you will get a speeding ticket that has to be paid in a nearby (or sometimes not so near) town before continuing your trip.

The same advice should be followed when driving through towns and cities. Be sure to notice the white signs warning that, upon entering the town, you will be in a different "Speed Zone Ahead." Be prepared to slow to the lower speed you will soon see posted on upcoming white signs. Some very small Texas towns are notorious for catching and fining drivers who have not slowed down quickly enough from the highway speed to the in-town 30mph (48kph) speed limit. You may not notice the local (variously colored and lettered) police car parked surreptitiously in an alley until it is too late.

Pay attention to other drivers flashing their lights at you; probably either an accident or speed trap is ahead. Some Texas motorists ask the gas station attendants if there are Highway Patrol cars ahead but they cannot always be relied upon.

Parking fees vary from town to town, with rates higher in larger cities and nonexistent in smaller towns.

A state law requires every passenger in a car to use a seatbelt, and there are also requirements that small children and babies be secured in youth or infant seats that have been fitted into the car seat. In Texas, a traffic ticket is a criminal offense. Penalties run from $150 for an expired registration all the way up to $1,250 for passing a school bus.

Texas state law requires that all drivers carry auto insurance policies. Auto rental companies offer insurance that runs from $10 to $25 per day, depending on coverage.

Texas has passed a statewide ban on texting while driving, but there is no state law that prevents drivers from talking on their cell phones while driving.. However, it may not be a good idea for travelers unfamiliar with the area, particularly in busy urban areas. The exception is during school zone hours, when the use of cell phones is illegal, unless the vehicle is stopped or you are using a hands-free device. Some cities have passed their own laws restricting any use of cell phones while driving, so be sure to check local ordinances to see the laws in a particular area.

Down Mexico Way

Current US State Department advisories caution against travel to certain areas in Mexico due to ongoing drug war violence and crime in border areas. Places like Colima, Guerrero, Michoacán, Sinaloa, and Tamaulipas are especially high-risk for violent crimes and kidnapping. During the last decade, murders in the major flashpoint area of El Paso-Ciudad Juárez have dropped considerably, after Mexico government crackdowns and a heavy military presence, and Mexican tourism officials are keen to encourage visitors to cross and enjoy all that the country has to offer. This is entirely a matter of informing yourself and exercising personal judgement, and keeping your wits about you. Thousands of people cross the border every day, with few problems, although with President Trump's migrant detainee and border wall initiatives, some people who traveled across the border, including US citizens, reported invasive and sometimes illegal searches of their belongings and technology. In any case, it's best to be aware of your legal rights and have numbers for your embassy or consulate on hand.

There are 28 border crossings in Texas; the main crossings are El Paso, Eagle Pass, Laredo, and Brownsville. Under Homeland Security rules, both US and non-US citizens must carry a valid passport to visit Mexico and to reenter the US by air or by sea (some US state-issued enhanced driver's licenses with embedded microchips are permitted, as well as Passport Cards, but don't rely on it) and, if applicable, an alien registration card (green card) to reenter the country. Be sure you have these on hand before making the trip to avoid big headaches at immigration. Short trips into the border zone (La Frontera), which extends approximately 25 miles (40km) south, are permitted.

If you're traveling further or staying over 72 hours, a Mexican tourist card, or *forma migratoria turista* (FMT), is required. These are free from immigration officials at the border and from Mexican consulates, Mexican government tourist offices, and travel agents. Drivers must obtain automobile permits, valid for 180 days, when going beyond the border region. These cost $44 from immigration officials.

It is mandatory to obtain Mexican insurance because in the event of an accident vehicles are usually impounded. Sanborn's Mexican Insurance (www.sanbornsinsurance.com) is a reliable company. At the border you will be given a temporary import permit after you show proof of ownership (photocopy of title will do), or the hire contract in the driver's name if you are driving a rental car, and the insurance policy. Keep these handy, as 12 miles (19km) into Mexico, every car without Mexico tags is stopped at the border checkpoints. Information is on www.banjercito.com.mx/registroVehiculos.

A – Z

A

Accommodations

Hotels

Whatever your budget, you should be able to find a suitable place to spend the night in Texas for between $50 and $150 per night. In addition to independently owned hotels and motels in every price range, even the many chains operating in Texas reach into some of its smallest towns.

At the expensive end of the scale there are Four Seasons, Ritz-Carltons, Intercontinentals, Rosewoods, Kimptons, Sheratons, Hiltons, Marriotts, and Hyatt Regencies. The Hotel ZaZa boutique chain is fairly expensive, as are most of the independent boutique properties in the larger cities. A more moderately price choice would be the Holiday Inns, La Quintas, Best Westerns, Ramada Inns, and Drury Inns. Quality Inns and Courtyards are reasonable; the Motel 6, Motel 8, Days Inn, Rodeway Inn, and Travelodge chains are at the budget end of the market.

Bed and Breakfast

Bed and breakfast rates in Texas are generally reasonable; plan on spending $100–150 per night. In historic districts or towns, there is not much of a distinction made between "bed and breakfast" and "historic inn," since they are much the same. For information and reservations at many Texas's B&Bs contact or visit the website of **Texas Bed and Breakfast Association**, 2629 19th Street, Lubbock, Texas 79410; tel: 979-836-5951; www.texasbb.org.

Campgrounds

There are hundreds of state, federal, or privately owned campgrounds throughout Texas. Federally managed campgrounds in national parks and national recreation areas (National Park Service), national forests (US Forest Service), and the 26 impounded lakes administered by the US Army Corps of Engineers, are all now on a central reservation system. Reserve at www.recreation.gov or call 877-444-6777. Reservations may be made up to six months in advance. Note: If you have not made a reservation (advisable during the busy summer season), most NPS and USFS campgrounds have a number of first-come-first-serve sites, but these go fast, so be sure to arrive early in the day to get a spot.

Around 70 Texas parks and recreation areas managed by the state allow camping within their boundaries. **Texas Parks & Wildlife Department's Central Reservations** (www.tpwd.state.tx.us/business/park_reservations; tel: 512-389-8900) can reserve sites anywhere within the state park system. A useful free booklet, *Texas Public Campgrounds*, is available from the Travel and Information Division, can be downloaded at https://ftp.dot.state.tx.us/pub/txdot-info/trv/campgrounds.pdf, or contact the Texas Department of Transportation,125 East 11th St. Austin, TX 78701.

The *RV Travel and Camping Guide to Texas*, a booklet listing private campgrounds in Texas can be downloaded at www.texascampgrounds.com. It is published by the **Texas Association of Campground Owners (TACO)**. In addition, the **Kampground Of America (KOA)**, www.koa.com, can provide a list of 25 member campgrounds around the state.

Vacation Rentals

Condominiums and beachfront/bayfront homes are available to rent in some areas, particularly on Galveston and South Padre Island. Check the Yellow Pages under "Realtors," or contact: **Island Services**, 3100 Padre Boulevard, South Padre Island, TX 78597; tel: 800-926-6926; www.pirentals.com.

Glamping has become popular in Texas over the last decade and includes accommodations like treehouses, teepees, tiny houses, safari tents, cabins, and more. While many glamping properties are privately-owned and provide booking on their websites, they often list on such sites like Glamping Hub, www.glampinghub.com, HipCamp, www.hipcamp.com, and Airbnb, www.airbnb.com.

Admission Charges

Some of Texas's most famous sights – the **Grassy Knoll** in Dallas, **the Alamo** in San Antonio – are free, and so are many museums in this wealthy state. Otherwise, most museums charge $5–10 per adult, although many have free entry days during the week or one weekend per month, such as the **Museum of Fine Arts, Houston** which is free on Thursdays. At the other extreme, the **Johnson Space Center** in Houston charges $29.95 (with a $5 discount for military and AAA members).

B

Budgeting for Your Trip

Texas has options both cost-conscious and luxurious in accommodations, food, and transportation. At one end lie budget motels for around $50 a night and national restaurant chains where dinner is about $10. Conversely, the major cities all have swanky restaurants and luxury hotels with penthouse suites whose daily rate runs up to $2,500. The average lies somewhere between. Travelers can expect to spend $100–150 per night for a room in a decent hotel or bed-and-breakfast; prices and selection drop in less urban areas. Allow $20–25 per meal, although Texas's excellent "home-cooking" restaurants, hole-in-the-walls, barbecue joints, and food trucks are cheaper. Dinner at a big-city restaurant with fine dining starts at around $60 per person.

Rental cars cost approximately $350 per week, including unlimited mileage, Texas tax and license, and a vague surcharge called a "facility fee." In addition, Texas applies higher add-on fees for cars rented from the airport than any other state, with mark-ups averaging more than 50 percent.

Greyhound is the major bus line, with routes to and from all of Texas's largest cities. One-way tickets range from $6 (Austin–San Antonio) to $15 (Dallas–Houston); to ride from Dallas to San Antonio is $18.

C

Children

Texas is a family-friendly state. Not only does every restaurant offer children's menus with smaller meals at reduced prices, but most attractions have discounted tickets for kids and free entry for those three years old or younger. Throughout the state, there are plenty of attractions specifically targeted to kids such as museums like The DoSeum in San Antonio and the Perot Museum of Nature and Science in Dallas, as well as aquariums, play zones, and theme parks like Six Flags and Legoland.

While there are family-friendly resorts like Great Wolf Lodge, which has an indoor water park, don't expect most Texas hotels or resorts to offer childcare services. They may be able to provide local babysitting services, though you'll probably have just as much luck finding your own on sites like Sittercity (www.sittercity.com).

Climate

What To Wear

For clothing, fabrics such as cotton, linen, and wool provide the best comfort in the Texas climate. Go particularly light in summer, but because of varying altitude and cool breezes, a sweater may be needed in the evening. The midwinters of Central and East Texas, the Coastal Prairie, and the Rio Grande Valley usually require only a lightweight coat. In the mountains, High Plains, and Panhandle, winters can be so severe that you need layers of warm clothes.

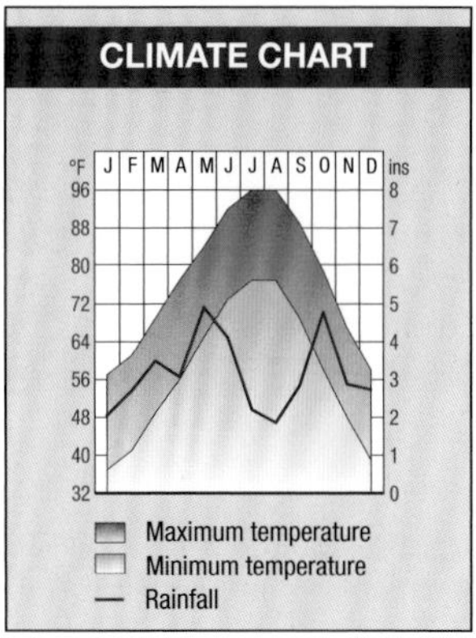

Texans are very casual dressers and away from the office blue jeans are the norm. They are worn almost anywhere, anytime of the day, dressed up or down by changing a shirt, sweater, jacket, or accessories. People in Dallas and Houston dress formally for some evening events, but casual pants and dresses for women and shirt-sleeves or tie-less shirts and jackets for men are acceptable almost anywhere you go.

With few exceptions, Western dress is informal and geared toward practical clothing for enjoying the outdoors. A pair of jeans or slacks, a polo or button-down shirt, and cowboy boots or shoes are appropriate at all but the fanciest places and events. Shorts and light shirts are suitable for most situations in the warmer months, though.

Year round, wear sunscreen with a SPF of at least 30, polarized eye protection, a broad-brimmed hat (cowboy hats are optional but very useful) to protect head and neck, layered clothing with sleeves and legs that can be rolled down as sun protection, and sturdy hiking footwear that secure the foot for walking on rough ground – flip flops are fine at the beach, but you won't want these when you are doing a lot of walking, wherever you are.

If you're hiking, a thin, inner polypropylene sock and a thick, outer sock will help keep your feet dry and comfortable. Blisters or sore spots can develop quickly. Cover them with moleskin or surgical tape, available at most pharmacies or camping supply stores. Bring a warm coverup and rainjacket; even in summer, as Texas weather is notorious for its unpredictability.

When To Go

A uniform description of either winter or summer weather in Texas is impossible: while it's snowing in the Panhandle, people wintering on the Gulf Coast may be getting a tan at the beach; Central Texas may be baking in the late-summer heat while the Guadalupe Mountains feel the early-fall chill.

Average temperatures of 32–50°F (around 0–10°C) in winter and 70–98°F (20–32°C) in summer do not vary greatly around the state, but the humidity factor and elevation affect the comfort level considerably. North Texas, West Texas, and Central Texas suffer from a dry heat and high temperatures over 100°F (38°C), though in the hottest months of July and August, it can occasionally get as high as 110°F (38°C), and sometimes 115°F (46°C). South Central Texas, East Texas, and the Coastal Prairie suffer from high levels of humidity, so it is usually very hot and sticky in the summer between May and October.

Although it doesn't usually snow or freeze in these areas, occasionally it does so in a big way. It is not unknown for cities as far south as Austin and San Antonio to be blanketed with snow, shutting down businesses and roads completely for the duration. North Texas cities are wont to suffer from ice storms, snow, and icy roads in the winter. In the Panhandle and the higher elevations of the Davis Mountains, the Guadalupe Mountains, and the Big Bend area, where fall comes earlier than in the southern part of the state, there is little humidity except snow, which is common in the winters, sometimes causing roads and mountain areas to be closed to the public.

"Tornado Alley" runs through the center of the state, stopping in Central Texas. However, that does not mean that other areas don't occasionally experience tornadoes. Peak twister season lasts from late spring to early summer. Texas has a top-notch warning system that

Sightseeing in summer calls for lightweight clothing.

involves TV, radio, and text notifications that describe the severity of tornadoes as "watches" (weather conditions could cause a tornado) and "warnings" (a tornado has been sighted in the area). Seek immediate coverage in a basement, center of a building, or a bathroom if you hear a tornado siren as this indicates immediate danger.

Annual rainfall ranges from 8–16 inches (20–40cm) in the dry Big Bend region, to over 48 inches (122cm) in the wettest parts of the state, such as Houston and East Texas.

The best time for statewide travel is Oct/Nov, March and April, and late May/early June. This will avoid, for the most part, Texas's hottest and coldest temperatures and the heaviest rainfall.

Crime and Security

While most people go about their business safely, the fact remains that like any large American cities, Houston, Dallas, Austin, San Antonio, and El Paso have their incidences of crime and violence. Do not walk a long way after dark in strange or deserted parts of town. Keep a watchful eye on your belongings. Do not leave your car unlocked in parking lots, and never leave your children alone. Smaller towns in Texas have much lower crime rates, but use the same precautions everywhere as you would in a big city. Be especially mindful in border regions, both in border towns and rural areas many miles inland. Due to heavy policing and international cooperation, the incidences of drug war crime have started to drop substantially in places like El Paso/Juárez, which used to be one of the most violent cities in the US. Other border crossings away from urban areas may not be as safe, however, so be careful.

Hotels usually warn you that they will not guarantee the safety of belongings left in your hotel room. If you have any valuables, you may want to lock them in the hotel safe.

To reach the police in an emergency dial **911**. For police non-emergencies dial **311**.

Customs Regulations

Everyone entering the United States must go through US Customs, often a time-consuming process. You may bring in duty-free gifts worth up to $100 ($800 for returning US residents). Visitors over 21 may bring in 200 cigarettes, 4.4lbs (2kg) of smoking tobacco, and 100 cigars; quantities permitted are higher for US residents. Those over 21 may bring in 1 quart (1 liter) of alcohol. Travelers with more than $10,000 in US or foreign currency, traveler's checks, or money orders must declare these upon entry. Among prohibited goods are meat or meat products, illegal drugs, firearms, seeds, plants, and fruits.

For a breakdown of the most up-to-date and current US Customs and Border Protection regulations, make sure to contact US Customs and Border Protection, 1300 Pennsylvania Ave. NW, Washington, DC 20229; tel: 877-227-5511; www.cbp.gov.

E

Electricity

Standard electricity in North America is 110–115 volts, 60 cycles AC. An adapter is necessary for most appliances from overseas, with the exception of Japan.

Embassies and Consulates

Australia 3009 Post Oak Boulevard #1310, Houston, TX 77056; tel: 832-962-8420.
Canada 500 N. Akard Street, Suite 2900, Dallas, TX 75201; tel: 214-922-9806.
5847 San Felipe Street, Suite 1700, Houston, TX 77057; tel: 713-821-1440.
United Kingdom 1900 North Akard Street, Dallas, TX 75201; tel: 214-978-8989.
254 Spencer Lane, San Antonio, TX 78201; tel: 210-735-9393.
1301 Fannin Street, Suite 2400, Houston, TX 77002; tel: 713-210-4000.

Emergency Numbers

For all emergencies requiring police, fire or ambulance dial 911.
Road conditions on state highways, tel: 1-800-452-9292.
Information on evacuation routes, shelters and special-needs transportation, tel: 211
Poison, tel: 1-800-222-1222 (Texas and national).
American Red Cross, tel: 1-888-733-2767.
Texas Roadside assistance, tel: 800-525-5555.
Texas crime stoppers, tel: 800-252-8477.
To report a missing person, tel: 911.

Etiquette

The key word here is "relaxed." Openness and natural friendliness rule. Don't be surprised when strangers smile broadly at you and ask how you are doing as you pass them in the street. You can expect almost everyone with whom you come into contact to ask how you are feeling, where you come from, where you are going and, if you prove to be a foreigner, whether you are married, how many children you have, what your job is, and why you are here. Or they may just ask how you're "doin'."

This is not inappropriate behavior, personally invasive, or presumptuous, not even an attempt to begin a long, intimate conversation. It is natural friendliness and goodwill that prompts these genial greetings and enquiries from passersby, waiters, and salespeople who suddenly become new Texas friends. Don't even be surprised at a congenial slap on the back to emphasize a point, or – particularly in South Texas – a friendly embrace in greeting.

Health regulations prohibit all animals, except service animals, in public eating places in Texas, however, there are exceptions with some restaurants allowing animals like dogs on restaurant patios.

H

Health and Medical Care

Depending upon the country from which you are traveling or through which you have just come, you may need an international vaccination certificate. Many types of over-the-counter (OTC) medications are readily available, but if you're using prescription medication, it's best to bring extra, along with a spare pair of prescription glasses if you use them. Tap water is fine to drink, but if you're out camping in the more remote parts of some of the state's national parks or national forests, it is best to bring your own or use purifiers.

Covid-19 pandemic

Texas has been hit hard by the Covid-19 pandemic causing millions of cases and tens of thousands of deaths. For ongoing restrictions, visitors to Texas should check the most up-to-date state guidance at www.hhs.texas.gov.

Emergency Medical Services

In the event of an emergency, **dial 911** (the operator will put you through to the police, ambulance, or fire services). The call is toll free anywhere in the US, including on cell phones. If you can't get through, **dial 0** for an operator. In national parks, it's best to contact a ranger.

Most cities have 24-hour pharmacies (drugstores), urgent care clinics, hospitals with emergency rooms, and poison control centers. Look in the Yellow Pages or the inside cover of the telephone book, or dial 411 for telephone operator assistance.

Precautions

Much of Texas is made up of wide open spaces (that is, all its small and sprawling cities together occupy only a tiny portion of the state), so anyone who spends much time exploring has a good chance of coming into contact with a poisonous snake or spiders. Don't forget: you are in their home territory, so avoidance is always the best strategy. If you are walking in a field, for example, cover up with loose clothing secured at neck, ankles, and wrists to discourage ticks and chiggers from finding a spot in which to embed themselves. Tall, thick boots help protect against stinging ground insects and reptiles. Watch out for loose mounds of dirt in grassy areas, which could house fireants. Once disturbed (test the area with a long stick), they will swarm at great speed and can be all over your legs in no time. Be careful with children as they may not think fast enough to brush off the ants once attacked.

Rabies: Raccoons, skunks, bats, and squirrels can all be found in Texas, but should not be touched; they are potential carriers of rabies, which is easily transmitted to people.

Insects: The bite or sting of a spider, ant, or scorpion is not usually fatal, but it can cause a lot of pain and itching and the area around it may swell. In most cases, discomfort gradually subsides. If extreme symptoms such as numbness, tingling, shooting pain, high temperature, low blood pressure, abdominal cramps, spasms, breathing difficulty, or problems focusing the eyes occur, see a physician at once. Remember that bringing the insect with you greatly aids the doctor.

In Texas, chiggers are often referred to as "red bugs." A salve from the drugstore may help relieve the itching, but you will just have to wait for it to go away. The same is true of the bite of the mosquito, which are found by the million around water in low-lying areas. Do try your best to avoid getting bitten by mosquitoes as out in the American West, they carry West Nile Virus.

Snakes: Snakes are not quite the omnipresent menace that strangers in Texas fear. They usually remain in fields or sand dunes and often hide under logs or in holes, waiting to hunt at night or early in the morning. In addition, most snakes in Texas are harmless and only strike in self-defense. Just entering a snake's territory and standing too close can agitate it enough to strike, so be cautious: walk in the open when possible, proceed with caution among rocks, sweep grassy areas with a long stick before entering, avoid dark or overgrown places where snakes might lurk, and shake out bedding or clothing that has been lying on the ground.

Coral snakes are abundant in Texas. Because of their beauty and relatively small size, youngsters frequently pick them up, so be sure to discourage children from picking up strange animals. Rattlesnakes and coral snakes have very different toxins: the toxin of the former attacks the nervous system, while the latter primarily affects the respiratory system. Treatment consists of injecting very different antivenins, so identification is extremely important.

If you are bitten, at least try to see what the snake looked like. A positive identification is extremely important for the physician making a treatment decision. Do not attempt any first-aid treatments such as freezing the limb, tourniquets, or the outdated cut-and-suck method. Instead, go to the emergency room of the local hospital at once.

Jellyfish: Portuguese man-of-war jellyfish are found in their hundreds on Padre Island. Washed ashore, their blue balloon-like forms with long tentacles continue to pulsate for a while. If you are stung by their tentacles – either on shore or in the water, where they are harder to avoid – you may develop rashes and red welts. A few sensitive victims go into shock or endure fever, cramps, and nausea. Some lifeguards treat these stings with meat tenderizer; others wash the area with sodium bicarbonate, boric acid, lemon juice, or alcohol. If symptoms are severe, you should see a physician.

Insurance

It's vital to have medical insurance when traveling. Although hospitals are obligated to provide emergency treatment to anyone who needs it, regardless of whether they do or don't have insurance, you may have to prove you can pay for treatment of anything less than a life-threatening condition. Know what your policy covers and have proof of the policy with you at all times or be prepared to pay at the time service is rendered. Your travel insurance should cover both yourself and your belongings. Your own insurance company or travel agent can advise you on policies, but shop around since rates vary. Make sure you are covered for accidental death, emergency medical care, repatriation, trip cancellation, and baggage or document loss.

L

LGBTQ Travelers

Texas's urban centers, especially Dallas, Houston, San Antonio, and Austin, have large LGBTQ populations, with corresponding businesses and services. In particular, Houston was the first large US city to elect an openly gay mayor, Annise Parker. Both Dallas and Houston have neighborhoods around which the LGBTQ community is centered: Oak Lawn in Dallas, and the Montrose district in Houston.

Dallas has a weekly publication that comes out every Friday called The Voice (https://dallasvoice.com). Houston has a magazine called OutSmart (www.outsmartmagazine.com); Austin has L Style G Style (www.lstylegstyle.com). In addition, Houston has a comprehensive online guide at www.mygayhouston.com.

Dallas, Houston, and Austin host annual parades in June. The Dallas Pride is referred to as the **Alan Ross Texas Freedom Parade** (https://dallaspride.org), while Houston and Austin calls their Pride events, Pride **Houston** (www.pridehouston.org) and **Austin Pride** (https://austinpride.org). Austin is home to the annual All Genders, Lifestyles, and Identities Film Festival (aGLIFF) every fall (August or September; www.agliff.org).

Dallas's **Cathedral of Hope** (www.cathedralofhope.com) is said to be the largest LGBTQ church in the world with a congregation of more than 4,000.

Local Dialing Codes

Abilene 325
Amarillo 806
Austin 512
Corpus Christi/Padre Island 361
Dallas 214, 469, 972
Del Rio 830
El Paso 915
Fort Worth 682, 817
Galveston 409
Houston 281, 713, 832
Lake Jackson 979
Laredo/McAllen 956
Lufkin/Huntsville 936
San Antonio 210
Tyler 903
Waco 254

Lost Property

Texas is too big and too hands-off organizationally to have a central repository for lost items. The best you'll find might be a form you can fill out such as the one offered by the Dallas Police Department (www.dallaspolice.net/report/lostppropertyreport).

M

Maps

Mapsco (www.kappamapgroup.com) is the big map company of Texas. It publishes thick, complex binders of most major Texas cities, much like London's A-Z. At approximately $45, they're not cheap, but their level of detail is useful for those who will be driving around a city and need an explicit, page-by-page street guide. The Roads of Texas is a more practical, one-volume set of detailed maps that covers Texas's entire road system.

The **Automobile Association of America** (see page 309) provides excellent road maps and personalized trip planning for its members.

The **Insight Fleximaps** to Dallas/Fort Worth, Houston, and San Antonio are laminated and immensely durable.

Media

Print

In this rapidly expanding era of electronic publishing and free information on the world wide web, print media has undergone a massive contraction. Yet most communities still publish print editions of newspapers, as well as electronic versions, and the opinions and endorsements of columnists and editorial boards continue to play an important role in community life. Dallas and Houston have more than one daily newspaper, covering local, national, and international news. There are also several weekly newspapers in most cities that cover local and, sometimes, statewide news. Local newspapers include: *Dallas Morning News, El Paso Times, Fort Worth Star-Telegram, Galveston County Daily News, Houston Chronicle, San Antonio Express-News, and Waco Tribune-Herald.*

In addition, Texas has some interesting and worthwhile alternative free newspapers, which usually offer a good source of information on local culture, politics, and community in each city. These include the *FW Weekly* (Fort Worth), *Byline Houston* (Houston), *Austin Chronicle* (Austin), *Dallas Observer* (Dallas), *Texas Observer* (Austin), and *San Antonio Current* (San Antonio).

The Texas Department of Transportation (125 E. 11th Street, Austin, TX 78701; tel: 800-558-9368; www.txdot.gov) publishes the state's official monthly travel magazine, *Texas Highways* (www.texashighways.com), an attractive color magazine, as well as a weekly online newsletter. *Texas Monthly* (www.texasmonthly.com), a great way to tap into the pulse of Texas, is available at most newsstands.

There are also magazines dedicated to a particular city, such as *D Magazine* in Dallas. Bookstores display a wide array of books about Texas, from the *Texas Almanac* – covering every conceivable subject – to comprehensive bed-and-breakfast listings and cycling trip guides.

Radio and Television

There are over 70 television stations and at least 550 AM and FM radio stations in Texas. Thanks to cable, satellite, or pay television, programs from all over the world can be seen almost any hour of the day or night. Some rental cars also come with commercial-free satellite radio. The installation of cable in most hotels and motels and many homes means that how a particular station is found depends on where it appears on the cable to which they subscribe. Consult the newspaper for television listings. Radio listings are sometimes given in Sunday supplements of newspapers.

Money

American dollars come in bills of $1, $5, $10, $20, $50, and $100, all the same size. The dollar is divided into 100 cents. Coins come in 1 cent (penny), 5 cents (nickel), 10 cents (dime), 25 cents (quarter), 50 cents (half-dollar), and $1 denominations. There is no Value Added Tax (VAT) in the US, but cities charge a sales tax, usually around 4–10 percent of the sale. Car rental companies charge both sales tax and service fees.

Nearly every tourist-oriented business in Texas accepts credit cards, but foreign visitors who prefer to use cash are advised to take US dollar travelers' checks, since exchanging foreign currency – whether as cash or checks – can prove problematic. You can seek out currency exchange facilities at busy centers like retail malls, but overall they're hard to find.

The easiest way to take out money is from an ATM (automatic teller machine) with a debit or credit card using your PIN. ATMs are readily available in the state, including at most supermarkets. The most widely accepted cards are Visa, American Express, MasterCard, Diners Club, and Discover. Maestro cards are often not accepted.

Be sure to check the rate of exchange and any other charges your bank may levy before using your card abroad. Some charge prohibitive rates. The ATM operators will usually apply a charge as well, though you will be notified of this on-screen before you complete the transaction.

Credit Cards are very much part of life in Texas, as in other parts of the US. They can be used to pay for just about anything. It is very common for car rental firms and hotels to take an imprint of your card as a deposit. If you rent beach equipment or bicycles you man have to leave your card at the counter. Car rental companies may oblige you to pay a large deposit in cash if you do not have a credit card.

If visiting Texas from another part of the USA or another country, make sure you tell your bank or credit card company that you'll be using your card out-of-state.

Tipping

Restaurant bills do not usually include a service charge unless you are in a group of six or more, when a gratuity of 18 percent may be added to the total and unless the service is dreadful, you are obligated; otherwise, tips of 15–20 percent are expected.

Fifteen percent is a good rule of thumb when tipping for any service, including taxi rides and haircuts, although some Texans have not got used to tipping barbers. Bellhops and parking attendants expect a dollar per bag or vehicle, shoeshiners more. If you stay more than a couple of nights in a better hotel, it is usually suggested to tip chambermaids a small amount for making up the room. Staff are low paid and generally rely on tips.

O

Opening Hours

Offices: Mon–Fri 8am–5pm.
Banks: Mon–Fri 9/10am–5pm (although most have drive-through facilities that stay open longer). Some banks are open on Saturday morning.
Retail shops: Mon–Fri 10/11am–5/6pm, except in large shopping malls, when hours are extended to 8, 9, or 10pm and weekends. A few retail stores are always open.
Museums: many are closed on Mondays.

P

Passports and Visas

A machine-readable passport, a visitor's visa, proof of intent to leave the US after your visit and (depending upon your country of origin) an international vaccination certificate, are required of most foreign nationals for entry into the US.

As part of the visa waiver program (VWP), visitors from the UK staying less than 90 days do not need a visa; however, it is compulsory for non-US residents from VWP countries to submit information about themselves online to the Department of Homeland Security and register via the website of Electronic System for Travel Authorization (ESTA) (https://esta.cbp.dhs.gov/esta) to be preapproved for travel to the United States at least three days before they actually travel.

Vaccination certificate requirements vary, but proof of immunization against smallpox or cholera may be necessary.

US citizens traveling by air between the US, Canada, Mexico, the Caribbean, and Bermuda must present a current passport; a birth certificate and photo ID are no longer valid proof.

Due to increased security, the precise regulations for entry to the US change often, and vary for citizens of different countries. It's a good idea to check on the current situation before you travel, on the US State Department website (www.travel.state.gov) or via a US Embassy or Consulate in your home country. Any non-US citizen wishing to extend their stay should contact US Immigration and Naturalization Service at 425 I Street, Washington DC 20536; tel: 202-501-4444 or 800-407-4747.

For the latest travel restrictions related to the Covid-19 pandemic, please check online at https://travel.state.gov.

Postal Services

First-class postage and priority mail are the same anywhere in Texas, or in the US, and bills arrive just as quickly in tiny Cut-and-Shoot

Public Holidays

Banks, federal, state, county, and city offices and private businesses often close during public holidays. Many stores remain open during weekends and holidays.

New Year's Day 1 January
Martin Luther King Jr.'s Birthday 15 January, although observed the third Monday in January
Presidents' Day Third Monday in February
Easter Sunday Late March/early April
Memorial Day Last Monday in May
Independence Day 4 July
Labor Day First Monday in September
Columbus Day Second Monday in October
Veterans Day 11 November
Thanksgiving Day Fourth Thursday in November
Christmas Day 25 December

as they do in big-city Dallas. Post offices open at 7, 8, or 9am and usually close at 5pm, Mon–Fri. Many of them are open for at least a couple of hours on Saturday mornings, but they are all closed on Sunday.

There may also be coin-operated machines that dispense stamps whether the office is open or not. Rates are usually listed nearby. There are US Post Office Information numbers in the phonebook, or call 411 and ask the operator.

Visitors can receive mail at certain post offices if it is addressed to them, care of "General Delivery," followed by the city name and (very important) the zip code. You must pick up this mail in person within a week or two of its arrival and will be asked to show some form of valid personal identification.

Public Restrooms

Public restroom facilities are generally limited to city parks and highway or interstate rest stops Stores, malls, restaurants, and gas stations are your best bet.

R

Religious Services

Texas's population is primarily Protestant in the North, Central, and East sections (with Baptists in the majority) and Catholic in the South and West. Other religions and ethical systems represented in the state include Baha'i, Buddhism, Hinduism, Islam, and Judaism. Consult the Yellow Pages or ask at the desk of your hotel for the nearest place of worship.

T

Taxes

There is no state income tax in Texas, but the state charges a sales tax of 6.25 percent on most purchases, from clothing to electronics to dining out. Individual cities then apply their own percentage, usually totaling approximately 2 percent. The only major nontaxable exception is food purchased from a grocery store. Remember that the price shown is typically without the tax added so don't expect to pay with only a $5 note for something priced $4.99.

Telecommunications

In this era of cell phones, you'll find fewer public telephones in hotel lobbies, restaurants, drugstores, garages, roadside kiosks, convenience stores, and other locations. The cost of making a local call from a payphone for three minutes is 50 cents. 800 numbers and 911 calls are free. To make a long-distance call from a payphone, use either a prepaid calling card, available in airports, post offices, and a few other outlets, or your credit card, which you can use at any phone: dial 800-CALLATT, key in your credit card number, and wait to be connected. In many areas, local calls have now changed to a 10-digit calling system, using the area code.

To call from city to city in Texas, you must first find out the area code. The state's size requires that it be divided into different three-digit codes. The numbers of people moving to Texas and the proliferation of cell phones in recent years has resulted in more and more areas being assigned new area codes, often not long after they have been changed, so don't be surprised if an area code has changed from the one currently published. To call from one area to another, dial 1 before the three-digit area code and the local seven-digit telephone number.

There are Western Union cablegram offices in most Texas cities. Look in the local telephone directory in the white pages (for major cities, there may be separate books for businesses and residences). Messages and money can be sent over the wires immediately. You must have identification, such as a driver's license, to receive money.

Watch out for in-room connection charges, especially in more upscale hotels; it costs less to use the payphone in the lobby, although some hotels may offer free local calls. Likewise, W-fi access is frequently free in hotel lobbies, but there is often a charge for it in guest rooms.

Time Zones

Texas spans two time zones: Central Standard Time (Greenwich Mean Time minus six hours) and, in the extreme western corner of the state, Mountain Standard Time (Greenwich Mean Time minus seven hours). Daylight Saving Time is observed in almost every part of the state and begins at 2am on the first Sunday in April when clocks are advanced one hour and ends at 2am on the last Sunday in October.

Tourist Information

Most cities in Texas have a Convention and Visitors Bureau (CVB), where staff will provide you with brochures and maps. Elsewhere you must rely on the local chamber of commerce. They are oriented toward business people, but the staff is usually happy to help, particularly in tourist areas.

The Media section (see page 315) gives details of Texas periodicals containing useful information for visitors to the state. Download a free *Texas State Travel Guide* from www.traveltex.com.

Travel Information Centers

Texas has 12 Travel Information Centers operated by the Texas Department of Transportation (125 E. 11th Street, Austin, TX 78701; tel: 800-558-9368; www.txdot.gov), and offering state and highway information, trip planning, information on scenic wildflower trails, and so on. They are located off the interstate at the main state entry points and other key points around the state: Amarillo, Anthony, Austin, Denison, Gainesville, Langtry, Laredo, Orange, Rio Grande Valley, Texarkana, Waskom, and Wichita Falls. You can download most of their publications from their website.

Main Tourist Offices

Austin, 602 E. Fourth Street, TX 78701; tel: 512-474-5171; www.austintexas.org.

Dallas, 325 North St. Paul Street, Suite 700, TX 75201; tel: 214-571-1000; www.visitdallas.com.

El Paso, 1 Civic Center Plaza, TX 79901; tel: 915-534-0600; https://visitelpaso.com.

Fort Worth, 111 W. 4th Street, Suite 200, TX 76102; tel: 800-433-5747; www.fortworth.com.

Houston, 701 Avenida de las Americas, TX 77010; tel: 713-853-8100; www.visithoustontexas.com

San Antonio, 203 S. St Mary's Street, Suite 200,TX 78205; tel: 210-244-2000; www.visitsanantonio.com.

Tour Operators

Gray Line bus tours are available in all the main Texas towns and cities, and also include specialty tours, such as a Hill Country Wine Tour by wine experts. For information tel: 800-472-9546, international direct 303-539-8502; www.grayline.com.

Specialty tour companies include:

Big Bend Far Flung Tours (tel: 432-371-2633; www.bigbendfarflung.com). This Terlingua-based company offers rafting trips on the Rio Grande through Big Bend National Park and Jeep tours.

Hill Country Wine Tours (tel: 830-329-9463; www.hcwinetours.com). Limousine tours from Fredericksburg to Hill Country wineries, hosted by experts.

Osprey Cruises (tel: 956-761-6655; www.ospreycruises.com). Sightseeing nature cruises and Deep Sea and Bay fishing excursions in South Padre Island.

Artist Boat Kayak Adventures (tel: 409-770-0722; www.artistboat.org). Ecotours of Galveston Island using art and natural history to teach about the wild shore ecosystem.

Travelers with disabilities

The 1995 Americans with Disabilities Act (ADA) brought sweeping changes to facilities across America. Even older and smaller inns and lodges may be wheelchair accessible, so it's best to always ask. For the sight-impaired, many hotels provide special alarm clocks, closed-captioned TV services, and security measures. To comply with ADA hearing-impaired requirements, there are often special procedures; local agencies may provide text telephone (TTY) and interpretation services.

Check with the hotel when you make reservations to ascertain the degree to which the hotel complies with ADA guidelines. Ask specific questions about bathroom facilities, bed height, wheelchair space, and availability of services.

Many attractions have wheelchairs for loan or rent; most parks today also offer barrier-free or accessible trails. Some provide special visitor publications for visitors with disabilities and interpreters and visitor guides. The Society for Accessible Travel and Hospitality (tel: 212-447-7284; www.sath.org) publishes a quarterly magazine on travel for people with disabilities.

W

Websites and Apps

As you travel through Texas there are a few websites and apps you'll want to use to make your visit memorable. Begin your trip by referencing Travel Texas (www.traveltexas.com), the go-to site for everything you need to know about exploring Texas.

Texas Time Travel (https://texastimetravel.com) is a great website to learn about the cultural and historical sites and attractions throughout Texas, especially those in small towns. You may also want to use this in conjunction with the Texas Historical Markers app on iOS or Android which will point out significant historical markers while on a Texas road trip.

The Texas State Parks Official Guide app (https://tpwd.texas.gov/state-parks/app) allows users to search for campsites, trails, and activities in Texas' state parks.

It's a good idea to check out the websites of local CVB or tourism boards to gain insight on the culture and activities available in that area. Some Texas cities even offer their own mobile apps, like El Paso's Visit El Paso Mobile App (https://visitelpaso.com/explore/app) which offers information on hotels, events, attractions, and themed itineraries in El Paso.

Weights and Measures

Despite past efforts to convert to metric, the US still uses the imperial system of weights and measures.

What's on Listings

Entertainment listings are published in many of the daily city newspapers (see page 315), and in alternative weeklies such as the *Dallas Observer*, the *Houston Press, the Houston Chronicle*, and the *Austin Chronicle*. Venues and events are also listed in *Texas Monthly*. *Dallas Morning News's* Live online newspaper (www.dallasnews.com) covers the Dallas/Fort Worth area. Fort Worth's free paper, *FW Weekly*, also has listings. For more information on San Antonio's nightlife, check out listings in either the *San Antonio Current* or the *San Antonio Express-News*. Local tourist offices also have information on what is going on locally (see page 318).

FICTION

Lonesome Dove by Larry McMurtry. Life in a frontier Texas town is explored in this romantic Western novel, part of a tetralogy.

Woman Hollering Creek and Other Stories by Sandra Cisneros. The Mexican-American author highlights the social role of women who live along the Texas-Mexico border.

Texas by James Michener. After moving to Austin to research his fictionalized account of Texas history, Michener liked it so much he stayed.

All the Pretty Horses by Cormac McCarthy. A gritty tale of the border country and its harsh realities published 16 years after McCarthy moved to El Paso.

Two for Texas by James Lee Burke. Known for his Dave Robicheaux Louisiana detective tales, Burke's historic novel is set during the Texas War for Independence.

The Devil Went Down to Austin by Rick Riordan. Fast-talking and hard-living P.I. Navarre, the detective with the PhD in literature, untangles dirty goings on in the state capital in this popular series.

Thyme of Death by Susan Wittig Albert. Small town New Age herbalist shop owner Chyna Bayles solves more mysteries than Miss Marple in this popular series by the prolific Hill Country writer.

All the Land to Hold Us by Rick Bass. An extraordinarily visionary novel by the petroleum geologist turned natural history writer. Set in West Texas's dusty oil country as the community and the landscape fall apart and unlikely alliances are made.

NON-FICTION

The Tex-Mex Cookbook by Robb Walsh. The Austin food writer brings to life the cuisine and colorful characters of border country.

The Wine Roads of Texas by Wes Marshall with forewords by Robert Mondavi and Fess Parker. This look at Texas's emerging wineries by wine expert Marshall with two celebrated vintners inspired the PBS series of the same name.

Friday Night Lights by Bud Bissinger. The true story of the high school football team that united a small town in Texas.

An Unreasonable Woman: A True Story of Shrimpers, Politicos, Polluters, and the Fight for Seadrift, Texas by Diane Wilson. A Texas Erin Brockavich, Wilson recounts the amazing story of her fight against pollution in the Gulf.

Molly Ivins Can't Say That, Can She? by Molly Ivins. The famed humorist rakes the Texas legislature (and others) over the coals.

The Tennis Partner by Abraham Verghese. Written by the well-known AIDS researcher (and author of the best-seller *Cutting for Stone*), this memoir poignantly captures his experiences caring for AIDS patients as a young doctor in El Paso in the 1980s.

Chinati: The Vision of Donald Judd by Marianne Stockebrand. A look at how New York artist Donald Judd transformed Marfa.

Texas Towns and The Art of Architecture by Richard Payne. A lovely photographic tour of the buildings in the Texan landscape.

Gone to Texas: A History of the Lone Star State by Randolph (Mike) Campbell. An engaging history of the last 10,000 years of Texas history through its waves of immigrants.

The Longhorns by J. Frank Dobie. This classic book about the history of Texas longhorn cattle helped save the breed.

Oil in Texas: The Gusher Age 1895–1945 by Diana Davids Hinton and Roger M. Oliens. How oil has made Texas wealthy.

The Years of Lyndon Johnson: The Path to Power by Robert A. Caro. The accomplishments of LBJ are explored by the famed political biographer.

Journey Through Texas by Frederick Law Olmsted. Essays by the celebrated landscape architect about his 19th-century travels through Texas.

Goodbye to a River by John Graves. The author and his dog float the Brazos River before it is dammed and reflect on its natural history.

A Field Guide to the Birds of Texas by Roger Tory Peterson. An invaluable handbook by the famed ornithologist.

Roadside Geology of Texas by Darwin Spearing. A look at Texas' geology and interesting landmarks from volcanic mesas to limestone plateaus.

Wildflowers of Texas: A Field Guide by Geyata Ajilvsgi. A perfect companion for spring wildflower travels.

Send us your thoughts

We do our best to ensure the information in our books is as accurate and up-to-date as possible. The books are updated on a regular basis using destination experts, who painstakingly add, amend and correct as required. However, some details (such as opening times or travel pass costs) are particularly liable to change, and we are ultimately reliant on our readers to put us in the picture.

We welcome your feed back, especially your experience of using the book "on the road", and if you came across a great new attraction we missed.

We will acknowledge all contri bu tions and offer an Insight Guide to the best messages received.

Please write to us at:

Insight Guides
PO Box 7910
London SE1 1WE

Or email us at:

hello@insightguides.com

OTHER INSIGHT GUIDES

Insight Guide titles cover nearly every major travel destination in North America, from Alaska to Arizona. City titles include *Boston, New York, Chicago*, and *San Francisco*. Regional and state titles include *California, Florida*, and *USA on the Road*.

CREDITS

PHOTO CREDITS

123RF 216, 247, 287
@PrettyATX/Visit Austin 151
Alamy 32, 60, 61, 241, 283
AWL Images 76
Bigstock 134, 250, 276
Bruce Bernstein, Courtesy of Princeton Library, NJ 28, 34
Carol M. Highsmith/Library of Congress 6BL, 7BR, 8T, 9BL, 17, 33, 50, 51, 52, 53, 56, 57, 58, 59, 67, 69, 70, 71, 74, 77, 82, 83, 84, 86, 87, 101, 102, 103, 121, 131, 156T, 162, 165T, 178/179T, 178BR, 179ML, 179BL, 194/195T, 197, 199T, 201, 203, 204T, 205, 206, 206T, 229T, 229B, 231, 232B, 236T, 243, 245T, 249T, 252, 255B, 255T, 257, 258T, 264, 265, 275T, 278B, 279, 284T, 293, 300, 302T
Corbis 54, 63, 90/91, 242
DVCB 7MR, 106, 108, 109T, 109B, 110, 111, 112
Fort Worth CVB 118, 119T, 120
Getty Images 7TL, 14/15, 18, 19, 22, 23, 37, 39, 42, 44, 45, 46, 55, 64, 65, 72, 80, 81, 100, 104, 114, 122, 124, 125, 127, 128, 135, 138, 139, 140, 142, 146B, 147, 157, 160B, 166B, 196, 200, 208, 211, 214, 215, 217, 219, 221, 222, 223B, 224, 225, 226, 227, 228, 235, 237, 239, 240, 246, 251, 256, 263, 268, 269, 270/271T, 270BR, 271BR, 271BL, 271TR, 281, 282, 296, 305
Greater Houston Convention and Visitors Bureau 6MR, 7TR, 47, 180, 181, 183B, 184, 185, 186, 187, 189T, 189B, 190, 191, 192, 306
iStock 4, 6ML, 7ML, 7ML, 9TR, 9TL, 20, 24, 25, 31, 36, 40, 41, 43, 79, 89, 115, 126, 129, 132B, 133, 136T, 141, 144, 145, 146T, 152, 158, 163, 165B, 166T, 173, 178BL, 179TR, 183T, 207, 213, 232T, 249B, 260, 261, 270BL, 271ML, 273, 275B, 278T, 280, 292, 294, 295, 297B, 297T, 301T, 301B, 302B, 304, 311, 319
Jim Turner/Lady Bird Johnson Wildflower Center/The University of Texas at Austin 150
Larry D. Moore 179BR
Library of Congress 29, 62
NASA 194BR, 194BL, 195ML, 195BL, 195TR
PA Images 262
Public domain 26/27, 30, 38
Shutterstock 1, 8B, 10/11, 48/49, 66, 94/95, 113, 168, 177, 195BR, 199B, 209, 230, 234
SuperStock 75, 210, 238, 245B
Texas Highway Department 35
The Art Archive 68
The Thinkery 148
Travel Texas 6MR, 12/13, 16, 21, 73, 78, 86, 88, 92/93, 94/95, 96, 105, 117T, 117B, 119B, 123, 132T, 136B, 137 143, 149, 153, 156B, 159, 160T, 161, 167, 170, 172, 176, 193, 202, 204, 218, 220T, 220B, 223T, 233, 236B, 248, 253, 258B, 259, 267, 272, 284B, 285, 286, 289, 298, 299, 308, 313
Visit San Antonio 155, 169, 171T, 171B, 175
Visit San Antonio/Carol Barrington 174
VisitHouston 85

COVER CREDITS

Front cover: Texas longhorn *Shutterstock*
Back cover: Austin *Shutterstock*
Front flap: (from top) Bishop's Palace, Galveston *Shutterstock*; Salt Lick BBQ *Carol M. Highsmith/Library of Congress*; Neon Texas state flag *Carol M. Highsmith/Library of Congress*; National Cowgirl Museum and Hall of Fame mural *Carol M. Highsmith/ Library of Congress*
Back flap: Texas Bluebonnets *Shutterstock*
E-book flap: West Texas country road *iStock*

INSIGHT GUIDE CREDITS

Distribution
UK, Ireland and Europe
Apa Publications (UK) Ltd;
sales@insightguides.com
United States and Canada
Ingram Publisher Services;
ips@ingramcontent.com
Australia and New Zealand
Booktopia; retailer@booktopia.com.au
Worldwide
Apa Publications (UK) Ltd;
sales@insightguides.com
Special Sales, Content Licensing and CoPublishing
Insight Guides can be purchased in bulk quantities at discounted prices. We can create special editions, personalised jackets and corporate imprints tailored to your needs.
sales@insightguides.com
www.insightguides.biz

Printed in China

First Edition 1986
Seventh Edition 2021

Every effort has been made to provide accurate information in this publication, but changes are inevitable. The publisher cannot be responsible for any resulting loss, inconvenience or injury. We would appreciate it if readers would call our attention to any errors or outdated information. We also welcome your suggestions; please contact us at: hello@insightguides.com

www.insightguides.com

Editor: Siobhan Warwicker and Zara Sekhavati
Author: Nicky Leach
Update Production: Apa Digital
Head of DTP and Pre-Press: Rebeka Davies
Picture Editor: Tom Smyth
Head of Publishing: Sarah Clark
Cartography: original cartography Colourmap Scanning Ltd, updated by Carte

CONTRIBUTORS

This new edition of Insight Guide Texas was thoroughly updated by Alex Temblador and edited by Siobhan Warwicker and Zara Sekhavati. It builds on previous editions written by Santa Fe-based travel writer Nicky Leach and other contributors, including Helen Bryant, John Davis, Eileen Mattei, Ann Mills, Ed Proctor, John Wilcock, and Christopher Walters. The text was proofread and indexed by Penny Phenix.

ABOUT INSIGHT GUIDES

Insight Guides have more than 45 years' experience of publishing high-quality, visual travel guides. We produce 400 full-colour titles, in both print and digital form, covering more than 200 destinations across the globe, in a variety of formats to meet your different needs.

Insight Guides are written by local authors, whose expertise is evident in the extensive historical and cultural background features. Each destination is carefully researched by regional experts to ensure our guides provide the very latest information. All the reviews in **Insight Guides** are independent; we strive to maintain an impartial view. Our reviews are carefully selected to guide you to the best places to eat, go out and shop, so you can be confident that when we say a place is special, we really mean it.

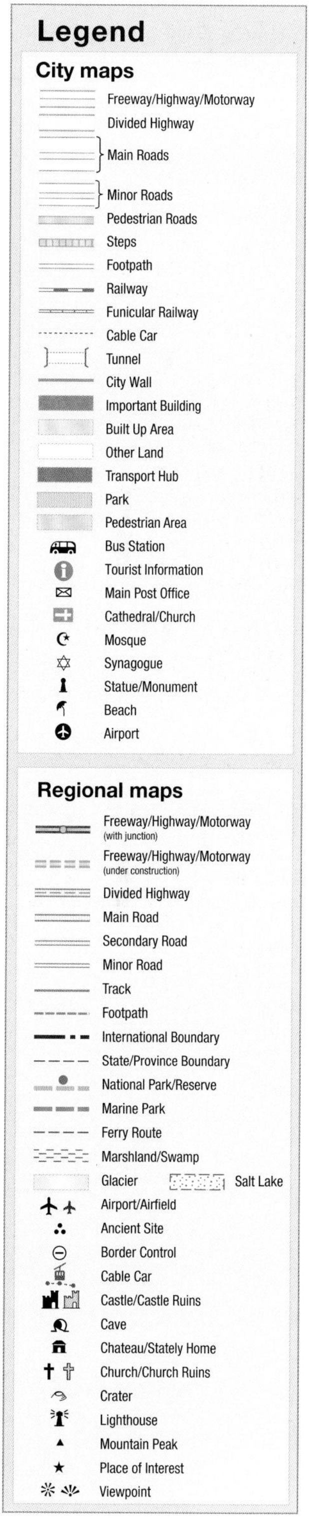

INDEX

MAIN REFERENCES ARE IN BOLD TYPE

C

H

N

T

Highland Park
Southfork Ranch
Oak Lawn Av.
Fairmount
Hood
Enid
Turtle Creek Drive
Carlisle St
Bowen St
Howell
Sneed
Oak Grove
North Haskell Street
Maple Avenue
REVERCHON PARK
Cedar Springs Road
Allen
Cole St
Vine
Laclede
McKinney Avenue
GREENWOOD CEMETERY
North Hall
Duff
Central Expressway
Watt
Thomas
Lucille
Lafayette
Ripley
Carver
Johnson
Caddo
Routh
Howell
Boll
Hugo
State
Ellis
McCoy
Munger Av.
Roseland
Washington Avenue
Ivan
Wolf
Bookhout
Randall
N. Pearl St
McKinnon Street
Harry Hines Boulevard
Alamo St
Hi Line Dr
Harwood
Hunt
Yeargran
Fairmount
Mahon
Worthington
Hiberna
State
Thomas
Clark
Allen
GRIGGS PARK
N. Hall
Ross Avenue
Pecos
Crescent Court Hotel
Leonard
Colby
Boll
Guillot
Vann
San Jacinto
Adolph
McCoy
Lakeheath
Villars
EXALL PARK
PIKE PARK
Maple Avenue
Pavillion
Trevolle
N. Houston Street
Payne
Alamo St
Wichita
Olive
KLYDE WARREN PARK
North Pearl Street
Morton H. Meyerson Symphony Center
Cathedral Santuario de Nuestra Guadalupe
Flora
Routh
Ross Avenue
Allen
Liberty
Carmel
Live Oak Street
Skiles
Stemmons Freeway
35E
American Airlines Center
Victory Ave
Slocum St
N. Akard
Caroline
Ashland
N. Field
Akard Street
Nasher Sculpture Center
Belo Mansion
North Hawkins
Old San Jacinto
Leonard
Crockett
75
Bryan
Montezuma
Florence
Oak
Dragon St
Field Street
St Paul
N. Harwood
Dallas Museum of Art
Crow Collectiob of Asian Art
J P Morgan Chase Tower
Cantegral
Swiss
Texas
345
Riverfront Boulevard
Perot Museum of Nature & Science
Woodall Rodgers Freeway
Munger
Fountain Place
Olive
Business Management Center
N. Good-Latimer
Avenue
Broom
Wells Fargo Building
North Avenue
First Baptist Church
Federal
Gaston
Monument
Indiana
JOHN B. CARPENTER PARK
Live Oak Street
Munger
Griffin
Ross
San Jacinto
Akard Street
Ervay Street
U.S. Post Office
Bryan
Dallas World Aquarium
Patterson
Field
Thanksgiving Square
Pacific Avenue
S. Central Expressway
Central Building
Lamar St
West End Historic District
N. Record
Bank One Tower
Elm Street
Main Street
Renaissance Tower
Neiman Marcus
Commerce Street
Sixth Floor Museum
Pacific Avenue
Elm St
Magnolia Hotel
J.N. Bryan's Cabin
El Centro College
Bank of America Plaza
Jackson St
South Harwood Street
North Pearl Street
Genard
Dallas Farmers' Market
Dealey Plaza
Main St
Earl Cabell Federal Building
Akard St
Ervay Street
Old Red Courthouse
Commerce St
Wood Street
Young Street
J.F.K. Memorial
Austin
Jackson St
South Griffin Street
Field
J. Erik Jonsson Central Library
Marilla
Market St
S.Record
Wood St
S. Houston Street
MUNICIPAL PLAZA PARK
Canton
Park
Union Station
Pioneer Plaza
Cadiz
South St Paul
St Louis
Commerce St
Young St
PIONEER PARK CEMETERY
Dallas City Hall
Corsicana
Reunion Blvd
Riverfront Boulevard
Stemmons Freeway
Reunion Tower
Austin
Lamar Street
Convention Center
Dallas Memorial Auditorium
30
REUNION PARK
Sports St
R.L. Thornton Freeway
Harwood
Reunion Arena
Drive
South Ervay Street
OLD CITY PARK
SAMUEL BEAUMONT PARK
St Paul
Park
Memorial
Blakeney
Beaumont
Fort Worth
Sports St
South Lamar Street
Powhattan
Wall
South Akard Street
Sullivan
Gano
Hickory
Lear
McKee
Browder
30
South Austin
Bellview
Gould
Beaumont
Seeger
Savannah
Holmes
Houston Street Viaduct
Cadiz
Cockrell
Wall
Gilks
Jefferson Blvd Viaduct
Roe
McKee
Alexander
TRINITY RIVER GREENBELT PARK
Austin
Buffalo
South Lamar Street
Trinity
Canton Street Viaduct
Cadiz Street Viaduct
Riverfront Boulevard
Corinth Street
Montgomery
Cockrell
Lamesa
Alma
Rock Island Road
Henning
Waco
35E